D0467470

Melville

BOOKS BY EDWIN HAVILAND MILLER

Walt Whitman's Poetry — A Psychological Journey
The Correspondence of Walt Whitman, Five Volumes
The Artistic Legacy of Walt Whitman
A Century of Whitman Criticism
The Professional Writer in Elizabethan England

A VENTURE BOOK

GEORGE BRAZILLER, INC.   ·   NEW YORK

EDWIN
HAVILAND
MILLER, 1918-

Melville

For information, address the publisher:
George Braziller, Inc.
One Park Avenue, New York, N.Y. 10016

International Standard Book Number: 0–8076–0787–8

Library of Congress Catalog Card Number: 75–7958
Printed in the United States of America
Designed by The Etheredges

mw 9/76 4012

To the Memory of My Father

Contents

Contents • *xi*

Illustrations

Preface

Herman Melville was not kind to biographers. A man of reticences and vulnerable sensitivity, he guarded himself in his letters except for the extraordinary ones he wrote in 1850 and 1851 to Nathaniel Hawthorne. For the most part he preferred not to verbalize his feelings or to share them. He shrank from people and the demands of intimacy, and he imprisoned himself, not always happily, in the family circle.

Melville kept no records during the early years of drift when he held one job after another and roamed on land and at sea, seeking without finding whatever he was searching for. For almost four years he accumulated experiences in the South Seas but kept no notes and told no "fibs." Only in the middle years did he keep journals during his travels, which consist, however, of jottings, terse, unpolished, obviously designed to jog his memory. Only at intervals did he relieve his monotonous notations to tell us how he felt, what excited his imagination or depressed his spirits.

This man of silences revealed his longings, his depressions, his hunger, his excitement, in the pages of his books. He prided himself that, like Ralph Waldo Emerson, he was one of the "divers." He dared to peer into the abysses of his own troubled, sensitive nature and to examine old wounds and old hurts. What he discovered at great pain and suffering he transmuted into an art which throbs and reverberates with the inner drama in an almost manic depressive rhythm.

And so, like *Billy Budd*, the work he wrote in the last years of his life, this biography is an "inside" narrative. It begins in the year during which he was struggling to shape a mammoth work about a white whale, and during which he was exhilarated and shaken to his depths by the presence of another genius, Nathaniel Hawthorne.

With humility and gratitude I acknowledge my indebtedness to a generation of Melville scholars who have established the record, biographical and literary, with exemplary thoroughness. The facts about his life and his family have been assembled in a brilliant compilation by Jay Leyda called *The Melville Log* (1951), which has provided the ballast for subsequent biographical and critical discussions. I hope that my work will do justice to the studies upon which it rests, to the research of Charles Roberts Anderson, Walter E. Bezanson, Merrell R. Davis, William H. Gilman, Harrison Hayford, Eleanor Melville Metcalf, Hershel Parker, Merton M. Sealts, Jr., G. Thomas Tanselle, and Howard P. Vincent. I have been deeply influenced by the interpretations of such critics and biographers as Newton Arvin, Richard Chase, Leon Howard, Alfred Kazin, Henry A. Murray, Robert Penn Warren, and Raymond M. Weaver.

It is a joy to pay tribute, inadequate as it may be, to the institutions whose resources I have used and to the librarians who are genuine and generous professionals. The New York Public Library is an extraordinary library with an extraordinary staff. I have drawn upon the manuscript collections, the Berg Collection, and the Annex. I am also indebted to the Melville Collection at the Houghton Library of Harvard University, to the Massachusetts Historical Society, and to the Boston Public Library.

I also take delight in acknowledging the friendly concern and excellent suggestions of my editor, Edwin Seaver, and of other members of the staff of George Braziller.

While this study was experiencing the usual growing pains, my students at New York University shared my struggles, my false starts, and whatever successes I may have achieved. I am grateful for their courtesy, their tolerance, and their disagreements.

Books are not written in libraries or in classroom lectures. This one grew week after week, year after year, in a study in New York and on a "poop deck" overlooking the Atlantic Ocean. In his lonely, troubled journey, Herman Melville repeatedly characterized himself as an Ishmael, a friendless orphan. I have been more fortunate: Rosalind has always been there.

E. H. M.

Rockport, Massachusetts

New Neptune
and
Mr. Noble Melancholy

The morning of August 5, 1850, was overcast. It was one of those typical summer days in Western Massachusetts when the sun struggles to emerge from the early morning haze rolling off the Berkshire Mountains, and even a native would not venture a prediction as to whether there would be rain or sunshine. In the New Haven Railroad Station at Pittsfield three men were walking about, bantering with the literary flourishes and analogies that often passed for wit in those days.

Shortly, another man "with a glazed India-rubber bag in hand" joined the three men, and the bantering continued until the engine puffed into the station and the four climbed aboard. "We are in the cars, and with a hurrah to the neighborhood from the steam-whistle we are away." They traveled only twelve miles to Stockbridge where a "stately" gentleman met them and conducted them "by horse-power, to his Umbrage in a hollow, in the skirts of Stockbridge."

These rather commonplace events were recorded in the pages of *The Literary World* later in the month. The magazine was established a few years earlier in New York for the purpose of proclaiming in immodest prose the advent of a literature worthy of the New World. The reporter's name was not given; he signed himself "Esteemed Correspondent." The immodest title, of course, provided no enlightenment to outsiders, but the readers of *The Literary World* knew at once the identity of the correspondent and presumably delighted in his "cultured" approach to reality, for he rarely stooped to names when allegorical and mythological epithets better served his purposes.

The "Esteemed Correspondent" identified the three men in the station as "New Neptune, Silver Pen, and our Humble Self." The latecomer was "Mr. Town Wit." The "stately" man of Stockbridge was not even provided with an epithet, not because he was undistinguished, but because he was not part of the literary clique.

"Humble Self" or "Esteemed Correspondent" was one Cornelius Mathews, a cantankerous man of incredible pomposity who spared no hyperbole in establishing his importance. One critic attacked his "pretentious imbecility" when he assumed "the arduous duties of wet-nurse to that sturdy bantling, the National Literature." At thirty-three, Mathews was the author of such forgotten books as *The Motley Book* (1838), *Behemoth: A Legend of the Mound-Builders* (1839), *The Career of Puffer Hopkins* (1842), *Poems on Man, In His Various Aspects under the American Republic* (1843), and *Big Abel and the Little Manhattan* (1845) — respectively, a collection of juvenilia, a romance, an urban novel, a collection of poetry, and a kind of fictionalized guidebook to New York City. The book of poems Elizabeth Barrett Browning had pronounced "as remarkable in thought and manner, for a vital sinewy vigor, as the right arm of Pathfinder" — a judgment which does justice neither to Mathews nor to James Fenimore Cooper, to say nothing of Mrs. Browning.

"Silver Pen" was Mathews's epithet for Evert A. Duyckinck, who, with his brother George, was the editor and proprietor of *The Literary World*. Evert was well established in New York as an editor and literary agent. He had an impressive personal library which Herman Melville made use of and which no doubt aided him in the compilation of the *Cyclopaedia of American Literature* (1855), in its day a most impressive scholarly study. He knew most of the famous literary figures of the era, and he was among the first to recognize the talents of Melville and Nathaniel Hawthorne. He had, however, serious critical lapses and one critical blindspot — his adulation of Mathews. This weakness was well known, and in a contemporary

satire Mathews is Mr. Ferocious and Duyckinck is Tibbings. One of
the characters in the play observes: "With what reverence Tibbings
bows to his substance, for he is but the shadow of Mr. Ferocious, and
how like a conscious idol Ferocious himself receives the adulation of
his worshipper."

Mathews and Duyckinck, "feeling the weight of brick and
mortar somewhat oppressively," had left New York for Pittsfield on
August 1. After spending the night in the Berkshire Hotel, in the
morning they had met their "welcomer in Berkshire, a retired Sea-
Dog, New Neptune by name." Apparently the readers of *The Literary World* needed only these two epithets to make the appropriate
identification. Herman Melville was New Neptune in the three installments in which Mathews indulged his fondness for circumlocutions
in recording his New England visit. Many people knew that Melville
had retired from the sea at age twenty-five and that he had published a somewhat notorious romance about the South Seas in 1846.
Duyckinck himself had arranged for the American publication of
Typee and had seen to it that the reviews were favorable. The Young
Americans, over whom Duyckinck and Mathews presided at what
they called "The Knights of the Round Table," praised each other's
writings immoderately. When Melville attached himself to the group
in the late 1840s, he enjoyed all the rights and privileges of a coterie
addicted to mutual admiration, as artful in self-promotion as another
journalist of the era with the name of Walter Whitman.

A month before the visit of Mathews and Duyckinck, in July
1850, Herman Melville had come to Pittsfield with his wife and their
eighteen-month-old boy Malcolm. They planned to spend the summer with Robert Melvill. This son of Herman's Uncle Thomas retained the original spelling of the family name. Herman's mother had
added the final *e* after the death of her husband, Allan Melvill.

Melville led his guests to his cousin's house, a large and once
elegant mansion called Broadhall. Mathews was ecstatic: "Old Broad-
Hall is a glorious fellow, and we could chant his claims and enjoy-
ments through a long summer day — the Benevolence, Beauty,
Worth, Wit, Genius — to say nothing of the ancient Family Portraits
and a small bottle of tea (reserved by an ancestor of the house) from
the dumpage in Boston Harbor." With no less enthusiasm than
Mathews, but more accuracy, Duyckinck wrote to his wife of
Melville's "rare place — an old family mansion, wainscoted and
stately, with large halls & chimneys — quite a piece of mouldering
rural grandeur — .... The farm has been sold." Neither writer apparently knew that Broadhall was purchased in 1816 by Major
Thomas Melvill, of Revolutionary War fame, and that his first-born
son, Thomas, Jr., occupied it until 1837. Unsuccessful as a farmer

and twice jailed for his debts, the son finally went West to Galena, Illinois, where he died in 1845. Robert eventually inherited the farm, but he was no more successful as a farmer than his father before him.

The tardy man at the Pittsfield station, Mr. Town Wit, was Oliver Wendell Holmes, who maintained a summer home in Pittsfield and was at the time Professor of Anatomy at the Harvard Medical School. As Mathews's title indicates, he was on his way toward the establishment of a literary reputation as a wit; he would become the "autocrat of the breakfast table" in the pages of *The Atlantic Monthly*. Holmes was one of a group of people, including William Cullen Bryant, Hawthorne, and Melville, who made the Berkshires an important literary outpost at mid-century.

It is conceivable that the audience of *The Literary World* identified the four literary men, but it is hard to see how they could have guessed from the description that the "stately" man was David Dudley Field, although he was well known in Stockbridge, Massachusetts, and in legal circles in New York City. Field came to Stockbridge as a boy of fourteen when his father began, in 1819, his pastorate of eighteen years at the Congregational Church, briefly served in the preceding century by Jonathan Edwards. The chimes in front of the church today were a gift of the son in his father's memory. The son followed his sire to Yale College, but chose the law rather than the ministry. In 1894 he was buried in the family plot in Stockbridge Cemetery across the road from his father's church. The impressive inscription reads: "He Devoted His Life to Reform the Law: To Codify the Common Law; To Simplify Legal Procedure; To Substitute Arbitration for War; To Bring Justice Within Reach of All Men." His brother Cyrus extended the "Reach of All Men" by means of the transatlantic cable.

In 1850 Field occupied a rambling two-story frame house on Main Street, about a half mile east of the Congregational Church, on the outskirts of the village and not far from Laura's Tower. Shaded by trees hundreds of years old and graced by homes aristocratic in their size and their well-bred simplicity, Main Street remains one of the most beautiful streets in America, a living monument to another way of life. In 1853 Field moved to a Stockbridge mansion and eventually bequeathed the house on Main Street to his daughter. Later known as Laura Cottage, it was occupied by Mathew Arnold when he stayed in the United States for a year in the 1880s. In 1953 the house was razed, and so with the passage of time Laura Cottage has become a photograph and a memory in literary history.

While Field's guests awaited the arrival of other "celebrities," who would join them in climbing Monument Mountain, the servants were preparing "turkeys and beeves" for an afternoon dinner as well as hampers of Heidseck champagne for a mountain "pic-nic" later in the morning. With understandable restlessness before "a Feast of Quidnuncs," Mathews wrote, "just by way of a rehearsal, for the grand climb, we take a run to the top of Sacrifice Mount, not far off." On their return "we have the mountain party completed, with the addition of the charming sketcher of New England mystic life, Mr. Noble Melancholy, and . . . his publisher, Mr. Greenfield."

Here Mathews's blithely undifferentiated prose failed its subject matter. Mathews conveyed to readers a straining effect of unrelieved excitement, but despite his work in the theater, he had little sense of drama. This meeting of Mr. Noble Melancholy and New Neptune was one of those rare dramatic moments when genius meets genius, or, more accurately, when genius collides with genius.

Mathews even failed to record the greetings when for the first time Nathaniel Hawthorne met Herman Melville.

Hawthorne came to Field's home from his modest little red frame cottage about halfway between Lenox and Stockbridge. There, in a converted farmhouse which Hawthorne himself termed "ugly," and on the shores of Stockbridge Bowl, one of the loveliest lakes in the Berkshire Mountains, he would shortly write *The House of the Seven Gables.* He was accompanied by James T. Fields, of the Boston publishing house, Ticknor & Fields. A few months earlier the firm had published *The Scarlet Letter*, which ushered in the greatest decade in American literary history. Hawthorne's romance was to be followed by *Moby-Dick* in 1851, *Walden* in 1854, and *Leaves of Grass* in 1855.

It was indeed a distinguished group that gathered on that cloudy Monday morning in August for the purpose of climbing Monument Mountain. But when a correspondent of *The National Intelligencer* wrote a glowing account of authors summering in the Berkshires, his publishers asked him to "permit them to suggest in friendliness that the great mass of their readers could not feel much interest in the private pursuits, habits & whereabouts of writers in the North of whom they have scarcely heard."

In addition to the men, there were three ladies in the party, Mrs. Field and her daughter Jenny, and Mrs. James T. Fields, "the new wife, who is the violet of the season in Berkshires." (According to Duyckinck, she was attired in "delicate blue silk," which was a pictorially satisfying accompaniment to her husband's "curled whiskers" and his "patent leathers.") There was one other male, who, as he noted years later, "enjoyed the distinction of being the only one of the party who had not written a book." Henry Dwight Sedgwick was of a distinguished Stockbridge family and was to become a local historian.

In 1895 Sedgwick wrote, "I remember little more of their conversation than that they talked prose apparently as unconsciously as *M. Jourdain* himself." In the pages of *The Literary World* Mathews did not have Sedgwick's mellowed detachment. According to "Humble Self," an almost maniacal exhilaration took possession of the participants, a mood which was sustained throughout the day. The party set out in three carriages, with Sedgwick on horseback, for the foot of the mountain about five miles away. Monument Mountain, which is part of a range near Stockbridge, is distinguished by a summit of rocks that form a white chimney on top of pine and white birch trees. (That fall, in his notebooks, Hawthorne likened Monument Mountain to "a headless sphinx, wrapt in a rich Persian shawl.") From the foot as one looks at the cliff of rocks the ascent appears difficult, but, despite Mathews's heightened prose, it can be climbed, even by women in the inhibiting habiliments of the nineteenth century, in an hour or a little more by following a ridge that taxes neither breath nor skirts, until the last fifty or so feet.

"Higher, higher up we go," Mathews wrote, his participles keeping pace, "stealing glances through the trees at the country underneath; rambling, scrambling, climbing, rhyming — puns flying off in every direction, like sparks among the bushes." In the privacy of a letter to his wife Duyckinck reported that Hawthorne and he were "in advance, talking of the Scarlet Letter." Mathews would have none of this matter-of-factness. He insisted that spirits mounted as the climbers reached the rocky top — "that watch-tower, so near up towards heaven."

There Holmes ventured a pun "and is, righteously, near losing his foothold and tumbling straight down a thousand feet." Since Monument Mountain is slightly over 1,600 feet above sea level, there was no possibility of falling a thousand feet, even for a bad pun, but the peak is not wide, the rocks are uneven, and the drop, viewed from the summit and with understandable acrophobia, appears to be a thousand feet or more.

Melville was "the boldest of all" and the wildest: "New Neptune is certainly fancying himself among the whalers of the Pacific, for he perches himself astride a jutting rock, like a bowsprit." As Melville "pulled and hauled imaginary ropes for our delectation," Holmes "peeped about the cliffs and protested it affected him like ipecac." Even Hawthorne, according to Duyckinck, lost some of his inhibitions on the magic mount, and "looked wildly about for the great carbuncle."

The day was not without ominous overtones, in the form of thunder clouds. "A black thunder cloud from the south," Duyckinck wrote in his imagistic prose, "dragged its ragged edges toward us."

Mathews was metaphorically more conventional: "The tempest . . . spreads his cloudy wings, which he presently shakes upon us, and compels us to a retreat, which, honored as the harbor of two lovely women, shall be henceforth known as the Fairy Shelter." There in the shelter, probably just below the pinnacle, since heavily skirted women could not have scrambled about on the rocky cliffs, Holmes "cut three branches for an umbrella and uncorked the champagne which was drunk from a silver mug." As Holmes posed with his improvised umbrella, the frock coats, the manicured whiskers, the blue silk, the patent leather shoes, the silver goblets, and the sparkling foam should have ravished the eyes of a nineteenth-century painter, if one could have been found, who could rise above the restraints of the culture to depict the hedonistic delights and colors of this pic-nic.

Inspired by the iced champagne and accompanied by "the vast organ-bass of the rolling thunder," Mathews read a poem written by William Cullen Bryant after a visit to Monument Mountain. "The Story of the Indian Girl" tells of a maiden "With wealth of raven tresses, a light form, / And a gay heart."

> She loved her cousin; such a love was deemed,
> By the morality of those stern tribes,
> Incestuous, and she struggled hard and long
> Against her love, and reasoned with her heart,
> As simple maiden might.

One summer day, accompanied by a friend, she climbed Monument Mountain, said farewell to her friends and her unlawful passion.

> But when the sun grew low
> And the hill shadows long, she threw herself
> From the steep rock and perished.

A strange poem to read over champagne, but stranger still would be a tale that Melville wrote a year later of a girl with dark tresses named Isabel who became a kind of wife to a half brother named Pierre.

After the storm and the champagne, "we walk about, in the new sun upon the mountain top, as though we were the angels of the time, and as though these airy ridges were our natural promenade." Eventually tiring of their "airy" superiority to the world below, the group slowly descended the mountain, passed the grave of the Indian maiden.

> There was scooped
> Upon the mountain's southern slope, a grave;
> And there they laid her, in the very garb

With which the maiden decked herself for death,
With the same withering wild flowers in her hair.

The picnickers boarded their carriages, and "with a cool gallop along the road . . . returned to the Umbrage," to Field's home.

The dinner, Duyckinck wrote to his wife, was "a three hour's business from turkey to ice cream, well moistened by the way." The most elaborately described guest at table was, to no one's surprise, Mathews himself: "an earth-monster, a perfect Behemoth, the mention of whose name has before now driven three critics crazy and scared a number of small publishers out of a year's growth; a mighty shadow, whose name we dare not mention." (Even Duyckinck's brother George found this too much: "Mathews' allusion to himself was in the usual execrable taste.")

At this point Mathews began a guessing game with the readers. "You would give the world to have an accurate account from so careful a pen as ours of what that picked company of wits and belles had to say to each other over the wine. But — we have sworn on oath — we have sealed a seal, never, never to divulge, no, never." Of course he could not refrain from hinting that among the topics was Holmes's contention that "in less than twenty years it would be a common thing to grow in these United States men sixteen and seventeen feet high; and intellectual in proportion." Three of the participants recollected that Dr. Holmes discoursed on "the superiority of Englishmen." Duyckinck, writing on the following day to his wife, claimed that Melville attacked Holmes vigorously, Hawthorne looking on.

In 1878, in *Yesterdays with Authors*, in a chapter devoted to his friendship with Hawthorne, Fields recalled that at dinner "Hawthorne rayed out in a sparking and unwonted manner," and that in the bantering exchange with Holmes, it was "Hawthorne stoutly taking part in favor of the Americans." It was undoubtedly Melville who took up the cudgels for the United States. Two weeks after the famous banquet, in *The Literary World*, he was to make a vigorous defense of American authors and to pull out all the emotional stops; and earlier in the year, in *White-Jacket*, he at one point sounds like a Fourth-of-July patriot, in a passage which begins, "And we Americans are the peculiar, chosen people — the Israel of our time; we bear the ark of the liberties of the world."

After three hours the participants, undaunted by, or perhaps stimulated by, food and talk, were ready for one more excursion to complete the kind of day which appealed to that muscular century. The party, apparently only the males this time, was guided by an after-dinner guest, John Tyler Headley, author of two-volume studies of *Napoleon and His Marshalls* and *Washington and His Generals*. The destination was Ice Glen, which Mathews declared, erroneously, to be three miles away. It is a gorge not far from Laura's Tower, perhaps a mile from Field's home, where boulders as well as trees have fallen in helter-skelter fashion, and some of the rocks, topped with ferns and green mold, form tunnels that make voices resound with doomlike intensity. There "you can have iced punches in their natural state in the middle of August," Mathews wrote. "A dark and slippery region, with oozing rocks for stairways, and rotten logs for bridges." Hawthorne was a trifle Gothic when he observed that Ice Glen looked "as if the Devil had torn his way through a rock & left it all jagged behind." When Melville a few months later was composing that extraordinary chapter in *Moby-Dick* entitled "A Bower In the Arsacides," he recalled "a wondrous sight. The wood was green as mosses of the Icy Glen; the trees stood high and haughty, feeling their living sap; the industrious earth beneath was as a weaver's loom, with a gorgeous carpet on it, whereof the ground-vine tendrils formed the warp and woof, and the living flowers the figures."

After the passage of twenty-eight years, Fields recalled that "Hawthorne was among the most enterprising of the merrymakers; and being in the dark much of the time, he ventured to call out lustily and pretend that certain destruction was inevitable to all of us." Mathews described the action somewhat differently: "Such face of melancholy we never in all our mortal life witnessed, as did our Boston Bibliopole [Fields] put on when he saw his two prize-producers — now under way with a volume each — the Essayist and Town Wit [Hawthorne and Holmes], engage in the neck-endangering progress through the treacherous gully, dripping with anxiety and mournfully repining at his own fat, which kept him from sallying forth. 'Ten per cent more to your authors on your next book, and *you'll* have less fat to complain of,' was quietly suggested to the struggling and perspiring book-man."

On the way back from Ice Glen the men tried "a pass or two with some scythes lying in the meadow," and then to Field's home and "coffee, conversation, Fay the Poodle taking an active part on his hind legs, and giving his opinion of the music in a jargonic howl equal to the most learned professor." It was almost ten o'clock. The "Feast of Quidnuncs" was ended — and stomachs, muscles, and wits must have been tired. Mathews pronounced a benediction in the pages of *The Literary World*:

Good-bye, friends, all round. Friends at the Umbrage, farewell — God speed you safely over the ocean in your new path of travel, and return you wisely and safely to the dear harborage of Stockbridge! Shake hands all round. Our kind and liberal entertainer sees us to the cars — away!

Hawthorne and the Fields returned to Stockbridge Bowl by carriage. Melville, Holmes, Duyckinck, and Mathews went to the New Haven Railroad Station less than a mile away. A friendly conductor named Conklin took pity on "three roving knights of the quill" — Melville, Duyckinck, and Mathews — stopped the train at a bridge before the Pittsfield station to save them "a footsore tramp at midnight. Be all conductors like him: and may every Berkshire Festival-Day, like this of ours, be provided with an Evening Star, like that, to rise upon the train and cheer us just when he is wanted." Holmes apparently continued on the train to the Pittsfield station.

On his return to New York Duyckinck sent his host a dozen bottles of Heidseck champagne and some cigars. In his reply, on August 16, Melville indulged in the literary camaraderie of Young Americans and *The Literary World*, with some semiblasphemous remarks as garnish. "What are you doing there, My Beloved, among the bricks & cobble-stone *boulders*? Are you making mortar? Surely, My Beloved, you are not carrying a hod? — That were a quizzical sight, to see any godly man, with a pen behind his ear, and a hod on his shoulder." From this parody of the Song of Solomon Melville turned to Milton and Cooper's Indians in acknowledging "the cigars! — The Oriental looking box! and the Antilles smell of them! And the four different thrones & dominations of bundles, all harmonizing together like the Iroquois." As for the champagne: "Twelve more beautiful babies than you sent me in that wicker cradle by Express, I have never seen. Uncommon intelligence was in their aspect, and they seem full of animation & hilarity. I have no doubt, if they were let alone awhile, they would all grow to be demijohns."

Mathews could not refrain from a second farewell in *The Literary World* on September 7 at the conclusion of what a contemporary journalist termed "somewhat Puffery Hopkinsy yava about Berkshire." Unlike Melville, he blended his overstrained literary frivolity with God-fearing, sentimental platitudes.

Parting in mirth and free hilarity — when shall we meet again! When will any two or three of that gay company, in memory and friendly talk, revive these scenes of innocent enjoyment? Long, long in this heart at least, as on a stage, will those happy scenes be re-enacted: one by one shall those dear friends come up and glide by, smiling on us once again, waving their friendly hands, and bid us God speed on our course: — God speed all, dear friends!

"Germinous Seeds"

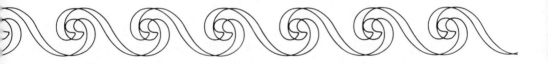

"The 5th of August was a happy day throughout, and I never saw Hawthorne in better spirits," James T. Fields wrote in 1878. In his journal entry for August 5, 1850, Hawthorne kept laconically and stubbornly to the facts.

> Rode with Fields & wife to Stockbridge, being thereto invited by Mr. Field of S. — in order to ascend Monument mountain. Found at Mr. F's Dr. Holmes, Mr. Duyckinck of New-York, also Messrs. Cornelius Mathews & Herman Melville. Ascended the mountain — that is to say, Mrs. Fields & Miss Jenny Field — Messrs. Field & Fields — Dr. Holmes, Messrs. Duyckinck, Mathews, Melville, Mr. Henry Sedgwick, & I. — and were caught in a shower. Dined at Mr. F's. Afternoon, under guidance of J. T. Headley, the party scrambled through the Ice Glen.

If he felt exhilarated by the outing, he kept the reaction to himself;

29

Hawthorne's prose was always as controlled as his person. A certain rigidity is evident not only in the coolness of the recital of events but also in the scrupulous observance of social hierarchies; Dr. Holmes, the most eminent of the participants, is given precedence, while for the most part names are given in alphabetical order. Even in the privacy of his diary Hawthorne seldom abandoned his self-protective reserve or recorded anything that might be offensive to eyes that, like Miles Coverdale's, pried into the depths of the human personality.

A few days later, on August 8, Hawthorne had visitors at his little red farmhouse overlooking Stockbridge Bowl, which Duyckinck termed "one of the most purely beautiful spots in the region." The guests met Mrs. Hawthorne, who, Duyckinck informed his wife, "resembles Margaret Fuller in appearance though more robust than she was." He praised the Italian prints on the walls, especially "a fine engraving of the Transfiguration presented by Emerson," and noted the "great taste" of a woman who knew intuitively how to smooth out any disparities between the artifacts of the Old World and the rustic simplicity of an American farmhouse. Hawthorne served champagne to his guests with the nervous elegance of a sybaritic puritan. In Duyckinck's most perceptive comment: "Hawthorne is a fine ghost in a case of iron — a man of genius and he looks it and lives it — He gave us some Heidsieck which a literary friend had presented to him, popping the corks in his nervous way."

In his journal Hawthorne noted his second meeting with Melville with customary (alphabetical) precision: "Messrs. Duyckinck, Mathews, Melville, & Melville, Jr., called in the forenoon. Gave them a couple of bottles of Mr. Mansfield's champagne, and walked down to the lake with them."

About this time Hawthorne lifted slightly the veil of reserve when he wrote to an old college friend, Horatio Bridge: "I met Melville, the other day, and like him so much that I have asked him to spend a few days with me before leaving these parts." The Melvilles planned only to spend the summer in the Berkshires and to return to New York City in the fall. As matters turned out, Hawthorne would leave Lenox in the fall of 1851 and the Melvilles would remain in Pittsfield for thirteen years.

So far as we know, Melville had nothing to say, directly, about the events that took place on August 5, 1850, or about this second meeting with Hawthorne. What he had to say in *The Literary World,* on August 17 and 24, in what was intended as a review of Hawthorne's *Mosses from an Old Manse,* was more personal and impassioned than anything in Mathews's three installments. While Mathews and Duyckinck were still enjoying the sights about Pittsfield, Melville found time to retreat to his study in "the *garret-way,* seated at that little embrasure of a window . . . which commands so noble a view of Saddleback," the tallest mountain in the Berkshires. There he wrote vigorously and rapidly, as though his life depended upon it — and indeed, in some sense, perhaps it did.

For months Melville had been working, in his usual fevered fashion, on *Moby-Dick,* and on June 27 he had informed his English publisher that it was almost finished, which was no doubt an over-statement. Shortly after he arrived in Pittsfield he discovered *Mosses from an Old Manse.* It was a moving experience. He recognized at once a kindred spirit, a man who said "NO in thunder." Then, un-expectedly, he met the celebrated author and cavorted with him on Monument Mountain and in Ice Glen. In his restless, searching eyes the timid, shrinking Hawthorne was transformed into a magnetic personality. No doubt Melville hesitated to express his feelings to Hawthorne in person, but he let the words explode in the pages of *The Literary World.* He was not a man given to temperate responses or to understatement. When he was moved, he was moved to the core of his being. He exposed his vulnerable heart everywhere he turned, without the self-protectiveness with which Hawthorne surrounded his equally vulnerable heart.

The review was unsigned. The sub-title read: "By a Virginian Spending July in Vermont." Melville had no Southern ties and he read Hawthorne's tales, as we know, in Pittsfield. In the second installment he added to the fiction: "I never saw the man; and in the chances of a quiet plantation life, remote from his haunts, perhaps never shall." The disguise served its purpose, at least for awhile, in deceiving the Hawthornes. Mrs. Hawthorne told her mother not to "wait an hour to procure the two last numbers of 'The Literary World,' and read a new criticism on Mr. Hawthorne. . . . I know you will enjoy the words of this ardent Virginian as I do." On August 24 Longfellow sent Hawthorne a copy of the notice, and commented: "I have rarely seen a more appreciating and sympathising critic; and though I do not endorse all he says about others, I do endorse all he says about you." To Evert Duyckinck Mrs. Hawthorne wrote, breath-lessly: "Who can he be, so fearless, so rich in heart, of such fine intuition? Is his name altogether hidden?"

Sophia Hawthorne's excitement was understandable. This was no ordinary review. Not only was her husband made into an Ameri-can Shakespeare, but the affective tone of the images and metaphors revealed an unusual personal involvement, as Longfellow noted, of the reviewer with his subject.

Mrs. Hawthorne felt the involvement — she characterized the tone as "ardent" — but, like most readers and many critics, she distrusted her emotional response, and saw the image pattern as literary embellishment, not as a "safe" mechanism for an author to reveal himself nakedly. Patterns of imagery sometimes reveal more than seemingly explicit confessions which often hide as much as they reveal because of the natural resistance of most men to public disclosure of inner secrets. Melville himself could not have realized, although he may have had intimations, how the emotional impact of Hawthorne upon him imposed an unconscious and consistant structure in a series of images that gradually led to the final climactic metaphor: "Already I feel that this Hawthorne has dropped germinous seeds into my soul. He expands and deepens down, the more I contemplate him; and further and further, shoots his strong New England roots into the hot soil in my Southern soul."

Mrs. Hawthorne and most readers, then and now, politely ignored the fact that the metaphor is an image of insemination. They refused, because they preferred to attribute artistic inspiration to nonphysical sources and to ignore the maternal and sexual components in the creation of an artifact. Geniuses seldom suffer from such blindness: it is their lot to see into themselves and into mankind, and to bear the burden of their insights. At the time Melville spoke of "germinous seeds" he was wrestling with Ahab's whale, and knew at first hand the ordeal of giving birth, which is a recurrent motif in the novel, from the opening words, when Ishmael is born, to the epilogue, when the orphan is rescued by the *Rachel,* and *Moby-Dick* is born.

A few days after he composed his article for *The Literary World,* in a letter to Duyckinck, Melville was still preoccupied with the subject. He labeled the twelve bottles of champagne "beautiful babies" in a "wicker cradle," and referred to the desk in "the *garret-way*" as "covered with the marks of fowls — quite white with them — eggs had been laid in it — think of that! — Is it not typical of those other eggs that authors may be said to lay in their desks, — especially those with pigeon-holes?"

The article opens conventionally — and prettily — enough, but before the conclusion of the first paragraph emotion breaks through.

> A papered chamber in a fine old farm-house, a mile from any other dwelling, and dipped to the eaves in foliage — surrounded by mountains, old woods, and Indian ponds, — this, surely, is the place to write of Hawthorne. Some charm is in this northern air, for love and duty seem both impelling to the task. A man of a deep and noble nature has seized me in this seclusion. His wild, witch-voice rings through me; or, in softer cadences, I seem to hear it in the songs of the hill-side birds that sing in the larch trees at my windows.

The language is reminiscent of Mathews's precious pictorial sense, but phrases like "has seized me" and "rings through me" indicate that Melville is not simply a passive recorder of literary and personal impressions. Hawthorne appears as a natural, even supernatural, force that enchants and hypnotizes, as Ahab mesmerizes the crew of the *Pequod*. Hawthorne himself recognized the impact of his writings upon the unknown reviewer when he commented to Duyckinck: "He is no common man; and, next to deserving his praise, it is good to have beguiled or bewitched such a man into praising me more than I deserve."

After the opening paragraph, Melville proceeds slowly and somewhat digressively — his often is the art of digression, sometimes magnificent, sometimes not — to observe that "on a personal interview no great author has ever come up to the idea of his reader" — which may be an oblique comment on his initial response to Hawthorne the person, or, more probably, another deliberate deception to conceal his identity. Almost at once he balances the remark with a reference to "the enchanting landscape in the soul of this Hawthorne, this most excellent Man of Mosses." He playfully explains the appearance of his review four years after publication: "It may be . . . that all this while the book . . . was only improving in flavor and body." A pleasant compliment, of course, an old book and an aged wine, but with the almost trite remark he inconspicuously introduces what will become a pattern of oral imagery.

> At breakfast the other day, a mountain girl, a cousin of mine, who for the last two weeks has every morning helped me to strawberries and raspberries, which, like the roses and pearls in the fairy tale, seemed to fall into the saucer from those strawberry-beds, her cheeks — this delightful creature, this charming Cherry says to me — "I see you spend your mornings in the haymow; and yesterday I found there 'Dwight's Travels in New England.' Now I have something far better than that, something more congenial to our summer on these hills. Take these raspberries, and then I will give you some moss." "Moss!" said I. "Yes, and you must take it to the barn with you, and good-by to 'Dwight.' "

> With that she left me, and soon returned with a volume, verdantly bound, and garnished with a curious frontispiece in green; nothing less than a fragment of real moss, cunningly pressed to a fly-leaf. "Why this," said I, spilling my raspberries, "this is the 'Mosses from an Old Manse.' " "Yes," said cousin Cherry, "yes, it is that flowery Hawthorne." "Hawthorne and Mosses," said I, "no more: it is morning: it is July in the country: and I am off for the barn."

If truth may intrude upon Melville's somewhat romanticized account, the book was given to him not by a Cousin Cherry, but by his Aunt Mary, the wife of his favorite uncle, Thomas Melvill, at whose desk in the next fifteen months he was to rewrite *Moby-Dick*. Cherry's name is appropriate for her function as mistress of the breakfast banquet and consistent with the nature and food imagery surrounding "flowery Hawthorne." The constant references to food are not accidental or picturesque, as Melville himself will make clear before the end of the article. When he sees the little green book, he unaccountably spills his raspberries. A playful detail perhaps, but in a significant scene in the last tale he wrote, Billy Budd spills his soup in a seemingly trivial episode which has tragic consequences and psychological meaning.

Early in the day, then, in fertile July, Melville is off to the barn, where food is stored, to absorb *Mosses from an Old Manse*.

> Stretched on that new mown clover, the hill-side breeze blowing over me through the wide barn-door, and soothed by the hum of the bees in the meadows around, how magically stole over me this Mossy Man! and how amply, how bountifully, did he redeem that delicious promise to his guests in the Old Manse, of whom it is written – "Others could give them pleasure, or amusement, or instruction – these could be picked up anywhere – but it was for me to give them rest. Rest, in a life of trouble! What better could be done for weary and world-worn spirits? What better could be done for anybody, who came within our magic circle, than to throw the spell of a magic spirit over him?" So all that day, half-buried in the new clover, I watched this Hawthorne's "Assyrian dawn, and Paphian sunset and moonrise, from the summit of our Eastern Hill."

> The soft ravishment of the man spun me round about in a web of dreams, and when the book was closed, when the spell was over, the wizard "dismissed me with but misty reminiscences, as if I had been dreaming of him."

On the surface, Melville appears to be playing with food imagery in an affected fashion, but a more subtle process is taking place. He speaks of "the rich and rare distilment of a spicy and slowly-oozing heart," but Hawthorne indulges in "no gross fun fed on fat dinners, and bred in the lees of wine." His "spiritually gentle" humor is "richly relishable," worthy of "an angel," but different from the jaded appetite of jaded adults. "The orchard of the Old Manse," Melville writes, "seems the visible type of the fine mind that has described it." Indirectly, but inevitably, he evokes Eden and the beginning of the race: "hushed in the noon-day repose of this Hawthorne's spell, how aptly might the still fall of his ruddy thoughts into your soul be symbolized by 'the thump of a great apple, in the stillest afternoon, falling without a breath of wind, from the mere necessity of perfect ripeness!' " Insistently, diction and images reiterate that Hawthorne's book provides nourishment, that it is blessed with maternal powers.

Gradually Hawthorne assumes a godlike role, combining male and female roles. He has "such a boundless sympathy with all forms of being, such an omnipresent love, that we must needs say that this Hawthorne is here almost alone in his generation." First there is the all-encompassing maternal love, and then "a great, deep intellect, which drops down into the universe like a plummet." Next Melville explores "this great power of blackness in him" which "derives its force from its appeals to that Calvinistic sense of Innate Depravity and Original Sin." "It is," he admits, "that blackness in Hawthorne . . . that so fixes and fascinates me," and this in turn leads to the assertion that Hawthorne is Shakespeare's equal. (Sophia confessed to her sister: "At last some one dares to say what in my secret mind I have often thought — that he is only to be mentioned with the Swan of Avon; the great heart and the grand intellect combined.")

One after another Melville invokes omnipotent figures — Hawthorne, Calvin, Shakespeare — extraordinary men who blended male potency and female creativity. "There are minds," he declares without naming them, "that have gone as far as Shakspeare into the universe. And hardly a mortal man, who, at some time or other, has not felt as great thoughts in him as any you will find in Hamlet." And then a seemingly conventional, democratic overassertion: "Believe me, my friends, that men, not very much inferior to Shakspeare, are this day being born on the banks of the Ohio." But surely he is referring to a man born in Albany, New York, on August 1, 1819, named Herman Melville.

And, as he later candidly admits, in praising Hawthorne "I have more served and honored myself, than him." Which means, if we follow the logic of his associations, that he ranks himself with Hawthorne, Calvin, Shakespeare. This admission leads him to acknowledge what too many critics want to deny, that writing is autobiography.

> And if you rightly look for it, you will almost always find that the author himself has somewhere furnished you with his own picture. For poets (whether in prose or verse), being painters of nature, are like their brethren of the pencil, the true portrait-painters, who, in the multitude of likenesses to be sketched, do not invariably omit their own; and in all high instances, they paint them without any vanity, though at times with a lurking something that would take several pages to properly define.

"Twenty-four hours," he tells us, "have elapsed since writing the foregoing. I have just returned from the hay-mow, charged more and more with love and admiration of Hawthorne." To express this deepening appreciation he reverts to the food analogy: "I found that but to glean after this man, is better than to be in at the harvest of others."

Now he arrives at his climactic statement. His own words reveal how inadequate Sophia Hawthorne's "ardent" is to summarize the effect of *Mosses from an Old Manse* upon Melville. "To what infinite height of loving wonder and admiration I may yet be borne, when by repeatedly banqueting on these Mosses I shall have thoroughly incorporated their whole stuff into my being, — that, I cannot tell." After the double entendre on "borne" — Melville himself finally finds the right word — *incorporated*.

The images coalesce in the word. *Incorporated*, on one level, implies absorption, the taking in of food or nourishment. On another level it implies *penetration*. And the next sentence inevitably makes Hawthorne the seedman, the penetrator: "Hawthorne has dropped germinous seeds into my soul." As in the earlier godlike analogy, Hawthorne assumes two active roles, maternal and paternal. Melville plays two passive roles, the child and the woman, the receiver and the ravished.

"He expands and deepens down, the more I contemplate him; and further and further, shoots his strong New England roots into the hot soil in my Southern soul." This statement, even with the defensive pun at the conclusion, is but the culmination of what he has twice hinted earlier: "how aptly might the still fall of his ruddy thoughts into your soul be symbolized by 'the thump of a great apple' " and "a great, deep intellect . . . drops down into the universe like a plummet."

Melville chose to disguise the "Southern soul" as that of "a Virginian." The South to Melville, whether Typee or the American South, was associated with fertility, love, freedom, the feminine principle. In his book review he is the receiver, the receptacle of Hawthorne's spiritual seeds. His pseudonym, which like most pseudonyms rests on mysterious unconscious sources, is feminine too — Virginia, virgin, spring.

"Hawthorne and His Mosses" is scarcely literary criticism in any ordinary sense. It is a love letter, a confession which Melville can make safely within what purports to be a book review. The article reverberates because it was charged with the writer's longings from his early years. Its reverberations were to be heard and felt throughout Melville's life.

A Growing Man
and
a Father Confessor

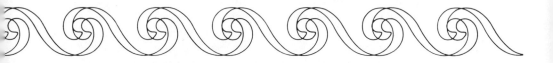

When they met on August 5, 1850, Hawthorne was forty-six, Melville thirty-one. The difference in age was significant. Even Mathews recognized the difference. In his allegory Melville was New Neptune, but Hawthorne was Mr. Noble Melancholy. The prefix attached to Hawthorne's disguise recognized the sobriety and maturity of middle age, as well perhaps as the achievement that was *The Scarlet Letter*. Although both writers resorted to nineteenth-century high jinks during the course of the excursions to Monument Mountain and Ice Glen, it was Melville who scampered to the end of a projecting rock while he played at being a sailor on a mountain bluff, with a reckless disregard for life and limb and an athleticism that distinguished him from his older, more dignified companions.

Perhaps I overemphasize the incident, but, as the relationship of Hawthorne and Melville unfolded, it foreshadowed the roles the two men were destined to play in ways which neither fully understood.

Of the two, Melville was the more masculine, physical presence: he was robust in appearance, forcefully muscular, and his bewhiskered, fleshy face had a ruddy virility. In Mrs. Hawthorne's words: "He is tall & erect with an air free, brave, & manly." Years at sea had left their mark, and one has no trouble seeing him at the masttop, climbing the rigging, or scrambling up a boulder on Monument Mountain.

Hawthorne was another kind of presence, his decorum matched by his slight, graceful, almost willowy body. There was something ethereal about him, as there is about his sympathetic "heroes," Arthur Dimmesdale, Miles Coverdale, the Reverend Mr. Hooper, and others. At this time Hawthorne had a magnificent high forehead, thinning hair, a long, ascetic face; the mouth was delicate and sensitive, the chin receding. The attire — the black coat, the high collar, the silken cravat — set off the fragile countenance. The tokens of middle age did not conceal the beauty — no other word will do — of that face which in youth and early manhood had almost a virginal delicacy and which in maturity wavered, as James Russell Lowell noted, between the beauties of the two sexes:

> When Nature was shaping him, clay was not granted
> For making so full-sized a man as she wanted,
> So, to fill out her model, a little she spared
> For some finer-grained stuff for a woman prepared,
> And she could not have hit a more excellent plan
> For making him fully and perfectly man.

Although we can hear in the background of Lowell's lines echoes of Shakespeare's hermaphroditic sonnet, number twenty, we must see and listen with a "third ear" in order to grasp the curious reversal evident in the Hawthorne-Melville relationship: Shakespeare is the older man in love with, or enamored of, a unisexual youth, but, in "Hawthorne and His Mosses" the younger, more overtly masculine man falls in love with a middle-aged Prince Charming. The pathos of age in pursuit of youth has often been told with understandable sympathy by artists like Shakespeare, Walt Whitman, and Thomas Mann, and, since the pursuit is at least in part the artist's attempt to recapture his own youth, the treatment of such delicate, personal material never sinks to the burlesque invariably present in a Chaucer or a Molière, for example, when an old man attempts to seduce or marries a girl young enough to be his daughter.

The drama in the Berkshires, as we observe the agitations of a thirty-one-year-old youth and of a middle-aged recluse, was more poignant and complex than the tales related in "The Sonnets," "Calamus," and "Death in Venice." The wounded narcissism of an aging artist in pursuit of what he knows to be a quixotic, elusive reincarnation of the irrecoverable, is haunting, elegiac autobiography. Hawthorne and Melville, however, were not artifacts, but men endowed, even overendowed, with all the vulnerabilities men, particularly artists, are heir to.

Despite his elegant manners and his soothing, sonorous voice, Hawthorne moved with nervous grace. As Duyckinck noted, in his hands champagne corks popped nervously. The veil Hawthorne drew around himself, and his characters — probably no writer has been so obsessed with veils, literal and figurative — camouflaged but directed attention to an inner restlessness. Externally he appeared as a kind of man of iron, but at what price we can only speculate. His prose was always under extraordinary control, even when he dissected the abysses of the human heart. He had difficulty in reading the finished manuscript of *The Scarlet Letter* to his wife, we are told in a famous story, but, as D. H. Lawrence and generations of readers have discovered, he unfolded his emotion-laden tale within a beautifully wrought artistic structure. The vertical thrusts of the three scaffold scenes, like the brush strokes of a painter, place throbbing emotion within a frame, at the same time emphasizing but containing it.

Everyone knows that Hawthorne after graduation from Bowdoin College returned to Salem, Massachusetts, and hibernated for seven years, reportedly emerging only at night from what must have been for a young man a house as gloomy as the seven-gabled mansion. After this period of incubation, when his journeys were mostly psychic imaginings, he contemplated going to sea at just about the time Melville was in the South Seas. Following his marriage to Sophia Peabody, he moved restlessly from place to place, from Salem to Concord, to Salem again, to Stockbridge Bowl, to West Newton, and eventually to England. The surface in Hawthorne's life and art always retained a kind of eighteenth-century coolness, like Henry Adams's prose, but the inner turbulence which made him the kin of Dostoevsky and Melville surfaces in the subject matter he deals with.

The cool grace of his prose veils his characteristic subject: the young male, usually in his twenties, paralyzed by fears of sexuality, matrimony, and social interaction. The "good" Mr. Hooper assumes a black veil, a kind of displaced fig leaf, to reveal tangibly and publicly his awareness of a universal "secret sin" and at the same time to escape marriage to Elizabeth. Goodman Brown loses faith in life and in his wife Faith after a journey into the forest, and lives out his days in morbid gloom. Giovanni, despite his amorous name, shrinks before Beatrice Rappaccini's passion. Arthur Dimmesdale holds his delicate white hand to his palpitating heart as he seduces his audience with his ministerial eloquence. Miles Coverdale, the poet-voyeur, retreats from the Blithedale experiment in communal living to his "cozy" bachelor quarters, where he asserts his love for Priscilla, now safely married to Hollingsworth. Everywhere is fear — of sexuality, of powerful male figures, and perhaps of life itself. Self-imposed isolation is the only escape, or evasion. There is peace only in death or sometimes, as in the last scaffold scene in *The Scarlet Letter*, at the bosom of a maternal figure like Hester Prynne.

Unlike Hawthorne, Melville moved with graceless, muscular energy which made visible the inner agitation Hawthorne concealed. In his teens he did not retire to a room for introspective self-analysis. Like Whitman, he tried one job after another, and drifted purposelessly. Like many of his contemporaries and his fictional heroes, he took to the sea, where he accepted incarceration in an all-male, rigorously hierarchical and harsh environment with crews that were ordinarily alcoholic and debauched dropouts in search of nothing so concrete, or crazy, as Ahab's anthropomorphic anti-god. Ishmael's "hypos" were his creator's. As Ishmael's prose expands and contracts in a kind of manic rhythm alternating between exhilaration and despair, between effervescent wit and abysmal blackness, so Melville's face and person vacillated with his mood-swings. Inner tensions surfaced and erupted, and then retreated. Some attributed his moody silences to contempt for people or to aloofness; few knew, although they are everywhere evident in his greatest works, the volcanic fires in his heart. When the despair of blackness strangled him, he was truly the American descendant of Ecclesiastes, who was one of his favorite authors, and his vision was as dark as the madness that consumes Ahab. In euphoric moods he was wildly playful, a delightful companion and a great comic writer, the only American descendant of Rabelais.

Because Melville viscerally identified with his material — his emotions were not recollected in tranquility — only rarely did he achieve the safety and detachment of Hawthorne's distancing. He plunged deep; Hawthorne veiled. Melville wore his heart on his sleeve. Hawthorne, like Dimmesdale, was fastidious. Dimmesdale, it will be recalled, attired himself in his Sunday finery before he ventured to the scaffold in the middle of the night, at Mistress Hibbins's witching hour, to make his "confession" before a nonexistent audience. Thunderingly, like Ahab and Pierre, Melville proclaimed in a letter to Hawthorne: "I stand for the heart. To the dogs with the head! I had rather be a fool with a heart, than Jupiter Olympus with his head." Hawthorne shared the sentiment, but not the inflated expression. The cost of Melville's genius was exorbitant, physically, emotionally, and artistically.

For approximately fifteen months Hawthorne and Melville were neighbors in the Berkshires. Melville went frequently to Stockbridge Bowl, to the red farmhouse. Though Hawthorne occasionally came to Pittsfield, the younger man, as "Hawthorne and His Mosses" foretells, was clearly the pursuer. Hawthorne doubtlessly recognized in Melville a wayward but fascinating genius, and perhaps secretly envied the younger man's vigor, as Owen Warland, the delicate artist in "The Artist of the Beautiful," secretly admires Richard Danforth's assertive masculinity. Melville, on the other hand, found in Hawthorne the living embodiment of an icon which appears in his earliest writings. Melville's letters present one-half of the engagement, and, not surprisingly, in his correspondence with a man who exerted a magnetic attraction upon his affections, he suddenly became a great letter writer, as he became a significant critic in "Hawthorne and His Mosses." He apparently destroyed Hawthorne's replies, with a reckless indifference to posterity, again not surprising for a man who shared Ahab's destructive tendencies and for whom the world was to become only five years later a sham, a "Masquerade."

The only other observer who left a record of this confrontation of genius was Sophia Peabody Hawthorne. In her own way, in letters to her family, Mrs. Hawthorne was as skilled a portraitist as either of the two men. Partisans of Melville have sometimes suspected her fairness in her eagerness to defend and almost to deify her husband, and she certainly kept out of her letters any indications of the disharmony within Hawthorne's nature. Although she undoubtedly colored her reports with her own unstinted love for her husband, she was enormously attracted to Melville, and her accounts have the authenticity of love which in legend and reality may be fickle but often comes closer than the unsympathetic mind to the essential truth of the human personality. She had discovered that Melville was the author of the extravagant review in *The Literary World*, when in September 1850 she wrote to her mother: "I am not sure that he is not a very great man — but I have not quite decided upon my opinion — I should say, I am not quite sure that I *do not think* him a very great man — for my opinion is of course as far as possible from settling the matter." Tentative as she was, she did not have to laud Melville at all; she did not know that posterity would one day peep over her shoulder to scan a letter she thought reserved for her mother's eyes.

Although Duyckinck, in 1850, considered her more robust than Margaret Fuller, Sophia Peabody had been a semi-invalid for many years. She was the daughter of a prominent Salem family that occupied one of those graceful houses which made the maritime center one of the architectural masterworks of the nineteenth century.

Sophia had a fragile, birdlike loveliness, not too different from her husband's. Because of her uncertain health, and perhaps because of Hawthorne's natural timidity — for complex reasons he, like Emerson and Poe, chose an invalid to be his wife — the courtship had proceeded for four years with the slow rhythm of not overly passionate participants. Hawthorne was thirty-eight when he led his "rose" to the altar. Marriage transformed Sophia: she regained her health and blossomed as wife and mother. She became pregnant about the time Hawthorne and Melville met, and their third child, appropriately named Rose, arrived on May 20, 1851, a month after the publication of *The House of the Seven Gables*.

While Melville wrestled with the white whale, Hawthorne wrote his epithalamion, a worthy companion of a poem by one of his favorite authors, Edmund Spenser. *The House of the Seven Gables*, which resembles a crewellike embroidery, pays a delicate tribute to Sophia's loveliness in the character of sun-kissed Phoebe. Holgrave, whose name syllabically resembles Hawthorne's, gradually allows his chilled heart to be thawed by Phoebe's warmth, and at the conclusion of the romance the two depart hand in hand from the blood-stained gabled house for a New Eden, where even the once sterile chickens will again breed and live happily ever after. At one point in the tale old Uncle Venner, a kind of cracker-barrel New England philosopher, embraces Phoebe with an image that reveals Hawthorne's search for the ideal mother: "you are somehow as familiar to me as if I had found you at my mother's door, and you had blossomed, like a running vine." Strangely, years later, in "A Monody," his epitaph to his former friend, Melville characterizes Hawthorne as a "cloistral vine," and in *Clarel* Hawthorne reappears in Melville's canvas as Vine.

For over a year Mrs. Hawthorne observed the friendship of the two men. Melville, and perhaps the relationship itself, puzzled her, but at last, in a letter to her sister Elizabeth Peabody, she arrived at a summation in the form of a graphic picture. "Nothing pleases me better," she wrote, "than to sit & hear this growing man dash his tumultuous waves of thought up against Mr Hawthorne's great, genial, comprehending silences." What Melville himself, in a letter to Hawthorne, labeled, with characteristically self-deflating wit, his "ontological heroics," she saw more sympathetically as "tumultuous waves of thought" dashing against "Hawthorne's great, genial, comprehending silences — out of the profound of which a wonderful smile, or one powerful word sends back the foam & fury into a peaceful booming, calm — or perchance not into a calm — but a murmuring expostulation — for there is never a 'mush of concession' in him. Yet such love & reverence & admiration for Mr Hawthorne as is really beautiful to witness — & without doing anything on his own part, except merely *being,* it is astonishing how people make him their innermost Father Confessor." A brilliant picture it is of an excitable son in the presence of a judicious father; and Sophia's intuition was inspired as far as Melville was concerned. But what she may not have fully perceived, taken in by Melville's virtual deification of the husband she too deified, was the fact that Melville's exuberance was almost an assault, and that the role of "Father Confessor" was a kind of anomalous paternity which forced Hawthorne to invade Melville's personality and at the same time open his own reserved nature to invasion. Hawthorne's tremulous characters shrink from such assaults, and surely his own fears made the unpardonable sin in his writings invasion or rape of another person.

"In the golden light of evening twilight," after she learned that he was the author of the articles in *The Literary World,* Melville confided in Mrs. Hawthorne. "He told me," she noted on one occasion, "he was naturally a silent man, that he was complained of a great deal on this account; but that he found himself talking to Mr. Hawthorne to a great extent. He said Mr. Hawthorne's great but hospitable silence drew him out — that it was astonishing how *sociable* his silence was." About this time Melville was describing a scene in *Moby-Dick* between a young man named Ishmael, a former schoolteacher, and a tattooed harpooner, Prince Queequeg among his own people. Despite cultural and linguistic barriers, and after a lot of farcical misunderstanding, the two men arrive at an understanding in one of the few tender moments in the novel. "Soon I proposed a social smoke; and, producing his pouch and tomahawk, he quietly offered me a puff. And then we sat exchanging puffs from that wild pipe of his, and keeping it regularly passing between us . . . and when our smoke was over, he pressed his forehead against mine, clasped me round the waist, and said that henceforth we were married; meaning, in his country's phrases, that we were bosom friends."

"When conversing," Sophia Hawthorne wrote in another letter, Melville "is full of gesture & force, & loses himself in his subject — There is no grace nor polish — once in a while, his animation gives place to a singularly quiet expression out of those eyes, to which I have objected." Here she captured the volatility of Melville's personality, but what eluded her, probably because it was foreign to her own temperament, was the virtuosity of a man who was not conventionally decorous, but who was capable of verbal brilliance and even scatological jokes beyond the powers of her husband. Melville was a lover of words and word-mongers like Rabelais, Sir Thomas Browne, and Thomas Carlyle. Words tumbled forth in abandon, sometimes uncontrollable abandon, as though he imagined that if he found *the* word he would find the *key* to existence. Yet, as Newton Arvin shrewdly observes, Melville's verbs are colorless and passive, not unlike in this respect his colorless, passive narrator-heroes. The images are often static, and to that extent passive, as we have seen in "Hawthorne and His Mosses," where amid hyperbole and extravagance emerge patterns of personal needs.

Sophia admired Melville's virile presence: "His nose is straight & rather handsone, his mouth expressive of sensibility & emotion." But she objected to the eyes, or perhaps, more accurately, was troubled by them. "He seems to see every thing very accurately," she wrote to her mother, "& how he can do so with his small eyes, I cannot tell. They are not keen eyes, either, but quite undistinguished in any way." Later she was again drawn back to those eyes — "an indrawn, dim look, but which at the same time makes you feel — that he is at that instant taking deepest note of what is before him — It is a strange, lazy glance, but with a power in it quite unique." Obviously perplexed but fascinated, Mrs. Hawthorne could not drop the subject until she finally groped toward insight: "It does not seem to penetrate through you, but to take you into himself." Once again she intuited more than she could probably have explained.

If in extant photographs and paintings Melville's eyes do not seem especially noteworthy, or for that matter small in the portrait Asa W. Twitchell painted about 1847, we had best trust to Mrs. Hawthorne's perception, since she was not examining eyes frozen in portraiture, but eyes which were as alive and mobile as the words that poured from the mouth of her "growing man."

Melville's small, restless eyes at sea and on land searched for an ideal beauty which was also a human ideal. The ideal in Hawthorne is always the beautiful embodiment of the ideal mother, as in Hester Prynne or Phoebe Pyncheon. Melville's ideal is male: the classical head, finely articulated muscularity, but usually with hermaphroditic attributes that soften the male body. Ordinarily the icon depicts a handsome youth of about the same age as the protagonist whose adventures are based on Melville's at about the same age, but sometimes the ideal figure is old enough to be the protagonist's father.

The sources of the icon are easily identified — the sculpture of Phidias, Apollo Belvedere, and the Narcissus legend. The sources, however, are not so important as the reasons for an attraction that appears in his first literary work in 1839 and reappears, with similar phraseology and imagery, fifty years later in the tale he was writing before his death in 1891. The icon blends Narcissus, Apollo, Ishmael — but also Jupiter, Jehovah, Abraham.

It was unveiled for the first time in his first published work, "Fragments from a Writing Desk," which appeared in *The Demo-*

cratic Press and Lansingburgh Advertiser on May 4 and 18, 1839, when Melville was a few months short of his twentieth birthday. "Fragments" is a letter addressed by a young man with the initials L. A. V. to an older man ambiguously identified as M. A wealthy, cultivated man of "beloved features," M. sits in his library in a "dear, delightful, old-fashioned sofa" with "luxurious padding" reading a "huge-clasped quarto." his "gentle protégé," the author, is attempting to prove in "the virgin purity and whiteness" of his letter that he has abandoned his "hang-dog modesty," and "that hereafter you shall not have occasion to inflict upon me those flattering appellations of 'Fool!' 'Dolt!' 'Sheep!' which in your indignation you used to shower upon me." He assures M. that he has rid himself of "this annoying hindrance": he has, in short, become a man. Or in L. A. V.'s coy words: "by coming to the conclusion that in this pretty corpus of mine was lodged every manly grace; that my limbs were modelled in the symmetry of the Phidian Jupiter; my countenance radiant with the beams of wit and intelligence, the envy of the beaux, the idol of the women and the admiration of the tailor." Suddenly, he declares, he finds himself "beautiful as Apollo, dressed in a style which would extort admiration from a Brummel, and belted round with self-esteem as with a girdle."

After asserting his beauty, but protectively in his self-conscious, half-mocking tone, L. A. V. does not proceed to become the village Casanova. Instead, he retreats into the role of the passive observer of the village belles — or the three graces of Lansingburgh, to be faithful to Melville's unoriginal mock-heroic device. Finally, he musters his malehood, but only when challenged by an "Inamorita," who sends him a *billet doux:* "Gentle Sir — If my fancy has painted you in genuine colours, you will on receipt of this, incentinently [sic] follow the bearer where she will lead you." In her apartment L. A. V. seizes her in his virile arms, "imprinting one long, long kiss upon her hot and glowing life" — only to be saved from a fate worse than that inflicted by Edgar Allan Poe upon his blonde heroines. "With a wild cry of agony I burst from the apartment! — She was dumb! Great God, she was dumb! DUMB AND DEAF!"

A trivial, banal piece of writing. We can mock, but we should not be too certain that Melville did not have a "wicked" sense of humor long before he wrote *Moby-Dick*. Nor should we make the mistake of most commentators and condescend to "Fragments from a Writing Desk" as unfortunate and mistaken juvenilia, the sooner forgotten the better. In their earliest efforts authors often write out of their personal experience more transparently than at the height of their powers when the reticences of age and the refinements of their well-filed art may somewhat disguise autobiographical disclosures.

Despite affectations, conventionalities, triviality, "Fragments from a Writing Desk" is an important document if we are to understand Melville personally and artistically. It unveils some of his major themes as well as some of his life-long preoccupations. The precious wit and affected prose cannot be dismissed simply because they were commonplaces in literary circles in the nineteenth century, as we can see in Cornelius Mathews's account of the meeting of Hawthorne and Melville. Periodically throughout his career, particularly in the pages of *Pierre,* Melville resorted to affected diction, not because he was incapable of other styles and other prose rhythms, but because the affectation permitted him to mock while he unveiled troubling emotional materials. Melville's prose styles reflect the complexities of his nature. That there is not a definable Melvillean style only points up the fact that Melville's is an elusive personality.

"Fragments from a Writing Desk" anticipates the later works in that it centers about a young man's relationship to an older, paternal figure. L. A. V. is apparently without a family, an orphan in other words, the first of the Ishmaels that will appear almost everywhere in Melville's writings.

L. A. V., as his literary effusion itself indicates, prides himself on his artistic talents and his cultivation. He separates himself from his peers, as the greenhorn sailors in the novels will isolate themselves from illiterate crews and pride themselves somewhat snobbishly on their intellectual and social accomplishments. L. A. V. is the forerunner of Redburn, White-Jacket, Ishmael, and Pierre, all young men proud of their ancestry and their cultivation and eager to establish relationships with their equals.

M., of "beloved features," is a bachelor, a father without a wife, who in turn — worse still — would be a mother. The idealized fathers in the later works — Jack Chase and Captain Vere, for example — will reject the matrimonial principle. M. is depicted in his library, and the revered fathers in the novels are invariably cultured men and sometimes, as in the case of Jack Chase, as affected as L. A. V. The model of M.'s library was no doubt the one which Melville had known in childhood, his father's, which contained an impressive collection of French books and prints.

The affected prose obscures somewhat the description of a rite of passage from boyhood to manhood, understandably so, since the rite of passage is unsuccessful. L. A. V. seeks to demonstrate his manhood, not to the Lansingburgh belles, but to M. Like the later greenhorn sailor protagonists of the novels, L. A. V. clothes himself in Apollo's beauty to attract M. and men. Note how he, unwittingly, orders his admirers: "my countenance radiant with the beams of wit and intelligence, the envy of the beaux, the idol of the women," and

"Apollo, dressed in a style which would extort admiration from a Brummel." When the exclamation points of the conclusion fade and the ordinary prose of uninflected reality asserts itself, L. A. V. has not established his manhood. He is at the conclusion as at the beginning a beautiful "child-man" acknowledging failure and still seeking the caresses of "those flattering appellations of 'Fool!' 'Dolt!' 'Sheep!' "

If we assume, as I believe we must, that there are few or no accidents in literary works, the initials L. A. V. may be a Melvillean word play on *laugh* or *love* or *lave,* words which characterize the seriousness behind the self-conscious mockery of the narrator, his craving for the affection and approval of M., and the desire to perpetuate the adolescent state. M. may stand for Melville, father or son, or, more probably, for both. For the sketch presents what in Melville is an ideal father-son relationship, a father worthy of a beautiful son and a son who grows beautiful in order to win and to deserve the father's love. The Apollo-like youth seeks the paternal bosom.

An almost unnoted aspect of nineteenth-century American art is the worship of Apollo. Benjamin West and the painters of his school depicted the human body according to the Apollonian idealization. George Catlin found Apollo in the wilds of America among the Indians, as did James Fenimore Cooper before him. Cooper knew little about Indians at first hand, but his sympathetic red men, Uncas in *The Last of the Mohicans* or Hard-Heart in *The Prairie,* are Apollos of a culture crumbling before the assaults of white "snivilization." These Indian Apollos reflect Cooper's disenchantment with a world which had no room for his archetypal bachelor-hero, Natty Bumppo, who, interestingly, is willing to play "father" only to these two beautiful young men. Everywhere in the nineteenth century there were plaster replicas of Apollo Belvedere and inexpensive engravings of the famous sculpture.

Melville journeyed to Rome for the first time in 1857. In his journal he devoted little space or attention to the seductive grace of Venus, but his prose becomes caressing before "Antinous, beautiful ... head like moss-rose with curls & buds — rest all simplicity — end of fillet on shoulder — drapery, shoulder in the mantle — hand full of flowers & eyeing them — the profile &c. The small bronze Apollo." (If we are reminded of Billy Budd, it is no mistake.) Later in the year, after his return to the United States, he joined the lyceum circuit, that nineteenth-century forerunner of adult education which attempted to bring enlightenment to a culturally underprivileged nation. According to the account of his lecture in the *Boston Journal* on December 3, 1857, "The lecturer next turned to the celebrated Apollo Belvedere. This stands alone by itself, and the impression made upon all beholders is such as to subdue the feelings with wonder and awe. The speaker gave a very eloquent description of the attitudes and the spirit of Apollo. . . . The Venus de Medici, as compared with the Apollo, was lovely and not divine." Melville probably did not appreciate the reporter's concluding sentence: "The lecture was quite interesting to those of artistic tastes, but we fancy the larger part of the audience would have preferred something more modern and personal." The journalist's response foreshadowed Melville's brief, unsuccessful career as a lecturer. Trained to observe externals, the newspaperman could not realize how "personal" and "artistic" the lecture actually was.

During his speech Melville alluded to a "native maiden, in the precise attitude of the Venus," to Fayaway, who in the pages of his first book assumes a graceful, almost seductive pose as the white sail of a canoe. But she is a sentimental confection, not a brown-hued embodiment of feminine sexuality. It is difficult for her to play Venus to Tommo, the adolescent narrator-hero who is perfectly content to be treated as a child by the natives. Fayaway's beauty pales before "one of the most striking specimens of humanity that I ever beheld" — a native named Marnoo, who, free of the rigid taboos of his society, wanders without check from tribe to tribe in the lovely islands of the Pacific.

> The stranger could not have been more than twenty-five years of age, and was a little above the ordinary height; had he been a single hair's breadth taller, the matchless symmetry of his form would have been destroyed. His unclad limbs were beautifully formed; whilst the elegant outline of his figure, together with his beardless cheeks, might have entitled him to the distinction of standing for the statue of the Polynesian Apollo; and indeed the oval of his countenance and the regularity of every feature reminded me of an antique bust. But the marble repose of art was supplied by a warmth and liveliness of expression only to be seen in the South Sea Islander under the most favorable developments of nature. The hair of Marnoo was a rich curling brown, and twined about his temples and neck in little close curling ringlets, which danced up and down continually when he was animated in conversation. His cheek was of a feminine softness, and his face was free from the least blemish of tattooing. . . .

Tommo is jealous when Marnoo usurps the attention of the natives which up to this time he has been enjoying exclusively. "The glory of Tommo is departed," he wails, but at the same time Marnoo's magnetic attraction forces him to play the role of a suitor. He offers a seat to the handsome native, whose only garment is "a slight girdle of white tappa." (The Lansingburgh Apollo, it will be recalled, is "belted round with self-esteem as with a girdle.") When "the stranger passed on, utterly regardless of me," Tommo feels like a spurned woman: "Had the belle of the season, in the pride of her beauty and power, been cut in a place of public resort by some supercilious exquisite, she could not have felt greater indignation than I did at this unexpected slight." As in "Fragments from a Writing Desk," the facetiousness is deceptive and self-protective. Melville is often most serious when he is most facetious; wild outbursts of farce and wit conceal depths of despair, which are related to personal hurts. Later Tommo wins Marnoo's favor and even his assistance in his plans to escape from the cannibalistic tribe. Tommo's "success" in his flight, in his escape from the tribe and Fayaway, now far away, is failure, for, like L. A. V., he fails to arrive at man's estate — and in the next romance tags along as the companion of Long Ghost, a peripatetic bachelor-amorist.

In Melville's fourth novel, Wellingborough Redburn, another greenhorn like Tommo, leaves behind in upper New York State his mother and three sisters, but carries with him what he considers to be the magical protection of his once distinguished family name, the symbol of which is the red hunting jacket that he purchases before he boards ship. Examining himself before a mirror, adorned in the red jacket, he is in his own eyes a Lansingburgh Apollo, a valentine, as it were, to the burly crew. He expects to become the pet of the sailors, the adopted "son" of solicitous fathers, while he is away from the solicitous care of his mother. Unfortunately his perception of his role in an all-male society is not that of sailors, who find his name amusing and pretentious. His jacket is a snobbish insult to the rough-and-ready camaraderie which mandates conformity in attire no less peremptorily than the ship rules impose conformity in conduct. Redburn is rebaptized Buttons, a name appropriately epicene in view of Redburn's confusion as to his sexual role when he courts the sailors. Buttons-Redburn becomes a kind of pet: like L. A. V., he enjoys the gratifications of abuse. But wanting more than this negative attention, which in this instance is without the counterbalance of M.'s affection, he eventually likens himself to Ishmael.

In Liverpool the "orphan" finds a "chummy" in a foppish young Englishman who, like Redburn himself, wavers between the sexes. Redburn is again the suitor: "I smoothed down the skirts of my jacket, and at once accosted him." Harry Bolton "was one of those small, but perfectly formed beings, with curling hair, and silken muscles, who seem to have been born in cocoons. His complexion was a mantling brunette, feminine as a girl's; his feet were small; his hands were white; and his eyes were large, black, and womanly; and, poetry aside, his voice was as the sound of a harp." Harry is too aristocratic, amoral, and effeminate to satisfy Redburn's "whole soul . . . when, in its loneliness, it was yearning to throw itself into the unbounded bosom of some immaculate friend." On the return trip to New York, while Harry replaces his friend as the butt of the crew, they find among the passengers a fifteen-year-old, "rich-cheeked, chestnut-haired Italian boy" named Carlo, a strolling musician whose appearance is as attractive as his songs:

> The head was if any thing small: and heaped with thick clusters of tendril curls, half overhanging the brows and delicate ears, it somehow reminded you of a classic vase, piled up with Falernian foliage.
>
> From the knee downward, the naked leg was beautiful to behold as any lady's arm; so soft and rounded, with infantile ease and grace. His whole figure was free, fine, and indolent; he was such a boy as might have ripened into life in a Neapolitan vineyard. . . .

(Or, interestingly, Carlo may have "ripened into life" in the character of Donatello in Hawthorne's *The Marble Faun*.) Redburn-Bolton-Carlo is one icon, of three youths bewildered and frightened in puberty, of a Lansingburgh Apollo who eventually returns home to a protective mother.

In *White-Jacket* the would-be sailor-hero assumes the name of the protective (maternal) garment or girdle he wears, and eventually finds the very model of paternity, not in Captain Claret, whose behavior is as intoxicatingly capricious as his name suggests, but in Jack Chase, "our noble First Captain of the Top." Chase is "a Briton, and a true-blue; tall and well-knit, with a clear open eye, a fine broad brow, and an abounding nut-brown beard." He has, we are told, "a bald spot, just about the bigness of a crown-piece, on the summit of his curly and classical head." Like White-Jacket he is an orphan of good birth: "Jack must have been a by-blow of some British Admiral of the Blue." Like M., he is a bachelor, a man among boys. Chase adopts the boy and takes him to his table, where he provides not only food for the body but also for the mind or soul. Chase, it turns out, is conversant with many languages and is better acquainted with poetry and literature than White-Jacket himself. This balding Apollo, then, fuses physical grace, well-defined masculinity, and culture. Like M., he is a product of the library, and speaks not like a sailor but like a preciously bookish man. With unconcealed delight White-Jacket becomes Chase's "pet."

Chase's impression upon Melville was deep and lasting. They met in August 1843 aboard the frigate *United States*. Melville eulogizes their relationship in *White-Jacket,* which he completed in

August 1849. When Melville returned to prose narrative after a silence of thirty years and delineated his last Apollo-Ishmael in the hermaphroditic perfections of yellow-haired Billy Budd, he dedicated the work to Jack Chase, "Wherever that great heart may now be / Here on Earth or harbored in Paradise."

White-Jacket was completed exactly one year before Melville met Hawthorne on August 5, 1850. Melville's "keen eyes" must have noted that Hawthorne had the classical head and the beauty of the sculptured figure he had fashioned in his icon. There was in Hawthorne the hermaphroditic quality of Marnoo, Bolton, and Carlo, and "the summit" of the "curly and classical head" was balding like Chase's.

It is of course coincidental, but not without interest, that Sophia Hawthorne likened her husband to Apollo. Shortly after her marriage she wrote to her sister: "Mr. Hawthorne has written a little, and cultivated his garden a great deal; and as you may suppose, such vegetables never before were tasted. . . . When Apollos tend herds and till the earth, it is but reasonable to expect unusual effects." In another letter a short time later she observed: "We have the luxury of our maid's absence, and Apollo helped me by making the fires. . . . Apollo boiled some potatoes for breakfast."

It is one of the ironies of the relationship of Hawthorne and Melville that in the drawing room of Hawthorne's red cottage at Stockbridge Bowl — what he facetiously called his Scarlet Letter — stood a wedding gift, a plaster cast of Apollo with his head tied on — a fractured witness to the dialog of the two authors.

That Melville saw Hawthorne as the realization of his icon was evident in one of Mrs. Hawthorne's first reports of the meetings of the two authors: "He said Mr. Hawthorne was the first person whose physical being appeared to him wholly in harmony with the intellectual & spiritual. He said the sunny hair & the pensiveness, the symmetry of his face, the depth of eyes, 'the gleam — the shadow — & the peace supreme' all were in exact response to the high calm intellect, the glowing, deep heart — the purity of actual & spiritual life."

At last, but all too briefly, wish and reality converged in Melville's life. It is no wonder that he became, like L. A. V., a "growing man" in the presence of a "Father Confessor." Nor is it surprising that manic exhilaration overcame Melville, as the straining prose in "Hawthorne and His Mosses" confirms. The exhilaration spilled over into the pages of *Moby-Dick*, which has verbal whirlpools aplenty, risings and fallings of mood and action.

Unfortunately, the living icon was but tremulous flesh — the flesh of a Salem recluse. Had Hawthorne been endowed with the virtues Melville attributed to him, he could not have fulfilled the expectations. For fifteen months the "growing man" and the "Father" acted out what could only become tragicomedy, long enough for Melville to rewrite *Moby-Dick* and for the first time to reveal the genuis of his wild imaginative energies. Then Hawthorne withdrew, no doubt with his characteristic and ingrained dignity but perhaps with some haste too.

The Apollonian icon originated not so much in Melville's knowledge of myth or sculpture as in his evaluation or misevaluation of the males in his own family. From his perspective, though he was by no means homely, he apparently saw himself in his early years as an ugly duckling, with large ears and with a heavy, stolid Dutch body. As Ezra Ames's portrait reveals and as the description of Mr. Glendinning in *Pierre* makes clear, Allan Melvill was a handsome man, with a sensitive and delicate face. Herman's older brother, Gansevoort, who was the favorite of both parents, was also unusually handsome. The Apollo figures in Herman's fiction have "delicate ears" and lithe limbs.

Since Herman had the opportunity granted almost only to artists, he was able to reconstitute his cosmos and to repair his damaged self-image. He gives to his young heroes an extraordinary attractiveness and through their Apollonian aura they win attention and favor. Except for Billy Budd his Apollos have Herman's brown hair, and they are inclined to dote over their charms before mirrors. The men to whom they are magnetically drawn have the same overpowering beauty. A woman who wrote to Melville sensed that he was indulging in what we would call wish fulfillment: "Are you the picture of him you so powerfully represent as the Master piece of all Gods works, Jack Chase?"

That Melville was not unaware of the implications of his icon or fantasy and his projections is indicated in his recourse to parody and to cloying sentimentality when his "lovers" meet and woo, or Melville makes love to himself. Such were the longings of his unrequited love that he was "predestined" to swoon before the icon. Yet in a significant passage in the first chapter of *Moby-Dick* Ishmael-Melville underscores the dangers of self-love.

> And still deeper the meaning of that story of Narcissus, who because he could not grasp the tormenting, mild image he saw in the fountain, plunged into it and was drowned. But that same image, we ourselves see in all rivers and oceans. It is the image of the ungraspable phantom of life; and this is the key to it all.

Abraham
—Allan Melvill

The world began for Herman Melvill on August 1, 1819, when Dr. Wright Post delivered him at 11:30 P.M. The delivery was performed at home, at 6 Pearl Street, not far from the New York harbor. On the following day the father informed his brother-in-law of the arrival of his third child.

> With a grateful heart I hasten to inform you of the birth of another Nephew, which joyous event occurred at 1/2 past 11 last night — our dear Maria displayed her accustomed fortitude in the hour of peril, & is as well as circumstances & the intense heat will admit — while the little Stranger has good lungs, sleeps well & feeds kindly, he is in truth a chopping Boy —

On August 19 the "little Stranger" was baptized Herman by the Reverend Mr. Mathews of the South Reformed Church. He was named after his mother's oldest brother, General Herman Gansevoort. On September 10 Mrs. Melvill took her three children to Albany to escape the annual New York cholera epidemic and remained with the Gansevoorts until November 18. The father stayed behind to watch over his import business: "the alarm of Fever has suspended the little Business doing, but I hope with the blessing of GOD, confidence will soon return & Business revive again."

With romantic hindsight some biographers have observed that Herman arrived in the world under inauspicious omens, not unlike those surrounding Ishmael when he sets sail on the *Pequod* on Christmas day. His father's business was none too secure, and nature, abetted by man's carelessness, was exposing one of her destructive moods that shake the confidence of some men. But for the "chopping Boy," fondled and catered to by presences he could not see, the world existed not in terms of man-made or natural fluctuations of business and epidemics, but in the more immediate fluctuations of satisfied and unsatisfied needs of his small body.

For a time he was a tyrant who made imperial and egomaniacal demands, like Ahab. Gradually, as his consciousness wakened and broadened, he was toppled from his "topmost greatness." His self-love had to embrace the unpleasing fact that the world did not begin with his birth; that parents were entities, sometimes whimsical and self-centered, not simply suppliers of his needs on demand; and that his tyranny was threatened by rivals. The disenchantment was inevitable and painful. Yet escape as he would — and later he was to abandon the prison of the green land for the illusory freedom of life at sea — Herman could not escape his cosmos which included, besides himself, Allan Melvill, Maria Gansevoort Melvill, and a brother and a sister, Gansevoort and Helen Maria.

The rich fantasy life and the innate talent of the genius permit him to achieve in art what is not permitted to Everyman in life: he reconstitutes his cosmos, peoples it to suit his purposes and pleasures, and restores himself to the central position all too briefly held in his earliest years before the unwelcome appearance of additional rivals in the form of brothers and sisters. In the eyes of many readers Melville is a writer of cosmic dimensions, an explorer of abysses and blackness, and a man with a tormenting, life-long quarrel with God. Although it sometimes seems that he deals only rarely and then indirectly with the human cosmos — the family with its relationships and interactions — actually the family and the child in relationship to his parents occupy a central place in his books through a unifying biblical myth. As John Milton universalized his blindness by recalling the blind seers of antiquity, so Melville universalized his canvas and his self-pity when he equated the pangs of his disenchantment and deprivations with those of the biblical "hero" who was sent from

home to wander in the wilderness. Melville's greatest narrator-pro-
tagonist has neither kin nor name. In three indelible words he supervises his own delivery and birth and his own baptism: "Call me
Ishmael."

When it was that Herman began to find parallels to his life
history in the biblical story of Abraham, Sarah, Hagar, Ishmael, and
Isaac, we do not know, but the myth appears in his writings for the
first time in *Mardi,* his third book, which he began in 1847 but did
not complete until 1849. Taji, a greenhorn narrator like Ishmael,
describes various kinds of sharks and their destructive propensities.
After observing that sharks and seraphs "were made by the same
hand," he continues: "No Fury so ferocious, as not to have some
amiable side. In the wild wilderness, a leopard-mother caresses her
cub, as Hagar did Ishmael." A short time later Taji introduces Samoa
and Annatoo. "Like the valiant captains Marlborough and Belisari-
us," he writes, the husband "was a poltroon to his wife. And Annatoo was worse than either Sarah or Antonina."

In his fourth book, Wellingborough Redburn, the bumpkin with
the pretentious name of which he is absurdly fond, becomes the
ship's fool. "I found myself," Redburn observes, "a sort of Ishmael
in the ship, without a single friend or companion; and I began to feel
a hatred growing up in me against the whole crew — so much so, that
I prayed against it, that it might not master my heart completely,
and so make a fiend of me."

When Pierre discovers himself in a situation in which he must
choose between his mother, the embodiment of middle-class respectability, and his half-sister, the illegitimate offspring of his father's
wayward sexuality, the narrator resorts to the biblical analogy: "Yet
was this feeling entirely lonesome, and orphan-like. Fain, then, for
one moment, would he have recalled the thousand sweet illusions of
Life; tho' purchased at the price of Life's Truth; so that once more
he might not feel himself driven out an infant Ishmael into the
desert, with no maternal Hagar to accompany and comfort him."
Even Israel Potter, the most pathetic of Melville's bumpkins, is an
Ishmael who after fifty years of wandering is denied a father as well
as a fatherland. In *Clarel,* the long poem which Melville wrote two
decades after he abandoned prose, once again the hero is an
"Omoo," or rover, and once again Ishmael is evoked:

> *And, in this land named of Behest,*
> *A wandering Ishmael from the West;*
> *Inherited the Latin mind,*
> *Which late — blown by the adverse wind*

Of harder fortunes that molest —
Kindled from ember into coal.

While the Apollo icon represents the hope for the restoration of
a state more perfect than the paradise lost, the Ishmael icon presents
the harsh reality of the rejected son, with his wounded pride and his
scarcely concealed self-pity.

Although Melville was one of eight children, in restructuring his
world fictionally, except in *Redburn,* he chose to deal with an only
child, usually an orphan, sometimes a bastard without definite
knowledge of his parentage, although he somehow knows that he is
of good birth. Ishmael is the logical, even obvious prototype for
slumbering resentments toward parents and brothers and sisters and
for public dramatization of a wounded ego. To Herman's questing
consciousness the legend acted as a magnet because of deeper, perhaps unconscious, parallels to his *feelings* about his life situation.

The recorder of the biblical tale slighted and failed to dramatize
the emotional core — the father's rejection of his son — because he
was not interested in the lot of the half-breed Ishmael, child of
Abraham and the Egyptian Hagar, but in the continuity of his people, the transmission of the heritage from Abraham to Isaac. Bowing
before the aged Sarah's insistence, Abraham banished Ishmael from
"civilization" to the wilderness, where his only companions were
Hagar and female attendants. The boy was about thirteen, on the
verge of puberty, when Abraham refused his blessing and deprived
him of a male model. Isaac had usurped the father's love, and
Ishmael not only felt himself cheated by the intruder but also in-
dicted himself as unworthy of his father's love. He felt betrayed and
unworthy, and at the same time he hated the man who rejected him,
and felt guilty before his hatred.

In Herman's adaptation of the ancient story, or, perhaps more
accurately, in his self-dramatization, he played the central role — the
rejected Ishmael, hungering for his birthright. Allan Melvill, however
ineffectual as a father and a provider, assumed the role of Abraham.
The rival for the father's affection was Gansevoort, Herman's older
brother. To Maria Melvill fell a more complex role because of the
adapter's ambivalence: she was Sarah, the tyrannical, emasculating
mother, but she was also Hagar, the mother worthy of the love
Herman-Ishmael wishes to bestow upon her and — more important —
to receive from her.

Like most fathers Allan Melvill was not especially deserving of
immortality. His life was short — he was forty-nine when the embers
burned out — and he had not distinguished himself in war or peace,

in art or business, or, for that matter, in the family as husband, father, and provider. In life he steadfastly maintained that he had done his "duty." In death his survivors were not certain that word had been wedded to performance. For, in truth, Allan was a failure, not the "happy failure" his son was later to describe in an unconvincing rationalization of a nonexistent state.

Allan Melvill was of a hardy race of Scottish warriors and brawny men that traced its ancestry to the thirteenth century. Although there was little of the soldier about him, he boasted of his lineage, the more so as his own achievements failed to match the glories of the past, which he tended to exaggerate in order to draw one of the morals to which he was addicted. The truth was that when the Melvills came to America in the eighteenth century, they, like most of the early settlers, had fallen on hard times in their native lands, and had sought a new beginning in what some termed a New Eden. Allan's father, Thomas Melvill, was left an orphan, and his climb to success owed nothing at all to his warrior ancestry, but a great deal to his industry and to chance. Greatness came to Thomas, and to his descendants, when, in the words of his son, he performed a "daring chivalric deed in the destruction of the Tea." The Boston Tea Party bore little resemblance to the heroics of the age of chivalry except in the eyes of a romantic son, but Thomas's involvement and his subsequent service to his country in the Revolutionary War earned him the title of major. Major Melvill never tired of recalling his day of greatness. He displayed a vial purportedly filled with tea, in the words of the *Boston Evening Transcript,* "with as much holy reverence as the miraculous robes of St. Bridget by the superstitious believer of the anti-Protestant faith." Cornelius Mathews saw the relic when he came to Pittsfield in August 1850. The tale was endlessly repeated by generations of Melvills.

In 1789 Major Melvill was appointed Collector of the Port of Boston by President George Washington. He held this comfortable sinecure for forty years, until Andrew Jackson relieved him and incurred the ire of his son. Snugly settled into the untaxing job, Major Melvill, like Rip Van Winkle, cultivated his eccentricities. Since for him time had stopped in 1773, he wore the tricornered hat and uniform of the era when the nation achieved its freedom. He became as time passed a delightful Boston anachronism, amiable, personable, and talkative. In one of his first poems, in "The Last Leaf," Oliver Wendell Holmes recalled how his "grandmamma" had said of Major Melvill

> That he had a Roman nose
> And his cheek was like a rose
> In the snow.

But now his nose is thin,
And it rests upon his chin
    Like a staff,
And a crook in his back,
And a melancholy crack
    In his laugh.

I know it is a sin
For me to sit and grin
    At him here;
But the old three-cornered hat,
And the breeches, and all that,
    Are so queer!

Holmes obviously delighted, and not maliciously, in a "queer" old man, but when Herman recalled his visits to his grandfather, he looked back with pride and nostalgia, as in this affectionate passage in *White-Jacket:* "Out on all furniture fashions but those that are past! Give me my grandfather's old arm-chair, planted upon four carved frogs . . . ; give me his cane, with the gold-loaded top . . . ; give me his broad-breasted vest, coming bravely down over the hips, and furnished with two strong-boxes of pockets to keep guineas in; . . . and give me my grandfather's gallant, gable-ended, cocked hat."

The public posture concealed the drive and shrewd business sense which enabled Major Melvill to accumulate a substantial fortune. His letters to Allan were no-nonsense affairs filled with references to business. Unlike his sons he had no time for sentimentality — or failure. Like Ben Franklin, Major Melvill was fond of aphorisms, but he never abdicated his common sense and critical judgment: he knew the limitations of the deity's involvement in human affairs. Unfortunately this knowledge, this acumen, was never transmitted to his sons. Early in their careers Thomas and Allan enjoyed brief periods of prosperity and independence and for a while had romantic dreams of success. The romances ended abruptly: long after they fathered large families they remained economically dependent upon their father. Thomas lived on, and mismanaged shamefully, a farm at Pittsfield which belonged to his father.

After Allan went into business for himself in 1818, he gradually in the next twelve years used up a potential inheritance in order to stave off bankruptcy. In 1821 he borrowed $2,000 from his father in March, and in May Thomas was imprisoned for debt. "Our afflictions," the first-born wrote to Allan, "are indeed great, very great, — we endeavour to believe they are for our own good, — here, or hereafter — for that purpose, they are undoubtedly intended, — and may He, who cannot err, vouchsafe to support us, under the heavy burthen." Thomas's pious words salved his pride, but the self-pity, which he chose to dignify as resignation to God's will, was the response of a man who was snuggling into failure and dependency.

After Allan's death Thomas befriended Herman and served as a kind of guide whose advice could be trusted in all matters except financial. Although he could not run a successful farm in Pittsfield or keep himself out of debtors' prison, Thomas was an intelligent man. (His father, however, had his doubts: "If he thinks at all, which I *very much* doubt, [he thinks] only of himself.") He was interested in education and offered the townspeople wise counsel which they unwisely chose not to heed. "His manners were mild and kindly," his nephew was to write, "with a faded brocade of old French breeding." Thomas had his father's eccentricities and always managed to fail with elegance.

Herman recalled the quaint spectacle of his uncle in the hayfields near the farm: "He never used the scythe, but I frequently raked with him in the hayfield. At the end of a swath, he would at times pause in the sun, and taking out his smooth-worn box of satin-wood, gracefully help himself to a pinch of snuff, partly leaning on the slanted rake, and making some little remark, quite naturally, and yet with a look, which — as I now recall it — presents him in the shadowy aspect of a courtier of Louis XVI, reduced as a refugee, to humble employment, in a region far from the gilded Versailles." Herman confessed that Uncle Thomas "impressed me as not a little interesting, nor wholly without a touch of pathos."

Allan, the second son, born in 1782, never fulfilled his father's praise, "my sheet Anchor . . . my hope." He started out with the supposed advantages of affluence when he took the American equivalent of the grand tour at the beginning of the nineteenth century. Allan stayed in Europe for some years, learned French, and gradually collected an impressive library of books and prints. A portrait painted in France about 1810 reveals him as an American rake abroad. The fashionable attire of a dandy became his soft, somewhat effeminate face and delicate curls better than the ancestral soldier's garb. If his son is not fabricating — which is a distinct possibility, given Herman's "wicked" sense of comedy — in the history of the Glendinning family in *Pierre,* Allan had an affair while he was abroad, which, like most Don Giovannis, he handled ineptly.

Allan's qualifications for a career were good looks, no small regard for his abilities, the gift of verbalization, and invincible optimism. Life should have rewarded him with a fortune or with a sinecure like his father's — his talents would have been an adornment, and the position would have provided a built-in stability which he lacked — but since life rarely smiled on him, he entered the import business in 1807 and was for the rest of his life associated with the clothing trade. For a time Allan was reasonably successful until a ship of which he was part owner was captured by the British in 1811. This was the first of the reverses which dogged him in his all too brief life.

Allan may have been a dandy abroad, but when he married he wed a most respectable young lady. In the course of business trips in upper New York State he met Maria Gansevoort, the only daughter of General Peter Gansevoort. The Gansevoorts, like the ancestors of Henry James, were a prominent, successful Albany family. This Dutch family came to New York in the seventeenth century, and from generation to generation son succeeded father in business and added to the family wealth and station. Allan was thirty-two when he married Maria Gansevoort in 1814.

When Allan was abroad in 1818 he confessed his love for Maria with an extravagance that may make the cynical distrust his fervor but that no doubt came from the heart. "There is so much about thee My Love," he wrote, "of all that the heart wishes, or the eyes look for in Woman. . . . I long to behold again the only object who ever reigned unrivalled in my affections." He informed her repeatedly — perhaps too often — that she could "confide implicitly in the constant fidelity, unchangeable love & undivided devotion of your husband & Lover." Although the young ladies in Liverpool wore their skirts too short, he found this "indecent & unbecoming exposure," and in Paris he denied himself the "diversions" of that attractive city because his heart "glows only with devotion to one earthly object." Allan had learned well from the writings of the sentimentalists, and he had quite a command of the well-turned, balanced sentence of sentiment.

In marrying Maria, Allan married the family, and for the next four years he lived with his mother-in-law and his brother-in-law. After the death of General Gansevoort in 1812, Peter Gansevoort, a lawyer and a graduate of the College of New Jersey (later Princeton University), became the head of the household, and eschewed marriage until after his mother's death in 1830. Peter managed the Gansevoort interests, but, interestingly, Allan wore General Gansevoort's ring. The family set Allan up in a dry goods business, but he was not satisfied for long in this role. In 1816 he was considering moving either to New York or to Boston to set up his own business. Two years later he went abroad, to Liverpool, Edinburgh, London, and Paris, to renew old acquaintances and to establish contacts in the trade. In November 1818 he was Allan Melvill, Esquire, Merchant, at 123 Pearl Street in New York City.

Although Allan worked hard for success, he relied from the outset too much upon the resources of his father and the Gansevoorts. His father may have been understanding, but Maria's family could hardly be without some serious reservations. Allan's incessant appeals for loans from the Gansevoorts in the 1820s abused his expectations. As aware as he was of appearances, he should have recognized the damage of his appeals to his image in the eyes of the Gansevoorts and Maria. His "success" in marrying Maria, in short, had a price; the General's ring became a symbol of his dependency.

The first two Melvill children were born in the Gansevoort house in Albany. Allan began to pay his debt when he allowed his first son to be named Gansevoort Melvill. No doubt the Gansevoorts were pleased, but the boy was to pay an awesome price for his mother's pride and his father's weakness. The second child, Helen Maria, was named after one of the Gansevoort ladies. In fact, the Melvill children until the appearance of the fifth one, Allan, were all to bear Gansevoort names — a trifling point perhaps, but trifles sometimes reveal relationships, dependencies, and sources of power.

Allan fathered a large brood at two-year intervals, except for the three-year spacing before the appearance of the last child in 1830. There were eight children in all. As the family multiplied, so did his problems in the import business. At times he was solvent and even sometimes successful but generally through the aid of loans he received from the Gansevoorts, his aging father, and an old classmate at Amherst Academy, Lemuel Shaw, who was to play an important role in the history of the Melvill family.

Like many businessmen, Allan was incurably opportunistic. When business was in the doldrums, he moved from one house to another, each one more expensive and fashionable than its predecessor. With his faith in God he kept his faith in upward mobility. He provided well for the children but sometimes with other people's money. He baptized them into the Dutch Reformed faith and dutifully filled their ears and souls with the truisms of Franklin and the Bible. He tried to be the human counterpart of the "almighty Parent." He failed to recognize, or concealed from himself, that his patriarchal moralisms were mouthed in a household that necessarily was matriarchal.

The Melvill ancestry was the only stability that Allan could cling to. And as his personal charm became as bankrupt as his business affairs, he clung pathetically. If he had nothing to look forward to with hope, to paraphrase Robert Frost's characterization of another failure, he could at least look backward with pride. With the kind of bravado and irrelevancy he was prone to, he preceded his seven-year-old son's visit to Albany with a note to Peter Gansevoort:

"I now consign to your especial care & patronage, my beloved Son Herman, an honest hearted double rooted Knickerbocker of the true Albany stamp, who I trust will do equal honour in due time to his ancestry parentage & Kindred." He would at least make Peter aware that donor and recipient were equals by birth, if not in the account books. A few weeks later, in August 1826, to a Melvill nephew about to leave for the Pacific he wrote with a patriotic and familial pride worthy of the warship on which the young man sailed:

> The name you bear should also inspirit you to services of the highest estimation in private society, & to deeeds of noble daring in public life; descended through a long line of respectable Ancestors, from a scottish Hero, who emblazoned by his achievements an hereditary title, which came down to him from remote antiquity, & who fell on Floden Field in defence of his Country's freedom; *your* great object with GOD's blessing must ever be, to preserve the Family name unsullied in social intercourse with the World, & render it conspicuous in the naval history of the Nation. . . .

> . . . and to sum up all in one emphatic sentence — perform your Duty "without fear & without reproach," and whenever this calls to action, seek honour with undaunted front amid the war of elements, or the din of battle, incur death rather than infamy & sooner return no more, than come back to us disgraced —

Captivated by the "noble daring" of his ancestors, he forgot as he wrote that a month earlier he had made an appeal to his father for a loan to shore up his ailing business. The Melvill name like a narcotic offered momentary solace as he retreated into a dream which failed to alter or to reverse reality. The glories in which he took much satisfaction must have been painful reminders of his own inadequacies.

The first child to be born after the family moved to New York was Herman, who, almost a century later, in the 1920s, was to restore the family to greatness. Two weeks after Herman's birth Allan informed his father that "business is absolutely stagnant, I am in fact doing nothing, & daily rejoice I have done no more, for those who have done little are the best off — we still have numerous failures & more anticipated." As always, Allan saw the worst in the best possible light. The summer epidemic which took Maria and the three children to Albany early in September 1819 was, as usual, much exaggerated, according to Allan, by those "whose interest it is to cry mad Dog at the appearance of a puppy." He was alone in the house on Pearl Street, and the epidemic had further dampened business, as he informed his father:

This is hard, very hard luck for me, who can so ill afford it, however, what cannot be cured must be endured, & there is no profit in repining at irretrievable calamities — though Fortune has played me many a scurvy trick, I will not complain of the fickle Goddess, who may yet be inclined to smile graciously upon me, & I will still endeavour to merit her future favours by patience, resignation, and perseverance — I am neither emulous of riches or distinction, they are both insufficient to ensure happiness, or purchase health, a man may do very well in private life with a mere competency, & if I can only provide for the rational wants of my beloved Wife & Children, I shall be content with my lot, & bless the hand from which all favours come. . . .

Like most nonrealists Allan rarely defined the abstractions by which he professed to live. He took what comfort he could in mellifluous sounds, which Herman was to translate into "wicked" parody in *Moby-Dick:* "This whole book is but a draught — nay, but a draught of a draught. Oh, Time, Strength, Cash, and Patience!"

If he had stooped to definition Allan would have admitted that "mere competency" meant a New York version of the Gansevoort style. When trade was somewhat better in the following year, he proudly announced to his brother-in-law that "we have hired a Cook & Nurse & only want a Waiter to complete our domestic establishment." He did not trouble to inform Peter Gansevoort when only six months later he appealed to his father for a loan of $2,000 to support his business and his "domestic establishment."

Allan persevered, but he knew where assistance lay. He asserted his integrity, and he was an honorable man, but practiced a naive version of Machiavellianism, which would have amused the Italian master, when he played off one backer against another. He may have fooled his eccentric father, but Peter Gansevoort did not wear a three-cornered hat and breeches of another world and time. As Allan moved his family up in the world of fashionable houses and magnificent debts, his business affairs moved with the inevitability of Fate to disaster. When one scheme failed, he tried another, with the same result. In 1827, when he was to become the father of his seventh child, its birth was heralded seven months earlier in an emotional letter to Peter Gansevoort:

Therefore as you value my present welfare & future existence, disappoint me not I beseech you, in an emergency fraught with all that is personally dear to me in life, & which ever involves the present & ultimate happiness of my Family — if you do, which kind heaven in mercy avert, I shall know not whither in this World to turn for succor in the very crisis of my fate, and all, all may be lost to me forever. . . .

In the following year the Melvills moved to 675 Broadway — "Maria is charmed with the House & situation." The home was papered with loans. In the course of the year he was offering Gansevoort's notes to Lemuel Shaw, as he paid off one debt and contracted another. By 1830 Maria was spending as much time in Albany as in New York.

Allan's creditors instituted legal proceedings on August 3, 1830, when Herman was two days past his eleventh birthday. Albany offered shelter in the prosperous shadows of the Gansevoorts, who took the impoverished family into their fold. Allan received a "Clerks Hire," but, as Peter Gansevoort informed Lemuel Shaw, "he & his family were dependent on us for their support." The situation, in other words, was in 1830 exactly what it had been when he married Maria sixteen years earlier. If Allan had been another kind of man, of greater stamina and independence, he would perhaps have gone elsewhere to make a new start. But such a venture would have involved a confrontation with Maria: as the bankrupt father of eight children he was scarcely in a position to be the victor in the confrontation. Such assertiveness was not his life style. Besides, twelve years in New York had undermined whatever resiliency and self-confidence he had. And so he accepted the humiliations of dependency and hoped that somehow the future would be kinder. No doubt his brother Thomas, who also knew failure at first hand, and had enormous skill in rationalizing his weaknesses, read Allan's mind correctly when he wrote to Major Melvill: "Being now among his connexions, possessing as they do, a very considerable fortune, I cannot but hope, he will yet be able, to retrieve past ill fortune."

The Gansevoorts set up Allan in the fur business, but he still had to borrow from them and his father. "$500," he wrote to the latter toward the end of 1830, "would save me from a world of trouble, & enable me to look forward with renewed hopes, in expectation of being afterwards able to support myself — which repeated losses & disappointments have prevented me from doing."

Business conditions were unfavorable in 1831. He journeyed to Boston to confer with his father, borrowed money from Peter Gansevoort to repay the Major, traveled to New York searching for a solution and credit, and barely had enough money for the return fare. The boat could not proceed past Poughkeepsie because of ice, and he crossed the Hudson River on foot with the temperature two degrees below zero. The last words in his diary were written on December 10, 1831: "Expenses to New York 75 cts / from New York 42." Sick and enfeebled by exposure, his spirits as bankrupt as his business, he feverishly attended to his affairs, as though one more effort would force the "fickle Goddess" to smile upon him.

He waited — as he had waited all his life. He read the Bible, and turned to Psalms 55:4-5:

> My heart is sore pained within me: and the terrors of death are fallen upon me.
> Fearfulness and trembling are come upon me and horror hath overwhelmed me.

On January 10, 1832, Peter Gansevoort informed Allan's older brother that "yesterday he occasionally manifested an alienation of mind. Last night he became much worse — and to day he presents the melancholy spectacle of a deranged man." Thomas came to Albany at once. He found Allan "at times fierce, even *maniacal. . . . I ought not* to hope. — for, — in all human probability — he would live, *a Maniac!*"

Allan rambled in that world where there is sound but no sense, hate and persecution but no love. His odyssey ended on January 28, at 11:30 P.M., at the same hour Herman was born twelve years before. Three days later he was buried. He owed his father $22,000, Peter Gansevoort $4,000.

The Gansevoorts assumed the business debts, and Peter began actively to guide the destinies of Allan's children. Even the name a few months later was changed to Melville.

As in most matters involving the subtleties of family interaction, where things unsaid and gestures are often more important than words, records are always scant. But the Melvill children made oblique comments. The three children who had offsprings ignored the paternal heritage but commemorated the mother's family, all except Herman naming the first girl Maria Gansevoort. Herman never referred, so far as we know, directly to the relationship of Allan and Maria, but when he depicted a family situation in his books, as he rarely did, he almost always painted a portrait of a dominant wife-mother. In *Pierre*, the imperious Mrs. Glendinning (the three syllables suspiciously resembling Gansevoort) bleached her husband's rakishness to pristine respectability, dressed him as the very model of gentility, and finally froze the image that she created in a conventional portrait that hung in the parlor. She created her artifact with a blue-stockinged attack worthy of her Dutch ancestors. She did not have to stoop to conquer; like Prufrock's ladies she simply raised a lovely eyebrow. Maria had not only a Dutch eyebrow but also the Gansevoort savings. If Allan resisted the eyebrow, he was impotent before the bank balance.

Apparently he wielded a heavy hand in family discipline. On the birth of his fifth child, the first to be named after the Melvills, he reported to Peter Gansevoort that Helen Maria, his oldest daughter, "says 'if Pa has many more children he will have to keep the rod in hand the whole time.' " Allan no doubt thought that Helen Maria was being "cute," but it is more likely that in her childish way she was acute. Allan evidently could dominate his brood not with the eyebrow but with tangible evidence of his uncertain power. On another occasion he reminded Peter of the virtues of discipline while the Melvills were visiting in Albany: "Uncle Peter though a great favorite with these blooming cherubs, will I trust ever prove an invaluable useful Friend, when love transcends *indulgence*, & who will rather consider their future welfare, then present enjoyment." It was the kind of reminder that Peter's authoritarian practicality scarcely needed as well as a justification of Allan's own tactics. On another occasion when he was in New York with the older children and Maria was in Albany with the others, he assured his mother-in-law: "my little Companions behave remarkably well, & pass their whole time in the house, or at school, unless they obtain leave to visit me at the Store, for I do not allow them to run abroad, or play in the street." Allan meant no harm, but he was keeping boys from being boys and from relationships with their peers, which is parental tyranny. (Herman, too, was to become a whimsical father, especially harsh and sometimes unreasonable in the treatment of his sons.)

Perhaps worse than the rod was the Sunday-school self-righteousness that accompanied it. The children did not record the paternal didacticism. Allan himself was the recorder, usually in letters addressed to the Gansevoorts, whose approval he needed for obvious reasons. One summer the children were vacationing in Albany, and he wanted the older two boys to return to New York and to resume their schooling for perfectly valid reasons. "We expect Gansevoort on Sunday . . . when we wish Herman also to be here, that they may recommense their studies together on Monday next, with equal chances of preferment, & without any feelings of jealousy or ideas of favoritism." But he had to mix psychology and morality: "besides they may thus acquire a practical moral lesson whose influence may endure forever, for if they understand early, that inclination must always yield to Duty, it will become a matter of course when the vacations expire, to bid a fond adieu to Friends & amusements, & return home cheerfully to their Books, & they will consequently imbibe habits of Order & punctuality, which bear sweet blossoms in the dawn of life, golden fruits in 'the noon of manhood,' & a rich harvest for the garners of old age."

When he lectured his children with this kind of soul-lifting eloquence, he usually spoke at the end of a day embittered by frustrations. Momentarily, rod in hand or nearby, and truisms on his lips, he had feelings of power and security in the truths of the ages and could even put out of mind tomorrow's ugly reality. But the children no doubt sensed in their intuitive wisdom that Allan, like Ahab, spoke in the irrelevant heroics of a dead era, and that the "golden fruits" were words untranslated into deeds. Try as he might to camouflage his economic lot, the children must have known of the recurrent financial crises. If nothing else, the mother's disappointed silences and illnesses, her trips to Albany, and Allan's hurried jaunts to Boston to see his father would have spoken loud. Parental anxieties and uncertainties always threaten the security of the family shelter, and the deceptions to which adults resort in order to protect their offsprings from unpleasantnesses undermine confidence and respect, and create vague fears. To see the father toppled from his eminence and revealed in his all-too-human weakness terrifies: his failure lays bare their vulnerabilities.

For Herman at least there was still another scar. Although Allan's comments indicate that he was not unaware of antagonisms between Gansevoort and his younger brother, he did not realize how Maria and he in their adoration of Gansevoort marked the life of the younger, brooding son. In 1826 Allan reported to Peter Gansevoort that Herman "is very backward in speech & somewhat slow in comprehension, but . . . of a docile & amiable disposition." Perhaps sensing Allan's unacknowledged bias, Peter on the following day wrote of the boy in very flattering terms. A year later, after the sons had spent the summer with Major Melvill, Allan contrasted the "charming spirits" of "our beloved Gansevoort" and the "less buoyant" responses of "his more sedate but not less interesting Brother." Six months later the boy "very backward in speech" surprised his father. "You will be as much surprised as myself to know," he wrote to Peter, "that Herman proved the best Speaker in the introductory Department, at the examination of the High School, he has made rapid progress during the 2 last quarters." After this somewhat astonished praise of Herman, Allan went on to enumerate Gansevoort's achievements: he "still ranks among the A^s N° 1 in the senior class," and in the dancing school which Helen Maria and Herman also attended "Gansevoort is said to have so much native grace (by his fair teacher Miss Whieldon) as to neglect his feet too much in the regular steps."

Apparently Maria and Allan had made an early determination, which would have the heartless consistency of dogmatism, as to the merits of their two sons. In 1824 Maria noted, with maternal finality, that Herman "does not appear so fond of his Books as to injure his Health" — a strangely premature judgment of a five-year-old boy. In 1830 Allan summed up the prospects of his second son, now eleven years old: "Herman I think is making more progress than formerly, & without being a bright Scholar, he maintains a respectable standing, & would proceed further, if he could be induced to study more — being a most aimiable & innocent child, I cannot find it in my heart to coerce him, especially as he seems to have chosen Commerce as a favorite pursuit, whose practical activity can well dispense with much book knowledge."

Herman's oratorical ability astonished his parents but did not change their opinions. They evidently did not stop to wonder why a boy "backward in speech" at home could distinguish himself as a public speaker. Although Allan did not use in Herman's presence the candid language he employed in his letters, the second son sensed that he was inferior intellectually, physically less graceful, "less buoyant" than his brother. Gansevoort cast a shadow over Herman's cosmos. To win his father's affection and esteem he was "docile" and "aimiable." No son aspires to such a passive state or to such epithets unless there is no other avenue open to him. The rancor Herman repressed erupted in one of Mrs. Glendinning's speeches in *Pierre*, where she recalls "that fine saying of his father's, that as the noblest colts, in three points — abundant hair, swelling chest, and sweet docility — should resemble a fine woman, so should a noble youth."

As a boy, then, Herman made himself worthy only of "Commerce," so that he could enter his father's "mansion," his business, and could presumably be his father's successor. In so doing he short-changed his natural talents and crippled his self-image. It was a kind of deliberate amputation, in order to obtain the favor of the father. Herman's efforts were in vain, for when his father died the family considered him too young to take over the business, and the blessing and the burden fell upon Gansevoort, who was shoved into manhood at the age of seventeen. Herman had no way of foreseeing that the seeming blessing was to be a curse. In his eyes Gansevoort's succession was further confirmation of his inadequacy.

The "power of blackness" enveloped Herman at an early age. He had to reconcile himself to what must have appeared as predestined inferiority to Gansevoort and to warp himself to fit the image created by the "almighty Parent." The father's approval exacted a fearful price for the love the son craved. At the same time the son was not unaware of the beloved father's weaknesses, particularly his tired moralisms, his forced optimism, his abounding faith in the Deity. Allan's pietistic bulwark cloaked overconcern with appearances and inadequate understanding of the needs of the human heart. If later Herman looked behind the pious declamations of missionaries in the South Seas and recognized their contempt for the people to whom they were bringing the God of love, he was but protesting the inconsistencies of his own parent.

In 1830, after the departure of Maria and the other children for Albany, Allan and Herman remained behind in New York to close their fashionable home and to settle whatever Allan could manage to settle. On October 9 father and son made their way to the harbor to board a boat for Albany. The journey was not a beginning but the end of Allan's dreams of independence. The father was as dependent as his son. Fifteen months later Herman saw his father stumble into the Albany home on a freezing December night, flushed, trembling, almost starved — a physical wreck after a frantic trip to New York in order to assuage his creditors. This time his incurable and sustaining optimism retreated into silence. As the children watched, Allan took to his bed, restlessly hurried to his place of business, and returned hours later murmuring vaguely about his affairs. Soon he remained in bed, asked for the Bible, and ranted in word and gesture. Adults whispered of a *maniac,* moved about the house stealthily, and tried to shelter the children from the awesome sight and the meaningless rhetoric.

Seven years later Herman wrote a Poe-like sketch for the *Democratic Press and Lansingburgh Advertiser.* The narrator reports seeing in a dream "THE DEATH CRAFT!" and "a human head covered with coagulated gore, and firmly griping between its teeth, a rusty cutlass!"

> I shrieked aloud: "Blast — blast my vision Oh God! Blast it ere I rave;" — I buried my face in my hands — I pressed them wildly against my eyes ... the ghastly appendage at the job-boom seemed fixing its ghastly eye-balls on me — each chalky remnant of mortality seemed beckoning me toward it! I fancied them clutching me in their wild embrace — I saw them begin their infernal orgies; — the flesh crisped upon my fingers, my heart grew icy cold, and faint with terror and despair, I lay prostrate on the deck. . . .

Then the narrator awakens and asks himself whether he has dreamed this horror. "Were these the scenes of my youth?" he cries, and answers himself: "No, no! they were far away across the bounding deep!" The external trappings of the sketch which came from nineteenth-century melodramatic prose should not conceal from us the fact that there was no reason to ask the question — "Were these the scenes of my youth?" — in the first place, unless his tale evoked memories from his past. The answer was an unconvincing rationalization, like Allan's, but a necessary one unless Herman were willing to voice publicly the pains of his childhood.

Years later, in 1849, in the pages of his fourth book Melville commented on the years of blackness through a thinly disguised autobiographical narrator. "But I must not think," Wellingborough Redburn writes, "of those delightful days before my father became a bankrupt, and died, and we removed from the city; for when I think of those days, something rises up in my throat and almost strangles me." In life there were two bankruptcies and two changes of address: in 1830 the Melvills moved from New York to Albany, in 1832 the survivors moved from Albany to Lansingburgh. In the novel the two events become one, as emotionally they are of one piece. Redburn's language reveals the complexity of his response: the strangled feeling of which he speaks may be repressed tears or repressed rage, or possibly both.

Melville did not recreate Redburn's early experiences with his father or dramatize the death scene, perhaps because the details were too painful to recall, but he had Redburn expose his wounded heart.

> Talk not of the bitterness of middle-age and after-life; a boy can feel all that, and much more, when upon his young soul the mildew has fallen; and the fruit, which with others is only blasted after ripeness, with him is nipped in the first blossom and bud. And never again can such blights be made good; they strike in too deep, and leave such a scar that the air of Paradise might not erase it. And it is a hard and cruel thing thus in early youth to taste beforehand the pangs which should be reserved for the stout time of manhood, when the gristle has become bone, and we stand up and fight out our lives, as a thing tried before and foreseen; for then we are veterans used to sieges and battles, and not green recruits, recoiling at the first shock of the encounter.

The harsh language — "bitterness," "mildew," "blights," "scar," "hard and cruel," "pangs" — makes clear that there is little sorrow for the fate of the unfortunate father. Redburn feels betrayed by a father who has not lived to play out his role as defender of the defenseless lad, and has pushed him into manhood before his time. The flower and oral imagery — "mildew," "fruit," "nipped in the first blossom and bud," "taste beforehand the pangs" — points up unmistakably the youth's feelings of deprivation. The imagery was to reappear constantly, sometimes with deathlike despair as in this passage, sometimes joyously as in his first encounter with Hawthorne's tales, and finally as a valedictory in the depiction of the last "blossom and bud," Billy Budd, whose life is snuffed out by another father figure.

Later in the novel, when Redburn reaches Liverpool, where he expects to use a guidebook found in his father's library in order to retrace his father's footsteps in that city, sorrow breaks through, and he fancies for a moment that he can overtake him and clasp his hand, until reality asserts itself: "But I soon checked myself, when remembering that he had gone whither no son's search could find him in this world. And then I thought of all that must have happened to him since he paced through that arch. What trials and troubles he had encountered; how he had been shaken by many storms of adversity, and at last died a bankrupt. I looked at my own sorry garb, and had much ado to keep from tears."

The sorrow here cannot obliterate the awareness in the earlier passage that the blackness cannot be lifted: "And never again can such blights be made good; they strike in too deep, and leave such a scar that the air of Paradise might not erase it." On that night in January 1832 Allan shattered Herman's cosmos and undermined his self-trust. When Allan's light went out, he left Herman an orphan. If the son later had little confidence in the optimistic credo of American society, in transcendentalism — or in life itself — his father's betrayal was in large part responsible. Allan never knew how his failures would reverberate in the life of his "docile" son. At least he was spared that knowledge; he was spared little else.

Abraham sent Ishmael off to the wilderness as the boy entered puberty, presumably when he was twelve or thirteen. Allan was no patriarch, just a flawed mortal who abandoned his son when he was but twelve years old. Not only did Herman become an Ishmael in his feelings of orphandom, but twelve was tattooed on his memory calendar, to commemorate the beginning of his mourning.

White-Jacket notes that in order to kill time aboard ship he likes "to lean over the bulwarks, and speculate upon where, under the sun, you are going to be that day next year, . . . so much so, that there is a particular day of a particular month of the year, which, from my earliest recollections, I have always kept the run of, so that I can even now tell just where I was on that identical day of every year past since I was twelve years old." White-Jacket, then, dates his life from age twelve.

Absorbed by the love-hate relationship with a white whale that consumes the captain of the *Pequod,* we forget that Ahab loses both parents before he is twelve months old, and that his mother, like Herman's father, sputters out her life in the drivel of madness. Toward the conclusion of *Moby-Dick*, just before Ahab sights the white whale, the *Pequod* meets the *Rachel.* Captain Gardiner asks Ahab to join the search for a small boat lost the day before in an encounter with Moby Dick. Only when Gardiner is confronted with

"Ahab's iciness," does he reveal that aboard the boat is one of his two sons: "a little lad, but twelve years old, whose father with the earnest but unmisgiving hardihood of a Nantucketer's paternal love, had thus early sought to initiate him in the perils and wonders of a vocation almost immemorially the destiny of all his race."

Pierre's father, who bears many similarities to Allan Melvill, dies when his son is twelve and abandons him to the care of a possessive mother.

Ginger-Nut, the twelve-year-old office boy in "Bartleby the Scrivener," is charged with keeping the clerks in the legal office supplied with food, until Bartleby in his suicidal depression refuses all nourishment. Herman was a clerk within a few months of his father's death, after being abruptly taken out of school in order to contribute to the support of the widow.

Ishmael vanished into silence. Herman recorded the blackness of his hurt, the legacy of a father who failed both himself and his son. Compulsively and endlessly the son quested for paternal companionship and guidance, for the ideal father no son ever finds.

While he was writing his great tale of Ishmael in 1850, he unexpectedly found the elusive ideal in the presence of Nathaniel Hawthorne.

Sarah
—Maria Gansevoort Melvill

Maria Gansevoort Melvill was the only daughter of General Peter Gansevoort. After distinguishing himself at Fort Stanwix during the Revolutionary War, he resumed his successful business career and continued until his death to be a prominent citizen of Albany, New York. Allan Melvill's father may have nursed his idiosyncracies and his vial of tea, but no Gansevoort became a "character." Life was a serious business and success was not to be trifled with by the assumption of anachronistic garments.

The Gansevoorts measured out their lives with sobriety. They were members in good standing of the Dutch Reformed Church, and Maria's children were baptized in that faith. Thomas Melvill's sons wandered restlessly and drifted here and abroad; the General's sons either entered business or, as in the case of Peter Gansevoort, went to college to prepare for a professional career which was not without its usefulness to the family business interests.

Maria grew up surrounded by those heavy, serviceable Dutch furnishings which perfectly blended faith in God and in the "good works" of mercantile success. Redburn at one point in his tale speaks affectionately of the Gansevoort home: "Why, no buildings here [in Liverpool] look so ancient as the old gable-pointed mansion of my maternal grandfather at home, whose bricks were brought from Holland long before the revolutionary war!" In this mansion there were always servants to ease Maria's easy life and to confirm her status among the religious and economic elite. Denied little in the way of material conveniences, she expected no denials. Her cultivation did not extend much beyond the truisms of generations of Gansevoorts. Nothing that she said or did offended the incontestable principles of her holy trinity – God, country, and the Gansevoorts. Perhaps the last was first in her affections. The creed was a monument and she foolishly tried to be a monument to it. She espoused her hierarchical faith and extolled the hierarchical family structure, where General Gansevoort ruled firmly. When Maria finally had to expose herself to reality, only then did she learn, as she was wont to say, that "the world is fleeting, changing, & most uncertain."

The tyranny Maria was to exercise over her children was also a disguise. Reared among men – she was the only female child – she incorporated their creed and drive for success and station, and accepted unknowingly the subordination of affection to these goals. Apparently she modeled her behavior on her father's, but she lacked the General's stamina and stability.

General Gansevoort died in 1812, and shortly thereafter Allan Melvill appeared in Albany. In accepting Allan's suit, in 1814, Maria acquired a husband with a worldliness, attractiveness, and amiability which she was unaccustomed to in her Dutch circles and her family, but she probably sensed that despite his veneer of sophistication Allan was malleable. Since he could not support her in the Gansevoort style, he could not take her from Albany. The couple had to move in with the General's widow and her son Peter. There Maria expected to domesticate the former dandy and world traveler. In accepting this living arrangement Allan surrendered some of his self-respect at a cost to himself as well as to Maria, who might have the satisfaction of molding him according to the Gansevoort formula, but in achieving her will reduced her husband in order to elevate him. She paid dearly, as it turned out, for her power.

After four years in the Gansevoort household Allan insisted on setting himself up in business in New York. Maria was twenty-seven when she left her sheltered environment for the first time. The rhythm of Allan's failure in the twelve New York years we have recorded. The rhythms of Maria's unsuccessful adaptation we must now relate in some detail, for these were the formative years of their son. The parental rhythms became Herman's.

Life in New York was not made easier by Maria's constant confinements. Gansevoort and Helen Maria were born in Albany; and in New York children followed with almost clocklike regularity, Herman in 1819, a year after their arrival, Augusta in 1821, Allan in 1823, Catherine in 1825, Frances in 1827, and Thomas in 1830. Such a steadily increasing family necessitated moves to larger accommodations and compounded the problems of the already rootless Melvills, most troublesomely in Maria's case. The Gansevoorts enjoyed an important niche in Albany society as well as the security and comforts of a large family circle. In New York the Melvills were without acquaintance or family. The Dutch tradition had managed in Albany to survive the Revolutionary War and the beginnings of industrialization. Most of the sturdy Dutch buildings of old New York were already buried in the rubble of a city that was to become a modern Troy. In Albany the Gansevoorts remained fixed in the family homestead; in New York the Melvills moved from one house to another. The only continuity was membership in the Dutch Reformed Church.

Allan's economic decline was paralleled by the deterioration of Maria's health. There may not have been a cause-and-effect correspondence, although it is a possibility, but family letters during the New York years were filled with references to her health and "nerves." There are all kinds of ways of handling unpleasant situations: by exertion of the will the heroic may sometimes subdue the flesh, but Maria was not of this cast. As her spirits crumbled, her body responded in kind.

Six years after the transfer to New York, in 1824, she was given, in her husband's words, to "unpleasant fainting fits." The slightest disruption in the family routine produced uneasy, petulant outbursts. A relative commented that trouble with domestics caused "that most terrible of all diseases to which she is subject — i.e. it makes her nervous." Maria suffered periods of depression. Allan referred to her "delicate condition" and her "low spirits," and a few months later Maria herself characterized her condition: "My strength of mind & Body is gradually returning — I for some time had serious fears for both & it was the cause of much sorrow to me [—] nobody can tell my sufferings when I appeared quick & ill Humour'd — Twas then I felt particularly my inability to controul myself & my great weakness." In 1828 she still suffered from her depressions: "My Spirits are better & I am a more agreeable companion than I have been for some time past."

In 1830, when Allan needed her moral and physical support before the final bankruptcy proceedings, Maria was as great a preoccupation and concern as his failing business. He wrote urgently, and with a good deal of insight, to his brother-in-law: "[Maria's] spirits are occasionally more than ever depressed, while the family requires extraordinary attention, & unless she soon obtains relief from mental excitement, by some favorable change in our condition & prospects, I fear that her health will suffer permanent injury – she is very desirous of removing to Albany, to enjoy once more the society of her connexions & friends & feel at home & if possible happy, which she never has been, & never can be here." In speaking of "permanent injury" Allan overstated, for Maria lived to a ripe age, but he probably did not exaggerate her discontent with life in New York. At the same time he had to overstate the case because neither he nor Maria could cope any longer with the situation. All that she could think of, when she learned that matters were beyond her control and strength, was retreat to the Gansevoort family.

She returned to Albany the wife of a bankrupt. The offspring of success, she had fallen into the hell of mercantile society. Her public image was her self-image. Her creed had been tested but had failed her because she had never realized how dependent she was upon her family and its protectiveness. Her body had exposed her weaknesses; her faith could not protect her from depressions. At the same time her physical and emotional state had commanded the attention of Allan and her family. In one way or another she exercised her power. Although he sometimes revealed insight in his letters, Allan did not fully understand the blows she had suffered during the twelve years in New York. He had his own humiliations to endure, and he had to rely on his own unreliable resources when she was unable to give him support or to manage the household. The children only dimly sensed what the collapse of Maria's world meant to her, nor could they understand how she strove to shore up the ruins.

In those vulnerable years when they needed understanding and guidance in order to establish themselves in their worlds, they experienced too many denials of loving care, too many outbursts from a "nervous" mother, and far too many instances of irrational tyrannies. They could have drawn up a bill of particulars, which, of course, none of them ever did. Like most children, they repressed the disappointments, the hurts they had to endure, although Herman was to render an indictment in his fiction.

Maria, with Allan's consent, had from the beginning placed the Gansevoort stamp upon the Melvill household. In her world view everybody earned through industry his ordained place, and, with an impatient flick of her Dutch wrist, she consigned to limbo those who did not measure up. A nephew deserved the fruits of his inadequacies — the sea — and the attire of his failure — the sailor's uniform. He, she wrote, "is ordered to be on board tomorrow morning dressed as a Sailor. . . . for my part I think it is the best thing that could be done with him, he does not appear to me to possess talents or inclination for study or improvement . . . it was not his destiny, if you will allow me the expression, to earn a subsistence by any means but that of Labour." Years later, in 1839, she was less dogmatic and snobbish when Herman went to sea for the first time. By then she had been thrice humbled, by the three bankruptcies of 1830, 1832, and 1837.

Like Allan, Maria preferred the first-born son, the one who bore her family name. As her derogatory comments about her nephew's status indicate, she revered "study or improvement." Although she did not expect Herman, then only five years old, to ruin his health by too much reading of books, he was obviously expected to give up play at that early age in order to improve himself. Success was fate. Infractions of her rules she punished vigorously. She denied two of the children vacation trips because they were "the most rebellious & ungovernable." That she was partly responsible for their conduct, their rebelliousness, undoubtedly never crossed her mind.

The most horrifying example of her power has come down in a family legend. Every afternoon Maria took a nap, as well-bred ladies were accustomed to do in a more leisurely century, but she did not retreat to the bedroom alone. She took along her eight children and had them sit on stools about her bed. She slept and they sat in complete silence, eight little guardian angels or eight little dunces. When she wakened, with a word, a verbal flick of the wrist, she restored them to childhood. Presumably she was refreshed by her nap and by renewed evidence of her power.

Maria was no monster, although she was imprisoned in her egomaniacal world. Her assertiveness sprang from her insecurity and her disappointments. Herman's appeared in his novels, markedly so in some of the richly farcical pages of *Moby-Dick*.

Ishmael seeks lodging for the night from Peter Coffin, the proprietor of the Spouter-Inn in New Bedford. Coffin tricks the young man into accepting as bed companion a tattooed cannibal harpooner named Queequeg. The two men are to share the inn-keeper's nuptial bed: "Sal and me slept in that ere bed the night we were spliced." With a great deal of difficulty and a lot of farce, Ishmael is reassured that the cannibal will not decapitate him. He falls asleep, and "Upon waking next morning about daylight, I found Queequeg's arm thrown over me in the most loving and affectionate manner. You had almost thought I had been his wife." After ex-amining "this arm of his tattooed all over with an interminable

Cretan labyrinth of a figure," he suddenly recalls a childhood experience.

> My sensations were strange. Let me try to explain them. When I was a child, I well remember a somewhat similar circumstance that befell me; whether it was a reality or a dream, I never could entirely settle. The circumstance was this. I had been cutting up some caper or other — I think it was trying to crawl up the chimney, as I had seen a little sweep do a few days previous; and my stepmother who, somehow or other, was all the time whipping me, or sending me to bed supperless, — my mother dragged me by the legs out of the chimney and packed me off to bed, though it was only two o'clock in the afternoon of the 21st June, the longest day in the year in our hemisphere. I felt dreadfully. But there was no help for it, so up stairs I went to my little room in the third floor, undressed myself as slowly as possible so as to kill time, and with a bitter sigh got between the sheets.

Later the boy goes to his stepmother and begs for "a good slippering for my misbehavior" — he is perfectly willing to accept "punishment" for his "crime" — but she, unrelenting, sends him back to his room.

> At last I must have fallen into a troubled nightmare of a doze; and slowly waking from it — half steeped in dreams — I opened my eyes, and the before sunlit room was now wrapped in outer darkness. Instantly I felt a shock running through all my frame; nothing was to be seen, and nothing was to be heard; but a supernatural hand seemed placed in mine. My arm hung over the counterpane, and the nameless, unimaginable, silent form or phantom, to which the hand belonged, seemed closely seated by my bedside. For what seemed ages piled on ages, I lay there, frozen with the most awful fears, not daring to drag away my hand; yet ever thinking that if I could but stir it one single inch, the horrid spell would be broken. I knew not how this consciousness at last glided away from me; but waking in the morning, I shudderingly remembered it all, and for days and weeks and months afterwards I lost myself in confounding attempts to explain the mystery. Nay, to this very hour, I often puzzle myself with it.

The juxtapositions in this scene are delicious and revealing. The innkeeper, whose name suggests the deathbed, provides Ishmael and Queequeg with his marriage bed. Ishmael's fears of the native are legitimate but are associated with castration anxiety. The fears dissolve — "never slept better in my life" — into caricatural nuptial delight. The dream deals symbolically, as Leslie Fiedler points out, with the boy's desire for intercourse with the stepmother and with the punishment he accords himself for his violation of the universal taboo. She thwarts, as dream censorship decrees, his genital desire as well as his oral need: she even denies him supper. The dream concludes with the mysterious hand, the boy's sexual arousal and possibly masturbation, with all the guilt society creates around pleasurable self-abuse. If Coffin cons Ishmael in the sleeping arrangement, Ishmael cons the reader in making the sexual object his stepmother and in disguising the incestuousness behind the dream. If we pursue the biblical analogy which Ishmael invokes in the choice of his name, the stepmother is Sarah, who forces Ishmael out of the household after the birth of Isaac. (The good mother in *Moby-Dick* will appear in the Epilogue not as Hagar, but as Rachel, who gave birth to Jacob's favorite son Joseph.) In addition to mythic logic, the episode has another logic: Melville avoids censure of the mother by transferring the love-hate to a stepmother.

As almost all commentators agree, Mrs. Mary Glendinning in *Pierre* bears curious resemblances to Maria Gansevoort, both in her name and in her military ancestry. Mrs. Glendinning tames her husband's waywardness and makes him worthy of her decorous parlor, and upon her husband's death she subdues her only son, not through illness, which is a weakness, but through the sexual ambience she creates in playing the role of sister to brother Pierre. She disguises, or at least renders somewhat innocuous, the incestuous bond by converting it into a brother-sister relationship. Upon Pierre's leaving the house one morning,

> "A noble boy, and docile" — she murmured — "he has all the frolicsomeness of youth, with little of its giddiness. And he does not grow vain-glorious in sophomorean wisdom. I thank heaven I sent him not to college. A noble boy, and docile. A fine, proud, loving, docile, vigorous boy. Pray God, he never becomes otherwise to me. His little wife, that is to be, will not estrange him from me; for she too is docile, — beautiful, and reverential, and most docile. Seldom yet have I known such blue eyes as hers, that were not docile, and would not follow a bold black one, as two meek blue-ribboned ewes, follow their martial leader. How glad am I that Pierre loves her so, . . . the fine, proud, loving, docile, vigorous boy! — the lofty-minded, well-born, noble boy; and with such sweet docilities!"

After this parodistic Shakespearean outpouring she quietly moves across the room and comes upon her father's baton. "She lifted it, and musingly swayed it to and fro. . . . Her stately beauty had ever something martial in it." Then she comments upon Pierre's possible loss of heroic manliness because of the "docility" she decrees. She hopes that somehow — she is, interestingly, vague — he will fuse both attributes in a bisexual combination not unlike her own nature: "So shall he remain all docility to me, and yet prove a haughty hero to the world!"

It is a masterly scene, and a complex one. As in the dream sequence in *Moby-Dick*, Melville undermines the action, or at least diverts attention, through the comic tone which permits him to dwell upon forbidden sexual desires. After the Shakespearean eloquence, Mrs. Glendinning reveals herself as the phallic woman, even assuming the male role in a kind of simulated intercourse. Melville gives Mrs. Glendinning his own verbal virtuosity, as he falls in love with her/his speech. Mrs. Glendinning is a consummate bisexual fraud whom Pierre loathes/loves. Isabel, a half-sister with whom he later establishes a strange "marital" arrangement, resembles his mother physically, although there is no blood tie between this bastard child and Mrs. Glendinning.

The ambivalence in the fictional portrait — Mrs. Glendinning is singularly attractive and at the same time intimidating in the exercise of her sexual powers — was traceable to a similar division in Maria's nature. She imposed her will upon the Melvills through fair and underhanded tactics, using her body in illness for her purposes, but as a young widow with eight children she assumed, of necessity, the role of father-mother and held the family together. Often she was irrational and impulsive, giving way to almost hysterical outbursts, but there was also a stubborn determination to protect her brood. She was not the lovable mother that Walt Whitman was to create in his poetic fantasies, nor was she Mrs. Pecksniff, as neighbors in Pittsfield were to allege. Outsiders judged, and not inaccurately from their detached points of view, the externals. The children knew that she was the only prop and anchor they had when their father's death deprived them not only of economic security but also of paternal guidance.

When Maria and the family moved to their home at 338 North Market Street in Albany in 1830, they had tangible evidence of the decline in their lot. The quarters were less pretentious than those to which they had grown accustomed in New York, where, despite Allan's difficulties, they had for twelve years constantly moved upwards. For Maria the new home provided a shabby contrast with the patrician splendor of the Gansevoort household. In Albany she probably expected a dramatic reversal in Allan's and her own fortunes since close by was the shelter of the Gansevoort position and affluence.

Allan's debts were formidable, and even the Gansevoort connection could not silence for long the demands of his creditors. One of Maria's acts in her grief was characteristically irrational but at once assertive. She decided, or decreed, that the name was to be changed from Melvill to Melville, which was the ancestral form. Perhaps she hoped that a change in spelling would magically alter the fortunes of the former Melvills and redeem the public image now twice-tarnished. The addition of the *e* to the name diminished poor, pathetic Allan Melvill.

Maria was not penniless at Allan's death, since the Gansevoorts had protected her modest inheritance from her husband's business follies. She attempted to economize by moving to cheaper, less fashionable quarters in Lansingburgh, a suburb about ten miles outside of Albany. Unable to descend into the depths of impecuniousness too abruptly, she retained one servant, although at the same time she did not shrink from making incessant demands for funds upon her brothers, particularly upon Peter, who was not exactly prospering in the uncertain business climate of the early 1830s and who, now past forty years of age, was about to marry.

A month after Allan's burial Gansevoort and Herman were taken out of Albany Academy. The older boy took over his father's business, and shortly Herman was a clerk at the New York State Bank. When a cholera epidemic broke out in Albany in the summer of 1832, Maria quickly gathered together her children and took them off for a visit to Allan's brother in Pittsfield. Her conduct was scarcely responsible from an economic viewpoint, and her brother indicated his disapproval when he ordered her to have Herman return at once to his duties in the bank. Peter had a point, but her impulsiveness was understandable. As a widow of six months, with her grief and her rage, and as the head of a household of eight children, she was holding on to all that was left, her children.

"Without Mr Melvill," as she lamented to Peter, she journeyed at the end of July from Pittsfield to Boston, to visit Major Melvill, now eighty-one years of age. In the Melvill household she collapsed:

> Haveing never travelled from Boston to Albany or on this road without Mr Melvill every object served to remind me of him — The absence of one to whom I *ever* was most sincerely attached, render'd my journey to Pittsfield, & Boston rather painful, I had need of all my fortitude to repress my feelings before Strangers — but when I enter'd the old Mansion, it was silent & dark as night, my feelings got the better of all restraint & I wept Hysterically for some time unable to controul them.

Less than two months after her visit to Boston the lovable, eccentric old man became indeed "The Last Leaf." On September 7,

1832, a fire broke out across the street from his residence. In the words of *The Firemen's Advocate*:

> The Major was active, and with his family were furnishing the firemen with refreshments, having an open house to all of them. But alas! by his exertions to relieve their wants at this fire, he took a violent cold, which terminated in the diarrhea; and owing to his advanced age, and the violence of the disorder, medicine had no effect in checking its progress. On Sunday evening, the 16th of September, at 9 o'clock, he sank into the sleep of death.

Daniel Webster eulogized his memory in an address before the National Republican Convention in October.

For Maria the Major's memory, like Allan's, became blemished. When the will was probated, the funds that remained went to the widow. One of the executors was Lemuel Shaw, Allan's friend from school days. On June 20, 1833, Maria wrote to Shaw:

> The apparent utter desertion of the Grandparents & Aunts of my children, since the Death of their Father, is singular, & to me seems inexplicable.

> Their Charities to Friends & Strangers to their Blood are known. Do you think it possible Mr Shaw that Allan's circumstances at the time of his Death, were unknown to his Parents, it can hardly be for the Major was here, and knew full well that my Brother was call'd upon to assist us immediately, for we had nothing — Could he have mention'd those things & been unattended to by Parental ears.

When she continued to make inquiries about the will, on February 12, 1834, Shaw had to remind her that Allan had begun drawing upon his inheritance in 1818, and then observed: "I trust, Mrs. Melvill, I need not reiterate any strong assurances, to convince you of the deep interest & solicitude I feel in the welfare of your children, and the children of one of my oldest & best friends. . . . I shall at all times & under all circumstances, do all in my power, to promote their best interests." Shaw made good his promise, but reluctantly Maria had to resign herself to the fact that she could expect nothing more from the Melvills.

There was still Peter Gansevoort, who since her father's death in 1812 had been the pillar of the family. He had lived with his mother until her death in 1830, and had dutifully accepted responsibilities not only for Mrs. Gansevoort but also for Maria and the Melvills. Although his wife was to nickname him "Tibbee Tee," he was a man of "duty" and discipline; he did not spare himself in his devotion to the family interests, but he also did not spare anyone else. Shortly after the Melvills moved to New York in 1818, he wrote to Allan:

> Gansevoort's deportment is greatly improved. — The effects of your too great indulgence have in great measure been corrected — He passed the ordeal with dignity and grandeur, often erroneously mistaken in a child for a perverse & contradictory spirit — He sustained a consistency throughout which justifies me in giving (which all men have not) character to the boy. I fear that I have incurred your displeasure, in having accepted his homage of superior respect, for he says that he loves me more than he does his father — I have however yielded to your injunction & endeavored to impress him with the truth that you are his liege lord.

Peter was scarcely knowledgeable of the behavior of children if he did not realize that Gansevoort's "homage" was the only way the child had to mitigate the inflexible character-building of his uncle. Allan was also imperceptive if he did not appreciate the fact that Peter used the child to show his lack of respect for his father.

In politics Peter was a Democrat and was at various times assemblyman and senator in the Albany legislature. More important, he knew all the major politicians and was able to obtain favors for the members of his family. He was also a friend of James Fenimore Cooper, and introduced Gansevoort and Herman to the writings of "our first national novelist," as Herman was later to describe the creator of Natty Bumppo. By all odds Peter was the most influential member of the family and also the one who did for Allan's children what the charming father could not do.

After Allan's death he was Maria's principal advisor. She did not hesitate to remind him of his responsibility. "Peter you have known me from Childhood," she wrote, "and have often heard Mamma say that we must always cling to each other as brothers and an only Sister should do." In her anxiety she was to make too many importunities to a man who would never abandon her or her children.

Maria, preoccupied as she was with her problems, could hardly be happy about Peter's marriage, on June 4, 1833, to a nineteen-year-old girl named Mary Sanford. It was a kind of betrayal of a sister who more than doted upon her brother. During the cholera epidemic of 1832, when she was safely away in Pittsfield, she wrote to him: "Do my dear Brother leave Albany if this weather continues, for you are the only person or Brother I should say, that I & mine have to depend upon for all things, yours is a valuable Life & not to [be] trifled with." She went on to say: "My dear Allan often use'd to say — 'Maria you love Peter better than me or your Children,' & I can assure you his Death has not made me love you less — you are every thing to me — & for my sake take care of yourself."

In closely knit families bonds are sometimes close and even intense, but in this case they take on added significance in view of the complex incestuous relationships Melville was later to explore in the melodramatic and farcical pages of *Pierre*, his most autobiographical work. Peter remained "married" to his mother until her death. Allan was aware, as Maria's letter divulges, that she had more than the ordinary sisterly attachment to her brother. If her children heard this tale, as they probably did in view of Maria's fierce pride in her family, Allan's image suffered still another blow in the eyes of his offsprings. It may even be significant that Maria named none of her boys after Peter, father or son — the General's name was Peter too — both of whom she kept for herself. It may also be more than coincidental that Melville had Mrs. Glendinning and her son act out a charade of brother-sister love: the son, curiously, was given the name Pierre. Perhaps Herman envied the fact that Peter enjoyed a love denied to him. Family involvements reappear in fiction in strange ways.

In 1832, with Peter always present in the wings, Gansevoort, her favorite son, became the means by which Maria was to revive the family fortunes and rehabilitate the family image. She launched the seventeen-year-old on a venture beyond his experience and capacities.

> This is to certify that my son Gansevoort Melvill, is carrying on the Fur, and Cap business in the City of Albany, on my account, and that I hold myself responsible for all debts contracted by my said son, in the course of said business —
> Dated Albany 28th March 1832 — Maria G. Melvill.

This certificate would probably have meant little to the Albany business community if it had not contained the endorsement of Peter Gansevoort. Gansevoort managed the business as best he could from March until July 14, when Maria hurried him off to Pittsfield, where for a month or more he was, in his mother's words, "employed, in raking & turning Hay, Fishing, rowing the Ladies across, & around a large pond back of the house, & is doing ample justice to the excellent Milk & delicious bread & Butter of the Farm." The boy was no doubt enjoying himself, since he was engaging in activities appropriate to his years, but he was hardly accumulating business experience. Yet at the end of September Maria noted that Gansevoort was anticipating that within two years the business would show "a Net profit of $10,000 a year." Gansevoort apparently shared his father's propensities for dreams and expansive statements.

For several years he had some success in the trade, and Maria promptly moved her family back to a fashionable address in Albany. When the economy tightened, Gansevoort's business began to topple. This time, unlike the last years in New York, when she managed to spend more time in Albany than at home, Maria had no place of retreat and was at the center of matters. In 1836 she was selling lots which she had inherited from her mother. Meanwhile, Gansevoort, like Allan years before, scrambled about seeking credit and called on his uncle for assistance. To no avail. Notice of bankruptcy was posted on April 15, 1837. Shortly thereafter, Gansevoort, humbled and chagrined, reversed his father's path: he took himself off to New York.

Maria had to remain in Albany to pick up the pieces. For the third time she endured the humiliation of bankruptcy, and once again she had to go through difficult readjustments. Peter raised $4,000, and Maria posted a bond "in the sum of Fifty thousand dollars" to the New York State Bank. At a family council held on June 5, it was decided to take Allan, now fourteen, from the Albany Academy and place him in Peter's law office. "The cause of this movement," Allan later wrote in his journal, "arose I believe from the fact that my superiors arrived at the conclusion that I was learning nothing at school and that this being the case the expense of my tuition ought to be saved to the limited exchequer of the family."

The following year the Melvilles changed houses, and probably landlords. "Economy was the object of this change of location," Allan reported in his journal, "and the only one which influenced my mother to forsake the 'place of her heart,' her early companions and old friends." Maria, predictably, was upset. Allan, also predictably, was becoming a young cynic: "But what ties are so sacred as not to be broken, or in some manner effected by the agency of gold & silver?"

Like most cynical remarks, Allan's was simplistic, but it contained several grains of truth. Family "ties" were "effected by the agency of gold & silver." The Melville family unit for the first time was not intact. Gansevoort was in New York, Herman taught school in Pittsfield, and Allan boarded with an "old maid" in Albany whose "house was not in the most agreeable part of the city." (The sons, not unlike their mother, clung in poverty to their former status.) The "ties" had to weaken because Maria had no alternative in her straitened circumstances but to place an excessive burden upon her three young men. When she begged her brother to provide a plan for "my support untill my Sons can do for me, & relieve my mind from an insupportable weight of uncertainty," her self-pity was not attractive, but respectable society and her patrician environment had decreed that respectable women belonged in the home and had "educated" her for economic dependency.

In her ordeal all she could do was to invoke God and motherhood, as she did in a letter to Allan in 1838. "My dear Allan, if you regularly attend the Sabbath School, & thereby obey your Mothers parting injunction, for be assured my beloved Boy the future usefulness of the Man depends much upon the foundation laid in boyhood. The instruction you receive in our Sabbath School is very important, *you are away from a Mothers care,* under a comparatively strange roof." Like her husband, she retained a faith in platitudes.

She continued to call upon Peter Gansevoort — too frequently. By this time he was the father of two children, and in a tight economy and encumbered with her son's indebtedness, he was not able to perform miracles. Maria was not unaware of Peter's strained resources, but preoccupation with her own plight did not allow for much sympathy or tact. When she expressed herself, everybody was supposed to listen — and to act. In June 1838 she demanded that Peter send her $100. "Do not fail so to do, for I owe for my last Barrel of Flour." Peter, this time provoked once too often, laid it on the line:

> I send by Mr Holme one hundred dollars as requested by your letter of Saturday last — You might rather have done without the blinds, than give your landlord or your neighbours the false unfounded idea that you have means to pay rent in advance — I do not object to the thing itself, so much as to the effect upon your comfort & peace of mind, which such an impression may produce — Your creditors are becoming impatient. . . . You ought to be aware of your true situation. . . .

> If the creditors hear that you are living handsomely at L[ansingburgh], and particularly that you pay rent in advance, they will be inclined to annoy you by a sale of your furniture. . . .

> I speak very plainly to you dear Maria, as I wish to avoid an occurrence, which I very much fear —

To the best of their limited abilities the sons knuckled under to their fate and to Maria, but her complaints and self-pity scarcely created a pleasant family environment. After a brief stay in New York as an apprentice in a law firm, Gansevoort came back to Lansingburgh a semi-invalid following an accident. Herman had only a one-year appointment as a teacher in Pittsfield. Late in 1838 he began to study surveying in order to qualify as an engineer, but failed, despite his uncle's efforts on his behalf, to obtain a position. Allan was having difficulties in Peter's law office. He alleged, probably not quite accurately in view of Peter's efforts to get employment for Herman, that his "Uncle was wishing to rid himself of all further expenses & responsibility on my account to obtain his object picked a quarrel with me, and my language (which he provoked) not being as he thought the most respectful towards him, he refused to notice me, & when I afterwards begged his forgiveness *if* I had offended him he told me I must leave him." (Allan underscored the *if,* blithely convinced of the rightness of his conduct.) In a huff, in May 1839, he went off to New York with Gansevoort, who at this time was sufficiently recovered to travel. On May 31 Gansevoort informed his family that he had arranged for Herman to sail to Liverpool aboard the *St. Lawrence.*

While Herman "sailed for Liverpool before the mast," in Allan's somewhat envious words, Gansevoort remained in New York and resumed his apprenticeship in a law firm. Allan returned to Peter's office, "but after two or three days his conduct towards me remaining the same I finally packed up what articles I had in the office and without exchanging a word with his lordship I left him." In July he found employment in another Albany law firm "on the miserable pitence of $5 per month." Maria, apparently recognizing that Gansevoort and Herman were escaping, tried to keep Allan in a state of "docility":

> My dear Allan while you live ever remember your Mother with *deep enduring affection,* and when you find you are about doing some thing which your inward Monitor Conscience — disapproves, let the recollection of your devoted Mother and her heartfelt advice come to strengthen the inward monitor, *crush not its voice,* & you — will triumph over temptations, my dear son I fear you feel too strong a confidence in your own strength. . . .

Poor Maria probably had not the faintest awareness of how a son, feeling his oats and his manhood, would respond to such advice.

About a month after his return from Liverpool, in October 1839, Herman was teaching at the Greenbush and Schodack Academy. This was the month in which, according to Peter Gansevoort, his sister was "entirely impoverished," and her furniture had been advertised for sale. Herman optimistically promised his mother "$150. to $200. a year," but since the school was in financial difficulties, he received only part of his wages. Again he failed Maria, who no doubt did not keep her disappointment to herself.

In 1840 Herman went West to seek his fortune and perhaps to escape from Maria and the responsibilities she placed upon libidinous and rebellious youth. He accumulated no fortune, only experiences which would reappear later in his fiction. On January 2, 1841, he set sail for the Pacific aboard a whaling ship — like Ishmael, "having little or no money in my purse, and nothing particular to interest me on shore."

For almost four years Herman gathered adventures and bequeathed Maria and her problems to Gansevoort and Allan, who served their apprenticeships in law offices devoid of adventures and exotic colorations. He was thousands of miles away from the sound of Maria's voice and only rarely received her moralistic letters. The two brothers heard her complaints and contributed what they could to her support.

In his old age Herman remarked to a niece that his mother "hated him." In Newton Arvin's perceptive observation, "What it meant . . . , in its hardly disguised way, was that Melville, on one side of his nature, hated his mother." But, as Hawthorne observed in a brilliant passage toward the conclusion of *The Scarlet Letter,* and as psychology was later to amplify, hate and love are opposite sides of the same coin: "Philosophically considered, therefore, the two passions are essentially the same, except that one happens to be seen in a celestial radiance, and the other in a dusky and lurid glare."

Herman's love and frustration appear in the dream sequence in *Moby-Dick* and in the incestuous antics of *Pierre.* The ambivalence present in the novels received legal confirmation in his own handwriting in 1852. He was the second son of a father who was also a second son. Herman's second son was born on October 22, 1851. When the new father filled out the birth certificate, he made an extraordinary oedipal slip:

First Name of Father	Maiden Name of Mother	Birthplace of Father	Birthplace of Mother
Herman	Maria G. Melville	New York	Albany

Herman's wife was Elizabeth Shaw Melville, who was born in Boston.

A few months after he filled out this certificate — such is the foreshadowing of seeming accidents — he began to write *Pierre,* which relates a tale of a son's infatuation with his mother and his foolish attempt to preserve the purity of his father's memory by passing off his half-sister as his wife.

The Ishmaels in Melville's writings flee from mother, but their flights confirm not only her attraction and power but also the feelings of rejection on the part of the sons. To dwell as Melville does on many occasions upon bastardy, even ennobling this anomalous and lonely state of disconnection, may be a covert attack upon motherhood, but more probably is a veiled cry for a connection never enjoyed in the perfect way these sons (and all children) craved.

Maria Gansevoort Melvill may not have been the model of motherhood — but one son at least never ceased to hope. She failed her son, as every mother does, the son in his self-enclosed world unable to appreciate how others in turn had failed her.

Isaac
—Gansevoort Melville

Gansevoort, the first born of the children, carried a heavy burden. He was baptized with his mother's maiden name. The darling of his parents, he suffered from the excesses of love. With the kind of paternal exuberance which flatters the parent as well as the child, Allan Melvill pronounced him "rather more than a genius." He grew up surrounded by loving parents, overwhelmed with attention, but burdened with expectations perhaps beyond his capacities. He received the family blessing, but in order to enjoy the privileges of the blessing he had to accept the mold his parents decreed though the mold might be at odds with his own desires.

Herman as the second-born son was Gansevoort's rival, and regardless of what he did, even when he won a speaking contest, he always played second to the older boy. It is easy to sympathize with Herman's self-effacement when he attempted to excel in ciphering and in business in order to gain parental approval, to win some of the affection away from his rival. But the two boys had to play out the roles which their parents and their own needs as offsprings imposed upon them. There was no escape from the drama of Isaac and Ishmael. The human drama was more complex and heart-rending than its mythic antecedent. The one who eventually assumed the role of Ishmael probably never realized that the recipient of the "genius" accolade suffered too. But Herman was the stronger, physically as well as emotionally. He survived long after Gansevoort burned himself out.

Family records are never as complete as one would like, since a family lives in the present, not in terms of a biographer's needs. But it is possible to reconstruct with reasonable accuracy aspects of life in the Melvill household, particularly in the case of Gansevoort. Family letters clearly establish that both Maria and Allan Melvill had an unwavering belief in Gansevoort's superiority to the other children. We also know that Allan at least was not insensitive to the rivalry between Herman and his older brother, and tried after his fashion not to exacerbate the situation, although it is doubtful that a parent can right this kind of "wrong" in the eyes of the rejected or neglected child.

Early in his life Herman vented his anger. The five-year-old boy, Maria wrote, "has turned into a great tease, & daily puts Gansevoorts Patience to flight, who cannot bear to be 'plagued by such a little Fellow.' " Teasing allowed his resentment harmless release. If his parents ordered him to stop, he had their attention for the moment, and Gansevoort was made aware of the "little Fellow." Children are intuitively Machiavellian masters of wonderfully human devices!

If Herman tried to topple Gansevoort, the latter worked hard to maintain his eminence. As soon as he entered school he distinguished himself and was almost always "A^S N^O 1" in his class, as his father observed. He was highly competitive and had few difficulties in adapting himself to the discipline and structure of the educational system, as later he was to adapt himself to the intricacies of the American political system. Not only was he what doting mothers term a "scholar," who won easily the battle of the report cards, but at an early age he also began to win prizes in oratory. On the platform he found himself the focus of all eyes, and there he could satisfy his competitive drives, with the approval of his audience, and sway them through his verbal facility. He was evidently an oratorical spellbinder at an early age. Even in dancing class, where he again made himself the center of attention, he cavorted with a grace beyond his years. And, finally, he was a beautiful lad, a charismatic youth.

No doubt in the family parlor this graceful, verbal, handsome boy was encouraged to perform before two parents who lived out their lives in terms of the public image. Their weakness became his. When later he excelled as a potential orator, he apparently confused the veneer of oratory with the reality of politics. Gansevoort had to assume and master conventional postures; individuality or rebellion would have cost him the favor of his parents and of the public. Since he could not abandon the center of the stage, he always had to be charming, pleasing, and noncontroversial. But as he succeeded in winning parental approval and later public favor, he became more and more dependent upon that favor. He needed the approval of a sympathetic audience more, unfortunately, than the audience needed him.

The death of Allan Melvill in January 1832 was a grave blow to the entire family, but especially to Gansevoort, who at seventeen had to take over the family business. On the one hand his self-importance was inflated by the assumption of a somewhat heroic role of entrepreneur while Herman, perched on a stool in the bank, added columns of tedious figures. But in losing Allan, Gansevoort lost a doting father who gave support to a youth more delicately knit than he imagined. Gansevoort did some strutting in his new role. From New York, where he had gone on business, he wrote: "I find that all the furriers in town know me; and ask me if I am the young man who lately began the cap manufacture in Albany." What Gansevoort did not tell his new associates was that as a manufacturer he was firmly under Maria's thumb and, even more important, under Peter Gansevoort's financial control. Maria treated him as a child, not as an entrepreneur, when she whisked him off from his business to Pittsfield during the cholera epidemic of 1832.

As a kind of replacement for his father in business and in the family Gansevoort assumed new powers, but often as his mother's spokesman. From Pittsfield he wrote to Uncle Peter: "Give Ma's and my love to Herman, and please to tell him that his mother desires him to be particularly careful of himself." Although the advice was well-intentioned in view of the epidemic, Gansevoort wrote with the platitudinous sanctimoniousness of his parents. Maria, about the same time Gansevoort wrote, praised Herman's penmanship, and told Peter that her son "must practise often, & daily." In another letter she sent her "best love to Herman, who I hope is a good Boy — & endeavours to make himself useful by writing — &c." It apparently never crossed her mind that Herman may have resented his dull servitude in the bank, especially when Gansevoort was cavorting in the Berkshires, and that he might have appreciated something more than "useful" advice.

For a time Gansevoort, who shared his father's euphoria, was exuberant about his prospects of success in the cap business. While he dreamed his romantic dreams, his uncle Thomas Melvill, who had once enjoyed great success but was now close to debtors' prison, had reservations when he wrote to Lemuel Shaw in 1833: "It is hoped Gansevoort is doing pretty well — But, on acct of his youth, & inexperience, I cannot cease to be anxious." Uncle Thomas had reasons to be "anxious," for by 1834 economic realities began to intrude. On March 24, for example, Gansevoort noted: "The most unpleasant thing I had to do was to get Hochstrasser, Denison & Guest to renew $400 of my note for $466 36/100 which will fall due on the 26th inst at the Mechanics & Farmers bank.... They consented but with a most miserable grace."

At the time the business was somewhat shaky, Gansevoort, with the advice of his uncle Herman, was consulting architects about plans for a new factory. He probably did not realize how closely he was duplicating his father's career. Financially he was too dependent upon Peter Gansevoort, and he met economic stringencies by concocting plans for further expansion. Unfortunately his expansiveness, like Allan's, had only verbal underpinnings. A fire in his store in May 1834, which produced a loss of about $2,000, was but another example of the machinations of Allan's "fickle Fortune."

The journal that he began to keep in this year is an interesting document, as much for what it says as for what it does not say. Although business matters intrude, particularly when the specter of failure became ominous, the jottings reveal clearly and even poignantly that the manufacture and sale of caps failed to satisfy his dreams and his romantic self-image. Books supplied Gansevoort with romance, models of rhetorical eloquence, and visions of power. While he was managing his father's business he continued to read with a passion not usually shared by manufacturers of caps, or even at this time by Herman himself.

"Slept in the store," he wrote in his journals in 1834, "before going to bed read part of the bride of Abydos." Later in the same month he "read the Prairie, was very well pleased with it — Characters of Ishmael Bush, Paul Hover & the trapper, well & powerfully drawn." Two months later he was reading "a work called 'Watts on the Improvement of the Mind,'" and he was particularly taken with Watts's emphasis upon power: "... let us for a moment consider the advantages which a highly cultivated understanding, the possession of extensive stores of useful knowledge an[d] unerring judgment, and the power of clear strong & conclusive reasoning will give a man; it will raise him above his fellows, it will make him their leader, in a word it will give him power — and with some minds the possession of power is in fact the possession of happiness."

Gansevoort also escaped from business when he joined the Young Men's Association for Mutual Improvement. This was one of those delightful, soul-satisfying institutions which flourished everywhere in the nineteenth century among idealistic youths who had unending faith in transcendental experiences, self-improvement, and universal brotherhood. In 1835 he was on the Executive Committee of the Association, and on January 23, 1836, he was elected president of the Debating Society. At the July 4th celebration at the Young Men's Association, the *Albany Argus* reported, "The Declaration of Independence was read, and well read, by Mr. G. Melville." Once again Gansevoort was the focus of all eyes: he had a place in the sun, where his charm had an appropriate setting and his oratory magnetized his audience. The family parlor had become a public platform.

His grace and beauty are evident in the only portrait which survives, a watercolor painted by an unknown Albany artist on June 13, 1836, when he was twenty-one. The feathery hair, the fastidious attire, the delicate, somewhat effeminate face resemble Allan Melvill's features in an oil portrait painted before his marriage (or the young Hawthorne for that matter). There is something epicene about the figure in the watercolor, not unlike the Apollo icon which haunted Herman. L. A. V., we recall, transforms himself into a Lansingburgh Apollo. Herman more closely resembled his stolid Dutch mother.

Toward the conclusion of a memorial notice in the *Washington Daily Union* after Gansevoort's death, the writer created an icon of a classical hero: "His figure was majestic — some might say colossal; his eye, large and black, with the glance of a Webster, and with a head and forehead whereon was stamped, by 'the seal of Nature,' the elements of a great and commanding character." The author may have overstated somewhat, obituaries not being noteworthy for their fidelity to fact, but Gansevoort was truly an impressive physical presence.

Three months after the watercolor portrait was made, on September 16, 1836, the Byronic young man had to write to Uncle Peter: "This morning I have been disappointed in receiving some money, on which I had calculated and which I shall not be able to get until Thursday next — This necessitates me to ask you to do me *another* favor — Will you be good enough to see the Cashier tomorrow morning & obtain permission for me to overdraw to the amt of say sixteen hundred dollars." On November 29 he complained that he could not pay the rent either on the store or on the house. The financial panic of 1837 finished the business. On April 15, 1837, Gansevoort was humbled in the cold, impersonal legalisms of bankruptcy:

> ...I, Gansevoort Melville...merchant for and in consideration of the sum of one dollar to me in hand paid by Benjamin L Collier of the City of Troy, Hatter and Furrier and Alexander W Bradford of the City of New York attorney at Law...do grant...and assign unto the said Benjamin L and Alexander...all my...goods and chattels merchandizes...and all sums of money due owing or belonging unto me the said Gansevoort Melville....

The liabilities amounted to $33,000, the assets to $17,000.

At twenty-two he was toppled from his precocious eminence. Neither the paternal attribute of "genius" nor his talents, misplaced in the business world, could protect him from public disgrace or, more important perhaps, from loss of face within the family. On April 26, 1837, he resigned from the Executive Committee of the Young Men's Association for Mutual Improvement, and left Albany for New York.

In New York he escaped from the family and public opinion, but he was not without protection, since he accepted shelter with Alexander W. Bradford, a former classmate at Albany Academy, and his new wife, a young lady from Albany. The son of the minister of the North Dutch Reformed Church in Albany, which the Melvills had attended before going to New York in 1818, Bradford had been spared Gansevoort's unromantic and subsequently deflating career. After leaving Albany Academy he went to Union College and then returned to became a member of the Young Men's Association for Mutual Improvement. Bradford encouraged Gansevoort "to take up a course of readings, evenings after I come home, Kent's Commentaries, & Blackstone." Bradford himself was admitted to the bar in 1837, and Gansevoort began to study in his offices in order to pursue a similar career.

Toward the end of 1837, or early in 1838, Gansevoort injured his ankle and took to bed. In June of 1838 he was in Lansingburgh, where the family had taken up residence again after abandoning more fashionable quarters in Albany. Maria, who took the "beloved" son in, attempted to describe his condition to her brother: "Gansevoorts Ancle is about the same in appearance as when he came up, he has much less pain when he moves, but is unable to bear the least weight on it. he is not able to leave his bed longer than to have it made."

The ailment, if it had been only physical, should not have incapacitated him for months. Maria's later comments indicate that the young man suffered a complete physical and emotional collapse. "His Symptoms," she wrote in October, "are more favorable, he is less irratable and capable of more self command." The "Symptoms" she described were not unlike her own "nervous" attacks in the New York years, and it appears that Gansevoort, unable to cope with his admittedly difficult plight, was "handling" matters by retreating to bed.

It was while Gansevoort was ill that Herman wrote "Fragments from a Writing Desk" for the *Democratic Press and Lansingburgh Advertiser,* in which he expressed a deep hunger for the loving guidance of an older man, a kind of successful father figure. The hunger was also so much Gansevoort's that one commentator has queried whether "Fragments" was written by the older son. A few years later, in a letter to Judge Lemuel Shaw, Gansevoort asked of his father's old friend what L. A. V. seeks from M. in "Fragments":

> ... From my Father's death it has been my misfortune that I have had no adviser of mature age, experience & knowledge of the world in whose purity of motive and soundness of judgment, I could place confidence — Am I too sanguine in hoping that the void, in matters of importance, will now be supplied by my Father's early friend — who on more intimate acquaintance will, I trust, be disposed to feel himself justified in transferring that confidence and affection to his son — To merit this adds another to the many incentives to virtuous & vigorous action which I now possess.

If in this appeal Gansevoort indulged in his father's pieties, it should come as no surprise that the young man needed not only Shaw's paternal affection but also his financial support, for he, like the rest of the family, was destined to be dependent upon Shaw.

It may be only a coincidence that in *Typee,* Herman's first book, the protagonist finds a buddy in Toby, who, like Gansevoort, is more of a leader than the emotionally passive Tommo. In a curious fictional reappearance of Gansevoort's illness and confinement, Tommo has a mysterious leg injury more psychosomatic than physical in nature. Because of the leg injury Tommo becomes a cradled child among the Typees, as Gansevoort was sheltered by Maria Melville during his sickness. Not only does Tommo bask in affection, but he also gains for himself time to weigh the qualities of civilized and primitive life styles without being forced, at least for the moment, to a decision that would commit him to either alternative or to deeply feared sexual involvement with the natives. He succeeds temporarily in stopping the chronological and psychosexual clock while he assesses his life.

For fifteen months Gansevoort relived and evaluated painfully the experiences of the seven hectic years between 1832 and 1839, during which he had lost his father, had succeeded him in business, then had watched himself fall into his father's abyss despite his charm, his rhetoric, and his unflagging efforts. During his convalescence he came to several decisions about himself and his future. For one thing he determined to resume his study of law in New York and to free himself from Maria's affections, which meant freeing himself from the tyranny of her favor. Although he dutifully continued to fulfill family obligations, Maria was in the future somewhat fearful of him, as we can see in a letter she sent: "How uncertain & changing are all things here below — but no more of this or you will stop reading." It would seem that Gansevoort was no longer cowed by her whining platitudes, but he apparently never realized that he had been so conditioned by these platitudes that he fell under their falsely comforting sway in times of decision and crisis.

When he returned to New York he may have had a feeling of emancipation from restraints, but, of course, he remained the same Gansevoort Melville. In fiction illness may be a great teacher, and epiphanies transform the pages as they redirect the lives of heroes, but life is more stubborn and infinitely less malleable than imagination. He still had recourse to the shibboleths of the age — "the many incentives to virtuous & vigorous action" — and soon he was to find platforms where he could fulfill his dreams of himself as an orator-savior, a youthful Daniel Webster. Yet the final seven years of his life, despite brief moments of glory, were to repeat the patterns and rhythms of the preceding seven years.

From New York he never shirked his responsibilities as the oldest son. He arranged for Herman's first voyage to Liverpool, but he pursued a dubious course when he continued to act as the conscience of his brother, now past twenty years of age. When Herman failed to respond to his letters, Gansevoort spoke about the matter "plainly" to his younger brother Allan: "I know no other reason for his remissness but laziness — not general laziness by any means — but that laziness which consists in an unwillingness to exert oneself in doing at a particular time, that which ought then to be done — . . . to illustrate — that disinclination to perform the special duty of the hour which so constantly beset one of the most industrious men of the age — Sir Walter Scott —"

Gansevoort's was not an easy lot. As he read for the law, he received only a pittance of a salary, and since Herman and Allan earned very little, the boys were unable materially to aid Maria and the five children. Gansevoort found some release from his burdens in 1840 when he made a number of speeches for the Democratic party. His responsibilities were not lightened when Herman gave up teaching and sailed aboard the *Acushnet* on January 3, 1841; and since he himself was not in good health he had to take, at Shaw's expense, "a voyage for the restoration of my health." He sailed on the *Teazer* to the West Indies in the same month that Herman was on a whaler bound for the Pacific Ocean.

On January 5, 1842, he was admitted to the bar. "On the 10th," he wrote to Shaw, "I put up my name as an Attorney at Law at 51 William St, a few doors from Wall, where I have a desk and the use of a library in offices occupied by two friends of mine — Alexander W. Bradford, & Theodore E Tomlinson." In the first six months he earned $375. "Moderate as these figures are," he informed Shaw, "I look upon them with thankfulness as the first fruits of a soil which shall not lack for any culture which it may be in my power to bestow." He somehow managed to sound like his father, perhaps in part because he was repeating Allan Melvill's relationship with Shaw. On July 22, 1842, he sent Shaw a note drawn on Bradford, "with the request that if convenient, you will do me *the very great favor* of discounting it."

Law, like business, could not contain Gansevoort's abilities and dreams. He found the New York equivalent of Albany's Young Men's Association for Mutual Improvement in the far more exciting atmosphere of Tammany Hall. He was establishing himself as a party orator before audiences numbering as many as four thousand of the faithful. "Do me the justice," he concluded, after a not altogether modest recital of his platform achievements, "Do me the justice to believe that these ephemeral successes, these triumphs of the hour, are neither over-estimated by me, nor tend to lure my time and thoughts from efforts towards those attainments, and that sterling efficacy of character which form the only true basis of deserved and lasting success —"

Apparently Judge Shaw, concerned that visions of success would seduce the romantic young man into characteristic Melville folly, tactfully reminded him of his responsibilities to himself and to his impecunious family, for in reply Gansevoort made a solemn pledge: "Your opinions as to speaking at popular meetings coincide exactly with those which I have ever entertained — I look upon my profession for the next 12 or 15 years *at least* as the leading object of my exertions — to which everything else must bend, and to the prosecution of which all other objects are mere accessories — With this idea steadily before me I trust to avoid the dangers of distracted and devious effort."

The pledge, sincere as it was, he could not keep. The public platform was an irresistible magnet: it fulfilled his dreams of his "genius" and made him the focus of thousands of eyes which restored the lofty eminence of his childhood when he was the center of an admiring family. At the end of the year when he was seeking appointment as Examiner in Chancery in New York City, his recommenders emphasized his "unrivalled" success as a political speaker. He probably received the appointment, however, not because of his oratorical brilliance, but for a more mundane reason. Peter Gansevoort intervened with an old political friend, Governor Bouck.

In respect to his affiliation with Tammany Hall, Gansevoort asked for "justice" but heeded neither friend nor kin. In 1843 Thomas Melvill, who had been skeptical about Gansevoort's talents for business, shared Judge Shaw's reservations about the young man's political aspirations: "I regret to learn by the public prints, that Gansevoort is aspiring to prominancy, in party politics, and especially that he is taking an active part, on the subject of 'repeal,' with which, as Americans, we have no concern. — Much better would it be for him to attend solely to his own concerns for 20 Years to come." Chauvinistic dreams of the enlargement of the United States through annexation of Texas coincided with Gansevoort's dreams. In the following year he was on the stump, speaking for the candidacy of James K. Polk in Tennessee, Ohio, Kentucky, New York, and elsewhere. At first his speeches were only two and one-half hours long, then lengthened to four hours, and finally he was declaiming "2½ hours in the afternoon & the same time again in the evening." One newspaper reported that "His language was chaste, refined and humorous withal, which like a charm, enlisted the undivided attention of the audience." Another newspaper toward the conclusion of the campaign said: "Though he appears to be only about 30 years of age, he probably has no superior as a political speaker in the country." The press was not in agreement about Gansevoort's abilities. Horace Greeley, in the *New-York Daily Tribune,* was not taken in by what the provincial papers pronounced "sparkling wit": "He develops too much gas and glory — talks too much of himself, Mr. Van Buren and Gen. Jackson — and says too little of the great questions before the People." No doubt Greeley was right, but Gansevoort could recall speaking in Cooperstown, New York, with James Fenimore Cooper on the platform.

At the peak of Gansevoort's success Herman returned to the United States after more than three and one-half years of adventure. In the yarn he later told of his return, in *White-Jacket,* toward the end of the voyage Captain Claret compels the seamen to shed their hirsute appendages, an order which almost causes mutiny. In life it was not the sea captain but Gansevoort who advised Herman to shave his whiskers and present himself as a "Christian" gentleman to Maria. If Herman had changed, convention still ruled the Melville family.

Herman settled in New York with Gansevoort and Allan, both of whom were now lawyers, and shortly began to write *Typee*. After the election of Polk, Gansevoort expected a reward for services rendered. He went to Washington in March 1845 to attend the inauguration, but nothing was forthcoming. Not content to trust to chance, he had his friends and political allies bombard the President with letters extravagantly asserting his credentials; thirty letters were written in April urging his appointment as Marshall for the Southern District of New York. The delay in the "payoff" was probably no mistake. Greeley's nasty reference to "gas and glory" indicated that Gansevoort could not conceal his egomania and that he was excitable and somewhat unstable. Or to put it another way, Gansevoort, like his father, wore his weaknesses on his sleeve. Politicians exploited his oratorical spellbinding but distrusted his judgment.

On May 7, 1845, he carried his case directly to Polk: "Although the entire failure of my application (for public employment) has injured me more seriously than you can imagine both in the present and the future and has fallen upon me with stunning force, yet having full faith that your personal feelings were throughout kind and friendly, and entertaining no doubt but that you have been guided in your decision by enlarged views of what you deem to be sound policy, I acquiesce in the result without a murmur." But he did "murmur" before he was finished: "In the sincere hope that those who have been adjudged to be more worthy than myself will prove themselves to be so, earnestly desiring that your administration may be honorable and triumphant, and your life prolonged prosperous and happy. . . ." The concluding remark was tactless and somewhat insulting, but behind the urgency of his own and his friends' appeals were his mounting debts. His platform successes had added to his fame, which had salved his ego and bolstered his confidence, but public acclaim provided nothing for his creditors, as Shaw had warned. Early in the year he was settling his debts "at ten cents on the dollar," and three weeks before he wrote to the President he had asked Shaw to discount a note for $500.

Finally, on July 16, he received an appointment as "Secretary of the Legation of the United States of America near her Brittanick Majesty." In accepting a minor consular post Gansevoort had also to accept a salary so small that he would have to live penuriously in London in order to pay off his debts. Perhaps he thought that "the fickle Goddess" would change her ways and smile on him, that, in other words, the minor governmental post would lead to a better one. Or perhaps he had no clear plan and simply reacted in character-istic Melville fashion and fled, with some vague expectation that if matters did not get better, at least they would not get worse. On July 30 Gansevoort asked Shaw to renew the note and on the following day he sailed for England. In his luggage was the unfinished manu-script of *Typee.*

On his arrival in London Gansevoort undertook to arrange for the publication of his brother's book, a duty which he fulfilled with energy and success. To the end he never neglected the family. But life in London lacked excitement. He was at the legation from ten or eleven o'clock until three in the afternoon, and he was without friends and funds. Because of obligations to his creditors he ate only in inexpensive restaurants and for more than six months presented no letters of introduction so that he could spare himself the expense of entertaining and being entertained. As a minor official his duties were unexciting and dull. Almost from the moment of his arrival in England he managed to antagonize the ambassador, Louis McLane, who began to send memoranda to James Buchanan, the Secretary of State, urging Mr. Melville's removal to Constantinople, Paris, or Le Havre — a transfer which "would not be more agreeable to me per-sonally, than advantageous to the public service."

Although the accounts of Gansevoort's behavior were written by his critics, they seem to include a great deal of truth. Gansevoort was almost manic and sometimes a little paranoid. "I have never seen him since he came here," McLane wrote to Buchanan, "that he was not in a mood painfully extravagant, as to all Men & all things." In the midst of delicate political negotiations, he was reported to have delivered "a Tammany speech" at a diplomatic dinner and to have concluded: "I was one who helped to place Mr. Polk where he now is, and I know that he will not *dare* to recede from 54.40." Under the circumstances it is not surprising that McLane complained: "I confess that I have never before met with precisely his parallel; and, with a rhetorical extravagance of speech & manner, and truthlessness the most extraordinary, he is constantly doing things that I will not venture now to hint at."

On March 19, 1846, Gansevoort complained in his journal of severe headaches, and a week later noted "little or no feeling of uneasiness or pain in the left eye, a mist still before it & quite unable to read even large type with the right eye closed." He was depressed when he wrote to Herman on April 3, 1846:

> . . . my thoughts are so much at home that much of my time is spent in disquieting apprehensions as to matters & things there. . . . I sometimes fear I am gradually breaking up. . . . I think I am growing phlegmatic and

cold. Man stirs me not, nor woman either. My circulation is languid. My brain is dull. I neither seek to win pleasure or to avoid pain. A degree of insensibility has been long stealing over me, & now seems permanently established, which, to my understanding is more akin to death than life. Selfishly speaking I never valued life much — it were impossible to value it less than I do now. The only personal desire I now have is to be out of debt.

As he fearfully watched himself "gradually breaking up," he must have recalled another scene fourteen years earlier. Allan quoted the Bible before the light of reason went out, and in this letter to Herman, Gansevoort seemed to be saying his farewell when he appended the death speech from *Measure for Measure*: "Ay but to die, and go we know not where":

> *The weariest and most loathed worldly life*
> *That age, ache, penury and imprisonment*
> *Can lay on nature, is a paradise*
> *To what we fear of death.*

On April 7 he notified the embassy "that he was threatened with a total loss of sight, and had been advised by Doctor Quinn . . . to withdraw immediately from his official duties." His superior, Ambassador McLane, wrote privately to the Secretary of State that Gansevoort did not face *"loss of sight!"* but that, according to his physician, "his disorder is in some degree connected with the brain, and a state of nervous derangement." Perhaps it was a brain tumor that was responsible for the "extravagant" mood swings. Like his father, Gansevoort lingered in the darkness of madness about a month. He paid his last installment to life on May 12, 1846. Allan Melvill's "beloved son" was allotted "30 years, 6 months and 6 days," the *Albany Argus* reported with cold exactness. Only twelve Americans attended the funeral services at Westminster Abbey.

Even death did not grant Gansevoort his "only personal desire . . . to be out of debt." He bequeathed to the family not only his old debts but also the cost of dying. Herman was compelled to write to President Polk: "Our family are in exceedingly embarrassed circumstances, and unless the measure which Mr McLane recommends is carried out, a great part of the expenses attendant on my brother's last illness and funeral will have (for some time at least) to remain unpaid." The request was granted; the humiliation remained. The body arrived aboard the *Prince Albert* on June 26. Herman was there to receive it. In 1830 Herman had sailed up the Hudson River to Albany with his bankrupt father aboard the *Swiftsure;* this time he made the lonely trek with his rival's coffin aboard the *Hendrick Hudson*.

Such is life's irony that in his farewell letter, with the quotation from *Measure for Measure,* Gansevoort enclosed the first English notices of *Typee,* which heralded the advent of a new author. With success – again the irony – came a new role for Herman as head of the household. There was no longer any reason for rivalry with the favorite son. Gansevoort's diligence in arranging for the publication of *Typee* and in seeing the galleys through the press should have settled the old score, but psychic scores are never settled.

Three years later Herman was in London to arrange for the publication of *White-Jacket* and noted in his journal: "No doubt, two years ago, or three, Gansevoort was writing here in London, about the same hour as this – alone in his chamber, in profound silence – as I am now. This silence is a strange thing. No wonder the old Greeks deemed it the vestibule to the higher mysteries."

Gansevoort reappears more or less directly in the fiction on at least two occasions. Redburn's older brother arranges for the lad's trip to Liverpool, and the youth stays overnight at the home of a friend (Alexander Bradford). In *White-Jacket* the narrator refers to a brother who "is at liberty to call personally upon the President of the United States, and express his disapprobation of the whole national administration," while "I am subject to the cut-throat martial law!" In view of Polk's reluctance to reward Gansevoort after the successful election campaign, this remark seems more boastful than accurate, giving White-Jacket an aura of importance.

In the late 1870s Herman composed a poem entitled "Timoleon," which describes a second son's feeling of loss:

> *Timophanes was his mother's pride –*
> *Her pride, her pet, even all to her*
> *Who slackly on Timoleon looked. . . .*

In 1890, a year before his death, Herman was reading Balzac's *The Two Brothers.* As he often did, he underscored memorable passages. In Balzac's novel he marked the following: "Phillippe, the elder of the two sons, was strikingly like his mother. . . . he was to her mind a man of genius; whereas Joseph, puny and sickly, with unkempt hair and absent mind, seeking peace, loving quiet, and dreaming of an artist's glory, would only bring her, she thought, worries and anxieties."

In his fiction Melville, like Marcel Proust and Henry James, freed himself from the rivalry of the older brother by relating tales of orphans. But he did not wholly free himself, since these orphans search for fathers or brothers as they attempt in fumbling fashion to reconstitute the family which they can live neither with nor without.

Ishmael
—Herman Melville

Herman never attempted, at least not directly, to deal fictionally with the short unhappy life of Gansevoort Melville. Yet on some level of consciousness he must have recognized that the dulling of Gansevoort's senses and mind in the last weeks of his life imitated Allan Melvill's physical and psychic death fourteen years earlier. He could not have blocked out the fact that his brother, like the Bartleby he was to create less than a decade later, preferred not to live. When Herman was troubled by eyestrain, as he often was, particularly during the strain of writing, he must have recalled Gansevoort's lot, and in his own manic swings he could not have overlooked the similarity to Gansevoort's gyrations.

Although Herman was doubtlessly not so shabbily treated by Maria and Allan as his injured pride declared, in matters of this sort objective evaluation is irrelevant. For Melville saw himself as a wounded Narcissus, an Ishmael. He grew up in Gansevoort's shadow, the rejected son who observed with envy and anger the older brother's oratorical brilliance, his charm, and his physical attractiveness. Although he rivaled Gansevoort when he won the oratorical prize which astounded his father, Herman devoted himself to ciphering and eventually won another first prize, pursuing a study in which Gansevoort was not superior and which would earn him, as it did, the approval of a father who had marked him for business. Unlike the artist-heroes in Thomas Mann's writings, who begin their rebellions against their businessmen-fathers in childhood and ambivalently identify themselves with the artistic interests of their mothers, Herman accepted the false and debased image his need for his father's affections decreed. He stooped but did not conquer.

Allan's final act was to cheat Herman by dying when he was too young to be his successor, and Herman had to observe his brother in a position of some prestige and favor. He found himself taken out of Albany Academy and placed in a bank, where he put his skill in ciphering to work in the passive and dull role of a clerk. More than the importance given to Gansevoort as Allan's successor in business, Herman must have resented the fact that his brother became Maria's surrogate. Gansevoort was young and prudish. Whether he informed his mother we do not know, but in his journal he noted on March 7, 1834, that in the middle of the afternoon "I was very much surprised to meet brother Herman in the bar-room at Davis' in company with Frederick Leake, and at first could not imagine the reason of his being there." Although he discovered that they "were unable to return that eve'g there being no cars," it is surprising that he troubled to record such a trifle, except that, after Allan's death, he always monitored Herman's behavior and personal appearance.

Evidently Herman endured his lot as a clerk in a bank for two years without too much complaint, but in the summer of 1834 he took himself off to the farm of his father's brother, Thomas Melvill, at Pittsfield, Massachusetts. For six months or so he had the kind of vacation that Peter Gansevoort denied him in 1832, when he ordered Maria to send him back to the bank. It was as though he was trying to escape the duty-ridden environment of the Gansevoorts and to reestablish some connection with his father's family. During the next six years, on at least three occasions Herman sought out Thomas Melvill, who had nothing to offer except his delightful eccentricity and his kind indulgences. (At Thomas's death in 1845 Judge Shaw had to provide for his debts.)

The escape to the farm was short-lived. Perhaps Maria or Peter recalled him to Albany, or perhaps he felt guilty about his retreat, a much likelier possibility, since Herman never, except for his adventures in the South Seas, managed to remain far from the family. At any rate he was back in Albany early in 1835. Toward the end of January he joined the Young Men's Association for Mutual Improvement and became a clerk in his brother's store. He imitated his brother when he joined the club in which Gansevoort was an officer and a shining oratorical light, and from his vantage point as a subordinate in the family business he observed during the next two years the denouement of a drama which repeated those of 1830 and 1832.

When Gansevoort hurried off to New York in 1837 after the official notice of bankruptcy, Herman remained behind in Albany and was once again the observer, this time of his mother's bond "in the sum of Fifty thousand dollars," which was drawn up to provide for Gansevoort's business debts. Although Gansevoort had fallen and fled, Herman at age eighteen was not ready to become his successor. The truth was that, except in his art, where his dependency takes another form, Herman was by nature and temperament dependent. Like L. A. V. he preferred to push off responsibilities upon others. Apparently on his voyages he was content with the status of a cabin boy or an ordinary seaman. Gansevoort oversaw the publication of *Typee,* and later his brother Allan made arrangements with publishers on his behalf. His wife was to manage the financial affairs of the family, partly because the money on which they depended came from her family, but also because Herman had little ability in such mundane matters. When he snuggled into the Custom-House in New York in 1866, he was content to be an inspector: he performed his tasks conscientiously and honestly but never aspired to rise in status.

With Maria's inheritance dissipated to meet obligations incurred by Gansevoort, Herman's responsibility was to provide income for the family. Since there was no longer a family business, he had to make his own way as best he could and with such limited experience and training as he had acquired in his first eighteen years. He drifted from job to job. Probably with the assistance of Thomas Melvill, who had interested himself in the problems of secondary education, he obtained a position in a school near Pittsfield late in 1837. "My scholars," he wrote to Peter Gansevoort, "are about thirty in number, of all ages, sizes, ranks, characters, & education; some of them who have attained the ages of eighteen can not do a sum in addition, while others have travelled through the Arithmatic: but with so great swiftness that they . . . are about as ignorant of them as though they had never passed that way before." The appointment was only for a year, and Herman, scarcely ideal as the mentor of recalcitrant young men, emerged unscathed from the experience, although, according to J. E. A. Smith, "some of the bigger boys undertook to 'lick' him — with what results, those who remember his physique and character can well imagine."

While he struggled to cudgel knowledge into stubborn school-children, he suddenly found himself engaged in a mud-slinging newspaper brawl in which the participants uninhibitedly dispensed abuse. So far as we can tell from letters in the *Albany Microscope,* at a hastily called meeting in January Herman had himself elected president of the Philo Logos Society, the debating club of the Young Men's Association for Mutual Improvement. The deposed president, with a name that easily lent itself to satire, Cornelius Van Loon, charged that "Hermanus Melvillian . . . with a ruthless hand severed the ties of friendship, wantonly injured the feelings of her most estimable members, . . . and forever destroyed her well earned reputation." In the exchange Herman responded with similar sophomoric invective. Van Loon's "incoherent ravings," he wrote, "remind me of the croakings of a Vulture when disappointed of its prey." In reply his antagonist pronounced "Herman Melville, a 'child of the devil, full of all subtility and all mischief.' " Most cutting of all, not once but twice Van Loon gave Melville "the title of Ciceronian Baboon," to which he uncharitably added: "and his personal appearance fully establishes the correctness of the title."

Van Loon singled out one of his adversary's most sensitive points. For years Herman had considered himself an ugly duckling in the presence of the graceful Gansevoort. The older boy had the Apollonian and hermaphroditic elegance of his father, while Herman was muscular and perhaps a bit stolid like the Dutch on his mother's side. To have his self-image confirmed in print was a bitter blow. When Herman looked in the mirror and saw an ugly duckling, he of course saw the image born of his hurts. When he informally launched his literary career in 1839, in "Fragments from a Writing Desk," it will be recalled, the piece centered about L. A. V.'s self-transformation into a Lansingburgh Apollo in order to win the favor of the fatherly man named M. Later protagonists — Tommo, Redburn, and White-Jacket, for example — reveal a similar concern with self-image: like "belles" they adorn themselves to gain the approval of males.

The passage of years, the death of Gansevoort, marriage, did not obliterate concern with a damaged self-image. It reappears in a famous passage written in reply to Hawthorne's lost comments after reading *Moby-Dick.* In this strange letter, sometimes assertive and at other times sycophantic and self-deflating, Melville wrote, seemingly about his masterpiece but actually about himself: "You were archangel enough to despise the imperfect body, and embrace the soul. Once you hugged the ugly Socrates because you saw the flame in the mouth, and heard the rushing of the demon, — the familiar, — and recognized the sound; for you have heard it in your own solitudes." In this ambiguous passage he identified himself with Socrates, a comparison not exactly modest, but at the same time, unconsciously, he made Hawthorne, the older man, into Alcibiades, the young beautiful warrior who wanted to seduce Athens' wisest teacher.

After one year as a teacher Herman was without a position. Gansevoort, suffering from a mysterious malady in his ankle, was an invalid in Lansingburgh, an additional expense to the family. On November 12, 1838, Herman enrolled in the Lansingburgh Academy to study surveying and engineering "at $5.25 a term." His motivations were explained in a letter which Peter Gansevoort sent on April 4, 1839, to William Bouck, one of the Canal Commissioners in New York State: "Herman Melville, a young man of talent & good education is desirous to obtain a situation in the Engineer department of the Canal. . . . He however submits his application, without any pretension & solicits any situation, however humble it may be, but he indeed would prefer a subordinate station, as he wishes to advance only by his own merit." Even Peter with his political connections could not obtain a position for his nephew.

And so Herman's newly acquired skill as a surveyor was to be wasted. He looked for other positions during April and May, but without success. About this time he thought of the sea. It was not the beginning of a romance, but a kind of last resort for a restless young man. Many youths in the nineteenth century went to sea for varying lengths of time. Herman could find examples on both sides of the family, since many of his cousins served at sea. Life aboard military or merchant vessels provided "time" for those who wanted to sow their oats and "find themselves," which may be another way of saying that after a "watery" fling they would be ready to reconcile themselves to society's molds.

Gansevoort, now sufficiently recovered to leave Lansingburgh and to return to his study of law in New York, made the arrangements. On June 5, 1839, "Aged 19, Height 5 feet 8½ inches," Herman "sailed before the mast," in Allan's words — aboard the *St. Lawrence* under the command of Captain O. P. Brown. His mother was not inaccurate when she said that "at heart" he was "rather agitated." The agitation revealed beneath the banalities of "Fragments from a Writing Desk," which was published just two months before he sailed, was not concerned with economic destitution but with the absence of an ideal father-son relationship, or personal destitution. When ten years later, in 1849, Melville recounted the voyage to Liverpool in *Redburn*, his hero sails not for romantic reasons but to retrace his father's footsteps. The narrator of *Redburn* informs readers: "I had learned to think much and bitterly before my time; all my young mounting dreams of glory had left me; and at that early age I was as unambitious as a man of sixty." This passage, as well as

others which refer to the bankruptcy of his father, possibly reverberates with an emotional overstatement of youthful disillusion and
of self-pity, but it probably approximates Melville's emotional state
in 1839.

The despair may be stated somewhat melodramatically, but the
young man's hurts were not small matters. Up to 1839 there had
been a series of false starts. Ciphering was hardly his vocation, nor
was teaching to be his career. Surveying he pursued probably at his
uncle's suggestion. Peter was trying to make the best of a difficult
situation for the Melville boys, and if Herman did not want to study
law as Gansevoort and Allan were doing, engineering was a respectable and remunerative profession. If Herman was "unambitious," as
the narrator of *Redburn* alleges, it was because he had found neither
direction nor solace for his emotional wounds.

Perhaps the most significant phrase in the passage from *Redburn* is the reference to feeling "as a man of sixty." In life and art
Melville was haunted by thoughts, fearful thoughts, of premature
aging and of death. Six weeks after his first adventures as a sailor
aboard the *St. Lawrence* he did not write a rollicking story of the
escapades of a greenhorn, although there was a market for sea stories
and comic anecdotes, but rather "The Death-Craft," a conventional
piece of sentimentality melodramatically preoccupied with death.
Redburn has a conspicuous death motif. As Herman was completing
Moby-Dick in 1851, he observed to Hawthorne: "I feel that I am
now come to the inmost leaf of the bulb, and that shortly the flower
must fall to the mould." His creative powers were most penetrating
in his engagement with the life-negating tactics of "heroes" like
Ahab, Pierre, and Bartleby.

Herman returned from Liverpool on September 30, 1839, his
exposures and images increased but with not much "confidence" in
his own talents and certainly without clarification of his goals. At the
moment he did not want to ship out on another vessel. But once
more he had to assume the burden of assisting Maria and the family.
Creditors were ready to foreclose, and there was the threat of having
the family possessions advertised to be sold at auction. In October he
was teaching again, this time at the Greenbush & Schodack Academy. Mrs. Melville was, prematurely as it turned out, "cheered by
Hermans prospects. . . . he has a great charge, & deep responsibility is
attached to the education of 60 Scholars." She expected that he
would soon "be able to allow me from $150. to $200. a year," but
was to be disappointed in her expectations since the school district
had difficulties in meeting Herman's salary. Soon he was forced to
beg for his wages.

When the school was closed in May "for want of funds until the winter," Maria explained to Peter Gansevoort, Herman "thinks of going far-west, as nothing offers for him here." She wasted little time on her son's ordeal which hers far transcended, as she made imperatively clear in the following sentence: "Oh that the Lord may strengthen me to bear all my troubles, & be pleased to sustain me under them."

On June 4, 1840, Herman left Albany accompanied by Eli James M. Fly, an apprentice in Peter Gansevoort's law office. If they were following Horace Greeley's call to go West, they were scarcely intrepid adventurers, since they did not travel farther than Galena, Illinois, where Thomas Melvill had settled in 1838. Herman's uncle, now sixty-four, had not found riches after leaving Pittsfield. His clothing was badly worn and his home modest, and since he could barely provide a livelihood for his family, he could do nothing for the young man. For a while Herman and his companion bummed about the Mississippi River and learned at first hand of the machinations of confidence men who sacrificed name and personality in order to wrest a precarious livelihood. He was accumulating experiences which would reappear in his novels, particularly in the pages of *The Confidence-Man*.

In November, short of funds, his hair long, his clothes shabby, he was in New York. "He has been & is a source of great anxiety to me," Gansevoort wrote to Allan on November 26, 1840. "He has not obtd a situation." But Herman was "in good health & tolerable spirits," with a good appetite, "as my exchequer can vouch." Most important of all to Gansevoort: "Herman has had his hair sheared & whiskers shaved & looks more like a Christian than usual." As a shorn Christian but an "omoo" in spirit, he searched in New York for an opening that might lead to a career, although he remained confused as to what he wanted. Forced to live off Gansevoort's meager funds, borrowed at that, and in effect to beg for his meals from his rival, he experienced once again, as he had so often before, the humiliation of dependency upon and subordination to Gansevoort. As he took stock of himself, he knew that drastic action was called for, not so much to relieve the family, although that was a consideration, as to salve his own pride. He decided to go to sea again.

Gansevoort assisted in the arrangements, accompanying Herman to Lansingburgh and Albany, where farewells were said to Maria and the Gansevoorts. About Christmas time the two brothers were in Boston to consult with Judge Shaw and also to borrow money for the trip Gansevoort was to make shortly for the sake of his health. Once more, as during Allan's struggle in New York and after his death, Shaw was in his familiar role as advisor to the family.

On December 26 Herman arrived in New Bedford, perhaps still in Gansevoort's company. (Ishmael arrives in New Bedford unaccompanied.) On December 31, his name appeared on the crew list of the *Acushnet,* a whaler on its maiden voyage which was expected to last three years: "Age 21, Height 5 feet 9-½ inches, Complexion dark, Hair brown." The *Acushnet* set sail for the Pacific on January 3, 1841.

If we can trust the narrator of *Redburn* to recreate the emotional climate at the time Herman went to Liverpool, we can probably rely upon the fidelity of Ishmael's narration in *Moby-Dick.* Like Ishmael, a former schoolteacher as well as the offspring of distinguished families, Herman had "little or no money in my purse." Probably he did not literally bring up "the rear of every funeral I meet" or seriously think of imitating Cato in throwing himself "upon his sword," but it was a "damp, drizzly November" in his soul before he went to sea on the *Acushnet.* At twenty-one he had succeeded at nothing; without employment he was in fact a burden to his impoverished family, and he had no prospects, partly because he had no defined goals. Worst of all, he found himself a failure, the true heir of Allan Melvill. Failure, he must have sensed, was to be an inflexible rhythm in the lives of the Melvilles, and fear of failure, though unstated, lies behind the uneasy actions of many of his fictional characters.

Herman knew, from the reports of relatives and from the books he had read, including Dana's *Two Years Before the Mast,* that when he signed on the *Acushnet* he was accepting a three-year imprisonment in a hierarchical society, where a despot ruled without check or constraint, where ordinary seamen like himself were treated more like objects than people, although life aboard ship was supposed to make men of those who did not become corpses. The grime and stench, the almost unendurable monotony, and the rigors of battling nature's caprices Melville never made as much of as Dana and others who lacked his genius but surpassed him in faithfulness to dull, harsh reality.

Perhaps at first the novelty of the voyage had some appeal for him, for after six months of sailing he had no complaints to make to Gansevoort, who summarized one of his brother's letters for Judge Shaw: "He was then in perfect health, and not dissatisfied with his lot. The fact of his being one of a crew so much superior in morale and early advantages to the ordinary run of whaling crews affords him constant gratification." Twelve months later the "constant gratification" had succumbed to contempt for the captain, disdain for a crew now consisting of illiterates and sexual athletes, and, probably most of all, insufferable boredom. On July 9, 1842, Herman and

Richard T. Greene (he became Toby in the pages of *Typee*) jumped ship at Nukahiva in the Marquesas Islands, and set out overland to a valley supposedly inhabited by a tribe of happy natives. By mistake they arrived among the Typees, supposedly awesome cannibals. In *Typee* Melville dressed up the facts, maintaining that his knowledge of the natives and their customs was based on a stay of four months, when in actuality he lived with the tribe about four weeks. The extent of Melville's fabrication is also evident in the fact that the two lads in the book take five days, climbing and descending one abyss after another, to get to a valley which was only four or five miles from the harbor where the *Acushnet* anchored.

On August 9, 1842, Herman escaped from a paradise which suddenly had become an inferno, when he discovered that the gentle, pleasure-loving natives banqueted on the flesh of enemies defeated in battle. In abandoning the ship he supposedly had left "civilization" behind, only to discover that "paradise" rested upon bloody underpinnings. He signed on the *Lucy Ann* (renamed *Julia* in his account of the events in *Omoo*), captained by a skipper who violated the rules of the sea, for he was not only incompetent but also effeminate. By the middle of September, the crew, reportedly led by one Herman Melville, mutinied, was placed under arrest, and eventually imprisoned on the beautiful island of Tahiti.

These escapades were recalled in *Omoo*, the happiest and most carefree of Melville's books. One of its early reviewers, Walter Whitman by name, was quite correct in his brief assessment in the *Brooklyn Eagle*: "We therefore recommend this 'narrative of adventure in the south seas' as thorough entertainment — not so light as to be tossed aside for its flippancy, nor so profound as to be tiresome."

After more mishaps as an "omoo" in the South Seas, Herman arrived in the Hawaiian Islands early in 1843, roamed about as a beachcomber, and finally found himself in Honolulu about the middle of April. There he tried his hand at various jobs, including "setting up pins in a ball alley," according to one report. On June 1 he signed an indenture in which he agreed to serve as Isaac Montgomery's clerk for one year, beginning July 1, 1843, in return for board and lodgings and a salary of $150. Herman must have been hard pinched at the time since Montgomery agreed to supply "board, lodging and washing" for the month preceding the contracted services. Weary of the South Seas, particularly when he was confronted with a clerkship which was probably no more exciting in Honolulu than it had been in Albany years before, he signed on August 17 on the frigate *United States* for three years or the duration of the cruise. It was his first experience aboard a naval vessel, an experience which he would draw upon in *White-Jacket*. Fourteen months later the

United States landed in Boston, and he was discharged on October 14, 1844.

While in the presidential campaign Gansevoort was basking in the accolades of partisan audiences and large segments of the American press, enjoying his brief days in the sun, Herman had to face the fact that he returned not as a hero or even as a successful sailor. He had accumulated adventures, had a fling in pagan society, sowing whatever oats he had to sow, but in the eyes of his family and society he was still a drifter. At twenty-five he had no job, no expectations, and meager, if any, savings. So far as anyone could tell, he had accustomed himself to the role of a passive, uncommitted observer. But if Allan Melvill and the family had consistently overvalued his "docility" in his youth, he was still little understood by his intimates, partly because he had found no outlet for his energies.

1844 was to be a pivotal year in Herman's life. Members of the family welcomed him, and he spun yarns about the South Seas. Shortly, if we can trust the legend, someone asked the inevitable question, "Why don't you put in book form that story of your South Sea adventures which we all enjoy so much?" Herman agreed at once. The story is probably apocryphal; it sounds suspiciously like the account of James Fenimore Cooper's sudden decision to become a novelist. Yet it may contain a grain of truth, for despite appearances Herman had been busy, perhaps obsessively so, ruminating about himself and his career. He had decided against business, engineering, teaching, or life at sea. Now that he was back on land, faced with the problems of supporting himself and making some kind of contribution to a family which still struggled to make ends meet, he had to arrive at some kind of decision. He may not have realized, or chose to ignore, that few authors at that time were able to support themselves, or he may have nursed romantic dreams about writing. But there were deeper reasons behind his decision. Years earlier he had proved he was Gansevoort's equal when he had won the oratorical contest at school. Now he would compete with Gansevoort once again and eventually prove himself the greatest wordmonger in the family.

It was as though he had been slumbering and had finally awakened. The first twelve formative years had been lived in the shadow of Allan Melvill, with all the false starts in order to capture his father's love, and had ended in the trauma of death. The next twelve and one-half years passed in further false starts and feelings sometimes of desperation. He could not have guessed that during the following twelve years, from 1844 to 1856, he would finally realize his dreams and establish a mastery in sharp contrast with his earlier passivity, though not without pain, and more trauma.

And so in 1844, he baptized himself Herman Melville, author. Melville himself used birth imagery to characterize the event in a famous letter to Hawthorne: "My development has been all within a few years past. I am like one of those seeds taken out of the Egyptian Pyramids, which, after being three thousand years a seed and nothing but a seed, being planted in English soil, it developed itself, grew to greenness, and then fell to mould. So I. Until I was twenty-five, I had no development at all. From my twenty-fifth year I date my life. Three weeks have scarcely passed, at any time between then and now, that I have not unfolded within myself."

There is no evidence that Herman had given much thought before 1844 to authorship as a career. Certainly he had served no literary apprenticeship, having written up to this time only "Fragments from a Writing Desk" and "The Death-Craft." Neither work revealed any more promise or hidden talent than countless other outpourings of now forgotten would-be writers. During his years aboard ship and his ramblings in the South Seas, he had not taken the trouble to keep a commonplace book or even a diary as he candidly admits in the preface to *Omoo*: "No journal was kept by the author during his wanderings in the South Seas; so that, in preparing the ensuing chapters for the press, precision with respect to dates would have been impossible; and every occurrence has been put down from simple recollection." If from an early age he had been haunted by dreams of glory as an author, we would suppose that he would have kept journals as Emerson and Thoreau did long before they published anything at all, or that, like Hawthorne, he would have started notebooks in which to jot down anecdotes that might later be expanded into tales or provide situations in novels. Curiously, the early journals in the family were kept by Gansevoort and Allan, Jr.

His birth as an artist brought about a transformation that must have amazed a family which had accustomed itself to Herman's "laziness" and general lack of ambition. When he found his purpose and decided to write, his energy was unbounded and his dedication almost maniacal. Hitherto passive and uncommitted, he suddenly was competitive and ambitious, and within a few years he would be competing with Hawthorne and Shakespeare himself. His drive for success was to be as frenzied as Ahab's pursuit of the whale.

When he sat down at his writing desk in 1844, he had only his recollections as he began to place his travels within the restrictions and forms of art. Recent research has confirmed that he had to assist his memory, to find crutches, by drawing upon secondary sources, sometimes appropriating whole passages from the writings of other travelers. Particularly in *Typee* he went about writing like a scholar with a well-stocked library at his elbow. In some respects he is the most bookish of the major American writers, but at his best, like all great borrowers, he transformed what he borrowed.

He became a writer to put money in his purse. The telltale signs are clearly present in *Typee*, beginning with the resounding, attention-getting opening sentence: "Six months at sea! Yes, reader, as I live, six months out of sight of land; cruising after the sperm-whale beneath the scorching sun of the Line, and tossed on the billows of the wide-rolling Pacific — the sky above, the sea around, and nothing else!" This is the kind of phony excitement and sentimentality the hacks of the era dished out. Melville could pander, or compromise, to be charitable, but also he could have refrained later from bitter and outrageously unfair comments about the readers he shamelessly courted at times and from dubious claims that their conventionality restricted his freedom of treatment and subject matter.

When in the first chapter of *Moby-Dick* Ishmael conjures up Narcissus, looking into the fountain, and observes, "this is the key to it all," he utters a profound truth about himself and Herman Melville. For Melville's subject was himself. In the first five books the first-person narrators relate tales and experiences based on the peregrinations of Herman's years of drifting. The point of view is that of the older Melville recalling the young Herman. The names of the heroes change, but the repetitions and patterns reveal that they are the same youth. Actually the autobiography began in 1839, in "Fragments from a Writing Desk."

L. A. V. is the first of the handsome young sailors, Billy Budd the last. Physically they are Apollos in search of other Apollos. The fantasy remains constant. If L. A. V. looks at himself in the mirror and finds himself handsome, the others do too. These lads are vain about their attire, sometimes adopting eccentric dress which may amuse or antagonize their peers but which makes them the focus of all eyes. One recalls that Allan Melvill was an importer of yard goods and in business was always associated in one way or another with clothing. If Herman saw himself as an ugly duckling next to the vibrant Gansevoort, in the fantasy of fiction he is beauty in search of beauty.

The greenhorns, even when they are bastards, as they sometimes are, invariably are of good stock, and more than a little snobbish. Herman could not hide that he was the son of the Melvills and the Gansevoorts. (Perhaps it is more than a little significant that the first of these youths, L. A. V., is in a sense born in a library which resembles Allan Melvill's.) The youthful protagonists dwell priggishly and lengthily on their hereditary, intellectual, and moral superiority to the motley members of democratic crews. White-Jacket associates only with those sailors who share his literary interests and his puritanical code. His intimate is Jack Chase, a bastard whose uncertain origins are immediately redeemed: "Jack must have been a by-blow of some British Admiral of the Blue." Ishmael tells us little about his background except to refer to his "sense of honor, particularly if you come of an established family in the land, the Van Rensselaers, or Randolphs, or Hardicanutes." In his last work Melville was still insisting upon the advantages of birth in the manuscript pages of *Billy Budd;* in fact he was almost quoting from *White-Jacket.* "Yes," he affirmed, "Billy Budd was a foundling, a presumable by-blow, and, evidently, no ignoble one. Noble descent was as evident in him as in a blood horse." Vere, also an orphan, was of aristocratic birth, perhaps even the father of the blonde Apollo.

These handsome youths are as prissy as they are snobbish. In *Typee* Melville writes satirically of "long-haired, bare-necked youths, who, forced by the united influences of Captain Marryat and hard times, embark at Nantucket for a pleasure excursion to the Pacific, and whose anxious mothers provide them with bottled milk for the occasion." Yet he was probably depicting the reactions he had when he left the maternal shelter for the sea and found himself unceremoniously introduced to the coarse jests and acts of his fellow sailors. Redburn, a member of the local temperance society and a stalwart product of the Sunday School, is an extreme example of the prude as a young man. Although Redburn eventually forsakes the temperance society to accept grog and smoke a pipe, never in word and certainly not in act does he indulge himself in libidinal delights. The bodies of these handsome sailors remain as virginal as mothers might desire.

The Apollo fantasy is an adolescent dream or homoerotic arrestment. For its fulfillment it requires a womanless society or at least some kind of protection from matriarchy and marriage. If women are conspicuous by their absence in Melville's writings, there is a reason. The lad hungers for friendship with another male, either young or old, fraternal or paternal, but in either case handsome and wellborn. In "Fragments from a Writing Desk" M.'s library is a bachelor's hall, markedly different from the ostentatious and blatantly seductive apartment of the deaf-and-dumb belle of Lansingburgh. In *Typee* the center of native life is the Ti, "which might be regarded as a sort of Bachelor's Hall, . . . a right jovial place. It did my heart, as well as my body, good to visit it. Secure from female intrusion, there was no restraint upon the hilarity of the warriors." Children were excluded, and "they allowed no meddlesome housekeepers to turn topsy-turvy those snug little arrangements they had made in their comfortable dwelling." Although King Mehevi indulges his amorous propensities as the occasion or need demands, he is "a confirmed bachelor," most at his ease with the "boys." Tommo too spends more time at the Ti than he does with the charming Fayaway. Surely one of the reasons that Melville's "microcosm" is the ship — and that he went to sea in the first place — is that life at sea was a man's world without "house-keepers."

The misogynistic note crudely struck in his first sketch — the absurd amorousness of the deaf mute — runs through his writings. His females are dolls like Fayaway in *Typee* or viragoes like Mrs. Glendinning in *Pierre,* implausible and unreal as characters, although they threaten the heroes by arousing fears surrounding either marriage and domestication or castration. Love, romantic or tragic, Melville could not handle except parodistically. The only successful "marriage" or love story in his books is that of Ishmael and Queequeg, in those deliciously farcical episodes in *Moby-Dick.*

The reestablishment of the son's relationship with the father, or friendship, was Melville's subject matter. The youths are fatherless and searching for the lost male model. Arrested in adolescence, the young men in story after story struggle toward man's estate, repeating the same struggles, fumbling and failing to complete the same rite of passage except in arbitrary conclusions imposed upon the materials. They remain orphans.

Melville was to play variations upon the theme from *Typee* to *Billy Budd.* His subject matter would not change, only the treatment, as more and more he found artistic powers worthy of his material and his deepening insight into himself. At first Melville the narrator laughed at himself while he compulsively recreated the same situations. The laughter was not without pain. Gradually he was able to create an Ishmael worthy of his mythic father.

A Child
in
Cannibal Land
—*Typee*

and *Omoo*

Typee delighted most of the early reviewers. They hailed it as "a very entertaining and pleasing narrative" and at once placed it with *Robinson Crusoe, Rasselas,* and *Two Years Before the Mast.* The notice in the *London Times* on April 6 concluded: "Enviable Herman! A happier dog it is impossible to imagine than Herman in the Typee Valley." Some reviewers doubted its authenticity, a few were troubled by its bias against missionaries and its immorality, but most agreed with Walter Whitman, who wrote in the *Brooklyn Eagle* on April 15: "A strange, graceful, most readable book this. . . . As a book to hold in one's hand and pore dreamily over of a summer day, it is unsurpassed."

In *Typee* Melville wrote for money and fame, and he did not consider the publisher's blurb offensive as long as it sold books: "A new work of novel and romantic interest. It abounds with personal adventure, cannibal banquets, groves of coco nuts, coral reefs, tattooed chiefs and bamboo temples; sunny valleys, planted with bread fruit trees, carved canoes dancing on the flashing blue waters, savage woodlands guarded by horrible idols, *heathenish rites and human sacrifices.* " When bowdlerizations appeared in the American edition, Melville did not protest, and after the publishing house requested extensive excisions, amounting to thirty-six pages of text, for the revised American edition in July 1846, he did not speak of artistic integrity and high purpose, or claim that he was the victim of society's hostility toward artists. On July 15, 1846, he wrote to his publisher:

> The book is certainly calculated for popular reading, or for none at all. — If the first, why then, all passages which are calculated to offend the tastes, or offer violance to the feelings of any large class of readers are certainly objectionable.

> —Proceeding on this principle then, I have rejected every thing, in revising the book, which refers to the missionaries. Such passages are altogether foreign to the adventure, & altho' they may possess a temporary interest *now,* to some, yet so far as the wide & permanent popularity of the book is conserned, their exclusion will certainly be beneficial, for to that end, the less the book has to carry along with it the better.

Realistically Melville adapted himself to the genteel standards of publishers interested in gaining the largest possible audience. He bent over backwards to demonstrate the authenticity of his narrative, even though he knew, or should have known, that the insertion of factual material about the Polynesian natives marred the story line.

After he decided to record his yarns about the South Seas, he went about the task with the kind of drive he had never exhibited before. Probably with the assistance of Gansevoort and perhaps of Evert Duyckinck, he assembled a collection of books dealing with the Pacific scene written by such men as Captain David Porter, C. S. Stewart, William Ellis, and Georg H. von Langsdorff. He familiarized himself quickly with all the available social and anthropological information. He kept a library of reference books near his desk as he wrote, and, as Charles Anderson observes, "it can be said almost without exaggeration that, with these sources open before him and with a lively imagination to body them forth, Melville might have written *Typee* without ever having seen the Marquesas Islands."

Melville did not approach publication like an amateur. While he wrote in New York between January and July 1845, he consulted with his own and Gansevoort's friends, who advised publication in England first, for two reasons: it was the best way to establish copyright and prevent pirated editions, and in that era of cultural inferiority, which Emerson had deplored a decade earlier in "The American Scholar," Americans looked to England for guidance in cultural matters. Melville wrote rapidly, and when Gansevoort left for England on July 31, 1845, he took with him an almost complete manuscript. Acting as his brother's agent, Gansevoort assumed full responsibility for the English edition and made all necessary arrangements. He began negotiations with John Murray, and, in order to satisfy the publisher's initial doubts as to authenticity, he assured Murray that Herman had "not even contributed to a magazine or newspaper" and that "adventurer, and the writer of the adventure, are one and the same person." He persuaded Herman to make the necessary alterations, and on December 3, 1845, Murray accepted the manuscript. In January 1846 Gansevoort began reading proofs, and in his journal he carefully documented the onerous task, which he completed early in February. He persuaded Washington Irving to read the first ten chapters in proof, and the gentle Squire pronounced portions of the work "exquisite," the style "graphic," "and prophesied its success."

On February 24 Gansevoort received bound copies of *Narrative of a Four Months' Residence Among the Natives of a Valley of the Marquesas Islands; or, A Peep at Polynesian Life,* as it was called in Murray's edition. The first favorable review appeared in the *Spectator* on March 1. At the time Gansevoort was reading proof he also arranged with G. P. Putnam for the American publication by Wiley and Putnam. When *Typee: A Peep at Polynesian Life* was published in New York on March 17, five "indelicate passages" were deleted.

Given the haste with which he wrote and the absence of a literary apprenticeship, *Typee* was a better book than Melville had any reason to expect. He had entertaining subject matter in his "Peep at Polynesian Life," particularly for an age which was charmed by exotic accounts of natives, and he was able to extract from his own experiences in the Marquesas enough of a yarn to integrate the factual materials, which comprise no small part of this book, with the escapades of Tommo in his attempts to survive as a prisoner of cannibals.

In this first-person narrative Tommo and his friend Toby are two greenhorns weary and bored after fifteen months on the *Dolly,* a whaler under Captain Vangs. These handsome young men are estranged from the rest of the crew because of their years, breeding, and prudishness. Jumping ship, they set off through the hills of Nukahiva in search of the Happars, a peace-loving tribe supposedly embodying Rousseau's fantasies of the "noble savage." In the course of their journey Tommo suddenly develops a mysterious swelling in one of his legs, but he manages with assistance from his companion to arrive in an idyllic valley occupied by the Typees, a tribe of cannibals. Life among the Typees turns out to be pleasant, although fear of cannibalistic propensities is always present. Tommo's leg refuses to mend, and Toby is permitted to leave for the harbor, in order to obtain medical supplies. When Toby fails to return, Tommo is filled with fears, but he is so well cared for by the natives that his leg ceases to trouble him. Like a child he basks in the attentions his "nurses," Fayaway and Kory-Kory, never fail to administer. When one day he stumbles upon Karky, the professor of the fine art of tattooing, who covets the opportunity of practicing his skill on an untouched white body, Tommo's leg at once begins to swell, and he again thinks of escape. At this time he discovers that the Typees do indeed feed upon the flesh of their enemies. Eventually he manages to escape with the aid of some natives sent out by the owners of the *Julia*, which is looking for additions to its crew. He effects his escape with an act worthy of the tyrannical Captain Vangs or of the cannibalistic tribe when he strikes the native chieftain Mow-Mow with a "boat-hook." The journey to paradise, then, ends in violence, in a blood-bath.

Typee suffers from Melville's inability to fuse conflicting personal and artistic desires. Although the work was "calculated for popular reading," as Melville himself acknowledged, he sensed, but not so clearly or confidently as he was to do later, that the journey motif at the center of the book, which had a realistic basis in his own experiences in the South Seas, could take on mythic and psychological dimensions. In 1845 he was not able to present simultaneously an authentic "Peep into Polynesian Life" and an allegory of Every Young Man.

Chapters 19 to 31, with the exception of the section on tattooing, are intended primarily to create verisimilitude, and serve this function admirably, but the tale of Tommo's existence among the Typees virtually stands still. Murray, his publisher, and readers interested in "facts" were satisfied, but at the expense of the mythic-psychological meaning. Artistically, *Typee* was not strengthened by the insertion in the first edition of an Appendix relating differences in colonial attitudes of the English and French in the 1840s, or by the inclusion in the revised American edition, in July 1846, of "The Story of Toby, A Sequel to *Typee*," which records the reappearance of Richard Tobias Greene. These additions, particularly the latter, after Greene confirmed in the *Buffalo Commercial Advertiser* the accuracy of the events recorded in *Typee*, may have silenced those who considered the book a romance rather than a true story, but detracted from the story of Tommo's evasive struggles with growing into adulthood.

When Tommo and Toby stumble into the valley of the Typees,

the natives want to know the names of the white intruders. They have no difficulty learning Toby's name — his "mellifluous appellation was more easily caught" — but the narrator does not divulge his name, "thinking that it might be difficult . . . to pronounce my real name," but "with the most praiseworthy intentions intimated that I was known as 'Tom.' But I could not have made a worse selection; the chief could not master it: 'Tommo,' 'Tomma,' 'Tommee,' every thing but plain 'Tom.' As he persisted in garnishing the word with an additional syllable, I compromised the matter with him at the word 'Tommo.' " In other words the "hero," out of suspicion or fear perhaps, refuses to identify himself and becomes an orphan in search of a family. King Mehevi baptizes him Tommo, "and by that name I went during the entire period of my stay in the valley." The diminutive form expresses exactly Tommo's psychological state, at the beginning and at the conclusion. He, like Billy Budd, remains a child among adults.

The child motif unifies the material and the experiences. When Tommo decides to flee the *Dolly* and Captain Vangs, he adopts Toby as a "brother," much as Ishmael later adopts Queequeg. The two lads make preparations, but, like children, fail to take along maps and provide only enough food to last them a day or two. They conceal the food they appropriate under their jackets, causing protuberances not unlike female breasts. In the midst of their struggle with bamboo reeds, storms, and rugged terrain, the narrator observes, "I could not avoid comparing our situation with that of the interesting babes in the wood. Poor little sufferers! — no wonder their constitutions broke down under the hardships to which they were exposed."

After they arrive in the valley, Mehevi notices the swelling in Tommo's leg and summons the doctor for an examination. The "old wizard" is, like all of Melville's doctors, a sadist and subjects Tommo to torture, "while Mehevi, upon the same principle which prompts an affectionate mother to hold a struggling child in a dentist's chair, restrained me in his powerful grasp." Like a protective mother Mehevi provides for Tommo's welfare by placing him in a household where he is the only "child" and Kory-Kory acts as a male nurse or older brother. The nurse, "as if I were an infant, insisted upon feeding me with his own hands. To this procedure I, of course, most earnestly objected, but in vain; and having laid a calabash of kokoo before me, he washed his fingers in a vessel of water, and then putting his hand into the dish and rolling the food into little balls, put them one after another into my mouth." Tommo takes baths under the natives' supervision. When he refuses to wash the lower part of his body in the presence of young ladies, Kory-Kory is outraged, "enjoining me by unmistakable signs to immerse my whole body. To this I was forced to consent; and the honest fellow regarding me as a froward, inexperienced child, whom it was his duty to serve at the risk of offending, lifted me from the rock, and tenderly bathed my limbs." The young ladies of the household "would anoint my whole body with a fragrant oil." At other times "I often lay for hours, covered with a gauze-like veil of tappa, while Fayaway, seated beside me, and holding in her hand a fan woven from the leaflets of a young cocoa-nut bough, brushed aside the insects that occasionally lighted on my face."

The natives, then, create a cocoon for the white child, a womb. Rather than give him a crutch to make him independent, Kory-Kory carries him on his shoulders. Although it is taboo, Tommo is permitted to have Fayaway in a canoe with him and to have her act as a sail. Everything he wants he has. He has all the attention the most omnivorous child has ever craved. The natives even permit Tommo to protect his ambiguous sexuality — or to deny his sex — since he is not expected to wear the girdle about the loins that exposes more than it conceals. Instead, hermaphroditically, he has "a few folds of yellow tappa tucked about my waist, descended to my feet in the style of a lady's petticoat." For the Feast of the Calabashes, Tommo, with the attention-getting desire of a child, pleases the natives by conforming to their style of dress. He removes his outer robe and remains "merely girt about with a short tunic descending from my waist to my knees." Delighted at this act, inhibited as it is, Kory-Kory "began more sedulously to arrange the folds of the one only garment which remained to me."

When Karky, the tattoo artist, wants to decorate his body, Tommo reacts with real and imaginary fears. He does not want to return to civilization with barbarous coloration, nor does he want to endure the physical pain of the "pricking" with "strange instruments" which "recalled to mind that display of cruel-looking mother-of-pearl-handled things which one sees in their velvet-lined cases at the elbow of a dentist." But fears aside, Tommo does not want to step out of his cocoon to man's estate. According to Melville, tattooing among the Typees is part of the religious rites, but, as Lévi-Strauss points out in *The Savage Mind,* native youths are often tattooed at puberty in order to indicate pictorially physical and sexual maturation. Tommo will have none of it.

His flight from the valley is facilitated by his exploitation of his childlike status. He can even deceive the unsympathetic chieftain named Mow-Mow, who is made more fierce in appearance by the absence of one eye: "He seemed indeed to regard me as a froward child, to whose wishes he had not the heart to oppose force, and whom he must consequently humor." When Tommo dashes the boat-hook at Mow-Mow's throat, his act is a perversion of the tattooing of the face, where the brief pain of the initiate is part of self-realization and the price of admission into adult society — a rite of passage within a cultural context — and where the ceremony is appropriately followed by an orgiastic community celebration. Tommo assaults a "bad father" and plays out, as it were, the horrors of the oedipal relationship.

Typee, then, deals with Tommo in a primitive setting and on a primitive psychological level. Tommo craves paradise, a return to the earliest human state when the child is completely sheltered by the parent. To recapture bliss, Melville recreates the world according to the elementary needs of a lad seeking "rebirth" as a child in an ideal environment.

With extraordinary consistency Tommo's drama is unfolded in terms of food and oral imagery. The Captain of the *Dolly* is Vangs, whose name suspiciously resembles Fangs and who, we are informed in the first chapter, is most gluttonous, saving the delicacies for his own table and compelling the crew to survive on "midshipmen's nuts." Tommo flees from Vangs only to find himself among cannibals. "Collectively," as Jean Jacques Mayou observes, they "constitute a kind of dark, gaping mouth ready to swallow him up." The word Melville himself used later to characterize his attitude toward Hawthorne, it will be recalled, was "incorporation." Not coincidentally, if perhaps unconsciously, Melville has Tommo strike the native who imperils his escape "just below the throat." Mow-Mow, who represents the tribe which wants to incorporate Tommo, has a name that appears to be an evil, destructive version, even in sound, of the unthreatening, blissful Moo-Moo.

In the first chapter the narrator introduces the reader to Pedro, the only chicken after a fifteen-month voyage to survive Captain Vangs's voracious appetite. "Poor Pedro's fate was sealed. His attenuated body will be laid out upon the captain's table next Sunday, and long before night will be buried with all the usual ceremonies beneath that worthy individual's vest." After Pedro's demise Vangs will be forced to land in order to find fresh meat for his table. "I wish thee no harm, Peter; but as thou art doomed, sooner or later, to meet the fate of all thy race; and if putting a period to thy existence is to be the signal for our deliverance, why — truth to speak — I wish thy throat cut this very moment; for, oh! how I wish to see the living earth again!" The mock-epic device so diverts our critical judgment that we may fail to recognize its significance: surreptitiously and comically it introduces a death motif. "Pedro's fate" is a comic foreshadowing of the cannibalism that later agitates Tommo, and Tommo's lack of an ethical view as to Pedro's death reasserts itself when Mow-Mow stands between him and freedom. Tommo's amorality is consistent with the child's amoral attitude toward its universe.

After he decides to jump ship, Tommo contemplates his release in oral images reminiscent of the child and the mother's breasts: "and so I straightway fell to picturing myself seated beneath a cocoanut tree on the brow of the mountain, with a cluster of plantains within easy reach." He also recalls stories of "bloody-minded Typees, whose appetites, edged perhaps by the air of so elevated a region, might prompt them to devour one." The preparations for escape involve almost a ritual of stuffing provisions "into the bosom of my frock" and causing "a considerable protuberance in front, which I abated in a measure by shaking the bits of bread around my waist." The removal of the food, after the two lads have been drenched by tropical storms, is also ritualistic: "In drawing this calico slowly from his bosom inch by inch, Toby reminded me of a juggler performing the feat of the endless ribbon." As the days go by and their food disappears, they suffer from hunger pangs and dream of "so glorious a valley — such forests of bread-fruit trees — such groves of cocoa-nut — such wildernesses of guava-bushes!"

When at last they arrive in the valley they find "a slender bread-fruit shoot perfectly green, and with the tender bark freshly stript from it." Soon they spy among the fruit trees in the grove a young native couple, presumably having just made love. The hungry boys try to make their need for food clear in "a complete series of panto-mimic illustrations" which are a parody of sexuality: Toby "opening his mouth from ear to ear, and thrusting his fingers down his throat, gnashing his teeth and rolling his eyes about, till I verily believe the poor creatures took us for a couple of white cannibals who were about to make a meal of them." Eventually they are taken to the "palace" of Mehevi, where their hunger is generously satisfied. Soon Tommo willingly sinks into the infantile state over which Kory-Kory "officiated as spoon." Partly perhaps because Melville knew little about the religious culture of the tribe, either from his brief visit or from his reading of secondary sources, the rites of the natives seem to be but excuses for gaiety and banqueting. The Feast of the Calabashes, to which Tommo goes in his inhibited approximation of native attire, is the most elaborately described festival. But the Ti, the bachelors' hall, is almost daily the scene of incessant gastronomic delights, Mehevi and the natives seemingly more interested in oral than genital gratifications — except that the situation is seen through the eyes of Tommo, who himself eschews genitality. The cultural feasts culminate in a scene to which Tommo is not invited — in fact, he is forbidden to attend — in which the Typees dine on some

Happars they have killed. Tommo, when he discovers the remains, has his fears confirmed and revived, that he himself will be consumed, like Pedro.

As in his later works, Melville in *Typee* establishes visceral rhythms. In the early pages when the boys are lost in the wilds of the island, "the gnawings of hunger became painfully acute." The contraction-expansion of the stomach muscles becomes extremely painful when Tommo is literally suffering from hunger, then there are no dilations during the months he is fed to satiety, but the sight of the gnawed human bones arouses fears for his life.

Paralleling the hunger pangs, rising and falling too, are the pains in his leg which he mysteriously injures and which throbs violently. "Cold shiverings and a burning fever succeeded one another at intervals, while one of my legs was swelled to such a degree, and pained me so acutely, that I half suspected I had been bitten by some venomous reptile." During the early stages of his sojourn among the Typees, "my malady began seriously to alarm me; for, despite the herbal remedies of the natives, it continued to grow worse and worse." Soon "I was almost a cripple, and the pain I endured at intervals was agonizing." After Toby disappears in search of medicine, Tommo gradually relaxes and basks in the attention he receives from natives who almost kill him with kindness. "My limb suddenly healed, the swelling went down, the pain subsided, and I had every reason to suppose I should soon completely recover from the affliction that had so long tormented me." Soon he wanders about the valley and achieves "an elasticity of mind" from which despair and fear are absent. He is able to "anticipate a perfect recovery." This euphoric state lasts about two months, until he meets Karky, the tattoo artist. Now his life "was one of absolute wretchedness. . . . It was during the period I was in this unhappy frame of mind that the painful malady under which I had been laboring — after having almost completely subsided — began again to show itself, and with symptoms as violent as ever." Then he adds, in phraseology that springs probably from the unconscious, "This added calamity nearly unmanned me." Ironically, tattooing is intended to make a man of Tommo.

And so the pain in the limb imitates the hunger pangs and goes through the same cycle — pain, remission, and pain again. The hunger is physiological, the swollen leg is both physiological and psychosomatic, and the dread or fear is both real and imaginary. The rhythm is the same in any case: at first he fears the Typees, then their kindnesses and their indolent life style allow him to repress his fear, but the tattooing and the cannibalistic banquet release the fears, which cause such anguish that he can stoop to murder to achieve freedom.

If the leg injury is, as Helen B. Petrullo posits, an instance of "hysterical paralysis" related to "the anxiety produced by the birth trauma," perhaps there are plausible grounds for the association of the contraction-expansion of the stomach and of the leg with the birth process, the most fundamental rhythm of all. Melville himself suggests the analogy when he depicts Toby performing as a juggler "the feat of the endless ribbon," which is a crazy umbilical cord of man's own making, of no great significance in itself except as an oblique preparation of the most elaborately described religious rite in *Typee*. This ceremony takes place in the Ti, in the absence of women who could only have laughed at male attempts to play at what comes to them naturally. Melville is aware of the comic aspects of the rites: "The whole of these proceedings were like those of a parcel of children playing with dolls and baby houses." The ceremony is supervised by Kolory, "a sort of Knight Templar — a soldier-priest," an allusion which reminds us that Knights Templars engaged in blasphemous rites and sexual deviations. Kolory carries about with him "what seemed to me the half of a broken war-club. It was swathed round with ragged bits of white tappa, and the upper part, which was intended to represent a human head, was embellished with a strip of scarlet cloth of European manufacture." A "mere pigmy in tatters," it is called Moa Artua. At the ceremony Kolory "bears the god Moa Artua in his arms, and carries in one hand a small trough, hollowed out in the likeness of a canoe. The priest comes along handling his charge as if it were a lachrymose infant he was endeavoring to put into a good humor."

> In the first place he gives Moa Artua an affectionate hug, then caressingly lays him to his breast, and, finally, whispers something in his ear; the rest of the company listening eagerly for a reply. But the baby-god is deaf or dumb, — perhaps both, for never a word does he utter. At last Kolory speaks a little louder, and soon growing angry, comes boldly out with what he has to say and bawls to him. . . . Still Moa Artua remains as quiet as ever; and Kolory, seemingly losing his temper, fetches him a box over the head, strips him of his tappa and red cloth, and laying him in a state of nudity in the little trough, covers him from sight. At this proceeding all present loudly applaud and signify their approval by uttering the adjective "motarkee" with violent emphasis. . . . After a few moments Kolory brings forth his doll again, and while arraying it very carefully in the tappa and red cloth, alternately fondles and chides it. The toilet being completed, he once more speaks to it aloud. The whole company hereupon show the

greatest interest; while the priest holding Moa Artua to his ear interprets to them what he pretends the god is confidentially communicating to him. . . .

Moa Artua having nothing more to say, his bearer goes to nursing him again. . . . the god is put tenderly to bed in the trough, and the whole company unite in a long chaunt, led off by Kolory.

This richly comic scene should not deflect attention from its importance in understanding the subterranean dimensions of *Typee* and the underlying unity of Melville's art. At the beginning of their adventures Tommo and Toby in effect dress up as women in a comic sexual reversal, when they conceal their provisions in their jackets. In the scene in the Ti we witness the male desire to assume the role and function of woman. Freudians have overemphasized "penis envy" at the expense, to use an equally unfortunate phrase, of "womb envy." Moa Artua, the absurd, patched-up phallus, enters the canoe, the womb, and emerges as a fetus-doll after its birth journey with a wisdom that delights the assembled natives. (The religious rite, interestingly, constitutes a variation upon the child motif as represented by Tommo, whose attire, like Moa Artua's, comically fuses two cultures, East and West, as well as both sexes.)

In the scene which nineteenth-century readers found most memorable, Tommo lies quietly in a canoe and Fayaway in her flowing white robes acts as a sail. Although the narrator alleges that she is a Polynesian Aphrodite, here as elsewhere she plays the role of a protective mother. In the canoe she not only towers over Tommo physically but literally provides a cradle for the incapacitated lad who may be impotent, asexual, or paralyzed by fears of castration. As Richard Chase suggests, the injury appears to be a sexual displacement.

The rhythms in *Typee*, then, ultimately are related to birth. Here Melville somewhat slyly and facetiously begins to deal with umbilical cords, mock-births, baptisms of the "new" child, and so forth. An older Tommo named Ishmael is born in the first sentence of Melville's masterpiece, and Ahab dies entangled in an umbilical cord of his own making which fatally links him to the white whale. Melville, like Whitman, dwells almost compulsively upon birth, its pangs, its similarities to death — the eternal recurrence of the journey from the womb to the tomb.

Toward the conclusion of the first chapter a native queen, magnificently tattooed, examines the "bright blue and vermilion prickings" of an "old *salt*": "She hung over the fellow, caressing him, and expressing her delight in a variety of wild exclamations and gestures." The crew of the French vessel is embarrassed, "but picture their consternation, when all at once the royal lady, eager to display the hieroglyphics on her own sweet form, bent forward for a moment, and turning sharply around, threw up the skirts of her mantle, and revealed a sight from which the aghast Frenchmen retreated precipitately, and tumbling into their boat, fled the scene of so shocking a catastrophe." The queen's frolicsome exposure of her tattooed buttocks — a hilariously aggressive act — is a devastating commentary upon the unnatural responses of civilized people eager to elevate themselves above bodily functions, but, even more important, the scene is not unrelated to Melville's own attitude toward his material. Throughout his career he simultaneously courts and attacks his audience. The assault he ordinarily conceals beneath a comic camouflage, comedy providing a socially acceptable form of aggression. His narrators, like Tommo, are seemingly passive observers of the action, but in their prose narrations they are anything but passive: they freely take up taboo materials and indulge themselves in sexual innuendoes. The psychologically primitive nature of such comic devices, of insult and hostility, fits perfectly with the struggles of the greenhorn narrators in environments which they deem hostile. They defend themselves by means of the primitive tactic of offense, or, to put it another way, since the narrators see themselves as helpless foundlings in an alien adult society, they resort to the crude physical assault of a child at bay. Comedy permitted Melville to take revenge not only on genteel society but, more specifically, on a family which always protected itself from reality and vulgarity by mouthing middle-class shibboleths. Much of his repressed hostility emerged in his art.

Melville did not hesitate to turn the same aggressive tactics against his art and the process of writing. Surreptitiously he often deflated the book he was writing while he was writing it, a reductionistic device which would achieve a crazy kind of perfection in *Pierre* and in *The Confidence-Man*, where his hostility was almost out of control. In *Typee* he was the serene young author, more or less, yet he could not conceal his unwillingness to be imprisoned within literary conventions which he found as restrictive as the moralistic platitudes of genteel society. At one point in the narrative Tommo indulges in a reverie about "centuries of progressive civilization and refinement" and other weighty matters, only to conclude: "The umbrageous shades where the interview took place — the glorious tropical vegetation around — the picturesque grouping of the mingled throng of soldiery and natives — and even the golden-hued bunch of bananas that I held in my hand at the time, and of which I occasionally partook while making the aforesaid philosophical reflections." Suddenly the bananas are more important than the plight of civilization, as indeed they are to a child.

The account of the struggles of Tommo and Toby during tor-rential downpours is abruptly reduced to inconsequence when Mel-ville explains, "I recommend all adventurous youths who abandon vessels in romantic islands during the rainy season to provide them-selves with umbrellas." What a wonderfully farcical picture — two youths carrying umbrellas on a tropical island! Even the romantic interlude with Fayaway, never too convincing at any time because of Melville's embarrassment in sentimental, heterosexual situations, finally ends in a thump of deflation: "Fayaway and I reclined in the stern of the canoe, on the very best terms possible with one another; the gentle nymph occasionally placing her pipe to her lip, and exhal-ing the mild fumes of the tobacco, to which her rosy breath added a fresh perfume. Strange as it may seem, there is nothing in which a young and beautiful female appears to more advantage than in the act of smoking."

In these three incidents the perspective is not that of Tommo, but of Melville placing the events in perspective and in the process undercutting the material. But the narrator is supposedly the older Tommo relating the events of his youth and assuming the overview of a comic writer. In *Typee* the juxtaposition is deliciously amusing, yet it is essentially defensive. Melville was providing himself with a defense, almost too neat, against criticism: comedy was not to be taken seriously. Whether he knew it or not, the deflationary tactics revealed his uncertain confidence in his role as author and, more important, in himself. Self-doubts, in other words, were reflected in his choice of literary tactics. If Melville's greenhorns, his handsome young sailors, are lost in a bewildering, seemingly hostile universe, they but reflect the personal struggle and the personal doubts.

Despite the attacks upon civilization and vague statements seeming to support Rousseau's romanticism, Melville did not take the French philosopher to heart: there was too much of the puritan and the Calvinist in his nature. Similarly he did not hesitate to insert a romantic interlude, but he only pretended to fall in love with Fay-away, who is a cream-puff out of sentimental novels transferred to an exotic setting. The sticky, self-conscious prose gives the whole "af-fair" away. Neither Tommo's nor Melville's heart was involved. De-cades later Gauguin came to these same islands. His women are not made of papier-mâché, for he embraced the land and its people not only with his mind and eyes but also with his heart. Melville neither looked too closely nor loved too deeply. Like Tommo he was afraid and fled.

He recognized, if not clearly in 1842 when he was in the South Seas, at least in 1845 when he was writing *Typee*, ironic contradictions in Tommo's and his own behavior. Hence the conclusion has a kind of logic and consistency. The product of so-called civilization cannot find a paradise among primitive peoples; there is no "passage to India" for the white man. Moreover, Tommo is a bit of a fraud, a con man, as it were. He lambastes the materialism, hypocrisy, and cruelties of religion and society, but when he wants to save his own skin he is prepared to murder.

Melville reports the fraud honestly, for if he cons his readers, he does not con himself. After his impulsive, murderous act, Tommo experiences no feelings of guilt. To the very end — such is the underlying unity of the book — he is an egocentric child. *Typee* fails to disguise the truth that Tommo has not gained insight: he merely reacts impulsively or fearfully to events.

About the time *Typee* was being published in England and the United States, Melville was thinking about, perhaps writing, another book. On April 3, 1846, from London, Gansevoort promised "to make some suggestions about your next book." Early reviews of *Typee* in both countries were favorable; only religiously affiliated publications protested the treatment of missionaries and the author's neutrality toward the sexual license of the natives. An anonymous notice in the *Salem Advertiser* on March 25 characterized the public response: "The book is lightly but vigorously written; and we are acquainted with no work that gives a freer and more effective picture of barbarian life. . . . He has that freedom of view — it would be too harsh to call it laxity of principle — which renders him tolerant of codes of morals that may be little in accordance with our own; a spirit proper enough to a young and adventurous sailor, and which makes his book the more wholesome to our staid landsmen. The narrative is skilfully managed, and in a literary point of view, the execution of the work is worthy of the novelty and interest of its subject." The reviewer was Nathaniel Hawthorne, to whom Duyckinck, always ready to further Melville's career, had sent a review copy. The paths of the two writers began to cross in 1846, four years before their meeting in Stockbridge.

On July 15, 1846, Melville informed John Murray, his publisher, of "another work now nearly completed which . . . embraces adventures in the South Seas (of a totally different character from 'Typee') and includes an eventful cruise in an English Colonial Whaleman . . . and a comical residence on the island of Tahiti. The time is about four months. . . . This new book begins exactly where Typee leaves off — but has no further connection with my first work." Again Melville wrote with great speed. In September he was ready to send Murray "enough of it to enable you to judge thereof." In December he gave Duyckinck the manuscript: "Relying much upon your literary judgement I am very desirous of getting your opinion of it & (if you feel disposed to favor me so far) to receive your hints." On December 18 he signed an agreement with Harper and Brothers and authorized John R. Brodhead on December 30 to act as his agent in negotiations with Murray. (Brodhead, a member of the American legation in London, was a childhood friend of Gansevoort.) On January 29, 1847, he wrote to Murray: "I think you will find it a fitting successor to 'Typee'; inasmuch as the latter book delineates Polynisian Life in its primitive state — while the new book, represents it, as affected by intercourse with the whites. It also describes the 'man about town' sort of life, led, at the present day, by roving sailors in the Pacific — a kind of thing, which I have never seen described anywhere." Murray accepted the manuscript on February 26, and it appeared in England on March 30 and about a month later in New York.

Melville sometimes was not accurate in his descriptions of his books to publishers, but in assuring Murray of the work's authenticity he "fibbed" only in that he neglected to say that *Omoo* was heavily indebted to William Ellis's *Polynesian Researches* (1833), and that, generally, it conformed to the dictates of popular taste more than its predecessor. He accurately characterized the picaresque form selected for the further adventures of Tommo and his own comic tone which made for entertainment rather than for exploration of his protagonist's emotional or psychological development. In the pages of *Omoo* Tommo relaxes and Melville does too. *Typee* is a wittier book than its successor, which is "comical" or farcical after the fashion of joke books.

The wife of Henry Wadsworth Longfellow was not completely off target when she wrote to her father that *Omoo* was "very inferior to *Typee,* being written not so much for its own sake as to make another book apparently." For Melville wrote *Omoo* while he was supervising a revised edition and agreeing to the bowdlerization of *Typee*. He evidently did not want the sequel to cause critical ripples, and he carefully qualified his comments on missionaries and dealt for the most part delicately or obliquely with the promiscuities of natives who managed to profess Christianity and at the same time to enjoy their sexual appetites. On the one hand, Melville was influenced by negative criticisms of *Typee* and the gentility of the marketplace, but at the same time he was faithful to his own experiences in Tahiti, when for a few months he bummed about in the company of one John Troy, who in the pages of *Omoo* became Doctor Long Ghost.

The *Julia,* which accepts Tommo after his escape from the

Typees, is misruled by Captain Guy, an effeminate fop who is called "Miss Guy," "The Cabin Boy," or "Paper Jack." "No more meant for the sea than a hair-dresser," Guy merits and receives little respect. He has to hide behind his burly mate, John Jermin, "the very beau-ideal of the efficient race of short, thick-set men," a fine sailor with "one failing: he abhorred all weak infusions, and cleaved manfully to strong drink." One day this lovable drunk chases the sun all over the deck at noon with an old quadrant at his eye — a kind of boozy Ahab. Long Ghost, the ship's "doctor," became an ordinary seaman after enjoying for a time the favors of Captain Guy, his drinking companion. "But once on a time they got into a dispute about politics, and the doctor, moreover, getting into a rage, drove home an argument with his fist, and left the captain on the floor literally silenced."

The crew suffers from the same alcoholic affliction as the officers. When Guy refuses to take the vessel into harbor, the sailors decide on mutiny but with the skills of a Tom Sawyer. While they are scheming to take over the *Julia,* they stumble upon some kegs and soon are so inebriated that they can only dance and sing like a bunch of good-natured adolescents. Guy and Jermin have no trouble in maintaining control of the ship. The rebels are eventually placed in a "Calabooza," or prison, presided over by Captain Bob, a "corpulent giant" of a native. The prison is an imitation of a prison as Bob is an imitation of a jailer. When the *Julia* finally leaves without the mutineers, the sailors are released from the "Calabooza" and roam aimlessly about the beautiful island seeking entertainment and booze until, bored, the inevitable occurs: they sign aboard another whaler.

Most of the book centers about the adventures of Tommo and Long Ghost, who lead the mutiny. After their release from prison they chum together. Long Ghost is a "doctor" primarily because he can read and can pose as a medical man. Since he has few pills to dispense and is not self-deceived about his professional skills, he cons no one. In appearance this middle-aged man is a version of Ichabod Crane: "He was over six feet high — a tower of bones, with a complexion absolutely colorless, fair hair, and a light, unscrupulous gray eye, twinkling occasionally with the very devil of mischief." His background is checkered, but, as Melville carefully informs us, "he had certainly at some time or other spent money, drunk Burgundy, and associated with gentlemen." He is a spinner of tales as tall as his own emaciated frame, but "he quoted Virgil, and talked of Hobbes of Malmsbury, beside repeating poetry by the canto, especially Hudibras." Yet the truth is, although we as readers are too charmed to be disturbed, that this middle-aged bachelor is arrested in adolescence.

Tommo and Long Ghost rename themselves, with somewhat

impoverished imagination, Paul and Peter before they set out on their tour of Tahiti. Most of their adventures and pranks are neither memorable nor more than mildly amusing. Overaged adolescence has only limited comic viability, to be ponderous about the matter, except to the participants. Long Ghost fancies himself a lady's man, and tries to play Romeo to Loo, a fourteen-year-old daughter of Po-Po, who puts an end to his clumsy, halfhearted advances by sticking him with a thorn. Tommo pretends to be "unmanned" when native women titter at his clumsy attempts to play Romeo, but he manages to survive his blushing retreats with little discernible pain. His feelings are much more ruffled when Kooloo, "a comely youth, quite a buck in his way," after assuring Tommo "that the love he bore me was 'nuee, nuee, nuee,' or infinitesimally extensive," shortly becomes "a retrograde lover; informing me that his affections had undergone a change; he had fallen in love at first sight with a smart sailor, who had just stepped ashore quite flush from a lucky whaling-cruise." So far as any emotion at all emerges through the comic detachment which Melville rigorously maintains, friendship constitutes the emotional or affective center of the book. Kooloo is more significant than Loo or the three maidens named Farnowar, Farnoopoo, and Marhar-Rarrar, which, translated, mean Day-Born, Night-Born, and Bright-Eyed. They are about as significant as their ridiculous names.

Much more significant is what happens to Tommo's leg. The limb incapacitates him during his sojourn among the Typees and flares up in pain whenever he feels himself threatened personally and sexually. It begins to mend almost miraculously as soon as he boards the *Julia*. Only in the first chapter is an ominous note struck, but facetiously in an oblique phallic pun, when one of the sailors says: "Ay, Typee, my king of the cannibals, is it you! But I say, my lad, how's that spar of your'n? the mate says it's in a devil of a way; and last night set the steward to sharpening the handsaw: hope we won't have the carving of ye." There is no "carving" or fear of castration when the friendship between Long Ghost and Tommo blossoms. After "the doctor and I lived together so socially," Tommo uses the leg to escape heavy duty aboard ship, until the officers get on to his "sojering," and soon there are no references at all to his limb.

There is no pain when life presents no threats. Appropriately, then, *Omoo* is stitched together with a series of escapades in which there is little suspense or tension. The structure is in its curious way married to Tommo's emotional state which recreates the euphoria Herman felt in 1843 when in Troy he found briefly the kind of chum he was in search of. Long Ghost is a more hedonistic and less intellectual version of M., the epicure of the library, more sensual (but safely so) than the youthful, but moody, Toby, and anticipates the camaraderie offered by the middle-aged Jack Chase in *White-Jacket*.

Omoo on its own terms is a success in its small way and scale. To ask for a richer, more varied comic work is no doubt unfair and ultimately beside the point. The book had to be written, both for the sake of money and experience. Filled with digressions, it is a digression from the subterranean materials Meville unveils in *Typee*. The interlude with Long Ghost-Troy is a digression in the life of Omoo-Herman — pleasurable but ephemeral, like an evening in a barroom. There is no hint, since reality rarely intrudes in *Omoo,* that Long Ghost-Troy will continue his digression from life and adulthood. Tommo will go on toward the uncertain enlightenment that maturity brings, nothing lost for what has transpired in his carefree escapades with Long Ghost, but nothing much gained either. At the conclusion of *Omoo,* Tommo is a bit older but not demonstrably wiser.

"The World
Revolves upon
an I"
—Mardi

If Tommo enjoys his ramble under the guidance and protection of Long Ghost, Herman himself enjoyed similar favors. His brother Allan bore the responsibility of providing for their mother and four unmarried sisters and relieved Herman of a duty he was quite incapable of assuming. In New York he enjoyed the friendship of Evert Duyckinck, who launched *The Literary World* on February 6, 1847, the first issue of which noted "a new work from the graphic pen of Mr. Melville, of Typee celebrity." In the next few months extracts from *Omoo* and a laudatory review, probably written by Duyckinck himself, appeared in the journal. On March 6 Melville published in *The Literary World* a review of J. Ross Browne's *Etchings of a Whaling Cruise.* Between July 24 and September 11 he wrote a series of political satires for *Yankee Doodle,* which was edited at the time by Duyckinck's friend, Cornelius Mathews. He established himself with a literary group who styled themselves Young Americans with a kind of literary chauvinism, which Melville himself mouthed bumptiously in *White-Jacket* and in his review of Hawthorne's tales in *The Literary World* in 1850, until disenchantment set in and he hatcheted the group in *Pierre*.

Although *Typee* was successful and produced, relatively speaking, a good financial return, Melville, perhaps on the advice of Uncle Peter Gansevoort, was about to take no chances. Armed with a letter from Peter, he went to Washington in February 1847 seeking a clerical position in the Polk administration. If he thought the president owed a debt to the family for the services performed brilliantly in 1844 by Gansevoort, he probably was unaware that his volatile brother had gained many enemies and few friends after demonstrating remarkable ineptitude in London. Like many other office seekers at the time he found all doors closed. He was spared knowledge of Polk's acerbic comment in his diary about the number of people who visited him "on the patriotic business of seeking office. Neither ice nor fire I believe would stop them. I am perfectly disgusted with the prevailing passion for place which brings crowds of persons to Washington. . . . How much better it would be if the horde of office seekers who infest Washington would apply themselves to some honest calling for a living."

Herman had sought to repay many family debts when he honored Shaw by launching *Typee* under his protection: "To Lemuel Shaw, Chief Justice of the Commonwealth of Massachusetts, this little work is affectionately inscribed by the author." Reading galley proofs of the book in London, Gansevoort was concerned: "I trust that the dedication to Judge Shaw will not be overlooked in the hurry of publication." On March 19, 1846, in an inscribed copy of *Typee*, Herman gracefully and feelingly acknowledged an extraordinary friendship which for more than sixty years remained faithful in word and deed to the Melvills and the Melvilles: "The dedication is very simple, for the world would hardly have sympathised to the full extent of these feelings with which I regard my father's friend and the constant friend of all his family."

Though portraits present Shaw as a portly man with a deeply furrowed face, almost too self-satisfied, and though his enemies had many harsh things to say about a man whose decisions and legal opinions were sometimes rigidly literalistic and self-righteous, there is no denying the fact that he was genuinely interested in Allan's family. He may have been rigid but he was also enormously loyal. Perhaps one of his most generous acts was his approval of his daughter's marriage to a man now in his late twenties whose "prospects" were not especially bright since he was determined to pursue the uncertain fortunes of a literary career.

In 1846 Herman began to court Elizabeth Knapp Shaw, who was a close friend of his sister Helen Maria. Elizabeth was three years younger than Herman. The only daughter of Shaw, she was born on June 13, 1822. The mother did not survive the birth of her child, whom the Judge baptized with the mother's name. With the best of intentions Shaw paid what he no doubt considered a tribute to his wife's memory, but his legal mind did not perceive the burden of guilt that he was placing upon the child. Fortunately, when she was five years old her father married Hope Savage, who proved to be an unusually generous stepmother.

The courtship continued for approximately eighteen months. Elizabeth spent about two months in Lansingburgh in the fall of 1846, and in March 1847 Herman was in Boston for a week or two. On June 1, after the appearance of the early favorable reviews of *Omoo,* he returned to Boston once again, this time to propose. Helen Maria was elated. Herman, she wrote to a friend, "has made arrangements to take upon himself the dignified character of a married man some time during the Summer, about the first of August. Only think! I can scarcely realize the astounding truth!" The wedding day was August 4, which was Helen Maria's birthday. The weather was "very pleasant," and Herman found a four-leafed clover in the forenoon, as he reminded his wife forty-four years later, in 1891, in the dedication of a collection of poetry which he did not live to see published. The ceremony was performed at the New South Church in Boston by Dr. Alexander Young. Three days later the *New-York Daily Tribune* carried an announcement written with characteristic nineteenth-century whimsey: "Mr. HERMAN TYPEE OMOO MELVILLE has recently been united in lawful wedlock to a young lady of Boston. The fair forsaken FAYAWAY will doubtless console herself by sueing him for breach of promise."

One month after the marriage, on September 22, 1847, Allan Melville married Sophia E. Thurston, and Herman, now a model of dignity and respectability, wore a "worked satin vest." A week or so later the two newly married couples set up housekeeping at 103 Fourth Avenue in New York — along with Maria Gansevoort Melville and the four unmarried sisters. They were able to purchase the house after Judge Shaw advanced $2,000. And so the Melvilles, except for the youngest child Thomas, who went to sea in 1846, were all together again in the city where Allan decades before had struggled in vain against the "fickle goddess."

In the early pages of his next novel, *Mardi,* in Chapter 3, Melville with immense comic exuberance introduces a theme which at first sight is not clearly related to the romance but which is surely not unrelated to the life situation: "All of us have monarchs and sages for kinsmen; nay, angels and archangels for cousins; since in antediluvian days, the sons of God did verily wed with our mothers, the irresistible daughters of Eve. Thus all generations are blended: and heaven and earth of one kin: . . . oh, be we then brothers indeed!"

Like *Moby-Dick, Mardi* evolved slowly, with changes of direction and lengthy additions, so much so that after two years of labor it came to over 600 pages. Apparently Melville began the work in January 1847, while *Omoo* was being set in type, with the intention of writing a sequel to his first two books. To Richard Bentley, the English publisher, on June 19, 1847, he characterized it as "a new work of South Sea adventure, . . . occupying entirely fresh ground," and made the same claim to John Murray on October 29, 1847. However, on January 1, 1848, he informed Murray that his book "clothes the whole subject in new attractions & combines in one cluster all that is romantic, whimsical & poetic in Polynusia. It is yet a continuous narrative. I doubt not that — if it makes the hit I mean it to — it will be counted a rather bold aim; but nevertheless, it shall have the right stuff in it to redeem its faults, tho' they were legion." Melville was vague and somewhat devious, for he knew that Murray would have nothing to do with fiction, and that the publisher was still troubled by the allegations of readers and critics that *Typee* and *Omoo* were romances more than factual narratives. On March 25 he tried to win over his hardheaded publisher with an outpouring of enthusiasm, which, as he perhaps did not recognize, resembled the vibrant prose of the romance he was writing:

To be blunt: the work I shall next publish will in downright earnest be a "Romance of Polynisian Adventure" — But why this? The truth is, Sir, that the reiterated imputation of being a romancer in disguise has at last pricked me into a resolution to show those who may take any interest in the matter, that a *real* romance of mine is no Typee or Omoo, & is made of different stuff altogether. This I confess has been the main inducement in altering my plans — but others has operated. I have long thought that Polynisia furnished a great deal of rich poetical material that has never been employed hitherto in works of fancy; and which to bring out suitably, required only that play of freedom & invention accorded only to the Romancer & poet. . . . Well: proceeding in my narrative of *facts* I began to feel an incurible distaste for the same; & a longing to plume my pinions for a flight, & felt irked, cramped & fettered by plodding along with dull common places, — So suddenly standing the thing alltogether, I went to work heart & soul at a romance which is now in fair progress, since I had worked at it under an earnest ardor. — Shout not, nor exclaim "Pshaw! Puh!" — My romance I assure you is no dish water nor its model borrowed from the Circulating Library. It is something new I assure you, & original if nothing more.

To this letter Melville received from Murray what he termed an "Antarctic" response. But at the same time he signed an agreement on November 15 with Harper and Brothers for the American publication, which, as usual, was to follow the English edition. At the end of January 1849 he had a complete set of proof sheets, which he sent to Murray. He asked for an advance of 200 guineas and requested that on the title-page he was not to be cited as the author of *Typee* and *Omoo*: "I wish to separate '*Mardi*' as much as possible from those books." The publisher's response was recorded by Brodhead, again acting as Melville's agent: "It is a *fiction* & Mr Murray says it don't suit him." Brodhead immediately took the book to Bentley, who on March 1 agreed to the financial terms, and published an edition of 1,000 copies on March 15. *Mardi* was officially published in New York on April 14, and a notice appeared in *The Literary World* on the same day. Duyckinck was a loyal friend.

Melville, as we have noted, described *Mardi* to Murray with an exuberance which reflected accurately not only his feeling about the work but also his euphoric state while he was writing. Toward the end of *Mardi* we have an account of a genius named Lombardo, who wrote a national classic called *Koztanza*. The portrait of Lombardo is Melville's own comically immodest portrait of himself as an artist, the first of many comments he is to make on the nature of art and creativity. Lombardo, we are told in the pompous prose of Babbalanja the philosopher, undertook *Koztanza* for two reasons: "Primus and forever, a full heart: — brimfull, bubbling, sparkling; and running over like the flagon in your hand, my lord. Secundo, the necessity of bestirring himself to procure his yams." Lombardo wrote like one intoxicated by his own words and fancies: "he was not his own master: a mere amanuensis writing by dictation. . . . it was a sort of sleep-walking of the mind." The result, Babbalanja continues, was that "the Koztanza lacks cohesion; it is wild, unconnected, all episode." After the critics attacked the violation of unities and the excesses of a prose run wild, Lombardo himself "almost despised it; but when he bethought him of those parts, written with full eyes, half blinded; temples throbbing; and pain at the heart — . . . He would say to himself, 'Sure it can not be in vain!'" Then later Lombardo had doubts: "Who will read me? Say one thousand pages — twenty-five lines each — every line ten words — every word ten letters! That's two million five hundred thousand *a*'s, and *i*'s, and *o*'s to read! How many are superfluous? Am I not mad to saddle Mardi with such a task?"

This portrait of Lombardo is a characteristically Melvillean mixture, on the one hand a defense of a romantic author who pours out his heart as he upsets all literary conventions, and on the other hand a witty criticism of a writer who argues romantically and irrelevantly that his visceral engagement in his art certifies its quality. Through Lombardo, Melville also anticipated the criticism of *Mardi* "as a monstrous compound of Carlyle, Jean-Paul, and Sterne, with now and then a touch of Ossian thrown in." Although Lombardo acknowledged the inordinate length of his creation, he took pride in the fact that *Koztanza* was to be a national epic. Melville had a similar aspiration, nourished no doubt by the Young Americans and by Duyckinck, who in his notice of the novel in *The Literary World* asked, "Is not this sign of a true manhood, when an American author lifts his voice boldly to tell the truth to his country people?" Both Melville and Duyckinck expected *Mardi* to be a great American novel.

During the "Winters of '47 & '48," Elizabeth Melville observed, "he worked very hard at his books — sat in a room without fire — wrapped up — wrote Mardi." Lombardo, Babbalanja reports, "never threw down his pen: it dropped from him; and then, he sat disenchanted: rubbing his eyes; staring; and feeling faint — sometimes, almost unto death." Although Mrs. Melville did not romanticize her portrait of an artist-husband, her account says a lot about his industry and his self-discipline in composing a work characterized by self-indulgence:

> We breakfast at 8 o'clock, then Herman goes to walk, and I fly up to put his room to rights, so that he can sit down to his desk immediately on his return. Then I bid him good-bye, with many charges to be an industrious boy, and not upset the inkstand, and then flourish the duster, make the bed, &c in my own room.... whatever I am about, I do not much more than get thoroughly engaged in it, than ding-ding goes the bell for luncheon. This is half past 12 o'clock — by this time we must expect callers, and so must be dressed immediately after lunch. Then Herman insists upon my taking a walk every day of an hours length at least.... At four we dine, and after dinner is over, Herman and I come up to our room, and enjoy a cosy chat for an hour or so — or he reads me some of the chapters he has been writing in the day. Then he goes down town for a walk, looks at the papers in the reading-room &c, and returns about half past seven or eight. Then my work or my book is laid aside, and as he does not use his eyes but very little by candle light, I either read to him, or take a hand at whist for his amusement, or he listens to our reading or conversation, as best pleases him.

Melville was determined to outgrow Mr. Typee and Mr. Omoo and at the same "to make as early a publication as possible, a thing of much pecuniary importance with me," as he confided to Murray. He wanted intellectual acclaim and large sales — God and Mammon. To achieve his purposes he imprisoned himself and recklessly poured out words and also his physical energies. One of the remarkable things about *Mardi*, despite its outrageous length, is its unflagging vitality, the author piling episode upon episode, one verbal display upon another. The plot is thin, at times lost in the verbiage; and the characters are verbal automatons without hearts or complexity; the proliferation of episodes is often not justified organically. The flood of words is a form of artistic narcissism, as though Melville is pronouncing not only Lombardo but also himself a "genius."

Mardi, as he anticipates in discussing Lombardo, received a mixed critical reception, the praise of those who could finish the book offset by the censure of those who often couldn't get through it. Many of the important literary journals were hostile, berating the "novelties" of which Melville was proud, but more important, readers, even in a century which sometimes seemed to worship three-volume novels, did not purchase his romance. About 2,900 copies were sold in the United States up to the time of Melville's death in 1891. The fears of Lombardo-Melville, then, were fulfilled.

As commentators have proposed, *Mardi* can be divided into three parts — a narrative, a romance, and a satirical travelog with metaphysico-socio overtones. The three parts reflect changes of purpose which Melville more or less stumbled into as he wrote, since he obviously began *Mardi* with no clear-cut plan. The sections may represent, loosely, three stages in man's growth, youth with its foolish recklessness, adolescence with its search for love and an ideal, and maturity with its resignation to the inevitability of death and acceptance of the status quo. But the difficulty with such a construction is that Taji, the central character, does not grow: he is foolhardy when he jumps ship at the beginning and no less foolhardy when he continues his wanderings at the end. Since Taji does not mature, but pursues his demon wherever it leads, there is no progression, or organic growth, and Melville in the third part has to shift attention to Babbalanja, who, despite his loquacity, does alter from a questing skeptic to a believer. Babbalanja mouths all the learning and the secondary sources that Melville was reading and consulting in the years after his birth as an artist. But Taji and Babbalanja are both given to excesses, the one to foolish acts and the other to lengthy monologs, neither capable of self-restraint. The book reflects this self-indulgence. In his admiration of his own cadences and inventions, Melville was so caught in the struggles of his own heart, his own world, that he forgot the reader's heart. His characters, including Taji and Babbalanja, do not engage us: they are simply verbalisms that may amuse us but do not stir our guts. Although the discussion of Lombardo reveals Melville's awareness of his artistic and structural problems, he seems not to have been completely aware of the book's psychic unity, the almost inevitable consistency of materials which superficially appear to be almost patternless.

The heart of *Mardi*, disguised as it may be by the introduction of extraneous matter, is the protagonist's search for the restoration, or reconstitution, of the basic human unit, the family. Aboard ship he vainly searches for "brothers," only to discover that "there was no soul a magnet to mine." He, as he admits, with deceptive levity, is an idealist, "an aerial architect; a constructor of flying buttresses." Which is to say that he wants a home where he can experience an ideal family relationship denied to him in his youth. Not until almost the conclusion of his tale does the narrator supply us with an invaluable piece of information: "I was . . . ill-provided young, and bowed to the brunt of things before my prime."

Because he is in flight from a family which has disappointed him, he refuses to divulge his baptized name: he chooses to be an Ishmael, an orphan. He will baptize himself and assume a name that will suit his purposes. (In this regard he is no different from Tommo, White-Jacket, or Ishmael.) To the end of the adventure he will remain a child defining or refashioning the cosmos in terms of his needs and seeking substitutes for those who have failed him. As Babbalanja observes, "The world revolves upon an I."

The *Arcturion* is under the command of a kindly captain, not one of the tyrants or "bad fathers" that usually appear in Melville's writings. Taji's life is not unpleasant, although monotonous; except that the "family" structure encloses him within a hierarchical system which provides security, without love, and holds him rigidly in a subordinate position among companions who are his equal neither socially nor intellectually. He decides to free himself from his servitude and to establish his own social order and structure with the assistance of Jarl. The youth's "leap" to freedom is a childish act, according to Jarl: "He entreated me to renounce my determination, not be a boy, pause and reflect, stick to the ship, and go home in her like a man." The youth scorns Jarl's clichés, the world's definition of manhood. The practical-minded Jarl fails to perceive that the crazy act releases the youth from the authoritarian patriarchal system and allows him to create a new world, a new family, in which he plays at being captain, admittedly only of a raft.

The lad shrewdly chooses a companion who is not only permissive but also obliged, despite his sensible reservations, to participate in the crazy act. Jarl is a bachelor, approaching middle age, who fulfills himself by seeking out an attractive young sailor who becomes his "son" as he plays the dual roles of father and mother. Like the boy, he has not established his own sexual identity and wants to "play house" with others in a similarly undeveloped or arrested state. "Unsolicited," the narrator reports, "he was my laundress and tailor; a most expert one, too; and when at meal-times my turn came round to look out at the mast-head, or stand at the wheel, he catered for me among the 'kids' in the forecastle with unwearied assiduity.... Yet in some degree the obligation was mutual. For be it known that, in sea-parlance, we were *chummies.*" Like Tommo and Long Ghost, they are boys together. "Nay," the youth continues, "could I even wrest from thy willful hands my very shirt, when once thou hadst it steaming in an unsavory pickle in thy capacious vat, a decapitated cask?" The intimacy of this passage, including its use of the "thou" form from another era of meaningful personal relationships, collapses comically with a sly but honest acknowledgment of the sexual impotency of these boy-men.

In planning the escape Jarl attends to matters of survival like food and water; and the youth, whose skills are primarily oral or verbal, perhaps artistic, ruminates about abandoning the "Maternal craft, that rocked me so often in thy heart of oak." The lot of the two under the circumstances can hardly be considered easy, the monotony of waiting for winds, the inadequate protection against the weather, the confinement within a small space; but everything is made far worse, and farcical to match the foolhardy deed, when the narrator suddenly discovers that the devoted Jarl is "afflicted with the lockjaw." Because Jarl's "intellects stepped out, and left his body to itself," the youth dominates the scene completely; he has what every child seeks – the center of the stage for himself. Jarl's silence also serves the author's purposes: he can luxuriate in verbal pleasures and avoid dialog, or dramatic interaction, which he can handle no more satisfactorily in his art than his characters can in the life they simulate.

Eventually Jarl and his friend come upon a ship seemingly drifting without captain or crew. They board the *Parki* and discover that the ship is inhabited by two natives named Samoa and Annatoo, who manage their domestic affairs as farcically as they handle the *Parki*. They have stumbled into marriage: one day Samoa, "thinking the lady to his mind, ... meditated suicide – I would have said, wedlock – and the twain became one." Theirs is a mockery of marriage, and family life, but so are all marriages in this misogynistic book, the admirable characters not marrying at all. Samoa and Annatoo, like Jarl and the youth, are sexually sterile, both keeping to "their separate quarters." In her little room Annatoo hoards the fruits of her kleptomania — she steals everything in sight — and before her loot performs "penance like a nun in her cell." Samoa contentedly and chastely occupies his bachelor quarters, allowing his wife to strip him of his possessions as earlier he has allowed her to amputate his arm, which now flies from the mast as a once-human banner.

Since Samoa and Annatoo are but overgrown children playing at marriage, the youth assumes control of the ménage and the farce. Jarl is placed at the helm of the *Parki,* "like some devoted old foster-father," and "As I stood by his side like a captain, or walked up and down on the quarter-deck, I felt no little importance upon thus assuming for the first time in my life, the command of a vessel at sea." The lad usurps the adult role, in effect replacing the captain of the *Arcturion,* but it is a masquerade, since without Jarl's skill and knowledge of the sea he is helpless. With his verbal skill, however, he surrounds himself with the aura of captaincy, even placing over his hammock the blade of a shark, "an aromatic sword; like the ancient caliph's, giving out a peculiar musky odor by friction. But far different from the steel of Tagus or Damascus, it was inflexible as Crockett's rifle tube; no doubt, as deadly." The narrator's mock-heroic words indict him as quixotic, the product of too much reading of books.

After a series of farcical mishaps, the *Parki* sinks and Annatoo dies; only one sentence is devoted to the demise of "Woman unendurable," "worse than either Sarah or Antonina," in contrast with several pages noting the ship's death throes. With Annatoo out of the way, the youth-captain dares to dress himself to suit his rank — "I had very strikingly improved my costume: making it free, flowing, and eastern. I looked like an Emir." In attire out of the *Arabian Nights' Entertainments*, the youth boards a boat on which Aleema, an old priest, has confined Yillah, a beautiful innocent who is about to become a human sacrifice. When Aleema menaces the youth with "his dagger, the sharp spine of a fish," he slays the priest and carries off Yillah.

The murder of Aleema — that it can be construed as self-defense is logical but irrelevant in view of the preceding events — is the climax of what now turns out to have been a systematic toppling of father figures by the "son," the lad without name. The latent oedipal conflict is now made explicit, for Yillah embodies the narrator's recurrent dream of an ideal mother: "For oh, Yillah; were you not the earthly semblance of that sweet vision, that haunted my earliest thoughts?"

As the narrator approaches shore with Yillah, he learns that the Mardians consider him a "white Taji, a sort of half-and-half deity, now and then an Avatar among them, and ranking among their inferior ex-officio demi-gods." On landing, he assumes divinity: "Men of Mardi, I come from the sun. When this morning it rose and touched the wave, I pushed my shallop from its golden beach, and hither sailed before its level rays. I am Taji." Yillah, it now appears, is a seraph from the sun. If, as Mildred K. Travis ingeniously argues, Yillah is Phoebe, Apollo's sister, and Taji is Apollo, the sun god, then the two are involved in an incestuous relationship — one more indication of the subterranean subject of this romance. Interestingly, Yillah is as blonde and blue-eyed as Jarl, whom she replaces, and he considers her "a sort of intruder, an Ammonite syren, who might lead me astray." Perhaps Jarl resents what appears to be Taji's assumption of genitality, or he is disgruntled that his masquerade as a mother fails when a woman appears on the scene, or he may be acting as a censor of the incestuous bond between the two young people.

If Jarl's motivations are difficult to clarify, it is more the fault of Melville than of the reader. For surreptitiously he has centered the action about the family bond and the oedipal relationship and has resorted to comic masquerade to disguise the fact. The consummation of the oedipal wish in the death of Aleema logically and psychically demands retribution and guilt. But given the mock-heroic development up to this point, *Mardi* cannot suddenly be transformed into a Hawthornian study of guilt. Melville continues his narration in the same comic vein for at least two reasons: *Mardi* is a romance, not a tragedy, and comedy allows him to disguise his intent and to deal with serious subject matter in a deviously offhand way. And so after the climactic murder he continues to present clowns or fools, including the misadventures of the biggest fool of all, Taji. "Solomon," he notes earlier, "more than hints that all men are fools; and every wise man knows himself to be one."

On a few occasions Taji reveals remorse, particularly when Aleema's sons appear out of nowhere in pursuit, but such moods, incompatible with comedy, are fleeting. Yet he must and does make payment for his deeds, the aggressions which culminate in the killing of Aleema. The punishment is subtle, in harmony with the comic framework of *Mardi,* and psychologically perceptive. Yillah stays with Taji only briefly, then disappears into the musical spaces whence she has come, her memory only a lovely echo. Taji is denied genital consummation, the taboo against incest taking effect. He does not replace the "father." When he sails in search of the maiden, no longer does he masquerade as a captain or a god. He is a boy among four adults — Media, Mohi, Yoomy, and Babbalanja — but they do not provide him with an audience. He is the observer and listener, as silent as Jarl. Taji, then, is dethroned from the throne to which he is not entitled.

Since *Mardi* is comedy and Taji-Melville can manipulate events in any way he chooses, the four elders, despite their philosophical pretensions and their adult status, are, like the youth, bachelors who form an all-male club, a Ti afloat, where, without women, they function primarily on an oral level. Their delights are threefold: eating, drinking, and talking. They neither aspire nor rise to genital adulthood, revering their cooks above women. To match their arrestment *Mardi* becomes in the third part a banquet, almost an orgy, of sounds. The chatter of the elders is at times no more sagacious than Taji's "leap" into the ocean, as much a masquerade of adulthood as Taji's assumption of divinity. In their cups these would-be philosopher-kings sound no more foolish than they do cold sober.

The most complex and amusing of the four is Babbalanja, who replaces Taji at the center of the work. The other men listen tirelessly to his sometimes tiresome speeches. Like Taji, Babbalanja has been wounded in his youth: "in my boyhood, my own sire was burnt for his temerity." Like the youth he is an almost compulsive talker, given to extreme self-indulgence in the tales he relates and in the attention he receives and in effect demands. If Taji is a boy and a pseudo-man, Babbalanja is a double, a sometimes ludicrous split personality. His Good Angel is an old philosopher named Bardianna, who has bequeathed to him a loquacious heritage of wisdom which is a combination of Ben Franklinisms and misogyny; his Evil Angel is a demon called Azzageddi, whose name, wickedly, recalls spaghetti, but who occasionally "dives" deep into human mysteries. Unlike Shakespeare, to whose fools Babbalanja has been compared, Melville deliberately keeps the extent of Babbalanja's wisdom in doubt.

Occasionally Babbalanja speaks like a transcendentalist: "When I place my hand to that king muscle my heart, I am appalled. I feel the great God himself at work in me." He proclaims, following his master, "Oro is life," but when a character asks, "And what is death?" he replies: "Death, my lord! — it is the deadest of all things." Babbalanja is as profound, and long-winded, in praising pipes as he is in discussing Oro, or God. "Like a good wife," he declares, "a pipe is a friend and companion for life. And whoso weds with pipe, is no longer a bachelor. After many vexations, he may go home to that faithful counselor, and ever find it full of kind consolations and suggestions." Which is a most evasive and comic way of extolling a substitute for family life and sexuality.

Yet Babbalanja also speaks the wisdom of Ecclesiastes, whom Melville himself professed to admire above all other writers.

All we discover has been with us since the sun began to roll; and much we discover, is not worth the discovering. We are children, climbing trees after birds' nests, and making a great shout, whether we find eggs in them or no. But where are our wings, which our forefathers surely had not? Tell us, ye sages! something worth an archangel's learning; discover, ye discoverers, something new. Fools, fools! Mardi's not changed; the sun yet rises in its old place in the East; all things go on in the same old way; we cut our eye-teeth just as late as they did, three thousand years ago. . . . Nothing changes, though much be new-fashioned; new fashions but revivals of things previous. In the books of the past we learn naught but of the present; in those of the present, the past. All Mardi's history — beginning, middle, and finis — was written out in capitals in the first page penned. The whole story is told in a title-page. An exclamation point is entire Mardi's autobiography.

At the conclusion of the book the doubting Babbalanja and his three companions prepare to settle in Serenia, under the loving protection of Oro and Alma. The names of the gods do not disguise the fact that they are "converted" to Christianity and to its limitations upon aspirations and reason. The four middle-aged hedonists, after all their talk and feasting, snuggle into Serenia, which sanctions their bachelordom and allows them to keep their all-male club intact.

Taji refuses to settle in Serenia and in effect rejects Oro and Alma. Bombastically he follows in the footsteps of Odysseus, but he sounds like an absurd Odysseus, or a mad Ishmael:

> ". . . Let *me*, then, be the unreturning wanderer. The helm! By Oro, I will steer my own fate, old man. — Mardi, farewell!"
>
> "Nay, Taji: commit not the last, last crime!" cried Yoomy.
>
> "He's seized the helm! eternity is in his eye! Yoomy: for our lives we must now swim."
>
> And plunging, they struck out for land. . . .
>
> "Now, I am my own soul's emperor; and my first act is abdication! Hail! realm of shades!" — and turning my prow into the racing tide, which seized me like a hand omnipotent, I darted through.
>
> Churned in foam, that outer ocean lashed the clouds; and straight in my white wake, headlong dashed a shallop, three fixed specters leaning o'er its prow: three arrows poising.
>
> And thus, pursuers and pursued flew on, over an endless sea.

And so Taji "leaps" once again, abdicates once more. He mouths at the end the rhetoric of romantic alienation. In the process he establishes his fooldom.

The conclusion of *Mardi*, like so much else in the romance, is inconclusive and ambiguous. Perhaps Taji, like Ahab, is punished for his arrogance; perhaps like Pierre he is a fool of truth; perhaps like both of these, he wills his own destruction. Or, if we follow the latent subject matter, he is to be an eternal wanderer, pursued by Aleema's sons, because of his "crime," his incestuous desires, permanently estranged like Ishmael from society. He appears destined to remain the eternal youth, locked in adolescence. If after his experience he has learned anything, it is difficult to know what. What Media says of Babbalanja has more validity if applied to Taji: "You everlastingly travel in a circle."

There will probably never be a satisfactory interpretation of *Mardi*. It will always remain a work in which the seams are showing, the symbols interpreted according to the disposition of the interpreter. There are delightful interludes, amusing discussions, some interesting satire. Yet it is a wild, undisciplined work as headstrong and as romantic as Taji himself. Melville muffles the psychological drama through comic tactics and through seemingly intellectual discussions, although the papier-mâché characters enthuse rather than think, indulge in sophomoric witticisms rather than in serious, logical discussion. Melville writes from no preconceived position; he is groping for answers as he writes. And so he wavers — and his romance follows suit — between Babbalanja's willingness to surrender to orthodoxy and Taji's wild desire to continue a quest which seems suicidal.

He sincerely believed that he had written a great book. "Had I not written & published 'Mardi,' " he wrote to Duyckinck, "in all likelihood, I would not be as wise as I am now, or may be." He assured Judge Shaw, "Time, which is the solver of all riddles, will solve 'Mardi.' " But the riddle has not been solved by interpreters. The fogginess which contemporary critics singled out with sometimes malicious glee was shared by Elizabeth when she wrote to her stepmother: "if the mist ever does clear away, I should like to know what it reveals to *you* — there seems to be much diversity of opinion about 'Mardi' as might be supposed."

Almost nightly during the early years of their marriage Herman read chapters from *Mardi* to his wife. When it was finished, she was pregnant. Perhaps she may sometimes have wondered why a new bridegroom-husband and a prospective father celebrated the pleasures of bachelorhood and of male clubs and relentlessly satirized and attacked women, marriage, and the family. Marriage, she must have realized, brought about no change in Herman's fictional subject matter, particularly in the handsome young man's search for a father-brother.

"A Little
Nursery Tale"

—Redburn

While Melville was reading the last proofs of *Mardi*, Elizabeth Melville
went to Boston to wait for her confinement. Melville journeyed between New York and Boston, and two weeks after he had finished
the proofs their first child, Malcolm, was born on February 16, 1849.
Two days later his brother Allan and his wife had a daughter, Maria
Gansevoort. In naming his son, Herman honored "Grandma Melville's
side of the house," and Allan paid his respects to his Gansevoort
mother.

Judge Shaw pronounced the boy "healthy, well grown, & in
every way promising. Elizabeth is recovering gradually but slowly,
from the severe trial, which however she sustained remarkably well."
During her recovery the first review of *Mardi*, in *The London Athenæum* appeared: "Matters become crazier and crazier — more and
more foggy — page by page — until the end . . . is felt to be a happy
release." Such critical brickbats hurt Herman's pride, of course, but,

worse, made his economic lot as husband and now as father even more precarious.

After Elizabeth and he were again in their home at 104 Fourth Avenue, he decided, following the advice of his critics, to exploit once more his experiences before the mast. He retreated to his study and virtually imprisoned himself as he wrote page after page. Within ten weeks he completed *Redburn*, which drew upon his first voyage to sea in 1839. On June 5 he informed Bentley that *Redburn* was "of a widely different cast from 'Mardi': – a plain, straightforward, amusing narrative of personal experience – the son of a gentlemen on his first voyage to sea as a sailor – no metaphysics, no conic-sections, nothing but cakes & ale. I have shifted my ground from the South Seas to a different quarter of the globe – nearer home – and what I write I have almost wholly picked up by my own observations under comical circumstances." While he was making arrangements for the publication of *Redburn* and reading proof, he started another book, and within two months completed *White-Jacket*, which is an account of his adventures aboard the frigate *United States* in 1843 and 1844. In less than five months, then, he completed two lengthy novels, one numbering over three hundred pages, the other over four hundred pages. Behind this herculean expenditure of intellectual and physical energy lay a monomaniacal frenzy that ignored fatigue and physical discomfort. Melville had a robust physique but he exploited it carelessly. Early in 1849, he complained of the strain upon "my eyes which are tender as young sparrows."

The physical strain and enervation were bad enough, but he wrote out of necessity with little satisfaction in what he was doing. For in following his critics he was not being true to his own aspirations. As he informed his father-in-law: "So far as I am individually concerned, & independent of my pocket, it is my earnest desire to write those sort of books which are said to 'fail.' " In the same letter, on October 6, he declared that the books "are two *jobs*, which I have done for money – being forced to it, as other men are to sawing wood. . . . my only desire for their 'success' (as it is called) springs from my pocket, & not from my heart." Nine months later, on May 1, 1850, he made the same point to Richard Henry Dana, Jr.: "did I not write these books of mine almost entirely for 'lucre' – by the job, as a woodsawyer saws wood." After reading a flattering review of *Redburn* in *Blackwood's Magazine*, Melville commented in his Journal on November 6, "It's very comical – seemed so, at least, as I had to hurry over it – in treating the thing as real. But the wonder is that the old Tory should waste so many pages upon a thing, which I, the author, know to be trash, & wrote it to buy some tobacco with." He did not alter his tune when on December 14, 1849, he wrote to

Duyckinck "about the book Redburn, which to my surprise (somewhat) seems to have been favorably received. I am glad of it — for it puts money into an empty purse. But I hope I shall never write such a book again. . . . What but a beggarly 'Redburn!' And when he attempts anything higher — God help him & save him! for it is not with a hollow purse as with a hollow balloon — for a hollow purse makes the poet *sink* — witness 'Mardi.' "

The anger behind Melville's bluster is transparent and understandable — he may have overreached himself in *Mardi*, but at least he strove for something more than an imitation of his earlier successes — but he was protesting too much. He exerted every effort to insure the success of his first three books and revealed a great deal of shrewdness in his arrangements for publication. He was harsher on his critics than they deserved. Except for *Mardi* his books had received exceptionally good presses. He was probably angry at himself for not having the courage to write another *Mardi*.

When he was not striking a pose and pitying himself, he even acknowledged that "in writing these two books, I have not repressed myself much — as far as *they* are concerned; but have spoken pretty much as I feel." Two months later, on December 14, he retracted: "What a madness & anguish it is, that an author can never — under no conceivable circumstances — be at all frank with his readers. — Could I, for one, be frank with them — how would they cease their railing — those at least who have railed." His charge that the public and publishers did not allow him to be "frank" was only a partial truth. He vented his spleen in biased attacks upon missionaries, he assailed society and institutions at will, and in dealing with sexuality he was not as discreet as most of his contemporaries.

Though he was not as bold as Whitman was to be a few years later, Melville dealt with most of the taboo subjects of his age, sometimes in a bawdy fashion. He self-righteously flayed the public, yet he could have refused to make excisions in *Typee*, just as he could have refused to write what he considered pot-boilers. Too often he wanted his cake and aura too. Yet in manic moments he was willing to ridicule himself as "H. M. author of 'Peedee,' 'Hullabaloo' & 'Pog-Dog.' "

Although Melville took peculiar delight in ridiculing *Redburn*, he played the role of Redburn himself when he went to London in the fall of 1849 to arrange for the publication of *White-Jacket*. Redburn's unusual attire, his hunting jacket and red shirt, is an attention-getting device which ends in antagonizing the crew. Aboard the *Southampton* on the voyage to London Melville wore an unconventional green coat, and before he left the ship at Dover, he noted a "mysterious hint dropped me about my green coat." A few days later, in London, he "went down to the Queen's Hotel to inquire about our ship friends — (on the way green coat attracted attention)." Redburn dons his outlandish attire to make a social call upon Captain Riga after the ship sails, and Melville deliberately flouted convention and appeared the buffoon when he called on his publisher, John Murray: "Rigged up again, & in my *green* jacket called upon Mr. Murray in Ablemarle St." Having acted out his hostility for a month, he eventually lost his nerve, or came to his senses, on December 14: "Then went & bought a Paletot in the Strand, so as to look decent — for I find my green coat plays the devil with my respectability here. Then went & got my hair cut, which was as long as a wild Indian's." Three months later, now back in New York, he again played the same game when "I mounted my *green* jacket & strolled down to the Battery to study the stars."

It is impossible to tell, even with the aid of William H. Gilman's exhaustive analysis of the novel, whether Herman went to sea in 1839 with the inappropriate attire that Redburn sports when he boards the *Highlander* or whether Herman was so foolish as to think the Captain of the *St. Lawrence* would be delighted to receive a visit from a cabin boy. The probabilities are that Herman, who was not unacquainted with sailors in his own family, made no such blunders, and that he fabricated these details. But his assumption of the Redburn role later surely points not so much to the fact that he made life imitate art, or that, like many artists, he took a childlike delight in assuming various disguises, as to the fact that *Redburn* not only had a literal autobiographical basis but also accurately reflected emotional attitudes and feelings of Melville himself.

In a letter to Dana, he hit upon the most accurate subtitle for *Redburn* — "a little nursery tale." For in this book he dealt not only with his "first voyage" but also with events from the earliest years of his life.

Redburn starts out from Lansingburgh, leaving behind a mother and three sisters, boards a ferry in Albany for New York, seeks the assistance of his brother's friend (Alexander W. Bradford) before he sails on the *Highlander*. Redburn's father was a New York importer of French goods and a traveler, his library contained French books and portfolios of prints, and he died a bankrupt in Redburn's youth. There are references to the Gansevoorts (called Wellingboroughs here), to his brother Gansevoort, as well as to Major Thomas Melvill, whose glass ship reappears in the novel. When Redburn declares, "Yes, I will go to sea; cut my kind uncles and aunts, and sympathizing patrons," he reflects Herman's lot before he sailed in 1839, when he was dependent upon Peter Gansevoort and others for support. As significant and personal as these details are, they pale before the depiction of Redburn's emotional state.

This is the story of a father and his son. Although he is dead, the father is the most important character in the book. The first two chapters are dominated by specific references to Redburn's father and descriptions of the "mildew" which falls upon "his young soul" after the father's death. "Cold, bitter cold as December, and bleak as its blasts, seemed the world then to me," Redburn writes. Allan Melvill stumbled back to Albany in December 1831, frozen, wretched, and demented before his death. Redburn ships to Liverpool in order to retrace his father's journey to that city, and in Liverpool attempts to relive his father's life by using a guidebook of the city from his library, only to discover that time dates guidebooks and that man has no external props, either a father of "sacred memory" or an infallible guidebook. "This precious book was next to useless. Yes, the thing that had guided the father, could not guide the son. And I sat down on a shop step, and gave loose to meditation."

Gansevoort Melville appears in the novel as the older brother, in ill health, who arranges for Redburn's trip and his stay in New York, all of which Gansevoort had dutifully done in 1839. Redburn goes to sea wearing his brother's hunting jacket. His unconventional and pretentious first name is traceable to a "great-uncle . . . Senator Wellingborough, who had died a member of Congress in the days of the old Constitution, and after whom I had the honor of being named." Surely it was not accidental that Melville in this account of father and son chose a name resembling that of Allan's favorite son, Gansevoort. Fictionally Melville could enjoy a relationship denied to Herman.

In *Redburn* Melville wrote an In Memoriam to Allan Melvill, and, despite the merry tales of a bumpkin's adventures at sea, the comedy, as in *The Adventures of Huckleberry Finn*, is played out against an insistent death motif. Early in the tale Redburn observes: "I almost wished I was there now; yes, dead and buried in that church-yard." On the night the *Highlander* sails from New York a sailor suffering from delirium tremens jumps overboard and drowns; worse still, "to my terror, I found that the suicide had been occupying the very bunk which I had appropriated to myself, and there was no other place for me to sleep in." References to death are rarely absent: he relates how Brutus ordered his son executed; funeral bells resound for Cock-Robin; the *Highlander* passes a ship to which are lashed "three dark, green, grassy objects, that slowly swayed with every roll, but otherwise were motionless." In Liverpool Redburn visits a cemetery and sees in Launcelott's-Hey a woman and her children slowly starving to death, and there is the reality of the stench of death. During "A Mysterious Night in London," Redburn and Harry Bolton visit the Palace of Aladdin, a gambling joint and possibly a male brothel, where his newly acquired "chummy" suddenly brandishes his dirk and shouts: "They serve suicides scurrily here, Wellingborough; they don't bury them decently. See that bell-rope! By Heaven, it's an invitation to hang myself." On the return trip of the *Highlander*, a sailor shanghaied in a Liverpool pub suffers an extraordinary death, "when, to the silent horror of all, two threads of greenish flame, like a forked tongue, darted out between the lips; and in a moment, the cadaverous face was crawled over by a swarm of wormlike flames."

The book comes full circle. In the early chapters Redburn records the death of his father, and in the last chapter, rather than describe his own later career, he recounts the death of Harry Bolton, who for a while acts as a brother to him. Redburn knows grief or loss at the beginning of his tale, and the conclusion leaves him again bereft. "But yet, I, Wellingborough Redburn, chance to survive, after having passed through far more perilous scenes than any recorded in this, *My First Voyage* — which here I end."

Redburn's nursery tale opens with a number of brilliant scenes. In the first chapter after describing the books in his father's library, Redburn mentions "an old-fashioned glass ship, about eighteen inches long" which "converted my vague dreamings and longings into a definite purpose of seeking my fortune on the sea." As Alan Lebowitz notes, the glass ship may be a variation upon the Narcissus legend: in looking into the glass ship Redburn explores the mysteries of the sea and the origins of life, which means that he is exploring the mysteries of the self. Redburn notes that as a child he had tried "to peep in at the portholes" to discover what was inside. "And often I used to feel a sort of insane desire to be the death of the glass ship, case, and all, in order to come at the plunder; and one day, throwing out some hint of the kind to my sisters, they ran to my mother in a great clamor; and after that, the ship was placed on the mantle-piece for a time, beyond my reach, and until I should recover my reason." Since the ship is named *La Reine* Redburn may in his "insane desire" have wanted to examine the mysteries of the mother and of birth and sexuality, the reference to buried treasure pointing to this interpretation. On the day he leaves home to go to sea, to separate himself from his mother, but at the same time to make himself worthy of her by imitating his father's journey to Liverpool, the "gallant warrior in a cocked-hat . . . fell from his perch." Then Redburn observes with comic evasiveness: "but I will not have him put on his legs again, till I get on my own; for between him and me there is a secret sympathy." If we observe the tenses carefully, we note that the older Redburn who is recording the adventures of his youth makes it quite clear that at the time of writing, years after the accident, he — but Melville too — did not feel that he stood on his own "legs" — or, to put it another way, that he — and Redburn too — had not completed the rite of passage to adulthood.

The rite begins comically when Redburn boards the ferry in Albany attired in his older brother's hunting jacket and patched clothes and carrying a fowling gun. Since he forgets to purchase a ticket before boarding the ferry and has little money either for his fare or food (a somewhat strange way for a protective mother to allow a son to face the world), he is forced back upon his own resources. Rather than conceal himself, he deliberately goes to the part of the ship occupied by wealthy passengers, where he flaunts his rags: "There was a mighty patch upon one leg of my trowsers. . . . This patch I had hitherto studiously endeavored to hide with the ample skirts of my shooting jacket; but now I stretched out my leg boldly, and thrust the patch under their noses, and looked at them so, that they soon looked away, boy that I was." When Redburn is asked for his fare, he attempts to bluster through the situation in a childish imitation of adult behavior, but when the glances of the spectators become too much for him, "I then turned to the next gazer, and clicking my gun-lock, deliberately presented the piece at him. Upon this, he overset his seat in his eagerness to get beyond my range, for I had him point blank, full in the left eye."

At the end of the chapter Melville undercuts the episode — "Such is boyhood" — and diverts attention from the subtleties of the scene. Redburn plays at being a man when, brandishing his fowling piece, he indulges in comic phallic exhibitionism. At the same time his hostility toward strangers — "I could not help it, I almost hated them" — is completely out of proportion until we realize that he projects upon the passengers his feelings about his father's twofold betrayal, through bankruptcy and death, which makes him a beggar among the wealthy and leaves him without a protective and affectionate male model. Yet the desire to be accepted by people he allegedly hates is confirmed again in several scenes in England when Redburn tries to worm his way into the citadels and affections of the affluent — still attired in his hunting jacket and disreputable sailor clothes. The rejection which he courts allows him the indulgence of self-pity but is a kind of punishment for his destructive, hostile desires.

As the *Highlander* makes its way out of the New York harbor, Redburn sees an island which years earlier he had visited in the company of his father and an uncle.

> But I meant to speak about the fort. It was a beautiful place, as I remembered it, and very wonderful and romantic, too, as it appeared to me,

when I went there with my uncle. On the side away from the water was a
green grove of trees, very thick and shady; and through this grove, in a sort
of twilight you came to an arch in the wall of the fort, dark as night. . . .
And there you would see cows quietly grazing, or ruminating under the
shade of young trees, and perhaps a calf frisking about, and trying to catch
its own tail; and sheep clambering among the mossy ruins, and cropping
little tufts of grass sprouting out of the sides of the embrasures for cannon.
And once I saw a black goat with a long beard, and crumpled horns,
standing with his fore-feet lifted high up on the topmost parapet, and
looking to sea, as if he were watching for a ship that was bringing over his
cousin. I can see him even now, and though I have changed since then, the
black goat looks just the same as ever; and so I suppose he would, if I live
to be as old as Methusaleh, and have as great a memory as he must have
had. Yes, the fort was a beautiful, quiet, charming spot. I should like to
build a little cottage in the middle of it, and live there all my life. It was
noon-day when I was there, in the month of June, and there was little
wind to stir the trees, and every thing looked as if it was waiting for
something, and the sky overhead was blue as my mother's eye, and I was
so glad and happy then. But I must not think of those delightful days
before my father became a bankrupt, and died, and we removed from the
city; for when I think of those days, something rises up in my throat and
almost strangles me.

Rarely does Melville paint such a landscape. Here he avoids the coyness and self-consciousness which often mar his writing when he
deals with deeply felt events. Melville filters out the tensions and
unpleasantnesses of his youth in order to paint, in John Seelye's
words, "a kind of Eden or Arcadia presided over by a loving, mother-
ly eye." It is, sadly, a remembrance of a past that never was.

This delicate memory follows a chapter in which "He is Initi-
ated in the Business of Cleaning Out the Pig-Pen, and Slushing Down
the Top-Mast." Here the greenhorn loses his identity as Wellingborough Redburn, and even his sexuality, when one of the sailors
christens him: "Who had the baptizing of ye? Why didn't they call
you Jack, or Jill, or something short and handy. But I'll baptize you
over again. D'ye hear, sir, henceforth your name is *Buttons*." And so
Redburn discovers that his impressive-sounding name does not im-
press the crew and that in virile eyes he is an epicene, either Jack or
Jill, as the sexually indeterminate name of Buttons suggests. After
the baptismal rite he is sent to "clean out that pig-pen in the long
boat; it has not been cleaned out since last voyage."

The sailors not only rob Redburn of his manhood, dubiously
asserted in the scene aboard the ferry, but also return him to the
"nursery" by emphasizing his infantile state, particularly his oral

needs. Redburn himself introduces the importance of food when he appears in a hunting jacket and carries a fowling piece. The inappropriate attire suggests his unpreparedness for man's estate. When he signs the ship's articles, his costume amuses and annoys the sailors, and one says, "Come here, my little boy, has your ma put up some sweetmeats for ye to take to sea?" Before he is baptized Buttons, the chief mate asks, "What's your name, Pillgarlic?" After the christening he is, as we have seen, consigned to the pigpen. Later, in one of his most foolish acts, Redburn decides to pay a visit to Captain Riga. After dressing himself artfully and dusting off his "shooting-jacket" in order to cut, in his own eyes, "quite a genteel figure," he ignores the guffaws of the sailors and Jackson's shrewd observation: "Let him go, let him go, men — he's a nice boy. Let him go; the captain has some nuts and raisins for him." The chief mate, of course, does not let him meet the captain, and warns him, "You are very green . . . but I'll ripen you."

Redburn takes his revenge on Captain Riga after the fashion of an angry child. He climbs the mast in his patched trousers which rip and split "in every direction, particularly above the seat": "So that I was often placed in most unpleasant predicaments, straddling the rigging, sometimes in plain sight of the cabin, with my table linen exposed in the most inelegant and ungentlemanly manner possible." At one point Redburn complains that the crew "took me to task about my short-comings: . . . for every one had a finger, or a thumb, and sometimes both hands, in my unfortunate pie." Later Redburn informs Max that it is "immoral" to have wives in Liverpool and New York, whereupon the sailor recalls that Solomon had "a whole frigate-full of wives," and warns: "so, mind your eye, Buttons, or I'll crack your pepper-box for you!"

Here, in a veiled castration threat, food has its traditional association with sexual appetite. Two other scenes in the novel make the same analogy. The only genuinely kindly older male that Redburn encounters in his voyage is a skipper in Liverpool, "a bachelor, who kept house all alone. . . . and there we sat together like a couple in a box at an oyster-cellar. . . . He looked so like a great mug of ale, that I almost felt like taking him by the neck and pouring him out." The skipper's pleasures are his ale and entertainment of young boys whom he invites, after the necessary alcoholic imbibing, to take "a nice little nap." But Redburn — "my conscience smote me for thus freely indulging in the pleasures of the table" — takes leave — or perhaps flight. The young men in Melville's books are most active when avoiding sexual commitment.

Throughout this "nursery tale" Redburn seeks relationships with father figures and with peers: "All of us yearn for sympathy, even if we do not for love." At first he attempts to bribe his way into the affections of the sailors. He spends his last penny to purchase "a red woolen shirt," then examines himself coquettishly "before the glass, to see what sort of a looking sailor I was going to make," and finally presents himself aboard ship in all his assumed splendor. In his self-love he sees himself as a valentine to the crew. He makes love to the crew, as it were, filled with "a sort of incipient love," but his attire is a criticism of the sailors and his pride in his morality, education, and genteel name is an affront. Although he wants relationships and affection, he makes certain that he isolates himself as an Ishmael; that, in short, he fails.

Though he is much attracted to Captain Riga and dresses himself up like a suitor to pay court, he gradually accepts the fact that Riga is as false as his dyed hair. Jackson, "the foul lees and dregs of a man," exerts an even greater attraction over Redburn, and here we see in embryo some of the dynamics of the Ahab-Ishmael relationship. Jackson is "such a hideous looking mortal, that Satan himself would have run from him," with a "cold, and snaky, and deadly" eye. "A horrible thing," he is "the best seaman on board" and rules over the sailors with an authoritarian brutality which Captain Riga himself cannot emulate, cursing and insulting the crew while he lies about doing nothing. Yet he is "dressed like a Bowery boy." If Redburn is an epicene fop in a red jacket, Jackson is an adolescent bully — their attire pointing to their arrestment. At times Redburn imagines that Jackson eyes him with "malevolence" because he is favored with health while Jackson has "an incurable malady." At other times Redburn feels that he is being ogled because "I was young and handsome, at least my mother so thought me." Redburn, in other words, eroticizes the relationship. In a brilliant scene Jackson, though a dying man, appears as a sexual force or monster. The lad watches with fascinated horror as he examines a sailor's teeth in order to determine his age. Jackson probes "a little with his jackknife": "I watched Jackson's eye and saw it snapping, and a sort of going in and out, very quick, as if he were longing to kill the man." The obvious sexuality of this scene, played out on an oral level, and taking the child's view of sexuality as violence or assault, establishes a bond between the two characters.

As James Schroeter observes, Redburn wears patched clothes, and Jackson is a patched up skeleton of a man; Redburn bullies the passengers on the ferry, and Jackson bullies the crew of the *Highlander* into submission; both are isolates and geldings in the virile world of sailors. The one is a "Cain afloat; branded on his yellow brow with some inscrutable curse; and going about corrupting and searing every heart that beat near him." The other is a self-styled

Ishmael, who is deeply moved by Jackson: "But there seemed even more woe than wickedness about the man; and his wickedness seemed to spring from his woe; and for all his hideousness there was that in his eye at times, that was ineffably pitiable and touching; and though there were moments when I almost hated this Jackson, yet I have pitied no man as I have pitied him."

Jackson embodies all the primitive fears that mankind has about evil eyes, snakes, and monstrous ugliness. He is a perversion of the human ideal, yet Melville, almost perversely, elevates him by giving him the aura of Salvator Rosa's "dark, moody" pictures and of Milton's Satan. He is depraved but also tragic, commanding more sympathy because of his primitive powers and his appeal to primitive emotions than he perhaps deserves. Jackson, then, embodies the destructive tendencies inherent in Redburn's and human nature. He cannot relate to another human, he can only brutalize. He cannot give a love which he has apparently never received. The "Bowery boy" is arrested in self-loathing. He "prefers not to" live or let live. In this portrait Melville for the first time drew upon dark fantasies which he ordinarily repressed. The passive young men, acted upon rather than acting, came from one part of his nature; in another part there were desires which could only be expressed by hypnotic, power-mad overmen who ruthlessly and monomaniacally exploited mankind with loathesome delight.

The gentler side of Redburn's nature reappears in Liverpool when he meets Harry Bolton, who is young and attractive in an epicene way, not unlike Redburn himself. The meeting follows the seductive pattern established in "Fragments from a Writing Desk" and *Typee*: "I smoothed down the skirts of my jacket, and at once accosted him." Harry, it soon turns out, is an orphan but also a fop and an immoralist, as suspect as Jackson. He frequents the Palace of Aladdin, where the wall decorations depict sexual abnormalities, and his handwriting, we are informed, resembles "the perfumed hand of Petronius Arbiter, that elegant young buck of a Roman." The attraction of Bolton is great, but Harry's dishonesty about his background and exploits "made me hold back my whole soul from him; when, in its loneliness, it was yearning to throw itself into the unbounded bosom of some immaculate friend."

In a sense the passage sums up the heart of the book. For the loneliness which Redburn knows before he goes to sea to retrace the footsteps of his dead father remains after his search proves vain. He has not known the "unbounded bosom of some immaculate friend" since his father's death, for in one way or another everyone he meets in his journey proves a disappointment. This is a "nursery tale" which, like the genre, establishes the sad, and frightening, truth that there is no nursery after childhood: there is only the memory.

Jackson spits out, almost heroically, his life as the *Highlander* approaches New York, and frees the crew from his tyranny — "*his* death was *their* deliverance." In the harbor when Captain Riga cheats Redburn of his wages, the lad is "delivered" from still another father figure. The crew and Redburn take their revenge on the Captain with a tactic worthy of boyhood. "In a few moments the captain sallied from the cabin, and found the *gentlemen* alluded to, strung along the top of the bulwarks, on the side next to the wharf. Upon his appearance, the row suddenly wheeled about, presenting their backs; and making a motion, which was a polite salute to every thing before them, but an abominable insult to all who happened to be in their rear, they gave three cheers, and at one bound, cleared the ship."

Riga may deserve this comic comeuppance, but Harry Bolton does not deserve to be abandoned in New York, a helpless, penniless foreigner, without any skill and without much stamina. Redburn hurries off to his home, never considering the possibility of taking Harry along with him. Like Tommo in *Typee*, he is quick to indict society, particularly the inhuman treatment of the starving mother in Liverpool and of the emigrants aboard ship, but when actions are more important than social sentiments, his performance is not equal to his verbalizations. No more than Jackson can he give love. He attempts to alleviate his coldness by eulogizing Harry in the final chapter — words come easily — but the final paragraph describing his own survival reveals a Redburn as self-contained in his own cocoon as at the beginning of his adventure.

Here Melville is mercilessly honest. The rite of passage or the initiation of Redburn does not progress to enlightenment or socialization: he does not grow or change in significant ways. The extent of his knowledge is that man cannot rely on mentors, that he must rely on his own unreliable resources, which is scarcely a profound insight.

Artistically *Redburn* makes a real advance, despite unfortunate padding at the center of the book and the decline of interest and tension in the third part of the work. With less haste, careful revision, and, most important of all, confidence in what he was doing, *Redburn* might have been a companion to *David Copperfield* or *Huckleberry Finn*. Some of the interludes are little comic gems; Jackson is a fascinating study in ambivalence; and the book penetrates psychic levels which he had not explored in earlier books.

Melville was not always a sound critic of his own writings. He overestimated *Mardi* and disparaged his "nursery tale," which is artistically better and truer than its predecessors. Melville had no reason to be ashamed of *Redburn*.

"The Jelly
of
Youth"

—White-Jacket

Although Melville took what would appear to be an almost perverse delight in disparaging *Redburn*, he deliberately set out to protect *White-Jacket* from critical attacks. Several months before its official publication, he wrote to Richard Henry Dana, Jr., whose "unmatchable" *Two Years Before the Mast* (1840) provided him with a model: "I shall be away, in all probability, for some months after the publication of the book. If it is taken hold of in an unfair or ignorant way; & if you should possibly think, that from your peculiar experiences in sea-life, you would be able to say a word to the purpose — may I hope that you will do so, if you can spare the time, & are generous enough to bestow the trouble? — Your name would do a very great deal; but if you choose to keep that out of sight in the matter, well & good."

Apparently Melville feared that his censure of flogging and of the tyrannical Articles of War would arouse indignation: "This man-of-war book, my Dear Sir, is in some parts rather man-of-*warish* in style — rather aggressive I fear." But he was not so "aggressive" as he imagined. He was not emulating Tom Paine when he placed his criticisms within a novelistic framework which gave readers an excuse for dismissing them. Nor were the allegations new, since Dana, to cite only one example, had penned an effective indictment of flogging in 1840, and the subject was under discussion in Washington as Melville wrote. Sincere as he was in indicting military abuses, he knew that the topicality of the subject would add interest to his book, meaning sales.

White-Jacket, as the subtitle explains, describes "The World in a Man-of-War." Based on his experiences aboard the *United States* in 1843 and 1844, the book has a ballast of factual material, not unlike *Two Years Before the Mast*, so that the reader becomes acquainted in detail with the harsh discipline and onerous but monotonous duties aboard a military frigate. Although the descriptions and the indictments of naval tyrannies occupy more space than the activities and interactions of the narrator-hero and his friends, Melville is once more presenting a variation upon subject matter by this time well established in his writings.

For the sixth time — in five novels and in "Fragments from a Writing Desk" — he presents a "nursery" tale or, to use a graphic phrase from *White-Jacket*, describes "the jelly of youth," when a lad attempts to cross that difficult bridge from boyhood to so-called manhood; for the sixth time he recreates and relives the experiences of his youth in New York and Albany and then during his years of flight as a sailor. Although the social commentary may point, as some critics have suggested, to the broadening of Melville's social sympathies, it is but peripherally related to the evolution of the central character — to the heart of the book.

White-Jacket is still another of the unformed youths locked in their egocentric worlds where they wrestle with the longings and tensions Melville himself knew painfully. Physically he is slight, handsome but almost effeminate, wavering between the two sexes as adolescent boys are sometimes prone to do. In the all-male world he inhabits, where desires are directed to available sexual objects, his sexual identity is threatened by a sailor named, curiously, Old Revolver: "I became alarmed at the old Yeoman's goggling glances, lest he should drag me down into tarry perdition in his hideous storerooms." Colbrook, "a remarkably handsome and very gentlemanly corporal" and later "a representative in the Legislature of the State of New Jersey," always hums *"The girl I left behind me"* when he passes the youth.

Though White-Jacket fears sexual assaults upon his chastity, he, like Redburn, unconsciously no doubt, provokes the advances by assuming in the male environment of the ship an attire that renders his own sexuality ambiguous. His jacket is even more absurd and provocative than Redburn's shooting jacket.

> Now, in sketching the preliminary plan, and laying out the foundation of that memorable white jacket of mine, I had an earnest eye to all these inconveniences, and resolved to avoid them. I proposed, that not only should my jacket keep me warm, but that it should also be so constructed as to contain a shirt or two, a pair of trousers, and divers knickknacks — sewing utensils, books, biscuits, and the like. With this object, I had accordingly provided it with a great variety of pockets, pantries, clothes-presses, and cupboards.
>
> The principal apartments, two in number, were placed in the skirts; with a wide, hospitable entrance from the inside; two more, of smaller capacity, were planted in each breast, with folding-doors communicating, so that in case of emergency, to accommodate any bulky articles, the two pockets in each breast could be thrown into one. There were, also, several unseen recesses behind the arras; insomuch, that my jacket, like an old castle, was full of winding stairs, and mysterious closets, crypts, and cabinets; and like a confidential writing-desk, abounded in snug little out-of-the-way lairs and hiding-places, for the storage of valuables.

Apparently Melville wore a jacket of this kind during his voyage on the *United States*, for in answer to a query from Dana he wrote: "I answer it was a veritable garment — which I suppose is now somewhere at the bottom of Charles river [in the Boston harbor]. I was a great fool, or I should have brought such a remarkable fabric (as it really was, to behold) home with me." White-Jacket attempts to demonstrate that he has created a useful garment, although it fails to shed rain, but in enveloping himself in a simulated breast, he outfits himself according to the rules of the most primitive form of comedy — the boy-man playing at being a woman, playing house. In a comic Ben Franklinism, he avers, "Every man's jacket is his wig-wam," which is a deliciously droll observation that mercilessly but comically exposes the regressive wish of the narrator.

At the same time, the jacket resembles a shroud and a white albatross, as Melville hints at two imporant and serious insights. The creation of the garment points to a kind of concealed death wish, a longing which almost comes to pass at the conclusion of the book. It also suggests the wearer's wounded narcissism. Lovingly he creates a breast, and snuggles into it, because he craves love and affection, but his creation cannot restore, or substitute for, the mother.

The crew of the *Neversink* does not draw fine psychological distinctions or appreciate the sensitivities and hunger of a youth like White-Jacket. The jacket makes him sexual game, which he wants but fears; at the same time that it attracts attention, and propositions, it creates a barrier between him and the crew. Like Redburn, he affronts the sailors when he plays the sartorial game according to his own narcisstic needs, since in scorning the clothing bond he implies his own superiority. But his choice of garment, his masquerade as a boy-woman, stamps him a fool. In this role, attired in motley of his own devising, he receives, and demands, attention, but he also frees the crew from his demands, since he encourages their scorn. As a fool he places himself in a subordinate or dependent relationship to the men. And so White-Jacket debases himself and at the same time punishes himself for his ambivalent desires and his aggressiveness in assuming the garment in the first place.

In a richly comic passage, it becomes clear that the jacket may simulate the female breast but leaves exposed the male genitals: "But, alas! these skirts were lamentably scanty; and though, with its quiltings, the jacket was stuffed out about the breasts like a Christmas turkey, and of a dry cold day kept the wearer warm enough in that vicinity, yet about the loins it was shorter than a ballet-dancer's skirts; so that while my chest was in the temperate zone, close adjoining the torrid, my hapless thighs were in Nova Zembla, hardly an icicle's toss from the Pole." Which may be a form of exhibitionism but which more than hints that the sexual urges and functions remain unsatisfied and undirected.

Behind this burlesque, which is self-parody since White-Jacket himself is the recorder of his comic lot, is his grim awareness of his inadequacy.

After White-Jacket plays out his farce with the crew, and is rejected and also terrified, he finds a home at a mess presided over in a somewhat dictatorial fashion by a middle-aged, balding Apollo, whose name is invariably accompanied by a homeric epithet, "noble Jack Chase." This is an elite group composed of "fellows of large intellectual and corporeal calibre," quite different from the "scores of desperadoes" aboard the *Neversink*. Chase and his circle do not speak after the fashion of mortals but in a heightened or poetic prose which sets them off from the illiterate and seemingly inarticulate crew. Pure of speech, they are pure of body, disdaining the crew's "most liberal notions concerning morality and the Decalogue." If, as White-Jacket alleges, "The Navy is the asylum for the perverse, the home of the unfortunate," "noble Jack" provides at his mess an artistic, almost mythic environment, a kind of nautical Olympus, where White-Jacket is "incorporated" and receives nourishment for his stomach and soul. This paternal shelter is more protective, and real, than the simulated breast.

Throughout the action White-Jacket enfolds himself in Chase's shadow. A passive observer of life on the *Neversink*, he moves toward maturity and independence neither in act nor in deed. He only reacts at a distance, a safe distance, and, unlike Ishmael or even Redburn, rarely engages in self-examination. Because he is in truth a nonenity, a cipher, a youth who really does not struggle with himself, he does not engage our hearts: he is memorable only because of the symbolism in which he is encased. But such are the demands of the fable, the rite of passage, that Melville must at the conclusion attempt to redeem his bumpkin.

At the end of the voyage, as the *Neversink* approaches the harbor, White-Jacket climbs the rigging in his familiar garment. Suddenly the ship lurches and he finds "the heavy skirts of my jacket right over my head, completely muffling me." In raising his arms to remove the jacket he loses his footing and plunges into the sea. The fall is like "a nightmare." For the first time he recalls "father, mother, and sisters," and thinks of death and even welcomes it. "Some current seemed hurrying me away; in a trance I yielded, and sank deeper down with a glide." When the flirtation with what he calls "the life-and-death poise" passes, he seeks "the blessed air." He begins to swim toward the ship; "but instantly I was conscious of a feeling like being pinioned in a feather-bed, and, moving my hands, felt my jacket puffed out above my tight girdle with water." He whips out his knife and rips the "jacket straight up and down, as if I were ripping open myself." Finally he is free of the "wigwam," "Sink! sink! oh shroud! thought I; sink forever! accursed jacket that thou art!" The crew, mistaking the jacket for a white shark, begins to hurl harpoons in order to protect the lad.

Here, in the most moving scene in the book, White-Jacket finally cuts the umbilical cord, extricating himself from the protective breast, which almost becomes his "shroud," and becomes his own man. Pictorially and symbolically the work ends where it begins, with the jacket, and Melville convinces the eye and fulfills the requirements of the fable he is telling. As in *Typee* and *Redburn*, however, he cons the reader and the fable, for his hero completes the rite of passage, not after he demonstrates his ability to stand on his own two feet and to accept the ambiguous burdens of maturity, but only after an accident shoves the passive youth into adulthood. The metamorphosis at the conclusion of *White-Jacket* is fictional or symbolic contrivance, a clever pictorial device.

Although *White-Jacket* was drawn in part from the author's personal experience, he also drew upon twelve or more sources, material from other writers appearing in thirty or more chapters, as Howard P. Vincent and Willard Thorp have recently demonstrated. The book, in short, has as many patches as White-Jacket's garment. Just as the clothing symbol reverberates on many levels, including the unconscious level, so the selection of incident or anecdote, whether derived from his own adventures as a sailor or at second hand from his reading, and the emphasis given to a scene, both in length and detail, reveal Melville's preoccupation with "the jelly of youth." The deep, personal, though sometimes deceptively distanced, involvement in the hero's development imposes a unity upon episodes which, observed separately, appear to be unrelated, or redundant.

Three scenes or subjects receive extended treatment: the flogging permitted by the Articles of War, the surgical sadism of Dr. Cuticle, and the fate of the beards which the sailors sport with inordinate pride. The three incidents record, seriously or comically, assaults upon manhood, humiliations imposed by tyrannical authorities or "bad fathers" upon the crew. The scars of flogging may be more painful emotionally than viscerally, the blow to the self-image doing incalculable harm. Dr. Cuticle relieves his victim of pain by "murdering" him in a public spectacle. Jack Chase says with his usual flamboyancy, "though you are about to shear off my manhood, yet, barber, I freely forgive you," or in the words of the narrator: "as the beard is the token of manhood, so, in some shape or other, has it ever been held the true badge of a warrior." Although the fears are perhaps greatest in "the jelly of youth," or puberty, some males — and the sailors aboard the *Neversink* are for the most part boy-men fleeing normal adult commitments and relationships — never cease worrying about their virility, never free themselves from castration anxieties.

Melville's fictional world is so insistently peopled with characters either scarred and dismembered or fearful of mutilation that it is reasonable to suggest that he was not reflecting reality so much as his own hurt inner landscape. From the beginning of his career he evidences a fascination with tattooing, which is a mutilation undergone by youths worried about their masculinity. Many characters are horribly scarred physically and emotionally, and some, like Captain Ahab, hobble about with the assistance of man-made limbs. Ahab is not only crippled but also disfigured by a scar on his face like a fissure. Tommo has his mysterious leg injury, narrowly escapes tattooing at the hands of Karky, and in *Omoo* is threatened, comically, with amputation: "the mate says it's in a devil of a way: and last night set the steward to sharpening the handsaw: hope he won't have the carving of ye." Amputation is burlesqued in *Mardi* when Samoa has his arm chopped off with the aid of his termagant wife, and the limb later waves at the mast — which leads Melville to a comic history of amputation. Jackson's face is as scarred as his personality, or, to put it another way, his satanism takes corporeal form, like Ahab's. Even the handsome Chase is flawed, lacking one finger, and his literary hero Camoens, the Portugese poet, lost his right eye in battle.

Melville's fictional world is a wounded world crying out to be reconstituted or made whole. His "heroes," those orphans in flight from parents to parental substitutes or ideals combining the wisdom of Socrates and the beauty of Apollo, are trying to put themselves together again, to be psychically healed. In treating physical and emotional mutilation Melville wavers; sometimes he is serious, but often he deflects attention from the severity of the wounds by means of his comic approach, his recourse to burlesque, parody, and carica-ture.

Until 1851 and the appearance of *Moby-Dick* his works are flawed by his indecisiveness and lack of confidence in his artistic skills. For example, in recreating his youth in the two novels he wrote in 1849, at age thirty, he seemingly enjoys the perspective and distance granted by age, by experience, and, perhaps most important of all, by art. Seemingly he can now give order to the amorphous and uncover patterns which as a young man he could not find. But this is an illusion, for the distance between author and character is not so great as it may at first appear. If a character like White-Jacket is too dependent, both upon a garment and the protective mantle of Jack Chase, the author is unwilling to trust his own observations and experiences and needs the support of secondary sources. If White-Jacket displays intellectual ingenuity in devising a substitute breast, foolish as the creation may be, Melville's prop is the symbolism which avoids exploration of emotional depths and substitutes for the personal drama. Despite his relationship with Chase's circle, White-Jacket for the most part does not interact in a meaningful way with the crew. Melville as author observes from a distance. The comic tactics he employs, when he makes his hero into a bumpkin and stereotypes the other characters, neutralize emotions and in effect mutilate.

The comedy in the early books is usually bland and not unkind, except in the treatment of missionaries and the scattered satirical thrusts at man's evils. The tone gradually changes in degree, if not in kind, particularly after the failure of *Mardi*. From the beginning Melville's obsession with amputation or disfigurement is paralleled by an appropriate artistic device or intellectual attitude — caricature. He had had unusual opportunities to observe a limited cross-section of mankind during his years at sea, as he notes in *Mardi*: "Now, at sea, and in the fellowship of sailors all men appear as they are. No school like a ship for studying human nature. The contact of one man with another is too near and constant to favor deceit. You wear your character as loosely as your flowing trowsers. Vain all endeavors to assume qualities not yours; or to conceal those you possess. Incognitos, however desirable, are out of the question."

Despite the opportunities the various protagonists are not perceptive observers. Dozens and dozens of people, literally hundreds, make brief appearances in these novels and then vanish, most of them difficult to recall later. With the notable exception of Jackson in *Redburn*, few emerge from the mold of types into complex humans. Even admirable or "noble" characters like Fayaway and Jack Chase spring from the literature of romance, not from life. Some are more or less memorable because their complex, contradictory humanity is reduced to a pleasant or unpleasant trait or abstraction. The good people are genteel and handsome, like the narrator himself. The "villains" are usually repellant and sadistic, the very models of "bad fathers" or termagant mothers.

Locked in his own fears and ambivalences, the protagonist-narrator can see others only in terms of their impact upon him: whether they are kindly substitutes for parents who have made him an orphan or threaten his tenuous security. The hero is self-protective both when he makes the "good" people into "noblemen" without ordinary human inconsistencies and when the "evil" are gargoyles.

Caricature disfigures personal dignity and amputates human complexity and diversity through subtraction and overemphasis upon a single trait. The caricaturist willfully and protectively dehumanizes, and delights in a public display of his virtuosity. He entertains in a socially acceptable way while he releases his aggressions and vents his hostility. Melville's caricatures become harsher after the appearance of *Mardi*. There are fools aplenty in the early works, including the narrators, but they are not harshly dealt with for the most part. But the edge of his rapier wit gradually becomes sharper, and the tone will gradually alter until in *The Confidence-Man* the cosmos itself is disfigured.

His disenchantment with himself and the world begins to emerge in *White-Jacket*, where his caricatural art spares no one, friend or foe. Unlike the earlier Apollos, Jack Chase is undercut not by the Homeric epithets with which he is adorned, or by the external descriptions, but by the speeches which he declaims with the intensity of a mad poet. Chase quotes *The Lusiad* of Camoens at every opportunity, but with extravagant flourishes that make the orator a wordmongering fool. When he makes the world's poets into sailors, he sounds like a historian or scholar gone a little daft.

> How many great men have been sailors. White-Jacket! They say Homer himself was once a tar, even as his hero, Ulysses, was both a sailor and a shipwright. I'll swear Shakespeare was once a captain of the forecastle. Do you mind the first scene in *The Tempest*, White-Jacket? And the world-finder, Christopher Columbus, was a sailor! and so was Camoens, who went to sea with Gama, else we had never had the Lusiad.... Old Noah was the first sailor. And St. Paul, too, knew how to box the compass, my lad! mind you that chapter in Acts? I couldn't spin the yarn better myself.

Delightful as this nonsense is — it is one of Melville's virtuoso performances — the most charismatic figure in the book becomes caricatural; his heroism reduced to precious prose, the kind of prose Melville will later parody devastatingly in the pages of *Pierre*.

The parting of the hero and his "pet" after the *Neversink* docks sounds less like the completion of a rite of passage — the maturing man welcoming the youth into manhood — than a scene from a jaunty musical comedy: "How I swayed and swung the hearty hand of Jack Chase, and nipped it to mine with a Carrick bend; yea, and kissed that noble hand of my liege lord and captain of my top, my sea-tutor and sire?" White-Jacket is still paying court, like a girl or an infatuated boy. It seems like an erotic charade of a youth in an ambiguous relationship, the latently sexual nature of which compels Melville to equivocate, to caricature his feelings. Caricature provides self-protection and partly conceals White-Jacket's continuing dependency.

The former ship's clerk on the *United States*, one Harrison Robertson, annotated his copy of *White-Jacket*, and arrived at the conclusion, "Most of the characters & incidents described are grossly caricatured, or exaggerated." No doubt Robertson was correct, but he neither allowed Melville poetic freedom nor understood the complexities behind the deliberate distortions.

White-Jacket is often an interesting description of naval life, but does not satisfy as a fictional work, not merely because it was written in haste and spleen, but because the "hero" is too passive. Melville improves his caricatural skills in the book, but fails to maintain a consistent viewpoint, because he is as indecisive as his protagonist. He berates the Articles of War and the United States Navy, but at one point sounds like a Fourth-of-July orator extolling Americans as "the peculiar, chosen people — the Israel of our time; we bear the ark of the liberties of the world." Perhaps because of public taste or because of his own wavering, he concludes the book with a banal passage —

For the rest, whatever befall us, let us never train our murderous guns inboard; let us not mutiny with bloody pikes in our hands. Our Lord High Admiral will yet interpose; and though long ages should elapse, and leave our wrongs unredressed, yet, shipmates and world-mates! let us never forget, that,

> *Whoever afflict us, whatever surround,*
> *Life is a voyage that's home-ward bound!*

— which could have been written by many of his contemporaries.

No one could have written *Moby-Dick*. On the basis of *White-Jacket* no reader or critic could have even guessed that Melville's next book would be his masterpiece, one of the world's great books. Though he flounders in *White-Jacket*, he is moving, almost imperceptively, toward the architectonics and tonalities of *Moby-Dick*. Flawed as the symbolic structure may be, it foreshadows his more elaborate experimentations later. His comedy is developing as a caricatural art which is to serve his evasive purposes admirably and which will provide him with licenses and freedoms he has up to this point only hinted at. In *White-Jacket* he uses dialog only sporadically, but practice is necessary before Ahab can unleash his extraordinary cadences or Ishmael can meditate from the mast. Jack Chase may be a hero of an outrageously literary ilk, but Melville is about to consummate the marriage of his reading and self-scrutiny and to free himself from his dependency upon authorities. The leisurely, undifferentiated style which blunts interest occasionally in *White-Jacket* and too often in *Mardi* is to be transformed into a digressive art unequalled in literature. Melville is about to digest Rabelais, Sterne, Cervantes, Browne, Burton, and Carlyle, those wordmongers he admires, and emerge his own man, with an authentic Melvillean voice.

He is about to flower as a genius, not in the shadow of Jack Chase, that middle-aged Apollo and pseudo-poet, but in the shadow of Nathaniel Hawthorne, who was also middle-aged and the greatest writer America had produced before 1850.

"A Book Broiled
in
Hell-Fire"
—*Moby-Dick*

Malcolm Melville, the first child, was born in Boston on February 16, 1849. In her confinement Elizabeth preferred to be in the family home on Mount Vernon Street, where she had the attention not only of a kind stepmother but also of a devoted family servant named Mrs. Sullivan. While Elizabeth slowly recovered, Herman had little to do: he had completed *Mardi* and had mailed the proofs to Murray in London, and in a household where help was generous he was an appendage.

A week or so before Malcolm's birth, on February 5, for the first time he heard Ralph Waldo Emerson give a lecture, one of a series on "Mind and Manners in the Nineteenth Century." "Say what you will," Melville wrote to Duyckinck, "he's a great man." Later he elaborated: "I was very agreeably disappointed in Mr Emerson. I had heard of him as full of transcendentalisms, myths & oracular gibberish; I had only glanced at a book of his once in Putnam's store – that was all I knew of him, till I heard him lecture. — To my surprise, I found him quite intelligible, tho' to say truth, they told me that that night he was unusually plain." If it seems unusual that Melville should neither have heard nor read the greatest American thinker of his era, we cannot forget that he was self-educated, somewhat unsystematic in his reading, and that he was not a New Englander, not one of those who made Concord, Massachusetts, into a national shrine. "For the sake of the argument," Melville observed, "let us call him a fool; — then had I rather be a fool than a wise man. — I love all men who *dive*." Here he recognized an affinity with Emerson, but also "notwithstanding his merit, a gaping flaw. It was, the insinuation, that had he lived in those days when the world was made, he might have offered some valuable suggestions. These men are all cracked right across the brow."

On February 12 and again a week later he attended readings from *Macbeth* and *Othello* given by Fanny Kemble Butler, a woman he found "so unfemininely masculine that had she not, on unimpeckable authority, borne children, I should be curious to learn the result of a surgical examination of her person in private." Her performances and the discovery in a book shop of an edition of Shakespeare "in glorious great type, every letter whereof is a soldier, & the top of every 't' like a musket barrel" led him to impassioned self-censure: "Dolt & ass that I am I have lived more than 29 years, & until a few days ago, never made close acquaintance with the divine William." With almost childlike excitement, as though he was the first to arrive at such a conclusion, he pronounced: "And if another Messiah ever comes twill be in Shakesper's person."

Apparently Duyckinck chided this sudden idolatry of Shakespeare, for Melville defended himself: "And do not think, my boy, that because I, impulsively broke forth in jubilations over Shakspeare, that, therefore, I am of the number of the *snobs* who burn their tuns of rancid fat at his shrine. No, I would stand afar off & alone, & burn some pure Palm oil, the product of some overtopping trunk." Similarly he had to defend his laudatory remarks about Emerson: "You complain that Emerson tho' a denizen of the land of gingerbread, is above munching a plain cake in company of jolly fellows, & swiging off his ale like you and me. Ah, my dear sir, that's his misfortune, not his fault. His belly, sir, is in his chest, & his brains descend down into his neck, & offer an obstacle to a draught of ale or a mouthful of cake."

The other literary discovery of 1849 was the most significant. Late in July he borrowed from Duyckinck's personal library a copy of Hawthorne's *Twice-Told Tales*. It was not quite correct, then, as he was to claim in *The Literary World* in 1850, that he had never read Hawthorne before. In describing the scuttle-butt in *White-Jacket* he makes a graceful allusion to an essay in *Twice-Told Tales*, "A Rill from the Town Pump": "And would that my fine countryman, Hawthorne of Salem, had but served on board a man-of-war in his time, that he might give us the reading of a '*rill*' from the Scuttle-butt."

Although his literary discoveries are of interest, and even at times of importance in establishing influences, the emotional climate is even more important in the case of a writer who transferred to his fiction not only his life experiences but also his fluctuating moods. Unfortunately, most of the personal details at this time come from his letters to Duyckinck, which deal primarily with intellectual chitchat in the stylized banter to which the Young Americans were given. On March 28 Melville complained of "the Fourth Day of the Great Boston Rain," and then, with typical facetiousness, revealed his depressed state: "I have a continual dripping sensation; and feel like an ill-wrung towel — my soul is damp, & by spreading itself out upon paper seeks to get dry." Shortly afterwards Duyckinck apparently informed Melville that Charles Fenno Hoffman, one of his associates on *The Literary World* and a member of the Young American group, had become "deranged." In reply Melville made a curious confession:

> This going mad of a friend or acquaintance comes straight home to every man who feels his soul in him, — which but few men do. For in all of us lodges the same fuel to light the same fire. And he who has never felt, momentarily, what madness is has but a mouthful of brains. What sort of sensation permanent madness is may be very well imagined — just as we imagine how we felt when we were infants, tho' we can not recall it. In both conditions we are irresponsible & riot like gods without fear of fate. — It is the climax of a mad night of revelry when the blood has been transmuted into brandy. — But if we prate much of this thing we shall be illustrating our own propositions. —

Melville was more than ordinarily troubled by the prospect of madness. He had never forgotten that time in January 1832 when his father mingled nonsense with biblical quotations before he passed over the abyss. Taji totters on the thin borderline between sense and no-sense as he intrepidly sails alone in search of he knows not what. In *Redburn* at least two sailors spit out their lives in alcoholic delirium, and Jackson, that satanic character to whom Redburn feels a closer affinity than to almost any one else, deteriorates in body and mind, figuratively coming apart at the seams as he wilts into silence before he is silenced forever. Dr. Cuticle is a physician gone berserk, the sadism which leads him to surgery finally completely out of control. And shortly Melville was to create the "crazy" Ahab, who "dives" and wills his own destruction. Other madmen were to follow, as Melville's world, like Bartleby's walls, closed in on him. Melville was able to "imagine" madness, and to depict it, in the course of the anxieties and depressions which made him feel "like an ill-wrung towel." He was infatuated with that final abandonment, that last deprivation, and sometimes in his despair, not unlike Bartleby, he preferred nothingness. The two states he could "imagine" — and his fiction supports his assertion — were madness and "how we felt when we were infants, tho' we can not recall it." The birth of Malcolm must have opened old wounds. He had sired an offspring, but he had no love for first-born males, after his forced subordination to Gansevoort. With the arrival of Malcolm he was abandoned by Elizabeth, who had other concerns than to cater to his needs, as she had done during the writing of *Mardi*. Similarly in his youth he had experienced the "loss" of his mother with the arrival of five sisters and brothers. Between February 24 and April 5 Melville wrote at least four letters to Evert Duyckinck without once mentioning the child or the mother.

During the late spring and early summer Melville wrote *Redburn* and *White-Jacket* with almost maniacal speed. After signing an agreement with Harper and Brothers on September 13, 1849, to publish *White-Jacket* in the following spring, he made plans to go to London. He wanted to arrange the best possible terms for the English publication, and since Brodhead was no longer in London he had no one to act as his agent. In addition, he was exhausted from writing, reading proofs, overseeing the publication of *Redburn*, and then repeating the process with *White-Jacket*. About September 12 he invited Evert Duyckinck to join him on an extended tour of Europe. "Melville put me all in a flutter the other evening," Duyckinck wrote to his brother George, "by proposing that I should go to Europe with him on a cheap adventurous flying tour of eight months. . . ." The notice of his sailing in the *New-York Daily Tribune* read: "It is his intention to spend a twelvemonth abroad."

If Melville was talking to Duyckinck about a trip lasting eight months or a year, he apparently was not telling quite the same story to Elizabeth, who, not surprisingly, was somewhat less than enthusiastic about a lengthy separation. On October 6 Melville reassured Judge Shaw and his wife: "Lizzie is becoming more reconciled to the idea of my departure, especially as she will have Malcolm for company during my absence. And I have no doubt, that when she finds herself surrounded by her old friends in Boston, she will bear the temporary separation with more philosophy than she has anticipated." On the same day he informed Richard Henry Dana, Jr., "I shall be away, in all probability, for some months after the publication of the book."

While Herman laid secretive plans, or indulged in dreams of flight, Elizabeth was occupied with the christening of their child. On September 30 Malcolm was baptized at home by Dr. Henry Whitney Bellows. Eleven days later, on October 11, Melville sailed aboard the *Southampton,* with only Allan Melville and George Duyckinck to see him off "during a cold violent storm from the West." For the first time he kept a journal in which entries for the most part were brief and unadorned. The terseness notwithstanding, it is a useful document, particularly in the case of a writer who left a legacy of fewer than three hundred letters and only two journals.

Melville had a stateroom to himself, "as big almost as my own room at home; it has a spacious berth, a large washstand, a sofa, glass &c. &c." Attired in a green coat, the counterpart of Redburn's red jacket, Melville cut a figure aboard the ship.

During the voyage he became intimate with Dr. Franklin Taylor, a cousin of Bayard Taylor, and Dr. George J. Adler, professor of modern languages at New York University. Soon he was discussing with Dr. Adler " 'Fixed Fate, Free Will, foreknowledge absolute.' " Melville may not have been educated at Harvard or Yale, but he explored insoluble metaphysical problems with a university professor who was recovering apparently from a psychotic episode: "He was almost crazy, he tells me, for a time." (Adler was committed to an asylum in 1853.) On the third day out, a passenger leaped into the stormy sea: "It afterwards turned out, that he was crazy, & had jumped overboard. He had declared he would do so several times."

Adler, Taylor, and Melville discussed cosmic matters at a length also bordering on the cosmic. The stimulation was intellectual and alcoholic. After a heavy "infusion" of whiskey — "Taylor 4 or five tumblers &c," the et cetera concealing Melville's consumption — "We had an extraordinary time & did not break up till after two in the morning. We talked metaphysics continually, & Hegel, Schlegel, Kant &c were discussed under the influence of the whiskey." That Melville was not well read in German philosophy was undoubtedly not noticeable in the convivial excitement. Five days later another passenger, T. F. McCurdy, the son of "a rich merchant of New York," invited the trio "to partake of some *mulled wine.* . . . Got — all of us — riding on the German horse again — . . . separated at about 3 in the morning." The high jinks continued until the end of the voyage, when "Taylor played a rare joke upon McCurdy this evening, passing himself off as Miss Wilbur, having borrowed her cloak, &c. They walked together." On the last night he "cracked some Champagne" for the last time with McCurdy, and landed at Deal on the following day, November 5. He recalled his first visit to England in 1839, "*then* a sailor, *now* H. M. author of 'Peedee,' 'Hullabaloo' & 'Pog-Dog.' "

In London Melville saw the sights, made calls on some of the people to whom he had letters of introduction, met his first English publisher, John Murray, and frequented bookstores. Like Gansevoort a few years earlier, Herman lived modestly and was "not in" to visitors: "I am obliged to employ this fashionable shift of evasion of visitors – for I have not a decent room to show them – but (& which is *the* cause) I cannot in conscience ask them to labor their way up to the 4th floor of a house." Because Richard Bentley was in the country and the English publication of *White-Jacket* could not be immediately arranged, he took the opportunity to go to the continent for the first time. On November 27 he left for Paris, where he met Adler, later visited Brussels, and went over to eastern Germany. He was back in London on December 13, and two days later, "Hurrah & three cheers! I have just returned from Mr. Bentley's, & have concluded an arrangement with him that gives me tomorrow his note for £200."

In Cologne on December 9, he wrote in his journal: "I feel homesick to be sure – being all alone with not a soul to talk to." On December 16 he was torn between sailing or remaining for three more weeks in order to accept the Duke of Rutland's "cordial invitation": "I am in a very painful state of uncertainty. I am all eagerness to get home – I ought to get home – my absence occasions uneasiness in a quarter where I most beseech heaven to grant repose." Later in the day he engaged passage. For public consumption he attributed the abandonment of his travels to the "inadequate proceeds of the English editions of his book." On December 19 he dined at one of the Inns of Court, on the fifth floor, "and had a glorious time till noon of night." He pronounced it "The Paradise of Batchelors," and in 1855 in a short story with that title, he revived that "glorious time" among men who "had no wives or children to give an anxious thought. Almost all of them were travellers, too; for bachelors alone can travel freely, and without any twinges of their consciences touching desertion of the fireside."

Melville sailed from Portsmouth aboard the *Independence* on Christmas day, the same day on which the *Pequod* was to sail in quest of the White Whale. Without the stimulation of congenial passengers and perhaps bored, he made only a few jottings in the journal during the return trip, confining himself to listing and commenting briefly on some of the books he had acquired. The *Independence* docked on February 1, 1850. On the following day *White-Jacket* was reviewed in at least three English journals.

Although the reviews were favorable and Melville had a substantial advance from Bentley, his economic situation was not fundamentally altered. Despite the critical attention he had received since 1846 he was by no means the author of best sellers. During his lifetime only 4,922 copies of *White-Jacket* were sold, and his profit over a period of forty years amounted to $969.44. And so almost at once he began another book, the sixth since 1844.

During the next six months he once again imprisoned himself in his study in the New York house, where there were now a grandmother, four unmarried sisters, two brothers, two wives, and two children, in addition to domestic help; and Allan's wife was pregnant again.

Melville referred to his new book for the first time in a letter to Dana on May 1, 1850: "About the 'whaling voyage' — I am half way in the work. . . . It will be a strange sort of a book, I fear; blubber is blubber you know; tho' you may get oil out of it, the poetry runs as hard as sap from a frozen maple tree; — & to cook the thing up, one must needs throw in a little fancy, which from the nature of the thing, must be ungainly as the gambols of the whales themselves. Yet I mean to give the truth of the thing, spite of this."

On June 27 he promised Richard Bentley the book in "the latter part of the coming autumn," but, perhaps because he was writing to his publisher, he made the work appear to be more conventional: "The book is a romance of adventure, founded upon certain wild legends in the Southern Sperm Whale Fisheries, and illustrated by the author's own personal experience, of two years & more, as a harpooner." This account was misleading, probably deliberately so, since *Moby-Dick* was not to have the literal autobiographical substructure of his earlier writings, *Mardi* excepted, and Melville never qualified as anything more than an ordinary seaman, certainly not as a harpooner.

About the middle of July he put the manuscript aside, or perhaps he was bankrupt of "fancy," and went to Pittsfield, Massachusetts, to visit his cousin Robert Melvill. *The New-York Morning Express* on July 20 announced that Melville "has gone on a cruise to Europe once more. Of course, another of his amusing and peculiar books may be anticipated as the result of his voyage." On July 18 and 19 he took a "rambling expedition" with Robert and spent a night in Lenox, not more than a few miles from Hawthorne's house. Either he did not know of Hawthorne's presence, which seems unlikely, or he was too modest to introduce himself, even though Hawthorne was an old friend of Duyckinck. Yet on the day he set out on this "expedition," Aunt Mary, Robert's mother, presented her nephew with a copy of *Mosses from an Old Manse*. Perhaps he did not open the book until he returned from his brief journey. The tale he told in *The Literary World* about his discovery of Hawthorne was much more dramatic, but then fiction often improves upon reality. On July 21 he visited a Shaker colony, and, like Hawthorne, was fascinated by this celibate sect which decried "the jealousies and evil surmises" arising "from the partial and selfish relations of husbands, wives and children," and whose guiding saint, Mother Ann, testified "against the lustful gratifications of the flesh, as the *source and foundation of human corruption.*" A few days later he returned to the city and escorted his domestic entourage to Pittsfield for a summer vacation.

The Melvilles had barely unpacked when Duyckinck and Mathews arrived and the strenuous activities began which would culminate on the rocky peak of Monument Mountain. On August 5 Melville had an experience granted to few men: an icon from fantasy transformed into flesh. His reaction to Hawthorne was visceral, and he confessed his "love" in *The Literary World*. He visited Hawthorne at least three times within a month, and the latter came to Pittsfield. Elizabeth and Helen Melville called on Sophia Hawthorne. Suddenly Melville wanted to settle in Pittsfield. Although he had no funds, Melville decided to buy the farm next to Broadhall, which Robert Melvill had recently sold to the Morewoods. On September 10 Judge Shaw was in Pittsfield to advance $3,000 for the purchase of the farm owned by Dr. John Brewster, Sr. The necessary official documents were signed on September 14, and Melville took possession of, in the words of his neighbor J. E. A. Smith, "a large quaint old house, built in the early days of the settlement of the town." He named the farm Arrowhead, "from some Indian relics which were turned up in his first plowing of its soil." Toward the end of September the family went to New York to pack their possessions, and early in October they were established at Arrowhead, which was to be home for the next thirteen years.

Hawthorne was the "magnet," to use one of Melville's favorite words, although the shy man from Salem would have shrunk from the epithet. Without any awareness on his part, he was the culminating link in a series of events and relationships which can be traced almost to the beginning of Melville's life. That Hawthorne was in Melville's eyes an ideal father was the most significant link, but that he should meet him near Pittsfield seemed an extraordinary accident. As a child, in the happier days when his father was still alive, Herman had visited Uncle Thomas's farm and had known the excitement of the city lad discovering rural life. In the summer of 1832 after Allan died he went to Pittsfield to escape an epidemic. In the summer of 1834 he threw up his clerkship — it was the first time he in effect jumped ship — and became "an inmate of my uncle's family, and an active assistant upon the farm." There for the first time since his father's death he spent happy months with this snuff-pinching "courtier," as eccentric as Major Melvill himself. His first teaching position was in a school near Pittsfield, probably on Uncle Thomas's recommendation. Before sailing to the Pacific aboard the *Acushnet,* he had visited his uncle, now transplanted to Galena, Illinois. Five years later he wrote "Hawthorne and His Mosses" at an "odd" desk, "an old thing of my Uncle the Major's, which for twelve years back has been packed away in the cornloft over the carriage house." It was at this table that Melville completed *Moby-Dick* and wrote all his major prose works.

On August 7, two days after the meeting on Monument Mountain, Duyckinck informed his brother that "Melville has a new book mostly done — a romantic, fanciful & literal & most enjoyable presentment of the Whale Fishery — something quite new." This would appear to be the book Melville had described earlier to Dana and Bentley. In the excitement following his encounter with Hawthorne he apparently put the work aside as he uprooted himself and his family and moved to Pittsfield, and then tried to ready his new home for the winter.

He returned to *Moby-Dick* about the first of November. Since no manuscripts survive, no one can be positive about the progress of the work or the extent of the revisions. It seems reasonably certain, however, that he in effect rewrote the entire book after his meeting with Hawthorne. The manuscript, supposedly finished in August 1850, was not completed until September 1851, and then in a scramble that must have vexed printer and publisher since the last chapters were not ready when type was being set. As he informs us in the text, he was writing or revising Chapter 85, "The Fountain," at "fifteen and a quarter minutes past one o'clock P.M. of this sixteenth day of December, A.D. 1850."

This comic reference to the process of composition disguises the fact that once again Melville had locked himself into a rigid writing schedule:

Do you want to know how I pass my time? — I rise at eight — thereabouts — & go to my barn — say good-morning to the horse, & give him his breakfast. . . . Then, pay a visit to my cow — cut up a pumpkin or two for her, & stand by to see her eat it — for it's a pleasant sight to see a cow move her jaws — she does it so mildly & with such a sanctity. — My own breakfast over, I go to my workroom & light my fire — then spread my M.S.S on the table — take one business squint at it, & fall to with a will. At 2 1/2 P.M. I hear a preconcerted knock at my door, which (by request) continues till I rise & go to the door, which serves to wean me effectively from my writing, however interested I may be. My friends the horse & cow now demand their dinner — & I go & give it them. My own dinner over, I rig my sleigh & with my mother or sisters start off for the village — . . . My evenings I spend in a sort of mesmeric state in my room — not being able to read — only now & then skimming over some large-printed book.

Despite the labored facetiousness, the passage exposes the discipline which Melville invariably imposed upon himself when he was writing.

While Melville unfolded the story of a monomaniac he neglected Elizabeth and Malcolm. Elizabeth found the winter of 1850-1851 even more difficult than the winter of 1847-1848, when *Mardi* was being born. Unable "to wean me effectively from my writing," she spent four or five weeks in Boston toward the end of the year. Apparently she found the rigors of existence in the Berkshires difficult after living in a comfortable urban home with plenty of servants in attendance. Years later Elizabeth recalled: "Wrote White Whale or Moby Dick under unfavorable circumstances — would sit at his desk all day not eating any thing till four or five o'clock — then ride to the village after dark — would be up early and out walking before breakfast — sometimes splitting wood for exercise."

"Taking a book off the brain," Melville wrote to Duyckinck, "is akin to the ticklish & dangerous business of taking an old painting off a panel — you have to scrape off the whole brain in order to get at it with due safety — & even then, the painting may not be worth the trouble."

After Melville settled in at Arrowhead and locked himself into his study, he saw Hawthorne less frequently than in the period immediately following the excursion to Monument Mountain. But in 1851 he wrote a series of letters to Hawthorne which "unfolded" a story as "true" as *Moby-Dick* and which counterpointed his fiction. The letters were tender, depressed, exhilarated, the moods in constant flux, not unlike the surface and subterranean rhythms of his masterpiece. Melville confided to Hawthorne what he exposed to no one else. He was eager to obtain the affection and approval of his "Father confessor," but the eagerness at times was so overasserted, so undisguised, that a note of desperation intruded, as though he feared rejection. The extravagant praise and, more specifically, the desire to "incorporate" Hawthorne constituted a kind of attack, yet at the same time, as in the article in *The Literary World,* he wrote as an equal of the man he termed the American Shakespeare.

Melville's love, then, was intertwined with rivalry. If he craved the warmth of a father figure, he was anxious now, unlike L. A. V., to demonstrate his worth by competing with the older man. The situation in life was not without parallels to the book which was to undergo a transformation from a presumably romantic account of "the Southern Sperm Whale Fisheries," based upon personal experience, into a study of the rivalry of the "son" (Ishmael) with the "father" (Ahab).

Melville forced himself on Hawthorne. On January 22, 1851, he appeared at the red farmhouse to invite the Hawthornes to Pittsfield. Sophia gave him "cold chicken," and Hawthorne presented him with copies of the third edition of *Twice-Told Tales* with a new preface composed in Lenox. Four days later Hawthorne finished work on *The House of the Seven Gables,* which he had begun after his arrival in the Berkshires and had completed while Melville continued to struggle with the "fin of the whale."

Melville playfully dismissed Sophia's explanation of why her husband could not return the visit as "that lady's syrenisms," and proceeded in somewhat peremptory fashion to dictate arrangements. He was ready to send his "best travelling chariot on runners," for "Your bed is already made, & the wood marked for your fire." He promised Hawthorne a Ti in the Berkshires: "Mark — There is some excellent Montado Sherry awaiting you & some potent Port. We will have mulled wine with wisdom, & buttered toast with story-telling & crack jokes & bottles from morning till night."

He confessed his disappointment to Duyckinck when Hawthorne turned down this second invitation, or summons ("I will send Constables after you"). "I had promised myself much pleasure," he admitted, "in getting him up in my snug room here, & discussing the Universe with a bottle of brandy & cigars. But he has not been able to come, owing to sickness in his family, — or else, he's up to the lips in the *Universe* again." By this time he had read *Twice-Told Tales,* which "far exceed the 'Mosses' — they are, I fancy, an earlier vintage from his vine. . . . Still there is something lacking — a good deal lacking — to the plumb sphericity of the man. . . . He does'nt patronize the butcher — he needs roast-beef, done rare." A shrewd reservation, although in his preface to his tales Hawthorne acknowledges their "lack of power" and "tameness." However, Melville still considered Hawthorne the only "profound" genius in American literature.

On March 12 Melville arrived at the red shanty "at dusk," Sophia noted in her diary, and was "entertained with Champagne foam — manufactured of beaten eggs, loaf sugar, & champagne — bread & butter & cheese." Hawthorne and his daughter Una spent the next two days at Arrowhead, but neither writer made a record of the feasting and the talk. About a month later, on April 11, Melville was again in Lenox; this time he received one of the few inscribed copies of *The House of the Seven Gables.* After a few days he returned the compliment in a warm letter playfully written like a formal "criticism" of the book, with phraseology reminiscent of the article in *The Literary World*. The romance "has delighted us," Melville wrote; "it has piqued a re-perusal; it has robbed us of a day, and made us a present of a whole year of thoughtfulness; it has bred great exhilaration and exultation with the remembrance that the architect of the Gables resides only six miles off, and not three thousand miles away, in England say." *The House of the Seven Gables,* he asserted, "for pleasantness of running interest, surpasses the other works of the author." He was particularly impressed by such "deep passages" as Judge Pyncheon's death scene and Clifford's contemplation of suicide. "Clifford is full of an awful truth throughout. . . . He is no caricature. He is Clifford."

As perceptive as his remarks on particulars were, he quickly moved to the general, away from the immediacies of the "heart" to the protective distancing and generalities of the "head" — a tactic to which he resorts frequently in his novels, when emotions are too much for him: "There is a certain tragic phase of humanity which, in our opinion, was never more powerfully embodied than by Hawthorne. We mean the tragicalness of human thought in its own unbiassed, native, and profounder workings. We think that into no recorded mind has the intense feeling of the visable truth ever entered more deeply than into this man's." Melville did not comment on the fact that the romance effects its miraculous conclusion because of the redemptive powers of Phoebe's sun-filled heart. Neither Ahab nor Bartleby has a woman to redirect his preference for death. Only Ishmael is saved by woman, not by one of flesh and blood — and love — but by a ship named *Rachel,* only a cold symbol of warm human love, although the conclusion of *Moby Dick* is in its way as miraculous as that of *The House of the Seven Gables.* Hawthorne revered the sun goddess Phoebe, Melville the sun god Apollo.

Carried away toward the conclusion of the letter Melville suddenly erupted in one of his most memorable outbursts: "There is the grand truth about Nathaniel Hawthorne. He says NO! in thunder; but the Devil himself cannot make him say *yes*. For all men who say *yes,* lie; and all men who say *no,* — why, they are in the happy condition of judicious, unincumbered travellers in Europe; they cross the frontiers into Eternity with nothing but a carpet-bag, — that is to say, the Ego. Whereas those *yes*-gentry, they travel with heaps of baggage, and, damn them! they will never get through the Custom House." Which is an impressive prose statement, but a simplistic and dubious formulation, like its counterpart in "The Try-Works" in *Moby-Dick:* ". . . the mortal man who hath more of joy than sorrow in him, that mortal man cannot be true — not true, or undeveloped. With books the same."

Melville urged Hawthorne to "walk down one of these mornings and see me," the six-mile distance being only a stroll in those days, but Hawthorne seemed to have preferred excursions in the hills about his farmhouse in the company of his two children, Julian and Una. Melville chose to forget, or to ignore, that as a father Hawthorne delighted in his children, even to retelling classical tales in *A Wonder-Book for Girls and Boys.* Melville lacked his friend's light, domestic touch, in life as well as in art. Although Hawthorne enjoyed the cigars, whiskey, and "ontological heroics" when they met, he avoided the intense relationship Melville sought.

Within a few months after his arrival in the Berkshires Hawthorne quite effortlessly attracted an intellectual coterie, others seeking him out as Melville did. His circle included such people as Fanny Kemble, the Shakespearean actress about whose sex Melville had nasty questions in February 1850; G. P. R. James, an English novelist, "conspicuous to all the world on his mountain-pile of history and romance," whom, curiously, Melville called upon after Hawthorne left the Berkshires; Catherine Maria Sedgwick, "our most truthful novelist, who has made the scenery and life of Berkshire all her own"; F. P. Whipple, a literary critic; and Oliver Wendell Holmes, to whom he sent a copy of *The House of the Seven Gables.* James Russell Lowell and his wife paid a brief visit in 1850. As much as the Hawthornes admired Melville, they did not share him with their circle. In the passage in *A Wonder-Book* describing many of the people mentioned above, Hawthorne pays his respects to Melville – "On the hither side of Pittsfield sits Herman Melville, shaping out the gigantic conception of his 'White Whale,' while the gigantic shape of Graylock looms upon him from his study-window" – respectfully but without the warmth of the account of Holmes which immediately follows. As an "isolato" Melville in that genteel group would have been an embarrassment. He was an exciting and excited conversationalist, or, more accurately perhaps, monologist, when he was interested; silent and even boorish when he was not.

The volatility and shifting moods which made Melville fascinatingly egocentric (perhaps more so at a distance) but problematical in a social situation were evident in a letter he wrote to Hawthorne about June 1, 1851. Despite its length he wasted no time inquiring about Rose Hawthorne, who was born on May 20, or about her mother. Birth was always a painful subject to a man who idealized bachelor heroes. After fifteen or sixteen months devoted to his "gigantic conception," he wrote like a splintered man, as splintered as Ahab, whose final suicidal pursuit of the monster he had yet to describe.

At the outset Melville apologized for not "rumbling down to you in my pine-board chariot," phraseology which recalls Ahab's likening his ship to "the sea-chariot of the sun," but "I had my crops to get in." Then came a curious remark, hostile and at the same time servile: "I mean to continue visiting you until you tell me that my visits are both supererogatory and superfluous." After referring to "a certain spontaneous aristocracy of feeling, — exceedingly nice and fastidious," — he made the application specific: "when you see or hear of my ruthless democracy on all sides, you may possibly feel a touch of a shrink, or something of that sort." After this painful admission, this awareness of Hawthorne's reaction to his turbulent ideas and personality, which may also have been a cry for sympathy, he struggled to bridge the gap between them, but in doing so his vulnerable pride became mixed with condescension. "It is but nature to be shy of a mortal who boldly declares that a thief in jail is as honorable a personage as Gen. George Washington." Shortly he tired of his "endless sermon" and admitted his physical and intellectual enervation. Within a week or so he planned to "go to New York, to bury myself in a third-story room, and work and slave on my 'Whale' while it is driving through the press. *That* is the only way I can finish it now. . . . The calm, the coolness, the silent grass-growing mood in which a man *ought* always to compose, — that, I fear, can seldom be mine. Dollars damn me; and the malicious Devil is forever grinning in upon me, holding the door ajar."

Suddenly in his letter Melville admitted to Hawthorne a despair so great that "a presentiment is on me, — I shall at last be worn out and perish, like an old nutmeg-grater, grated to pieces by the constant attrition of the wood, that is, the nutmeg." (The same image reappears on the second day of the pursuit of Moby Dick when Melville describes the wrecked boats of Stubb and Flash: "the odorous cedar chips of the wrecks danced round and round, like the grated nutmeg in a swiftly stirred bowl of punch.") For the second time within six months ("you have to scrape off the whole brain in order to get at it with safety") he more than suggested that in his case creativity teetered on madness. If Ahab's body and mind throb with maniacal schemes for revenge upon the leviathan that has "dismasted" him physically and emotionally, Melville's being throbbed as he lamented that the public crippled him by "banning" through not purchasing the books he wanted to write, with the result that "all my books are botches," or he might have said, amputations. "Four blisters on this palm," he punned, made him "sore" and "write a little bluely." This punning led in its agitated way to another version of a recurrent fantasy.

Would the Gin were here! If ever, my dear Hawthorne, in the eternal times that are to come, you and I shall sit down in Paradise, in some little shady corner by ourselves; and if we shall by any means be able to smuggle a basket of champagne there (I won't believe in a Temperance Heaven), and if we shall then cross our celestial legs in the celestial grass that is forever tropical, and strike our glasses and our heads together, till both musically ring in concert, — then, O my dear fellow-mortal, how shall we pleasantly discourse of all the things manifold which now so distress us, — when all the earth shall be but a reminiscence, yea, its final dissolution an antiquity. . . . Let us swear that, though now we sweat, yet it is because of the dry heat which is indispensable to the nourishment of the vine which is to bear the grapes that are to give us the champagne hereafter.

In this comic and soul-wrenching passage, Melville once more created an oral framework about Hawthorne which recalled the champagne served in silver goblets at their first meeting on Monument Mountain and the imagery of his article in *The Literary World*.

Next he returned to "talking about the 'Whale,' " which he had not worked on for "some three weeks." "I'm going to take him by his jaw, however, before long, and finish him up in some fashion." The bravado wilted immediately into despair: "Though I wrote the Gospels in this century, I should die in the gutter." Then followed an apology, mixed with characteristic self-abasement: "I talk all about myself, and this is selfishness and egotism. Granted. But how help it? I am writing to you; I know little about you, but something about myself. So I write about myself, — at least, to you. Don't trouble yourself, though, about writing; and don't trouble yourself about visiting; and when you *do* visit, don't trouble yourself about talking. I will do all the writing and visiting and talking myself." Yet, also characteristically, the self-abasement managed to censure Hawthorne's coldness and remoteness.

The censure turned abruptly into praise of "Ethan Brand," which he had recently read, particularly of the "frightful poetical creed that the cultivation of the brain eats out the heart." He continued to praise as he recalled that in his recent visit to New York he had heard "many flattering (in a publisher's point of view) allusions" to Hawthorne's new books. "So upon the whole, I say to myself, this N. H. is in the ascendant." Hawthorne's ascent recalled his own loss of popular favor: "What 'reputation' H. M. has is horrible. Think of it! To go down to posterity is bad enough, any way; but to go down as a 'man who lived among the cannibals'!"

Then came another painful confession in this heart-exposing, life-weary letter:

My development has been all within a few years past. I am like one of those seeds taken out of the Egyptian Pyramids, which, after being three thousand years a seed and nothing but a seed, being planted in English soil, it developed itself, grew to greenness, and then fell to mould. So I. Until I was twenty-five, I had no development at all. From my twenty-fifth year I date my life. Three weeks have scarcely passed, at any time between then and now, that I have not unfolded within myself. But I feel that I am now come to the inmost leaf of the bulb, and that shortly the flower must fall to the mould.

In his despair he remembered Goethe's commandment, *"Live in the all."* "What nonsense!" he exclaimed, especially if one had "a raging toothache," and concluded: "As with all great genius, there is an immense deal of flummery in Goethe, and in proportion to my own contact with him, a monstrous deal of it in me." He quickly signed the letter "H. Melville," and just as quickly added a postscript: " 'Amen!' saith Hawthorne." The comic deflation was a transparent defense, a witty dismissal of the fact that he had laid bare his heart.

He could not bring the letter to a conclusion. It possessed him as the whale possesses Ahab. The bubbles of fantasy and the gyrations in mood finally collapsed into common-sense awareness: "N. B. This 'all' feeling, though, there is some truth in. You must have often felt it, lying on the grass on a warm summer's day. Your legs seem to send out shoots into the earth. Your hair feels like leaves upon your head. This is the *all* feeling. But what plays the mischief with the truth is that men will insist upon the universal application of a temporary feeling or opinion." At last he concluded the letter with a final postscript: "P. S. You must not fail to admire my discretion in paying the postage on this letter." The attempt at wit was lame.

How Hawthorne reacted to this "crazy-witty" confession, disorderly in its struggle to reveal but not to reveal too much, moody in its rapid shifts from seriousness to self-conscious, protective jests — we shall — alas! — never know. Seldom before and only once again, in another letter to Hawthorne, was Melville to give so much of himself, to expose his vulnerabilities. The letter was an uneasy gift of love, a cry for understanding and affection, but to a man who like his characters needed the protection of veils, it could only be a burden and a threat.

From June 14 to 29 Melville was in New York driving himself to conclude his novel and to supervise the printing. Weary of the delays and "disgusted with the heat and dust of the babylonish brick-kiln of New York, I came back to the country to feel the grass — and end the book reclining on it, if I may." That final clause indicated uncertainty and lack of self-confidence. Yet he was in better spirits, he claimed, the pleasant weather having "now for weeks recalled me from certain crotchetty and over doleful chimearas, the like of which men like you and me and some others, forming a chain of God's posts round the world, must be content to encounter now and then, and fight them the best way we can." That in wrestling free of some "chimearas" he clung to another — "a chain of God's posts round the world" — demonstrated, at least to those who listened carefully to what his verbalisms revealed and concealed, that, if his agitation was great, his aspiration was no less so. His awareness that *Moby-Dick* was to be one of the world's great books, one of "God's posts," did not lighten his ordeal.

"Come and spend a day here," he wrote, "if you can and want to; if not, stay in Lenox, and God give you long life." The wit offered Hawthorne an excuse for not coming but was not without an undercurrent of hostility. "When I am quite free of my present engagements," Melville observed, "I am going to treat myself to a ride and a visit to you. Have ready a bottle of brandy, because I always feel like drinking that heroic drink when we talk ontological heroics together."

"Shall I send you a fin of the *Whale,*" he jested, in the pattern of imagery he established in his article in *The Literary World,* "by way of a specimen mouthful? The tail is not yet cooked — though the hell-fire in which the whole book is broiled might not unreasonably have cooked it all ere this. This is the book's motto (the secret one), — Ego non baptiso te in nomine — but make out the rest yourself." Although the letter was calmer than the preceding one, Melville was not inaccurate: "This is rather a crazy letter in some respects, I apprehend."

A few weeks later the "fin" was cooked and *Moby-Dick* was finished. On July 22 he wrote to Hawthorne "not a letter, or even a note — but only a passing word said to you over your garden gate." He thanked Hawthorne for his "easy-flowing long letter (received yesterday) which flowed through me, and refreshed all my meadows." The affected diction, bordering on the coy, was perhaps excessive, but so was the strain of completing his book. "The earliest good chance I get," he declared, "I shall roll down to you, my good fellow, seeing we — that is, you and I — must hit upon some little bit of vagabondism, before Autumn comes. Graylock — we must go and vagabondize there. But ere we start, we must dig a deep hole, and bury all Blue Devils, there to abide till the Last Day." The letter was signed, "Goodbye, his X mark." Melville here assumed the role of Queequeg, the prince-harpooner, who, after a "honeymoon" with Ishmael in New Bedford, decides to sail with the young man, and signs the register of the *Pequod* with an X. In the letter as in the novel Melville sought the safety of farce to disguise the intense emotional attachment; the tenderest and most intimate scenes in all his writings are those between Ishmael and the cannibal. Whether Hawthorne understood or not, Melville here exposed his love-starved heart, but, typically, the jesting tone took both men off the hook. The proposal for "some little bit of vagabondism" also revived memories of the carefree life in Tahiti with Long Ghost and of *Omoo,* where "Blue Devils" are not in evidence. But Melville in his manic exhilaration and in his affection misjudged Hawthorne, who shared little of Long Ghost's "vagabondism" or Queequeg's freedom from New England inhibitions.

On July 29 Melville signed an agreement with Richard Bentley to publish *The Whale* in England. Now he was ready for mad capers. On Melville's thirty-second birthday, on August 1, Hawthorne noted in his journal that after a visit to the post office he started home and sat down "to read the papers. While thus engaged, a cavalier on horseback came along the road, and saluted me in Spanish; to which I replied by touching my hat, and went on with the newspaper. But the cavalier renewing his salutation, I regarded him more attentively, and saw that it was Herman Melville!"

No doubt by chance Melville had come across a Spanish costume somewhere in the attic, perhaps one of the garments worn by Thomas Melvill in his prosperous and romantic days abroad before he became an unsuccessful farmer at Pittsfield. That he decided to wear the outfit was not accidental. As his works testify, he was unhappy with his lot as Herman Melville early in life and delighted in assuming new roles and in baptizing himself with new names. Nor was it accidental that he decided to visit Hawthorne as a cavalier, a lover. It was by chance, though, that when he rode to Lenox, Hawthorne happened to be sitting in "Love Grove." The loom of fate was more subtle than even Melville assumed. For the Spanish costume recalled the heroics of Jack Chase recorded in the book Melville wrote before *Moby-Dick,* where, coincidentally, he referred for the first time to Hawthorne. Chase, that other middle-aged Apollo, jumped ship and joined the Peruvian army. One day he returned, we learn in a chapter entitled "Jack Chase on a Spanish Quarter-deck," "clad in the Peruvian uniform, and with a fine, mixed material and naval step, a tall, striking figure of a long-bearded officer." Later in the voyage Chase "regaled us, in his own free and noble style, with the *Spanish Ladies,*" drawing presumably upon his amorous exploits as a Don Juan.

Later that evening the two men indulged in "ontological heroics." For the first time Hawthorne described the scene. "After supper, I put Julian to bed; and Melville and I had a talk about time and eternity, things of this world and of the next, and books, and publishers, and all possible and impossible matters, that lasted pretty deep into the night, and if truth must be told, we smoked cigars even within the sacred precincts of the sitting-room." Sophia was not at home to protect her "sitting-room," but Elizabeth Melville was at home while her husband celebrated his birthday with the kind of male camaraderie that delighted him more than domestic bliss, particularly with a wife who, as her pregnancy advanced, was anxious and highstrung. Two days after the male celebration Elizabeth could not complete a letter to her stepmother: "I cannot write any more — it makes me terribly nervous — I don't know as you can read this I have scribbled it so."

Elizabeth's nervousness did not interfere with her husband's vacation from his literary labors. On August 6 Evert and George Duyckinck arrived, almost on the anniversary of the visit of Mathews and Evert. Immediately Mrs. Morewood, as on the earlier occasion, became the hostess of sometimes frenzied festivities. On August 8 the Duyckincks and Melville called on Hawthorne and after drinking "our only remaining bottle of Mr. Mansfield's champaigne" went to the Shaker Settlement at Hancock, Julian joining the men. Hawthorne was so stimulated after the departure of his guests that "I would rather have ridden the six miles to Pittsfield, than have gone to bed." The next day he still "felt the better for the expedition of yesterday," and Julian affirmed "that he wanted to go again, and that he loved Mr. Melville as well as me, and as mamma, and as Una."

Late in August Melville received an advance of £150 from Bentley. His brother Allan, like Gansevoort years earlier, conducted most of the arrangements. He sent off the proof sheets to Bentley on September 10, and two days later acted as his brother's attorney in the formal agreement with Harper and Brothers for publication in New York after the appearance of the English edition.

At about this time Melville made two changes in his book. He altered the title from *The Whale,* although it was to retain that name in England, and, more important, there was a new dedication —

In Token
of my admiration for his genius,
This book is inscribed
to
NATHANIEL HAWTHORNE.

Moby-Dick was truly a "token" not only to the "genius" but to the "presence" of a man who fulfilled a life-long dream. In the pages of *The Literary World* a year earlier Herman proclaimed Hawthorne's "genius" and the impact upon his being of a "magnetic man." The letters he wrote after the meeting on August 5, 1850, demonstrated the almost child-like trust he placed in one to whom he confided his inner secrets with a candor not characteristic of a nature schooled in self-protective evasions. During the year Melville and Ahab wrestled with the white whale, he knew that only six miles away was a fellow artist who also had entered the dark abysses of the human soul but who was willing to engage in "ontological heroics" over cigars and to listen as he poured out metaphysics as hopelessly entwined to his psychic needs as Moby Dick is to Ahab's soul. Hawthorne was there as a quiet monument of strength, beauty, and success — or paternity. He was also there as a rival who offered an unspoken challenge to the "growing man" or "son."

The subject matter of *Moby-Dick* was established before he met Hawthorne. There may be traces of Hawthorne's influence upon the novel, similarities to "Ethan Brand" and *The Scarlet Letter,* for example, and a preoccupation with monomaniacs and "the power of blackness," but in the creation of Jackson in *Redburn,* which was written before he read or met Hawthorne, Melville was already moving toward *Moby-Dick.* Shakespeare and Milton were more important as literary influences than Hawthorne, but Hawthorne was not a book, but a presence, perhaps a kind of shrine against which he tossed his ideas while his novel was broiling in hell-fire. As he labored to give birth to *Moby-Dick,* Hawthorne was there to steady him, perhaps not so much in fact as in Melville's hungry imagination.

Stimulated to emulate and rival, Melville acquired greater control over his undisciplined pen, and finally brought the discordant elements of his genius into glorious harmony. It may have been a happy accident that Melville met Hawthorne, but it was not an accident that Hawthorne immediately assumed a "leviathanic" aura in Melville's eyes. *Moby-Dick* was a gift worthy of the giver and the receiver.

"Infants,
Boys, and Men,
and
Ifs Eternally"

—Moby-Dick

"Call me Ishmael." The words reverberate like the opening chords of Beethoven's *Fifth Symphony*. If the vowels are lengthened and intoned in low register, there is the crooning of death or tragedy. If the voice is lightened and the intonation unforced, the five syllables rock gayly, heralding birth, life, and, above all, the joys of art. Either reading is appropriate; both harmonies, of life and death, comedy and tragedy, resound in the words themselves. Now after five experiments master of his art, Melville will write in the elementary rhythms of the erotic and dying body, moods alternating from suicidal depressions to euphoric delights, the swings or gyrations of the manias which characterize man and his artifact, civilization. The book will mirror the characters, the characters the book, the destroyer becoming the creator and the creator the destroyer. The book will not arrive at stasis; nothing remains stationary or fixed, in life or in art. "There is no steady unretracing progress in this life,"

Major Thomas Melvill.
Oil portrait, Francis Alexander.
Old State House.
Photograph: Barney Burstein.

Allan Melvill (1810).
Watercolor, John Rubens Smith.
The Metropolitan Museum of Art,
bequest of
Miss Charlotte E. Hoadley,
1946.

Lemuel Shaw,
Chief Justice of Massachusetts.
Daguerreotype by
Southworth and Hawes (1851).
The Metropolitan Museum of Art,
gift of Edward S. Hawes,
Alice Mary Hawes,
Marion A. Hawes, 1938.

Allan Melvill (c. 1820).
Oil portrait, Ezra Ames.
Henry E. Huntington Library
and Art Gallery.

Gansevoort Melville.
Gansevoort-Lansing Collection,
Manuscripts
and Archives Division,
The New York Public Library,
Astor, Lenox
and Tilden Foundations.

Maria Ganesvoort Melvill (c. 1820).
Oil portrait, Ezra Ames.
The Berkshire Athenaeum,
Pittsfield, Massachusetts.

Elizabeth Shaw Melville (c. 1847).
Daguerreotype
—*The Berkshire Athenaeum,*
Pittsfield, Massachusetts.

Herman Melville (c. 1847).
Oil portrait, Asa W. Twitchell.
The Berkshire Athenaeum,
Pittsfield, Massachusetts.

Monument Mountain, near Stockbridge, Massachusetts
— scene of the meeting of Melville and Hawthorne on August 5, 1850.

The Melville children (c. 1860). Stanwyck, Frances, Malcolm, Elizabeth.
Photograph: The Berkshire Athenaeum, Pittsfield, Massachusetts.

athaniel Hawthorne (c. 1852).
il portrait, George P. A. Healey.
ew Hampshire Historical Society.

Nathaniel Hawthorne (1860).
Oil portrait
from photograph taken in 1860.
*Essex Institute,
Salem, Massachusetts.*

Herman Melville (1861).
*Photograph: Rodney Dewey.
The Berkshire Athenaeum,
Pittsfield, Massachusetts.*

Herman Melville (1870).
*Gansevoort-Lansing Collection,
Manuscripts
and Archives Division,
The New York Public Library,
Astor, Lenox
and Tilden Foundations.*

Herman and Elizabeth Melville (1885). *Photographs by Rockwood.*
New York Public Library, Gansevoort-Lansing Collection.

Grave of Herman Melville.
Woodlawn Cemetery,
Bronx, New York.

HERMAN MELVILLE.
Born August 1. 1819,

Ishmael will note as he tells a story without end; "we do not advance through fixed gradations, and at the last one pause: — through infancy's unconscious spell, boyhood's thoughtless faith, adolescence' doubt (the common doom), then scepticism, then disbelief, resting at last in manhood's pondering repose of If. But once gone through, we trace the round again; and are infants, boys, and men, and Ifs eternally."

In the opening chord the narrator dies, his identity a well-kept secret, and is reborn as Ishmael. Unlike the earlier narrators he does not wait for natives to baptize him Tommo or sailors to christen him Buttons. Ishmael performs the baptismal rite himself, and names himself after a mythic outcast fated to wander in the wilderness far from the protective mantle of Father Abraham. Over his rebirth he officiates gayly with banter and jest which do not quite hide the loneliness and the absence of a comforting social or family structure.

> Call me Ishmael. Some years ago — never mind how long precisely — having little or no money in my purse, and nothing particular to interest me on shore, I thought I would sail about a little and see the watery part of the world. It is a way I have of driving off the spleen, and regulating the circulation. Whenever I find myself growing grim about the mouth; whenever it is a damp, drizzly November in my soul; whenever I find myself involuntarily pausing before coffin warehouses, and bringing up the rear of every funeral I meet; and especially whenever my hypos get such an upper hand of me, that it requires a strong moral principle to prevent me from deliberately stepping into the street, and methodically knocking people's hats off — then, I account it high time to get to sea as soon as I can. This is my substitute for pistol and ball. With a philosophical flourish Cato throws himself upon his sword; I quietly take to the ship.

This comic recital masks reality, that Ishmael goes to sea not only because he is without funds but also because he is afflicted with "hypos," or depressions. The paragraph expands and contracts, euphoric in its comic tone and depressive in its subject matter, the verbal and structural equivalents of the rhythms upon which the book rests.

The *Pequod*, named after a fierce Indian tribe which the Christians of New England extinguished in the name of God, sails on Christmas day, that festive season of joy and birth of a child without an earthly father, on a mission of death, the destruction of whales, "in order to light the gay bridals and other merry-makings of men, and also to illuminate the solemn churches that preach unconditional inoffensiveness by all to all." It is captained by a man who buries himself in his cabin — "It feels like going down into one's tomb," he observes, "for an old captain like me to be descending this narrow scuttle, to go to my grave-dug berth" — until the year is reborn in the spring, at Easter time, that festival of death which culminates in rebirth.

The crew leaves behind the green land for "that rocking life imparted by a gently rolling ship; by her, borrowed from the sea; by the sea, from the inscrutable tides of God." The ship is a cradle endlessly rocking, providing escape from family and release from responsibility, as well as livelihood; but, exposed to the whims of the elements and to the dangers that whale-killers will fall victim of killer whales, it is also a coffin endlessly rocking. In Ishmael's words, "you cannot sit motionless in the heart of these perils, because the boat is rocking like a cradle, and you are pitched one way and the other, without the slightest warning; and only by a certain self-adjusting buoyancy and simultaneousness of volition and action, can you escape being made a Mazeppa of, and run away with where the all-seeing sun himself could never pierce you out."

Before Captain Ahab emerges from his cabin-tomb and becomes a presence and a voice, he is only a sound: "Soon his steady, ivory stride was heard, as to and fro he paced his old rounds, upon planks so familiar to his tread, that they were all over dented, like geological stones, with the peculiar mark of his walk." Ahab hobbles on a leg made of a whale's jawbone, "a living thump and a dead thump." The resonance of his feet is married to the life-death rhythm of the sea. "And had you watched Ahab's face that night, you would have thought that in him also two different things were warring. While his one live leg made lively echoes along the deck, every stroke of his dead limb sounded like a coffin-tap. On life and death this old man walked."

Ahab's step is "nervous," wavering more uncertainly than he is wont to admit except in rare moments when he briefly unveils the ravaging inner drama, between the frenzied propulsion to take vengeance upon a white whale and the heart-awareness that this pursuit dehumanizes him, robbing him of the joys of wife and child whom he has abandoned in Nantucket. In laming him the whale lames his universe, and compels him in his age to replay the oedipal drama of his youth. The "nervous" step is but an external manifestation of "moody Ahab," a fifty-eight-year-old sea captain who has spent forty years, not seeking the Promised Land, but in "the masoned, walled-town of a Captain's exclusiveness . . . fed upon dry salted fare — fit emblem of the dry nourishment of my soul." "In his inclement, howling old age," Ishmael observes, "Ahab's soul, shut up in the caved trunk of his body, there fed upon the sullen paws of its gloom!"

The "dry nourishment" begins when he is but twelve months old with the death of his father followed shortly by the death of his mother. (The parallel to Melville's own lot is hardly accidental.) He has been cheated by his parents: so like his father he cheats "the young girl-wife" he has "wedded past fifty," making her "a widow with her husband alive!" and like his mother he abandons the son. If the whale lames him he takes his revenge in laming his son, who, like Ishmael at the close of the tale, will be but "another orphan." Worse still, it is seemingly predestined that Ahab cannot succeed as father-husband where his own parents failed.

Ahab is in his own words "a forty years' fool — fool — old fool." He marries as death beckons, flees his bride after a one-night honeymoon to the captain's cabin where the world conforms to a familiar, masculine structure and shortly loses his leg in an unsuccessful attempt to kill a white whale. Ironically, Ahab physically resembles the whale. Wrinkled, humped, and disfigured, he bears the scars of his "elemental strife at sea"; "Threading its way out from among his grey hairs, and continuing right down one side of his tawny scorched face and neck, till it disappeared in his clothing, you saw a slender rod-like mark, lividly whitish. It resembled that perpendicular seam sometimes made in the straight, lofty trunk of a great tree, when the upper lightning tearingly darts down it, and without wrenching a single twig, peels and grooves the bark from top to bottom, ere running off into the soul, leaving the tree still greenly alive, but branded." The whale bears scars of wounds inflicted by man's destructive instincts, has a hideously deformed lower jaw, and in its flanks carries harpoons hurled into its mammoth but defenseless body. As the whale writhes from the pangs of foreign matter which it is powerless to remove, so Ahab suffers the prickling twinges of his missing leg — "a dismasted man never entirely loses the feeling of his old spar."

The whale inflicts the punishment which Ahab seeks after his attempts at sexuality and fatherhood — the loss of a leg or castration. The wound, as in Tommo's case, frees Ahab from the "interrelatedness" and unwelcome responsibilities of heterosexuality and restores an egocentric infantile world, where Ahab rules his "family," the crew of the *Pequod*, like a willful child. To his undernourished soul is given the power of speech which elevates him above other weather-logged New England captains of whalers. He glories in maniacal outbursts of rhetoric that reverberate beyond the unheroic confines of nineteenth-century profit-and-loss and the language of an industrial age which shrinks diction to its own unimaginative, pragmatic purposes. In speech Ahab evokes the verbal glories of Shakespeare, Marlowe, Milton, and the Bible, of those heroic ages when great men died with grandeur in a divinely ordered universe. The oversized rant corresponds to Ahab's oversized purpose, so all consuming and one-directional that it takes on a "crazy" kind of greatness because sane men are usually incapable of his intellectual and visceral dedication, his incredible attention span. Yet at the same time the rhetoric parodies what is essentially not a tragic view of life, but monomaniacal reductionism and oversimplification. His madness feeds upon the rhetoric as the rhetoric in turn feeds upon the madness.

Madness pervades the book, sanity vying with insanity as in Ishmael's witty opening paragraph. It is also Ishmael who says, "we are all somehow dreadfully cracked about the head, and sadly need mending." "Gnawed within and scorched without," Ahab is given to outbursts of self-inflation so outrageous, particularly in his Elizabethan diction, as to render paranoia poetic. He is ready to hurl his thin, gnarled body against the sun itself, to assume Prometheus' mantle, and to ape Milton's Satan in his warfare against the deity. Such is the boundless aggression born of his depressions and seething rage. Ahab's paranoia is traceable to his first year of life when he suffered the loss of his father and nursed at the breast of a "crazy, widowed mother" until she too died. This deprivation almost at birth produces the "dry nourishment" of his maturity and anxiety about his sanity long before he is attacked by the whale.

Before Ishmael and Queequeg board the *Pequod* they meet a prophet named Elijah, who hints darkly about "Old Thunder." Ishmael dismisses Elijah, "You must be a little damaged in the head." At the first meeting of Ahab and his officers, Stubb, the jolly man who handles problems by stuffing his gullet, is called "a dog." Stubb protests the epithet and is almost ready to strike Ahab. "He's about the queerest old man Stubb ever sailed with," he says to himself. "How he flashed at me! – his eyes like powder-pans! is he mad?" Here Stubb quietly makes explicit what "cracked" Elijah only hints. Soon Ahab informs the crew of his scheme to take revenge in a wild speech that hypnotizes the men, including Ishmael, to accept Ahab's madness as their sanity. Only Starbuck, the first mate, protests: "Vengeance on a dumb brute! ... that simply smote thee from blindest instinct! Madness! To be enraged with a dumb thing, Captain Ahab, seems blasphemous." Later, alone in his cabin, Ahab declaims with psychotic brilliance: "They think me mad – Starbuck does; but I'm demoniac, I am madness maddened!" Also alone, at the mainmast, Starbuck admits, "My soul is more than matched; she's overmanned; and by a madman!" The crew, under the influence of the grog which Ahab freely dispenses, bursts into song and dance – "Merry-mad!" in the words of the French Sailor.

Ishmael reacts to Ahab's speech with "a wild, mystical, sympathetical feeling," surrendering himself to the captain's will, but not wholly, for at the same time as narrator he begins what at first sight appears to be an objective analysis of Ahab's madness. "All that most maddens and torments; all that stirs up the lees of things; all truth with malice in it; all that cracks the sinews and cakes the brain; all the subtle demonisms of life and thought; all evil, to crazy Ahab, were visibly personified, and made practically assailable in Moby Dick. He piled upon the whale's white hump the sum of all the general rage and hate felt by his whole race from Adam down; and then, as if his chest had been a mortar, he burst his hot heart's shell upon it." Ahab has not lost "his great natural intellect," Ishmael avers. "If such a furious trope may stand, his special lunacy stormed his general sanity, and carried it, and turned all its concentred cannon upon its own mad mark; so that far from having lost his strength, Ahab, to that one end, did now possess a thousand fold more potency than ever he had sanely brought to bear upon one reasonable object."

As the cruise continues, Ahab's madness deepens and seems almost to infect the environment. The *Pequod* meets the *Jeroboam*, which has in its crew a man named Gabriel, who, like Elijah, predicts Ahab's doom and "in his gibbering insanity" pronounces "the White Whale to be no less a being than the Shaker God incarnated," a remark no less absurd than Ahab's projection of his despair upon the whale. Aboard the *Pequod* is a little black boy named Pip, not much of a sailor but an entertainer on the tambourine. The chapter entitled "The Castaway," one of the most poignant in the book, records the plight of this frightened, cowardly lad who for the second time falls out of a boat in pursuit of a whale and, according to established custom, the whale being more important than the fate of a crew member, is abandoned in the middle of the ocean, an infinitesimal mortal in the vast, blank sea. Finally he is rescued: "The sea had jeeringly kept his finite body up, but drowned the infinite of his soul." Pip dies and is reborn a Shakespearean fool, "crazy-witty." Or, to put it another way, Pip emerges from an American genre painting with its racial stereotypes, and in his lunacy, like Ahab, assumes the grandeur of another time, another place. "Pip saw the multitudinous, God-omnipresent, coral insects, that out of the firmament of waters heaved the colossal orbs. He saw God's foot upon the treadle of the loom, and spoke it; and therefore his shipmates called him mad. So man's insanity is heaven's sense."

This episode of traumatic isolation is followed by "A Squeeze of the Hand," which presents a hilarious picture of Ishmael, so overcome by the aroma of the sperm that he bathes his hands in the globules along with the other sailors. Soon "a strange sort of insanity came over me; and I found myself unwittingly squeezing my co-

laborers' hands in it, mistaking their hands for the gentle globules."
Unlike Pip, he has a vision of universal brotherhood: "let us all
squeeze ourselves into each other; let us squeeze ourselves universally
into the very milk and sperm of kindness." In the midst of what
approximates an autoerotic experience, he claims to see "long rows
of angels in paradise, each with his hands in a jar of spermaceti" — a
projection as "crazy" as any of Ahab's. But a short time later, in
another light, the fiery glow about the try-pots where the sperm is
rendered, Ishmael swings to another, less emotional perspective:
"There is a wisdom that is woe; but there is a woe that is madness."

Ahab befriends Pip, even shares his cabin with a "son" who has
experienced betrayal similar to his own. Yet Pip is "too crazy-witty
for my sanity," he avers. Nothing, not even this pathetic relationship,
keeps Ahab from his mission, from being Ahab, the betrayer of his
"sons." The ship begins to draw water. "Let it leak!" he screams to
Starbuck; "I'm all aleak myself." Later as "moody Ahab" watches
the sparks of the blacksmith's forge, he ruminates: "In no Paradise
myself, I am impatient of all misery in others that is not mad. Thou
should'st go mad, blacksmith; say, why dost thou not go mad? How
can'st thou endure without being mad? Do the heavens yet hate thee,
that thou can'st not go mad?" As the time approaches for the encounter with the whale, his brain throbs, his newly fashioned leg
twitches, and his wounded groin simulates orgasm. To Pip he cries:
"Pip, we'll talk this over; I do suck most wondrous philosophies from
thee! Some unknown conduits from the unknown worlds must
empty into thee!" From poor Pip he seeks what fifty-seven years
earlier his mother denied him — the consolation of the breast.

The manic alternations in speech and mood, running the gamut
of hysterical excitement to paralyzing depression, reflect anxieties
and repressions difficult to articulate. The speeches resound with an
agonizing, pounding sense of loss, and since the book, despite
Ishmael's disclaimers, is on one level "a hideous and intolerable
allegory," even the bodies reflect the deprivations. In speech and act
the characters struggle to reconstitute their dismembered bodies and
emotions, the allegory confirming the psychological need at the
center of the book.

Stripped of his bombast, Ahab is mostly patches, his mind and
body scarred from the moment he becomes an orphan in his first
year. Ishmael, another orphan, seeks at sea to regain emotional and
intellectual equilibrium, to reconstitute his shattered self-image
which has led him to contemplate suicide. Except possibly for the
tattoo on his right arm, Ishmael bears no physical scars of psychic
loss, but other characters are as wounded in one way or another as
the whale itself and its pursuer. Elijah's left arm is withered or

missing, and his face resembles "the complicated ribbed bed of a torrent" because of the "confluent small-pox." During the journey Ahab meets Captain Boomer, who has "a white arm of sperm whale bone, terminating in a wooden head like a mallet." Because Boomer is also a victim of Moby Dick, Ahab greets him eagerly, with a comic sense not usually in evidence: "With his ivory arm frankly thrust forth in welcome, the other captain advanced, and Ahab, putting out his ivory leg, and crossing the ivory arm (like two sword-fish blades) cried out in his walrus way, 'Aye, aye, hearty! let us shake bones together! — an arm and a leg! — an arm that never can shrink, d'ye see; and a leg that never can run.' " The blacksmith has lost "the extremities of both feet" because of exposure during a bout of drunkenness.

More traumatic than these bodily wounds are the psychic losses. Bulkington, a sailor of Michelangelesque proportions, "with noble shoulders, and a chest like a coffer-dam," is cursed by "some reminiscences that did not seem to give him much joy," and, like Ahab, cannot tolerate existence on land. Starbuck has lost a father and brother at sea. Pip abandons in the indifferent sea what little sanity he is born with. Perhaps worst of all — and most prophetic — is the plight of Captain Gardiner of the *Rachel.* Only the day before meeting the *Pequod*, he sent out boats in pursuit of Moby Dick, but when darkness set in, one boat was missing, bearing his twelve-year-old son. Gardiner begs Ahab to join him in search of the lad, but Ahab refuses "in a voice that prolongingly moulded every word — 'Captain Gardiner, I will not do it. Even now I lose time. Good bye, good bye. God bless ye, man, and may I forgive myself, but I must go.' " Slave to his purpose, although the voice reveals his conflict, Ahab cannot take time out to pity a twelve-year-old youth any more than the world had time to waste on a twelve-month-old orphan. In betraying the youth he plays out the role of Father Abraham, but since the lad is the young Ahab, it is self-punishment. In spurning Captain Gardiner's pleas he retaliates upon his own father, but his frenzy to go on to his own destruction may be an unconscious recognition of his feelings of guilt.

Paternal rejection lies behind the first sentence when Ishmael evokes the myth of Abraham and the son's loss. Although the narrator reveals little about his own background, except that he, like his predecessors in Melville's writings, is of good stock, the history of Ahab's youth, brief as it is, establishes a bond of mutual loss between the two characters. The fate of Gardiner's son later becomes, then, the third allusion to Melville's own lot at age twelve when Allan Melvill lost his wits and gave up his unhappy life. "Call me Ishmael" can also be translated, "Call me Allan Melvill's son."

Unlike the biblical Ishmael, who journeys into the wilderness attended by Hagar, and finally fathers races of men, the fictional Ishmael has, according to Melville's invariable formula, to seek a "bosom friend" to replace both Hagar and Abraham. Ishmael is attracted, like L. A. V. and White-Jacket, to an older man and, like Tommo, to a South Seas native, a prince named Queequeg, who leaves his home to seek experience in the "civilized" world and in his flight avoids matrimonial and social responsibilities. With this tattooed cannibal, who sells heads in New Bedford, and swaggers about with his harpoon — "George Washington cannibalistically developed" — Ishmael experiences a farcical "marriage" and "honeymoon." This caricature of marriage and parenthood is played out in the bedroom of Peter Coffin (a name of obvious significance), on the bed on which he and his wife Sal consummated their union and conceived their children. Ishmael assumes the feminine role and Queequeg asserts, with the usual male duplicity, "I wont touch a leg of ye." In the morning the youth finds himself locked fast in an embrace and a "tomahawk sleeping by the savage's side, as if it were a hatchet-faced baby." As Queequeg dresses and puts on his boots, Ishmael passively watches, playing the voyeur, and Queequeg leaves "sporting his harpoon like a marshal's baton." The episode, with its phallic puns and innuendoes, mocks sexuality and birth, not unlike the rite in *Typee*. The hilarity conceals how intricately it is tied to the subsequent action: to the unnatural behavior of Ahab, who has as "his bedfellow . . . a stick of whale's jaw-bone for a wife," to Ishmael's sterile fantasies in "A Squeeze of the Hand," to the phallic rites in "The Cassock" chapter, which also burlesque fertility and birth, and, finally, to the narrator's arrestment at the conclusion in a state which does not foreshadow the passage of "another orphan" into adult sexuality.

After their "marriage" Ishmael goes to hear Father Mapple preach in a chapel containing marble markers to honor sailors who have died at sea. Before the sermon the congregation sings a hymn describing the "dismal gloom" of a man inside a whale and the delivery eventually granted by God. After ascending his elevated pulpit, pulling up a rope ladder behind him, and enclosing himself in a kind of womb or approximation of a whale's stomach, Mapple retells the story of Jonah, embellishing it with nautical details for his audience of sailors, their families, and survivors. He begins with a significant interpolation, that Jonah is sought by the authorities as a "parricide," and concludes with a paean to the "delights" of service to the Lord. Jonah's is a story of death and rebirth and oral incorporation.

Many commentators have seized upon Mapple's sermon as the

moral cornerstone of the book, ignoring the fact that Melville is an artistic confidence-man, who, in what he called a "wicked book," invites all interpretations but leaves them all in doubt. Jonah first appears in the narrative in the form of a bartender at the Spouter-Inn, where he "dearly sells the sailors deliriums and death." Later there are two travesties of Mapple's seeming eloquence, Fleece's sermon which Stubb forces him to deliver after he dines on the whale's phallus, and the chapter entitled "Jonah Historically Regarded," which is another parody of a subject mocked earlier in *Redburn*: "Jonah himself must have been disappointed when he looked up to the domed midriff surmounting the whale's belly, and surveyed the ribbed pillars around him. A pretty large belly, to be sure, thought I, but not so big as it might have been."

What most effectively undercuts Mapple's sermon is the following scene in which Ishmael and Queequeg, snug in the bedroom, worship the native's little god of "polished ebony" named Yojo, which, spelled backward, proclaims, "O joy." On first seeing Yojo in the Spouter-Inn, Ishmael "almost thought that this black manikin was a real baby preserved." In worshipping the idol they whittle at his nose with mutual "delight." Since Yojo is obviously a phallic deity, and is later linked with the whale's "grandissimus," the whittling takes on other overtones and makes Ishmael's abandonment of his Presbyterianism even more hilarious and outrageous to religious sensibilities. They celebrate Ishmael's conversion with a "social smoke."

The conclusion of the chapter — "Thus, then, in our hearts' honeymoon, lay I and Queequeg — a cosy, loving pair" — contrasts with the preceding one in which Mapple, after heralding the "delight" of service to God, waves the benediction, and, in illustration of the self-denial he espouses, kneels "till all the people had departed, and he was left alone in the place." His parishioners leave with only the memory of his beautiful rhetoric, but in his worship Ishmael "felt a melting in me. No more my splintered heart and maddened hand were turned against the wolfish world." The "topgallant delight" of Mapple's isolation parallels Ahab's incarceration in his own cabin, where he nurses what later he will call his "topmost greatness." But the contrast must be qualified, like most remarks about *Moby-Dick*, for the "melting" of the "honeymooners" is adolescent sexual by-play, as amusing — and sterile — as the antics of Tommo and Long Ghost in *Omoo*.

If the Queequeg-Ishmael relationship parodies marriage, the great scene on the quarter-deck in the spring of the year is also a grim mockery of the life process. Here hate rather than love dominates and sterility and regression suffuse the scene. As Ahab, abstracted and moody, is pacing the deck with "his nervous step," Stubb whispers, "D'ye mark him, Flask? . . . the chick that's in him pecks the shell. T'will soon be out." Assembling the thirty men in the crew for the first time, Ahab cries, "What do ye do when ye see a whale, men?" They shout, "Sing out for him!" "Strangely and fiercely glad and approving," Ahab nails a gold doubloon to the mainmast and promises it to "whosoever of ye raises me a white-headed whale with a wrinkled brow and a crooked jaw. . . . whosoever of ye raises me that same white whale, he shall have this gold ounce, my boys!" Tashtego, one of the native harpooners, mentions the name of the white whale, and at this fateful moment Moby Dick is born. (Later an astonished Spaniard asks, "Sir sailor, but do whales have christenings?") Starbuck establishes the connection, that Moby Dick has "dismasted" Ahab, and the captain confirms the fact with "a terrific, loud, animal sob, like that of a heart-stricken moose." He quickly recovers from his pain and self-pity, and "with measureless imprecations" gives birth to his plan for revenge upon Moby Dick: "That is what ye have shipped for, men! . . . What say ye, men, will ye splice hands on it now?" These "sons of bachelors," as the ship owner describes them when they set out from Nantucket, "marry" themselves to Ahab's "crazy" purpose.

To celebrate the "splicing" Ahab orders grog for the sailors, and with "the bloodshot eyes of the prairie wolves," he supervises what is a perversion of "a noble custom of my fisherman fathers before me." With the grog the boy-men "incorporate" his will. Starbuck, aware that he is "overmanned," deplores "such a heathen crew that have small touch of human mothers in them!" and endeavors, but in the safety of monolog, to reassert the normal order of birth and fertility. Stubb laughs "because a laugh's the wisest, easiest answer to all that's queer," and, thinking of his wife, wonders, "What's my juicy little pear at home doing now?" At midnight the sailors are still drinking, singing sea chanties, dancing, some of the men in the darkness playing at being women. At the height of an orgy which recalls the landscape of boyhood, the English sailor makes the regression explicit: "Blood! but that old man's a grand old cove! We are the lads to hunt him up his whale!" And all shout, "Aye! aye!" The child Pip has, ironically, the last word in this "Merry-mad" scene — "that anaconda of an old man swore 'em to hunt him! Oh, thou big white God aloft there somewhere in yon darkness, have mercy on this small black boy down here; preserve him from all men that have no bowels to feel fear!"

"I, Ishmael, was one of that crew," he records; "my shouts had gone up with the rest; my oath had been welded with theirs; and stronger I shouted, and more did I hammer and clinch my oath, because of the dread in my soul." Ishmael soon finds not only the right words to characterize the response of his "*greedy* ears" to Ahab's "*quenchless* feud," but also an explanation for the behavior of the sailors. The whaleman, he alleges, "is wrapped by influences all tending to make his fancy *pregnant* with many a mighty *birth*." Lonely and superstitious, sailors "*incorporate* with themselves all manner of morbid hints, and half-formed *foetal suggestions* of supernatural agencies." Hence they "hearken with a *childish* fire-side interest and awe, to the wild, strange tales of Southern whaling." Once again, as in his account of his "incorporation" of Hawthorne, Melville in his diction exposes the psychic need and the deprivations behind the seemingly impulsive and even melodramatic behavior of his characters. At another point Ishmael likens the combat between man and whale to the child's misconstruction of sexuality as assault and to the struggles of a fetus emerging from the womb: "amid the chips of chewed boats, and the sinking limbs of torn comrades," whalehunters swim "out of the white curds of the whale's direful wrath into the serene, exasperating sunlight, . . . as if at a birth or a bridal."

What Ishmael does not articulate is that Ahab's elemental appeal is not only verbal but also physical. For the missing leg is a wound near the genitals, "The dead thump" a constant reminder of castration. In joining Ahab in pursuit of Moby Dick, the crew reveals unconscious castration fears, that loss of malehood which the "bad father" threatens. Ahab's actual loss is the universal fantasized loss. If Ahab is avenged, they are reassured of their masculinity.

The book constantly parodies the birth process, partly because art itself is a parody of fertility, a self-parody as it were, but also because *Moby-Dick* like its principal characters is fixated upon elemental processes. Queequeg, as marked with tattoos as Ahab is with scars, demonstrates "great skill in obstetrics" on two occasions. On the way to Nantucket, Queequeg rescues a "poor bumpkin" who falls overboard. Later when Tashtego plunges into the mouth of a whale, Queequeg goes to his assistance: "He averred that upon first thrusting in for him, a leg was presented; but well knowing that that was not as it ought to be, and might occasion great trouble; — he had thrust back the leg, and by a dexterous heave and toss, had wrought a somerset upon the Indian; so that with the next trial, he came forth in the good old way — head foremost." Queequeg joyfully functions as an obstetrician because he sees the birth process not as a threat to human survival but as a bond with the mother that must be severed in the natural course of events.

Ahab, on the other hand, is fixated upon the potential disasters at birth: "Born in throes, 't is fit that man should live in pains and

die in pangs!" His half-truth, vomited out of his racking despair,
rationalizes his self-destructive dedication to a life in which he spits
out his hate as the mother in his warped view spits out the child.
Ahab's perspective is clouded and distorted by his earliest experience, parental betrayal, which he turns into self-hatred but cloaks
even perhaps from himself with his paranoid self-aggrandizement. He
is helplessly entwined and his actions tragically predetermined. The
most meaningful bond of his pained life is his "crazy" love-hate
relationship with a whale, the most colossal of God's creations but
indifferent to man's existence, as colossal and indifferent as parents
seem to a child. Ahab is fated to witness on the last day of the chase
a terrifying confirmation of his fears. Fedallah, a faithful but mysterious aide who, like the witches in *Macbeth*, utters ambiguous proph-
ecies, disappears on the second day. On the following morning the
captain again sights Moby Dick and beholds Fedallah strangled in a
man-made umbilical cord: "Lashed round and round to the fish's
back; pinioned in the turns upon turns in which, during the past
night, the whale had reeled the involutions of the lines around him,
the half torn body of the Parsee was seen; his sable raiment frayed to
shreds; his distended eyes turned full upon old Ahab." Fedallah's
staring, dead eyes do not turn Ahab to flight; his course is fixed, his
life too painful to bear. "The harpoon was darted; the stricken whale
flew forward; with igniting velocity the line ran through the groove;
— ran foul. Ahab stooped to clear it; he did clear it; but the flying
turn caught him round the neck, and voicelessly as Turkish mutes
bowstring their victim, he was shot out of the boat, ere the crew
knew he was gone." There is only silence — not even a final scream —
as, entwined in the cord, Ahab experiences once more the throes-
pains-pangs of birth-death.

After Ahab nails the doubloon to the masthead, various members of the crew comment on the symbols on the gold coin, each one
interpreting them in terms of his life experience and self-image. Similarly attitudes toward birth and sexuality are refracted in narcissistic
mirrors. Ishmael joyfully participates in playful sexual parodies both
in his "honeymoon" and in the sperm-squeezing scene, the experiences conforming to adolescent homosexual attractions prior to heterosexual engagements. The manic tone of the episodes accords with
the carefree sterility of the actions and protects them from serious
analysis. Melville appears to impose upon the latter episode more
than the egocentric pleasures of masturbation allow, except in foolish rationalizations, when he has Ishmael assert that "attainable felic-
ity" is not "in the intellect or the fancy; but in the wife, the heart,
the bed, the table, the saddle, the fire-side, the country" — all of
which Ishmael flees when he goes to sea in pursuit of the "white

phantom," just as Melville himself avoids such subject matter in his books except in *Pierre*, which is a strange and "mad" version of the domestic novel.

Immediately after the solitary pleasures of "A Squeeze of the Hand," follows "The Cassock," where there is a nineteenth-century whaling-ship version of ancient phallic rites without precedent in American literature before Walt Whitman, except for mild intimations in Hawthorne's "The Maypole of Merry Mount." The mincer wears "canonicals" made of the whale's "unaccountable cone" or "grandissimus," which is the same color as Queequeg's phallic god Yojo and not unlike Father Mapple's attire. He is "arrayed in decent black; occupying a conspicuous pulpit, intent on bible leaves; what a candidate for an archbishoprick, what a lad for a Pope were this mincer!" The pun and the reference to the mincer's youth keep the episode in an adolescent framework, where sexual exhibitionism is part of the growth process. But when Ishmael alludes to the idols worshipped by Queen Maachah and King Asa, as described in 1 Kings 15, he underscores the blasphemy and the social destructiveness of priapic cults. Such awareness, however, does not diminish one whit his pleasure in this Rabelaisian scene.

Similarly, Ishmael delights in the sexual suggestiveness and innuendoes in "A Bower In the Arsacides," where his exploration of the whale's skeleton resembles sexual intercourse, and his interest in measurements is not without phallic overtones. Although the Arsacides are a group of islands in the South Seas, the name must have delighted him on two scores: it provides another opportunity for an anal joke, the first of which appears in the opening chapter, and "Arsacides" suspiciously resembles "parricide," a subject introduced by Father Mapple and of particular interest to "sons of bachelors" who have not outgrown castration fears. "A Bower In the Arsacides" operates on a primitive anal, oral, and genital level.

These scenes of "simple child's play" indicate clearly Ishmael's recognition of the infantile sexual play in which he indulges. Ahab is devoid of a sense of play; his boundless aspiration to become a "manmaker" affords him no pleasure. Unlike Ishmael, Ahab is unaware of how he perverts the myth of Narcissus. When the carpenter is fashioning another leg for him — for the third time his limb has been shattered — he conjures up "that old Greek, Prometheus, who made men, they say." Swept away by his vision, he sees himself as a god: "While Prometheus is about it, I'll order a complete man after a desirable pattern. Imprimis, fifty feet high in his socks; then, chest modelled after the Thames Tunnel; then, legs with roots to 'em, to stay in one place; then, arms three feet through the wrists; no heart at all, brass forehead, and about a quarter of an acre of fine brains;

and let me see — shall I order eyes to see outwards? No, but put a sky-light on top of his head to illuminate inwards." Then, as though in retaliation for his heartless aspiration, he is humbled and humanized by the pain he feels where once there was a leg ("Canst thou not drive that old Adam away?"); he cries: "Oh, Life! Here I am, proud as Greek god, and yet standing debtor to this blockhead [the carpenter] for a bone to stand on! Cursed be that mortal inter-indebtedness which will not do away with ledgers." Finally, his exhilaration crumbles into self-abasement and a longing for death: "I'll get a crucible, and into it, and dissolve myself down to one small, compendious vertebra." After the captain leaves, the carpenter muses that "he's queer — queer — queer."

When the *Pequod* enters the South Sea, Ishmael is enraptured by the "serene Pacific": "Lifted by those eternal swells, you needs must own the seductive god, bowing your head to Pan." The captain, "standing like an iron statue at his accustomed place beside the mizzen rigging," has "but few thoughts of Pan" as he looks at "that sea in which the hated White Whale must even then be swimming." In the demonic light of the blacksmith's forge, Ahab ironically refers to "Mother Carey's chickens," which are "birds of good omens," before he orders Perth to fashion a special harpoon of his own devising for the destruction of the white whale. Ahab will not even permit Perth to temper the weapon in water: "I want it of the true death-temper."

The creation of this instrument of death represents the peak and nadir of Ahab's creativity. The mincer harmlessly indulges in phallic play in "The Cassock" episode, but Ahab out of his emotional wounds fashions a monstrous, destructive phallus, a totem of his perversion. His words unwind asymmetrically in the dissonance of madness: " 'Ego non baptizo te in nomine patris, sed in nomine diaboli!' deliriously howled Ahab, as the malignant iron scorchingly devoured the baptismal blood." This, Melville informed Hawthorne, is "the book's motto (the secret one)."

The captain, now more mad than heroic as the time for the encounter with the whale approaches, begins to strip away what few vestiges of humanity he has permitted himself in his fifty-eight years of hate. Early in the narrative he throws away his pipe. Now he destroys the quadrant. "No longer will I guide my earthly way by thee," he cries, a foolish act which is part of his foolish self-aggrandizement. In his chilled universe of absurd "self-reliance" he trusts no one. "With his own hands" he rigs "a nest of basketed bowlines," and orders himself hauled to the masthead, where he rocks, a friendless orphan, an isolate, in a man-made womb. A "red-billed" sea-hawk swoops down upon the "nest" and steals Ahab's hat

— an appropriate rebuke to his inhuman aspirations and a kind of decapitation (or displaced castration) which the captain blithely ignores as his eyes scan the seas for his enemy-lover.

Before the white whale is sighted, the sea asserts the erotic principle, Ishmael matching his prose amorously to "The Symphony."

> It was a clear steel-blue day. The firmaments of air and sea were hardly separable in that all-pervading azure; only, the pensive air was transparently pure and soft, with a woman's look, and the robust and man-like sea heaved with long, strong, lingering swells, as Samson's chest in his sleep. . . .
>
> Aloft, like a royal czar and king, the sun seemed giving this gentler air to this bold and rolling sea; even as bride to groom. And at the girdling line of the horizon, a soft and tremulous motion — most seen here at the equator — denoted the fond, throbbing trust, the loving alarms, with which the poor bride gave her bosom away.

Briefly, for the first and last time Ahab unburdens his heart to Starbuck — "the step-mother world, so long cruel — forbidding — now threw affectionate arms round his stubborn neck." He articulates his impoverishment — "the dry nourishment of my soul" — and bewails the forty years palsied by his foolhood. Suddenly he wants to be touched, to be caressed, and speaks to Starbuck out of a childish vanity: "Here, brush this old hair aside; it blinds me, that I seem to weep. Locks so grey did never grow but from out some ashes! But do I look very old, so very, very old, Starbuck?" The mood, this unnatural-natural desire for an attention he cannot endure, passes quickly, and he snuggles into his mythic grandeur: "I feel deadly faint, bowed, and humped, as though I were Adam, staggering beneath the piled centuries since Paradise." But guilt and self-punishment immediately follow: "God! God! God! — crack my heart! — stave my brain!"

Deceived by this sudden transformation of Ahab into humanity, and thinking that Ahab shares his desire for reunion with his family, Starbuck imagines that the captain is ready to "head for Nantucket." His emotional cry — "See, see! the boy's face from the window! the boy's hand on the hill!" — wells out of his empathic heart, but Ahab cannot tolerate the sight and touch of Starbuck's son, who by extension is his own son — and the young Ahab. "But Ahab's glance was averted; like a blighted fruit tree he shook, and cast his last, cindered apple to the soil." (In the background one may hear the contrasting words which Melville wrote about Hawthorne's spell, "how aptly

might the still fall of his ruddy thoughts into your soul be symbolized by 'the thump of a great apple, in the stillest afternoon, falling
without a breath of wind, from the mere necessity of perfect ripeness!' ") After Starbuck steals away, the captain "crossed the deck to
gaze over on the other side; but started at two reflected, fixed eyes in
the water there." In Narcissus' watery image he sees his own death.

On the following day the chase begins. While Ahab plots murder, the whale cavorts in the smooth sea — "his entire dazzling
hump . . . in a revolving ring of finest, fleecy, greenish foam." Moby
Dick seems to personify the erotic principle, or Pan: "Not the white
bull Jupiter swimming away with ravished Europa clinging to his
graceful horns; his lovely, leering eyes sideways intent upon the
maid; with smooth bewitching fleetness, rippling straight for the nuptial bower in Crete; not Jove, not that great majesty Supreme! did
surpass the glorified White Whale as he so divinely swam." The whale
raises its "marbelized" body out of the water in "a high arch, like
Virginia's Natural Bridge" and "warningly" reveals himself as "the
grand god" before he disappears.

Ahab pursues. Soon Moby Dick's deformed jaw is "within six
inches of Ahab's head," but only shakes the boat "as a mildly cruel
cat her mouse." Moby Dick's dallying only maddens "that monomaniac Ahab, furious with this tantalizing vicinity of his foe," and in
his rage he attempts hand-to-hand combat with the whale's jaw, only
to have his boat upset. The whale withdraws and raises its forehead
"twenty or more feet out of the water" — again erotically but also
"warningly." It playfully circles round and round the wreck until
Ahab orders Starbuck to drive the *Pequod* on Moby Dick. After he is
rescued, "the eternal sap runs up in Ahab's bones again!" — his
monomaniacal rhythms, his love-hate, once more pitting him against
the erotic rhythms of the whale.

On the second day the crew of thirty men, united, as in the
quarter-deck scene for destruction and death, share Ahab's frenzies
which have "worked them bubblingly up, like old wine worked
anew." This time the men see "the wondrous phenomenon of
breaching. Rising with his utmost velocity from the furthest depths,
the Sperm Whale thus booms his entire bulk into the pure element of
air, and piling up a mountain of dazzling foam, shows his place to the
distance of seven miles or more." They witness a wondrous sight
which elicits from Ahab only another murderous curse. This time all
three boats place harpoons in the whale, but the whale's gyrations
cause the crews to become entangled in the lines, and soon the
wrecks "danced round and round, like the grated nutmeg in a swiftly
stirred bowl of punch." Flask bobs up and down "like an empty
vial" near the whale's jaw, Stubb sings out "for some one to ladle

him up," only Ahab's boat is momentarily free to pull into "the creamy pool." (The imagery is truly extraordinary in this scene of birth-death.) Soon Ahab's boat turns over, and when he is saved for the second time, his ivory leg is "but one short sharp splinter." The captain is as unchanging as fate. "Ahab is for ever Ahab, man," he announces. "This whole act's immutably decreed. 'Twas rehearsed by thee and me a billion years before this ocean rolled. Fool! I am the Fates' lieutenant; I act under orders."

The third day dawns "fair and fresh" — "a new-made world," Ahab declares, "and made for a summer-house to the angels." "Here's food for thought," he continues, "had Ahab time to think; but Ahab never thinks; he only feels, feels, feels; *that's* tingling enough for mortal man! to think's audacity." When he discovers that the *Pequod* has "oversailed" the whale, he changes course and steers directly toward Moby Dick's jaw. Once more, for the last time, the whale rises from the water to a height of thirty feet, "leaving the circling surface creamed like new milk round the marble trunk of the whale." Even after he sees Fedallah chained eternally to the whale's belly, Ahab madly pursues. This time the "predestinating head" of Moby Dick attacks the *Pequod* itself. Stubb, true to his nature, cries "for one red cherry ere we die!" Ahab, also true to his nature, orders Tashtego to hammer the red flag to the mast, and then his voice reverberates in a moan, "Oh, lonely death on lonely life! Oh, now I feel my topmost greatness lies in my topmost grief." He girds his loins and voice to pour forth his unending spleen at "thou all-destroying, but unconquering whale": "from hell's heart I stab at thee; for hate's sake I spit my last breath at thee."

As his last "crazy" gesture, no less futile than all the gestures of his life, he hurls at nature's greatest creation a harpoon studded with his hate and fashioned in his pain. At the end as at the beginning of his life there is no illumination, no clarification of his "madness." Ahab is but an intractable child, a fool of fate. There is only the sound of the sea which continues to roll "as it rolled five thousand years ago."

"And I only am escaped alone to tell thee," Ishmael, quoting from Job, writes in the Epilogue, "On the margin of the ensuing scene," he observes the vortex which swallows the *Pequod*. "Round and round, then, and ever contracting towards the button-like black bubble at the axis of that slowly wheeling circle, like another Ixion I did revolve. Till, gaining that vital centre, the black bubble upward burst; and now, liberated by reason of its cunning spring, and owing to its great buoyancy, rising with great force, the coffin life-buoy shot lengthwise from the sea, fell over, and floated by my side. Buoyed up by that coffin, for almost one whole day and night, I floated on a soft and dirge-like main."

Again the birth ritual is reenacted. Queequeg's tattooed coffin emerges from the sea like the whale or a fetus to become Ishmael's cradle, Captain Gardiner does not find his lost son but takes Ishmael aboard the "devious-cruising Rachel," and the mood shifts from death and hate to resignation and perhaps qualified affirmation. For art, despite its subject matter or the artist's predisposition, has "a predestinating head" like Moby Dick. It is fated to affirm, not because it imposes an uncertain but inevitable order upon seeming chaos, in the depiction both of external and internal landscapes, but because the artist himself has a love-hate relationship with life and mortality. As helplessly as Ahab must pursue his fantasy the artist must "scrape" his brain, even when it feels like a nutmeg grater, and harness his emotional and intellectual energies to the creation of an artifact, with a "crazy" rejection of the pleasure principle. Art is after its fashion always a love story.

When Ahab dies and Ishmael is spared, one generation succeeds another according to the ancient formula. In a real sense Ahab fathers Ishmael. If Ahab warps life by fixating his fifty-eight years of hurts upon a whale, he bequeaths his fixation to "another orphan" who in turn will narrate a tale of this "leviathanic" projection of megalomania, self-hatred, and life-hate, and which he will eventually christen *Moby-Dick*. Aboard the *Pequod*, in a patriarchal environment which sanctions his caprices, Ahab is lord, and Ishmael an insignificant seaman, the one active and the other passive. In recording Ahab's fate Ishmael reverses the order and replaces his rival.

Although Ahab and Ishmael never engage in dialog during the cruise, Ishmael enters the other's mind empathically. Like Ahab he himself not only bears the name of a biblical outcast but also worships non-Christian gods and finds companionship with one of an alien culture. Both are foundlings in search of a white phantom, impelled by imperious narcissistic needs, "isolati" from civilization, religion, and family. Ishmael, after falling under Ahab's magnetic sway, gradually in his active-passive reflective way, in monologs and digressions, frees himself and establishes his own identity. Yet the bond between the two is deep, the similarities great. As master of the narrative Ishmael is a match for the master of the *Pequod*. Both are tyrants.

In rage and deprivation but in heroic diction Ahab distorts the cosmos to conform to his own self-image. Not without awareness, although he is powerless to change, he acknowledges his warped perspective: "So far gone am I in the dark side of earth, that its other side, the theoretic bright one, seems but uncertain twilight to me." Ishmael as narrator provides only a partial corrective to Ahab's imbalance. In the midst of the "The Grand Armada" chapter, where the crew observes the mating and nursing habits of whales deep in the sea, Ishmael, looking deep into himself, admits the fissure within: "amid the tornadoed Atlantic of my being, do I myself still for ever centrally disport in mute calm; and while ponderous planets of unwaning woe revolve round me, deep down and deep inland there I still bathe me in eternal mildness of joy."

When Ahab speaks of the "theoretic bright" side of life, almost denying the existence of the sun for the sake of the darkness which harmonizes with his wounds, and Ishmael recognizes the "eternal mildness of joy," a difference in attitude (and art) emerges, although the distinction cannot be drawn too sharply without producing new distortions. Ahab commands not only by means of authoritarian decrees but also by means of his overpowering rhetoric with its magical evocations of timeless fears and tragedies. He strikes verbal postures in borrowed clothing, his language as irrelevant as Don Quixote's silver Latin in the Renaissance wasteland, and like Cervantes' immortal fool he pursues windmills with no time permitted for comedy which of course would undermine his megalomania.

Ishmael, however, is given, as he confesses in the first chapter, to "wild conceits," to salacious jests and scabrous puns, to burlesque and farce, to witty digressions and satire, and often to hilarity, sometimes as manic as Ahab's depressions. He does not serve as an old-fashioned comic norm, a common-sense corrective to Ahab's extremism. There is too much of Ahab's madness in Ishmael's nature for that, but, in true comic fashion, he invokes the unholy trinity, anal, oral, and genital. He ordinarily physicalizes what Ahab sublimates into abstractions and cloaks in the poetry of another time, another place. Yet the resolution of the novel points to the central axiom of the comic perspective, the triumph and survival of the son.

From his evocative opening sentence Ishmael is a virtuoso performer, in his antics witty and sometimes as mad as Ahab, as greedy for a well-turned phrase as the captain is for vengeance. Like Ahab, Ishmael follows a "predestinated" course: "doubtless, my going on this whaling voyage, formed part of the grand programme of Providence that was drawn up a long time ago." At the outset he playfully, but madly, reveals his suicidal course when he burlesques the drama he is about to unfold:

"Grand Contested Election for the Presidency
of the United States.
"WHALING VOYAGE BY ONE ISHMAEL.
"BLOODY BATTLE IN AFFGHANISTAN."

In a few lines he accomplishes three things: he minimizes his own "performance" as an artist, ridicules the narrative, and undercuts Ahab's and his own greatness. Such artistic courage is audacity or "madness," or possibly a little bit of both, certainly worthy of Ahab himself. Psychologically the burlesque is appropriate since it reflects Ishmael's personal instability and covers his aggressiveness with a comic overlay.

After the introductory chapter Ishmael presents a farcical account of his adventures before the ship sails. He falls in and out of bed with Queequeg, juxtaposes Presbyterianism and Yojo-ism, as well as a cannibal and a man of God, introduces a "cracked" prophet in Elijah and "cracked" shipowners in Bildad and Peleg, two Quakers whose religious views clash with their materialistic aspirations. Except for frequent intimations of doom sounding in the background, the first thirty-one chapters are maniacal in their rapid mood shifts and situational changes, picaresque in the seeming random and tentative organization, although the looseness is an artful contrivance in deliberate contrast with the eventual fixation of the book and the two central characters upon the white whale. The farce accords with the nonmanipulative role Ishmael assumes at this point in the narrative both in his passive relationship with Queequeg and in his seemingly offhand attitude toward his narrative.

After Ahab appears and makes his first speech there is a change in Ishmael's role. Beginning with Chapter 32, "Cetology," Ishmael the would-be sailor begins to recede from the center of the farcical stage and Ishmael the artist takes over as a witty commentator and a manipulator of the narrative. In his lengthy discussion of cetology and his casual but essentially systematic anatomy of the whale, he reveals a concentration and obsession equal to Ahab's. As the captain scans the waters in search of Moby Dick, Ishmael surveys all history in his cetological commentary. Where Ahab bears the scars of the ages, weighing the book down with his grandiloquent tragic viewpoint, Ishmael is light in his touch, seemingly balanced in his perspective. At first Ishmael succumbs as completely as the rest of the crew to Ahab's rhetoric, when he publicly announces his quest for the white whale — he, too, is "overmanned" — but gradually he frees himself from the "magnet" and establishes his own voice, or appears to do so, since his "free and easy sort of genial, desperado philosophy" is ultimately Ahab in another key.

Ishmael is truly genial-desperate. After Ahab's performance on the quarter-deck, Ishmael appears to be a corrective commentator when he analyzes the captain's madness; he answers Ahab not in analysis but in a virtuoso chapter called "The Whiteness of the Whale." If Ahab seduces the crew, Ishmael seduces readers — by almost identical tactics — into accepting his irrational analysis of whiteness as logical discussion. By incantatory appeal to superstitions and by factitious analogies he posits that the hue of whiteness "strikes more of panic to the soul than that redness which affrights in blood," which culminates, after an orgy of emotionally charged language and allusions, in the undemonstrable assertion that whiteness is the "colorless, all-color of atheism from which we shrink."

In the course of an exposition which is quietly hysterical he asserts that the whiteness of the polar bear or of the albatross is demonic in the terror it arouses. But the terror is more verbal than real. Red bears against a white glacier or red birds, like the sea-hawk at the conclusion, can be equally terrifying. Atheism, regardless of the color given to it, terrifies only if one is imprisoned in religious fears and presuppositions about the nature of the cosmos and the afterlife — or if one is willing to suspend rational judgment. Although many commentators have singled out the profundity of this chapter, they appear to slight the fact that Ishmael undercuts it at one point in an imaginary conversation with readers: "But thou sayest, methinks this white-lead chapter about whiteness is but a white flag hung out from a craven soul; thou surrenderest to a hypo, Ishmael." And then he has the delightful effrontery to resume in the same vein, alleging that "here thou beholdest even in a dumb brute, the instinct of the knowledge of the demonism of the world"; and that "Though in many of its aspects this visible world seems formed in love, the invisible spheres were formed in fright."

"The Whiteness of the Whale" is a tour de force wittily and wickedly calculated by an artist who keeps all his ambiguities open and his readers off rational balance. Its appeal is as primitive as Ahab's rhetoric and as simplistic as the projection of evil and deity upon the innocent back of a white whale. Ishmael, like Ahab, reduces the cosmos to false dualisms which capture the emotions by denying rational distinctions and gradations. The chapter is no more profound than Mapple's sermon or Fleece's parody; it is but another, highly romanticized, way of surveying the multiform variety of life. "The Whiteness of the Whale" illustrates "madness maddened," the artifice of a wit who, while seeming to undercut the central character, constantly reenforces him and reveals the emotional affinity when he in turn projects his own frightened life experience upon the universe.

Ishmael begins mock-innocently in his comic course when he reduces to manageable and human proportions both whales and bibliography by speaking of Folio Whales, Duodecimo Whales, and so forth. But the wit disguises the fact that he is attacking the making of books, again mocking both himself and his narrative. After he is exposed to death when the whaling boat he is in capsizes, he does not lose his wits as Pip is to do later; rather he laughs with a calculated leer in "The Hyena," when he arrives at a conclusion strikingly like Ahab's except for the language he employs:

> There are certain queer times and occasions in this strange mixed affair we call life when a man takes this whole universe for a vast practical joke, though the wit thereof he but dimly discerns, and more than suspects that the joke is at nobody's expense but his own. However, nothing dispirits, and nothing seems worth while disputing. He bolts down all events, all creeds, and beliefs, and persuasions, all hard things visible and invisible, never mind how knobby; as an ostrich of potent digestion gobbles down bullets and gun flints. And as for small difficulties and worryings, prospects of sudden disaster, peril of life and limb; all these, and death itself, seem to him only sly, good-natured hits, and jolly punches in the side bestowed by the unseen and unaccountable old joker. That odd sort of wayward mood I am speaking of, comes over a man only in some time of extreme tribulation; it comes in the very midst of his earnestness, so that what just before might have seemed to him a thing most momentous, now seems but part of the general joke.

The good-natured tone of the passage tends to minimize despair while actually reenforcing it, and at the same time camouflages Ishmael's continuing transformation from passivity to assertiveness. More and more he will play the role of "the unseen and unaccountable old joker." Ishmael's aspirations match Ahab's.

His latently aggressive nature emerges as he adds satire to his comic arsenal. Presbyterianism and Quakerism are diminished farcically in the first part of the book. The satirical harpoons are no less effective, perhaps more destructive, even though he hurls them unsystematically, even casually, or so it seems. Sometimes they are directed at topical matters like phrenology ("The Nut") or at cruelty to animals (he singles out ganders, not whales). Gradually he takes on more significant subject matter when he attacks man-made syntheses, the collective philosophical wisdom of the ages. The complexities of the age-old analysis of free will and chance are outrageously simplified when both become balls of yarn for a "mat-maker" who, when startled, drops "the ball of free will." On one occasion the *Pequod* is balanced in the waves — once more the dualistic approach — by two dead whale heads christened Locke and Kant. "So, when on one side you hoist in Locke's head, you go over that way," Ishmael writes; "but now, on the other side, hoist in Kant's and you come back again; but in very poor plight. Thus, some minds for ever keep trimming boat. Oh, ye foolish! throw all these thunder-heads overboard, and then you will float light and right." At another point he comments: "How many, think ye, have likewise fallen into Plato's honey head, and sweetly perished there?"

In "The Fountain" one paragraph converts some of the world's greatest minds into spray: "And I am convinced that from the heads of all ponderous profound beings, such as Plato, Pyrrho, the Devil, Jupiter, Dante, and so on, there always goes up a certain semi-visible steam, while in the act of thinking deep thoughts." If ancient "wisdom" becomes vapor, so too does Ishmael's satirical assertion of the fact, for immediately he holds himself up to ridicule, almost in punishment for his aggressions against the "fathers": "While composing a little treatise on Eternity, I had the curiosity to place a mirror before me; and ere long saw reflected there, a curious involved worming and undulation in the atmosphere over my head. The invariable moisture of my hair, while plunged in deep thought, after six cups of hot tea in my thin shingled attic, of an August noon; this seems an additional argument for the above supposition." His "genial, desperado philosophy" leaves a lot of wreckage in its wake, not unlike Ahab's monomania.

Just as Narcissus' watery image, which is "the key to it all," mirrors the fluctuations and rhythms of the two characters, the "gloomy-jolly" book itself reflects the author's deliberate assaults upon literary conventions. *Moby-Dick*, like the whale itself, bears its scars. Out of the wreckage Melville shapes his incredible artifice. Early, in the farcical phase, Ishmael justifies a digression with this comment: "But no more of this blubbering now, we are going a-whaling, and there is plenty of that yet to come." Later the tone is mock-heroic when he states his "less celestial" purpose, "I celebrate a tail," or when he observes: "But is the Queen a mermaid, to be presented with a tail? An allegorical meaning may lurk here." At another point he notes that some people "will scout at Moby Dick as a monstrous fable, or still worse and more detestable, a hideous and intolerable allegory." (Later, in January 1852 he confessed to Sophia Hawthorne that "I had some vague idea while writing it, that the whole book was susceptible of an allegoric construction, & also that *parts* of it were" — surely one of the most disingenuous statements that he ever made.)

He shatters fictive illusion when he deliberately and comically makes us aware of the process of writing. In the midst of a serious commentary on Ahab's "madness" he refers to "a furious trope" in the preceding sentence. He introduces the last sentence of a paragraph filled with pretentious historical and mythic allusions, with the phrase, "In plain prose," which topples his stylistic inflation. "The foregoing chapter, in its earlier parts," he asserts in "The Affidavit," "is as important a one as will be found in this volume" — which at best is but a partial truth. In the interpolation called "The Town-Ho's Story," which in some respects is *Moby-Dick* in miniature, he notes: "For my humor's sake, I shall preserve the style in which I once narrated it at Lima." In the midst of his ridicule of Locke and Kant he satirizes his satire: "Here, now, are two great whales, laying their heads together; let us join them, and lay together our own." At the conclusion of "Cetology" he suddenly writes: "God keep me from completing anything. This whole book is but a draught — nay, but a draught of a draught. Oh, Time, Strength, Cash, and Patience!" The irrelevancy of the two sentences — the ingenious comment upon the writing process and his own (meaning Melville's) financial need — is relevant since it lays bare all the author's manipulative control of his "crazy" structure. Later he asserts that he does not wish to proceed "methodically," and at another point he suggests that "There are some enterprises in which a careful disorderliness is the true method."

On still another occasion he presents his version of Emerson's organic theory of art: "Out of the trunk, the branches grow; out of them, the twigs. So, in productive subjects, grow the chapters." It is an impressive statement — until we recall that this is the first paragraph of a chapter entitled "The Crotch." Just as Queequeg associates the markings on the doubloon with his genitals, reducing the symbolism to its sexual origins, so Ishmael hints at the sexual underpinnings of art, somewhat in the fashion of Whitman's emphasis upon the phallus as seedman. He sexualizes a reality which Ahab seeks to desexualize, although his projection of the world's evil upon the whale that wounds him in the groin confirms the biblical association of evil and sexuality. Even the name Moby Dick may be a phallic pun.

Ishmael's dissection of the whale begins with the head, eventually concentrates upon the phallus in hilarious scenes like "Stubb's Supper," "A Squeeze of the Hand," and "The Cassock," where he transforms native bawdy humor into art, and finally arrives at the fundament, the skeleton of a divine whale in Arsacides. In this brilliant episode which devitalizes the majestic monster of the sea into the inevitable collection of bones after death, Ishmael employs reductionistic and regressive imagery. The locale is a bower reminiscent of similar settings in Spenser's *Faerie Queene* or of the first bower, the Garden of Eden. In the preface to the scene Ishmael the artist appropriately assumes the role of a parent, specifically a mother, and the artifact, the history of the life and death of a whale, becomes a child: ". . . it behoves me now to unbutton him still further, and untagging the points of his hose, unbuckling his garters, and casting loose the hooks and the eyes of the joints of his innermost bones, set him before you in his ultimatum; that is to say, in his unconditional skeleton." In the process of describing the scene, Ishmael, after the fashion of Jonah and Theseus, reenacts the birth process by reversing it to enter the womb. "To and fro I paced before the skeleton — brushed the vines aside — broke through the ribs — and with a ball of Arsacidean twine, wandered, eddied long amid its many winding, shaded collonades and arbors." (At the same time he reexperiences Eve's birth from Adam's rib.) Inside the whale he takes "admeasurements" which, he informs us with playful pseudo-realism, "are copied verbatim from my right arm, where I had them tattooed; as in my wild wanderings at that period, there was no other secure way of preserving such valuable statistics."

The accuracy of his measurements is of little significance except perhaps to a literalist without a sense of humor or psychological imagination, the absence of which prevents empathy with Melville's "performance." To miss the joke evidences insensitivity to Melville's duplicitous art, his wild sense of comedy, and the profundity underlying it, and it is to succumb to Ahabitry, which is narcissistically arrested in an egocentric and humorless view of the universe. In order to arrive at the dimensions, Ishmael, the artist-parent that gives birth to and guides the manuscript omnisciently, must become for the time being the child that supplies the material and is the source of the manuscript. Here Ishmael assumes the perspective of a fetus surveying the "womb." The measuring duplicates the child's curiosity not only about the uterine state it has had to abandon forever except in moments such as this, but also about the proportions of the adult body, particularly of the mother, which from its diminutive perspective it regards as the ultimate mystery and ultimate fascination. It is a deliciously droll example of a child's searching out in its intuitive and irresistible desire for sexual knowledge.

At the conclusion of his examination, after all the wonderful indirections, Ishmael finds "forty and odd vertebræ in all" which lie "like the great knobbed blocks on a Gothic spire. . . . The smallest, where the spine tapers into the tail, is only two inches in width, and looks something like a white billiard-ball." Which brings us once more to the fundament (Arsacides again) and to the child's misunderstanding of the sexual passageways. "I was told," Ishmael adds with superfluous literalness, "that there were still smaller ones, but they had been lost by some little cannibal urchins, the priest's children, who had stolen them to play marbles with" — which is a wry way to assert the eternal cycle. The last sentence, masterly in its wit and in its psychic as well as artistic appropriateness, reveals Ishmael's complete awareness of his artistic manipulations: "Thus we see how that the spine of even the hugest of living things tapers off at last into simple child's play."

The reductionism here and elsewhere enables Ishmael to mask his "tornadoed" feelings and his alienation. The wit, often aggressive and hostile, is encased in a socially acceptable form. Ishmael does not knock off hats literally, but wittily. With impunity he punishes the world that has punished him. Like Ahab he takes his vengeance. Both are frightened boy-men. If Ahab is "unbuttoned" and assumes a quixotic kind of heroism, Ishmael's comedy not only "unbuttons" the whale but the readers and himself. A contemporary reviewer in *The Literary World* in November 1851 speaks, perceptively, of "Ishmael, whose wit may be allowed to be against everything on land, as his hand is against everything at sea." His verbal aggression undermines orthodoxy, philosophy, mythology, and human aspiration. In reducing everything to "a great practical joke," he secretly baptizes the book in a subversive comic norm — nothingness.

Ahab's magnificent rant transfigures his bankrupt life and impoverished sensibility, and grants him in his twilight years an unearned heroic stature, not because of his humanity but because of his "crazy" courage. He so poeticizes his self-hatred and his destructive tendencies that we forget that the lonely, emotionally and physically crippled captain, with whom in our own loneliness we empathize, hungers for the lullaby of death.

When Ahab craftily universalizes his "madness" by evoking infantile fears of the parent, his rhetoric hides from the crew, and readers too, a basic lack of confidence or trust in himself and in life itself; his bombast cloaks the impotency of his fears which he seeks to subdue through verbal and physical aggressiveness. He observes that he "only feels, feels, feels." In his own way he wallows in self-pity. When he goes on to exclaim, "to think's audacity. God only has that right and privilege," he exposes an intellect arrested in childish despair and primitive superstition. At one and the same time he cannibalizes the deity and abdicates intelligence to a creation that mirrors his hurts and tyrannizes over his imagination as he in turn tyrannizes over his docile crew. Fatherless, he accepts the hierarchical structure of life at sea, and eventually becomes captain or "father" in a patriarchal order built on fear rather than on love, which is the seemingly inevitable outcome of the tragedy of his first year. Beneath his authoritarian posture Ahab conceals his wounded ego.

Ishmael, on the other hand, although he too as an orphan is crippled and goes to the sea to ward off suicidal tendencies, can "marry" Queequeg, which at least establishes his ability, limited though it may be, to relate to others. More important, he can "divorce" himself from the limitations of Ahab's monomania which is lifeless and affectless. Where the captain broods compulsively on vengeance upon the white whale, or death, Ishmael meditates not only upon Thanatos but also upon the erotic continuity of the human condition. Unlike Ahab, he finds a nondestructive outlet for his destructive tendencies. His aggressions he harnesses to a wit which will imperil no lives. Even the negations of the satiric attacks fall into place in the context of *Moby-Dick*.

In his lonely study, where the shades of his artistic predecessors reassert the continuum, Ishmael the artist-creator modulates and manipulates his narrative, with the tender control of a fond parent over a wayward child. Tied as he is to the nihilism of Ahab and harried by his own hurts, Ishmael finds a form which encompasses and subdues chaos. Unlike Ahab, who reduces existence to conform to his own agony, Ishmael's art mutes and transforms his despair into a celebration of multi-faceted life.

In the Epilogue we see the cradle-coffin endlessly rocking, the maternal principle in the form of the ship *Rachel* timelessly reasserting itself. Ishmael the son survives Ahab the father, to tell a tale of death and rebirth. Such is the continuity of life and art. The sun and the son must ever rise.

From the womb of Melville's life experience and the blackness of his hurts, painfully, joyfully, maniacally, emerges a book which expands/contracts in the birth-death throes with which it begins. Before he finished writing, Melville, like Ahab, staggered beneath the pain and had trouble bringing it to a conclusion. The price of reactivating and reliving earlier pains and of rivaling Hawthorne was truly great intellectually and emotionally.

Moby-Dick is an exhilarating, frightening experience — perhaps the loveliest, most terrifying, "crazy-witty" meditation in the lonely American landscape.

"The Toddler Was Toddling, Entirely Alone"

—*Pierre*

Ishmael triumphs in the pages of his masterpiece but remains "another orphan," and the author himself was exhilarated but exhausted after what had turned out to be an eighteen-month gestation. Once again Melville attempted to recoup his energies by taking care of the chores on his farm. There was another winter coming and wood was needed for the fireplace which, he informed Duyckinck, "swallows down cords of wood as a whale does boats."

On October 22, 1851, Elizabeth Melville gave birth to her second son, Stanwix, and her husband, himself the second male child, confused son and father when on the birth certificate he made Maria Gansevoort Melville the mother of Elizabeth's child, or, to put it another way, his mother and he gave birth to Stanwix—which, of course, would be to make too much of a slip of the pen, if the implicit subject of his next romance, *Pierre*, was not incest.

Some time late in October Hawthorne was reading *Moby-Dick*, and at the same time Sophia and he were planning to move to West Newton after a mysterious and abrupt change in their plans. About November 16 Hawthorne sent what his friend called a "plain, bluff letter," which, unfortunately, Melville must have destroyed later. Melville's reply on the following day was almost like a chapter in *Moby-Dick* in its manic swings. For the first and last time in this correspondence he signed himself "Herman." "I say your appreciation is my glorious gratuity. In my proud, humble way, – a shepherd-king, – I was lord of a little vale in the solitary Crimea; but you have now given me the crown of India." Abruptly the euphoria gave way to self-deflation: "But on trying it on my head, I found it fell down on my ears, notwithstanding their asinine length – for it's only such ears that sustain such crowns."

The defensive wit was followed by what Melville called a "pantheistic" feeling, but what can be more accurately described as an explicit statement of the "incorporation" he had written of in *The Literary World* in 1850. Then a rival, now an equal, he fantasized an eternal "honeymoon" in the Pantheon.

> But I felt pantheistic then—your heart beat in my ribs and mine in yours, and both in God's. A sense of unspeakable security is in me this moment, on account of your having understood the book. I have written a wicked book, and feel spotless as a lamb. Ineffable socialities are in me. I would sit down and dine with you and all the gods in old Rome's Pantheon. It is a strange feeling—no hopefulness is in it, no despair. Content—that is it; and irresponsibility; but without licentious inclination. I speak now of my profoundest sense of being, not of an incidental feeling.

The platonic eroticism of the passage abruptly descended to earth and to conventional morality when he intruded one significant phrase—"but without licentious inclination."

He clarified the phrase when in the next paragraph, the most ardent and doubtlessly one of the most painful he was ever to write, he candidly and boldly laid bare his love,

> Whence come you, Hawthorne? By what right do you drink from my flagon of life? And when I put it to my lips – lo, they are yours and not mine. I feel that the Godhead is broken up like the bread at the Supper, and that we are the pieces. Hence this infinite fraternity of feeling. Now, sympathizing with the paper, my angel turns over another page. You did not care a penny for the book. But, now and then as you read, you understood the pervading thought that impelled the book – and that you praised. Was it not so? You were archangel enough to despise the imperfect body, and embrace the soul. Once you hugged the ugly Socrates because you saw the

flame in the mouth, and heard the rushing of the demon, — the familiar, — and recognized the sound; for you have heard it in your own solitudes.

What an extraordinary passage it is—saturated in oral imagery, reflecting basic needs which he defensively projected upon his friend! As "my angel" turned the page, Melville changed his mood and put denigrating words into Hawthorne's mouth, which expressed his own fear, with traces of hostility emerging, as he pleaded for reassurance. Then, in contrition, Hawthorne became an "archangel," again a maternal-paternal symbol, who ignored "the imperfect body" of the book and its author, and embraced "the soul." But, as the last sentence made clear, Melville wanted the body embraced too: like "ugly Socrates" — he was still the "ugly duckling" of his youth — he desired to be "hugged" by a beautiful man — by an Alcibiades or an Apollo. Like Ahab, he sought the comfort of touch.

Now doubt and depression overtook him. Although he was to sign the letter "Herman," he did not dare to use the intimate form in addressing Hawthorne; part of him wanted to retain the child-parent relationship. "My dear Hawthorne," he wrote, while he mitigated as he admitted his ardor:

> the atmospheric skepticisms steal into me now, and make me doubtful of my sanity in writing you thus. But, believe me, I am not mad, most noble Festus! But truth is ever incoherent, and when the big hearts strike together, the concussion is a little stunning. Farewell. Don't write a word about the book. That would be robbing me of my miserly delight. I am heartily sorry I ever wrote anything about you—it was paltry. Lord, when shall we be done growing? As long as we have anything more to do, we have done nothing. So, now, let us add Moby Dick to our blessing, and step from that. Leviathan is not the biggest fish;—I have heard of Krakens.

It was time to say "Farewell," but he could not stop. The verbal repetitions indicate that Melville deeply resented the separation that was to take place. "Lord, when shall we be done growing?" now becomes—

> Lord, when shall we be done changing? Ah! it's a long stage, and no inn in sight, and night coming, and the body cold. But with you for a passenger, I am content and can be happy. I shall leave the world, I feel, with more satisfaction for having come to know you. Knowing you persuades me more than the Bible of our immortality.
>
> What a pity, that, for your plain, bluff letter, you should get such gibberish! Mention me to Mrs. Hawthorne and to the children, and so, good-by to you, with my blessing.
>
> Herman

For the third time in the letter he professed to be "content," although ambiguous references to death and immortality intruded in what he chose to call "gibberish." But perhaps no higher, and more tender, tribute was ever paid to Hawthorne.

Melville could not end the letter which was to mark the end of a relationship.

> P.S. I can't stop yet. If the world was entirely made up of Magians, I'll tell you what I should do. I should have a paper-mill established at one end of the house, and so have an endless riband of foolscap rolling in upon my desk; and upon that endless riband I should write a thousand—a million—billion thoughts, all under the form of a letter to you. The divine magnet is on you, and my magnet responds. Which is the biggest? A foolish question—they are *One*.

> P.P.S. Don't think that by writing me a letter, you shall always be bored with an immediate reply to it—and so keep both of us delving over a writing-desk eternally. No such thing! I sh'n't always answer your letters, and you may do just as you please.

Behind the words lay the despair of all his years. If Ishmael needs Ahab to fill a void in his life, Melville needed Hawthorne. The son may have triumphed in the Epilogue to *Moby-Dick*, but life rarely confirms fantasy.

Just when Melville heard of his friend's departure we do not know. He may not have been aware that for months Hawthorne had been informing friends of his dissatisfaction with life in the mountains. Given his reserved nature and timidity as well as his awareness of Melville's intense attachment, he may have kept his plans secret until almost the last moment.

The Hawthornes left Lenox on November 21, 1851, "in a storm of snow and sleet," as he noted in his journal. Melville could scarcely have missed life's irony: Ishmael drives off "the spleen" by going to sea "whenever it is a damp, drizzly November in my soul." Shortly before their departure Sophia sent Melville a memento — an engraving of her husband based on the portrait of C. G. Thompson. The gesture was intended as a kindness, but whether it was of any comfort to the recipient is problematical. The portrait was no substitute for the presence of a man who in fifteen months had taken hold of his heart. Melville must have intuited what in fact was to happen. When Hawthorne retreated from Lenox, he retreated from Melville. How Hawthorne felt his reticences keep us from knowing, but his friend wrestled with the problems and nature of the relationship almost until the end of his life.

And so Hawthorne went his way, and Melville remained behind

— an "orphan" in the Berkshires — with, in the words of Pierre, "mutilated shadowings-forth of invisible and eternally unembodied images of the soul."

It was about this time he began his new novel. Once more he imprisoned himself in his study and wrote with his usual fury and dedication. At Christmas time his neighbor, Mrs. Morewood, informed Duyckinck, "I hear that he is now engaged in a new work as frequently not to leave his room till quite dark in the evening — when he for the first time during the whole day partakes of solid food — he must therefore write under a state of morbid excitement which will soon injure his health — I laughed at him somewhat and told him that the recluse life he was leading made his city friends think that he was slightly insane — he replied that long ago he came to the same conclusion himself."

On March 1, 1852, Elizabeth Melville's physician, Amos Nourse, wrote to Judge Shaw: "Her husband I fear is devoting himself to writing with an assiduity that will cost him dear by & by." On January 21 his brother Allan was arranging a contract with Harper and Brothers for the publication of *Pierre*, and on February 20 Melville received an advance of $500. In February Herman, or perhaps Allan, wrote to Richard Bentley about English publication. Bentley was unwilling to make an advance payment because losses from the last four books amounted to £453.4.6, and he proposed that profit be tied to sales. Meanwhile, Melville worked at *Pierre* with his customary fury. The book was finished about the end of March, and on April 16 he sent a set of proofs to Bentley, accompanied by a letter rejecting the publisher's financial scheme. "My new book," he averred with almost monumental inaccuracy, possesses "unquestionable novelty, as regards my former ones, — treating of utterly new scenes & characters; — and, as I beleive, very much more calculated for popularity than anything you have yet published of mine — being a regular romance, with a mysterious plot to it, & stirring passions at work, and withall, representing a new & elevated aspect of American life."

Melville was either deliberately inaccurate or was indulging himself in a "wicked" joke. *Pierre* is by any definition scarcely "a regular romance." The "stirring passions" are incestuous passions and oedipal cravings. Few contemporaries would have considered it "a new & elevated aspect of American life," either in its depiction of the rural gentry or in its forced diction and strained syntax which had nothing in common with American prose rhythms, written or oral.

He was a little more accurate in his first extant reference to *Pierre* in a letter to Sophia Hawthorne early in January 1852: "My Dear Lady, I shall not again send you a bowl of salt water. The next chalice I shall commend, will be a rural bowl of milk." For *Pierre* is a domestic romance, though perhaps the strangest one in our litera-ture. At the same time Melville was informing Mrs. Hawthorne that, as her husband followed *The Scarlet Letter* with *The House of the Seven Gables*, so was he turning from yarns of the sea to another genre. Whether he knew it or not, he was continuing the rivalry which showed through in the pages of *The Literary World*. After detailing the excellences of Shakespeare's rival in the New World, Nathaniel Hawthorne, he admitted, "however great may be the praise I have bestowed upon him, I feel that in so doing I have more served and honored myself, than him." But in this new contest he was no match. Melville was not a domesticated person; his artistic skills did not include the intimacies of domestication or the realistic detail of this genre. In *The House of the Seven Gables* Hawthorne is the limner of love. In *Pierre* Melville is the limner of pain.

The pain is Pierre's but also Melville's. For what he did not acknowledge to Mrs. Hawthorne, to Bentley, or to anyone else, was that *Pierre* was more than a romance: it was an account of the tormented inner life of a man baptized Herman Melville.

When he retreated to his study to begin *Pierre*, he had not allowed himself sufficient time to recuperate from the "leviathanic" struggles involved in producing *Moby-Dick*, to adjust himself to the added responsibilities of his larger family, or to place Hawthorne's unexpected and hasty departure in perspective. As Melville brooded over the plot of his new book and the character of his new "hero," he dove deep into his own life, as the following passage makes clear:

> Not yet had he dropped his angle into the well of his childhood, to find what fish might be there; for who dreams to find fish in a well? the running stream of the outer world, there doubtless swim the golden perch and the pickerel! Ten million things were as yet uncovered to Pierre. The old mummy lies buried in cloth on cloth; it takes time to unwrap this Egyptian kind. Yet now, forsooth, because Pierre began to see through the fast superficiality of the world, he fondly weens he has come to the unlayered substance. But, far as any geologist has yet gone down into the world, it is found to consist of nothing but surface stratified on surface. To its axis, the world being nothing but superinduced superficies. By vast pains we mine into the pyramid; by horrible gropings we come to the central room; with joy we espy the sarcophagus; but we lift the lid — and no body is there! — appallingly vacant as vast is the soul of a man!

The setting of the romance is Saddle-Meadows, which resembles Arrowhead, from which he could see the saddle-like humps or crowns of "Greylock's most excellent majesty." It is the ancestral home of a family named Glendinning, which resembles Gansevoort. Pierre's grandfather, General Glendinning, died in 1812; General Peter Gansevoort died on July 2, 1812. "Pierre's was a double revolutionary descent," we learn, as was Herman's, from General Gansevoort and Major Melvill.

Mary Glendinning is "nearly fifty years of age." Maria Gansevoort Melville was forty-eight when Melville was nineteen. The description of Mrs. Glendinning could serve for Mrs. Melville:

> She was a noble creature, but formed chiefly for the gilded prosperities of life, and hitherto mostly used to its unruffled serenities; bred and expanded, in all developments, under the sole influence of hereditary forms and world-usages ... his mother's immense pride: — her pride of birth, her pride of affluence, her pride of purity, and all the pride of high-born, refined, and wealthy Life. ... He too plainly saw, that not his mother had made his mother; but the Infinite Haughtiness had first fashioned her; and then the haughty world had further molded her; nor had a haughty Ritual omitted to finish her.

Pierre's father married at thirty-five; Herman's at thirty-two. Mr. Glendinning has a "fastidious" library, like Allan Melvill's. The romance makes much of two portraits of Mr. Glendinning, one before marriage in which he appears as a dandy and another after his wife domesticates him. Two similar portraits of Allan Melvill still exist.

"Chestnut-haired, bright-cheeked," and with "chestnut eyes," Pierre resembles Melville in appearance, and has the small hands and muscular arms of the Apollo icon in his earlier novels. At the beginning of the tale he is in love with Lucy Tartan, who — like "Lizzie" Shaw — is the daughter of "an early and most cherished friend of Pierre's father." Pierre's schoolday chum is named Glendinning Stanly, a cousin and an orphan. The model was Stanwix Gansevoort, Melville's cousin who was "orphaned" after the early death of his father.

Most important, Pierre was twelve when his father died "of a fever" and "wandered in his mind." Halfway through the romance we suddenly learn that Pierre had enjoyed a few years earlier a great deal of literary popularity after the publication of some poems about the South Seas. It becomes, then, quite apparent, as a number of critics have noted, that Pierre is writing a work that resembles *Pierre.* Or, to put it another way, Melville was writing about Melville writing a book based on his own experiences and repressed longings.

For *Pierre*, as Newton Arvin was perhaps the first to observe, unfolds the tale of an only child who, after the death of his father, enjoys the exclusive possession of his mother. Pierre is pampered, petted, and fed by a mother who provides him with an oral paradise. The son is her "brother" and she his "sister," in the titillating little game they play with erotic, if incestuous, undertones.

The choice of the name Pierre is the most extraordinary confirmation of Herman's hunger for his mother's affection. Many critics have pointed out that Pierre stems from *petros*, or stone, and have noted the importance of the Memnon Rock scene and the dedication to Mount Greylock. A few have pointed to St. Peter, the stone upon which Jesus established His church, but it was also Peter who thrice betrayed his master on the night of the crucifixion. *Petros* or *Peter* also evokes *petrify*, or death, as well as *salt-peter* or *penis*. Such jugglery, relevant as all the associations may be to the symbolic substructure of the romance and to the clarification of its subterranean meanings, pales before a simple fact. Peter Gansevoort, the General's son, took over after Allan Melvill's death, and for years guided and infuriated the Melville boys as they struggled toward manhood. But, more important, as everyone in the family knew, Maria Gansevoort Melville loved him more than her own husband.

As Melville scraped this painful story out of the depths of his longings and frustrations, he projected his despair upon the universe, reducing almost all relationships to incestuous attachments. Late in the novel the narrator recalls the fable of Enceladus: "Old Titan's self was the son of incestuous Cœlus and Terra, the son of incestuous Heaven and Earth. And Titan married his mother Terra, another and accumulatively incestuous match. And thereof Enceladus was one issue." On the last day of Pierre's life his former fiancée Lucy stands before "The Cenci of Guido," and the narrator notes "the two most horrible crimes (of one of which she is the object, and of the other the agent) possible to civilized humanity — incest and parricide."

And so in *Pierre* Melville unfolded his attachment to his mother as well as unresolved oedipal rivalries. Locked in an environment polluted by deviant longings, Mrs. Glendinning and Pierre act out an incestuous charade. He ties the ribbon about her perfumed neck before she descends to the dining room, where she presides over the table while Pierre gorges himself beneath "the proud, double-arches of the bright breastplate of thy bosom." Mrs. Glendinning approves of his marriage to Lucy because "I hope to have a little sister Tartan," and because Lucy poses no threat to her dominant position. Later Pierre "marries" his half-sister Isabel, the offspring of his father's liaison before his marriage, in order to protect his father's memory and to legitimatize the illegitimate girl. Isabel not only bears her mother's name, as Pierre bears his father's — thus duplicating Mr. Glendinning's liaison — but in her brunette beauty she resembles Mrs.

Glendinning — thus allowing Pierre to "possess" his mother and his father's mistress. The narrator in effect makes the point, in his convoluted diction, when he observes that "the latent germ of . . . his proposed extraordinary resolve — nmely, the nominal conversion of a sister into a wife — might have been found in the previous conversational conversion of a mother into a sister; for hereby he had habituated his voice and manner to a certain fictitiousness in one of the closest domestic relations of life."

The portrait of Mrs. Glendinning is a cruel one. The narrator relentlessly depicts her as a phallic woman, an American bitch. Haughty and arrogant, she utters her "docility" speech with the fervid sterility of Lady Macbeth. When she suspects that Pierre is keeping secrets from her she picks up a fork and in a rage hurls it; "hanging by the side of Pierre's portrait, she saw her own smiling picture pierced through, and the fork, whose silver tines had caught in the painted bosom, vibratingly rankled in the wound." As evidenced by the formal portrait she commissions, she makes her husband respectable, which is to say asexual, and by molding Pierre into a "docile" lad she renders him impotent. The atmosphere of Saddle-Meadows is perverse with the seductiveness of a woman, as an unkind text informs us, "not very far from her grand climacteric." At menopause Mrs. Glendinning stimulates desire but at the same time blocks Pierre's normal sexual development. She keeps him "docile," but, in a wickedly hilarious speech in which she fondles "the old General's baton," surely revealing her own incestuous wishes, she wonders: "Yet but just now I fondled the conceit that Pierre was so sweetly docile! Here sure is a most strange inconsistency! For is sweet docility a general's badge? and is this baton but a distaff then?" As she wavers between sexual roles, so Pierre wavers.

Although Pierre speaks floridly of his great passion for Lucy, the words mimic both Shakespeare and, more important, his own libidinal drives. He chafes momentarily when his mother postpones his marriage day, yet later on the same day, after observing the fragile body of Lucy, he indulges in a speculation which would never occur to a man of passion: "This to be my wife? I that but the other day weighed an hundred and fifty pounds of solid avoirdupois; — I to wed this heavenly fleece? Methinks one husbandly embrace would break her airy zone, and she exhale upward to that heaven whence she hath hither come, condensed to mortal sight." The speech is silly, but it is silliness born of sexual fear. "It can not be," he continues, "I am of heavy earth, and she of airy light. By heaven, but marriage is an impious thing!" The sexuality absent in the Lucy-Pierre relationship appears in the scenes with his half-sister, who substitutes for the other "sister." Isabel's luxurious hair enfolds her and Pierre as she tells her lonely story, and she invites him to look into the guitar (a womb symbol, as Henry A. Murray points out), where her name is inscribed. When the erotic rhythms reverberate too threateningly, she says: "I am called woman, and thou, man, Pierre; but there is neither man nor woman about it. . . . There is no sex in our immaculateness."

After "He Crosses the Rubicon," which is the narrator's mocking description of his decision to inform Lucy and his mother that he is about to marry, he returns to Isabel at the farmhouse. She "sprang forward to him, caught him with both her arms round him, and held him so convulsively, that her hair sideways swept over him, and half concealed him." As they embrace, "Over the face of Pierre there shot a terrible self-revelation; he imprinted repeated burning kisses upon her; pressed hard her hand; would not let go her sweet and awful passiveness." Then: "they changed; they coiled together, and entangledly stood mute." Such are the ambiguities of the diction that sexual desire may have been consummated or only simulated because of incestuous fears.

Probably there is only the frustration of ungratified desire since "passion" is juxtaposed against images of mutilation. After Pierre learns of Isabel's life, "the long-cherished image of his father now transfigured before him from a green foliaged tree into a blasted trunk." When he struggles futilely over his own writing, "he began to feel that in him, the thews of a Titan were forestallingly cut by the scissors of Fate. He felt as a moose, hamstrung." Before the final death scene Pierre has a vision of "Enceladus the Titan, the most potent of all the giants" and an offshoot of incest, who tries to seize power from his father — "still, though armless, resisting with his whole striving trunk, the Pelion and the Ossa hurled back at him." In the garden at Versailles Balthazar Marsy created a replica of this giant with arms and converted the mouth into a fountain. But "Nature, more truthful, performed an amputation, and left the impotent Titan without one serviceable ball-and-socket above the thigh." Which is Melville's not very veiled way of noting castration and punishment for filial aggression.

Pierre is no Enceladus. He shoots Glen Stanly in cold fury. In prison Pierre proclaims, "I long and long to die, to be rid of this dishonored cheek." When Isabel and Lucy enter, Pierre banishes them. "Pierre is neuter now!" he proclaims. After Lucy's death he seizes "Isabel in his grasp . . . and tearing her bosom loose, he seized the secret vial nesting there." Impotent, fed with "death-milk" from Isabel's breast, his life-long hunger satisfied, he is finally "docile."

But there is one more scene — a brilliant one. Lucy's brother appears and demands of the turnkey: "Hath any angel swept adown and lighted in your granite hell?" The jailer, weary of distracted prisoners and inane questions, wheezes to another turnkey, "Broken his wind, and broken loose, too, ain't he?" After this frightful anal pun, he answers Lucy's brother — "jerking his stumped thumb behind him."

When the unheroic hero exclaims, "Pierre is neuter now!" he completes the process begun at puberty with the death of the father. Mr. Glendinning cripples his twelve-year-old son when his life sputters out in delirious wanderings: "My daughter! my daughter!" The boy cries, "thou hast not a daughter, but here is thy own little Pierre." The "unregardful voice in the bed" wails again, "My daughter! — God, God! — my daughter!" As Pierre grasps one of the dying man's hands, he sees, or thinks he sees, that "the other hand now also emptily lifted itself, and emptily caught, as if at some other childish fingers." Pierre's rejection, then, is twofold: his father abandons him but not before introducing a rival who robs the lad of the paternal blessing, as Gansevoort robbed Herman of Allan Melvill's favor.

After he receives Isabel's letter, the narrator addresses Pierre directly, almost cruelly: "Ay, Pierre, now indeed art thou hurt with a wound, never to be completely healed but in heaven; . . . thy sacred father is no more a saint; all brightness hath gone from thy hills, and all peace from thy plains." Pierre groans as he removes the portrait from the walls, "I will no more have a father." He knows that in protecting Isabel he will estrange his mother. "Then Pierre felt that deep in him lurked a divine unidentifiableness, that owned no earthly kith or kin. Yet was this feeling entirely lonesome, and orphan-like . . . so that once more he might not feel himself driven out an infant Ishmael into the desert, with no maternal Hagar to accompany and comfort him." The words *once more* acknowledge the previously unacknowledged rejection on the deathbed, and reveal that now he will even lose "Hagar." At the Black Swan he burns his father's portrait. "Henceforth," he declaims in the third person, "cast-out Pierre hath no paternity, and no past; and since the Future is blank to all; therefore, twice-disinherited Pierre stands untrammeledly his ever-present self! — free to do his own self-will and present fancy to whatever end!" Here, as elsewhere, Pierre is wrapping himself in romantic rhetoric. In burning the portrait he punishes the father who has punished him and Isabel, but he does not admit his resentment of his father's sexual success both with Isabel's mother and Mrs. Glendinning. His "burnt and blackened" hand is punishment for his aggression.

In deciding to become an author Pierre thinks he is transcending the "docile" bond with his mother. Yet, as he begins to write, he recalls that as a "toddler" mother and father rescued him when he stumbled. "Now," when he leaves Saddle-Meadows, to play father-brother-husband to Isabel, "cruel father and mother have both let go his hand, and the little soul-toddler, now you shall hear his shriek and his wail and often his fall." Worse still, "seated at his book . . . he began to feel the utter loss of that other support, too; ay, even the paternal gods themselves did now desert Pierre; the toddler was toddling, entirely alone, and not without shrieks."

Soon he shrieks "vehemently," "This book makes me mad," a cry which resembles Ahab's "crazy" attribution of the world's evil to a whale. Both Ahab and Pierre are toddlers, terrified that like their parents they will cross into the darkness of insanity. Pierre is haunted by "infantile reminiscences — the wandering mind of his father." Later his mother dies mad and alone — the son not learning of her death until twenty-five days later. As he retells his story in the book he is writing, Pierre is subject to eyestrain, perhaps reminiscent of Oedipus' self-punishment for his incest; to fainting fits, not unlike those of Melville's mother in periods of emotional stress (as Leon Howard observes); and to psychotic interludes when his mind wanders ("his own hereditary liability to madness").

But he must write the book that makes him mad and live a life that maddens him. In killing Glen Stanly, "his own hand had extinguished his house." " 'Tis speechless sweet to murder thee!" he screams. In murdering his childhood friend, then, he commits symbolic parricide, for Glen inherits Saddle-Meadows after the death of Mrs. Glendinning and thus is his father's successor. The punishment Pierre metes out to himself fulfills moral and psychological mechanisms.

Pierre is an act of self-punishment. The recreation of Pierre's youth provides catharsis neither to Pierre nor to the narrator — nor to Melville. The description of Pierre writing a book is an account of Melville writing *Pierre*. The walks alone, the eyestrain, the self-isolation — these are fictional but also real. The publisher who spurns Pierre's book corresponds to Bentley's refusal to make an advance payment for *Pierre*. The literary luminaries at the Apostles are the New York coterie presided over by Evert Duyckinck.

Pierre is paranoid and so is the book. It flails at parental figures, and old friends. Pierre assails readers for worshipping "Mediocrity and Common Place." He attacks artistic coteries, like the Young Americans, who "discuss, in glorious gibberish, the Alpha and Omega of the Universe," and, by indirection, deflates his own posturings and rant. Fiction consists of "mutilated stumps," great books are "mutilated shadowings-forth." Pierre empties the world of meaning and meaningful interaction, in an arrogant but frighteningly narcissistic projection of his own despair. The cosmos is shriveled to reflect his own self-evaluation: "I am a nothing," and "Pierre is neuter now!" This is an infantile whine for sympathy.

The narrator boasts, "I write precisely as I please" — only to reveal that he is capable of Pierre's self-deception. The utterance is the child's boast, "I do as I please." The truth is, as the narrator asserts, that "a fœtal fancy" beckons Pierre to look into the well of childhood, but the narrator proceeds, as he admits in a pun, "perambillically." Which is to say, in his own words, books reflect the "mutilated stumps" of the author's personal experiences: "It is impossible to talk or to write without apparently throwing oneself helplessly open; the Invulnerable Knight wears his visor down."

Pierre is disjointed like the life it records. It violates fictional structure, shifts points of view at will, takes a comic attitude toward noncomic matters like incest, and introduces a cacaphony of styles scarcely conceivable to the ordinary writer or reader but justifiable in *Pierre*. The style is Pierre.

And yet in a crazy kind of way the book is a virtuoso performance. For despite the narrator's understandable confusion as to whether he is an objective observer, a stand-in for Pierre, or Melville's voice, there is real control of the disorderly materials and an underlying logic. At times the narrator allows speakers to overindulge in verbalisms, and at times his own digressions are longwinded and even tedious. The incestuous parody at the beginning mocks the relationship between son and mother even as it reveals it; like the Queequeg-Ishmael episodes, comic tactics camouflage its deviancy. The pseudo-Romeo-and-Juliet atmosphere points up the absence of genuine passion in the Lucy-Pierre relationship. Mrs. Glendinning's rhythms, particularly in the "docility" speech, do not make her a heroine, but indicate that, like Lady Macbeth, defeminization is weakness, not strength. When Isabel, a young lady who has had no formal education, speaks to the accompaniment of a guitar in Elizabethan periodic prose, she makes herself worthy of Pierre and his quixotic idealism, but she is more than a little absurd, as is Pierre's idealism.

Pierre's extreme veneration of his father's memory is married to an inflated prose that may be a tribute but, more likely, an admission of the son's feeling of abandonment (and loss of paradise) or even guilt, since he has replaced the father in the affections of the mother. The melodrama which he creates as he sets out to right his father's wrong, and in the process to replace the father, reflects his anger as well as his guilt. Without observable remorse he kills mother, friends, and finally himself. The loss of control, which borders on a psychotic state, is reflected in the novel itself, making logical and even mandatory irrational distortions. The novel seems about to fall apart, as does Pierre. Finally, Pierre is a failure as son, "husband," lover, author: he is encased in a book that can only fail.

In final analysis, *Pierre* is an unattractive, sometimes repellant romance. Although it contains acute psychological analysis — certainly there are few competitors in nineteenth-century American literature — it fails to breathe. The unrelieved emphasis upon Pierre's emotional gyrations, which are psychologically logical and plausible, is a strength but also a weakness; the book is locked into Pierre's closed world. Its truths, in other words, constitute a falsehood, life being more varied and even contradictory than this almost clinical dissection allows. Unlike *Moby-Dick* it is monochromatic and eventually monotonous. Paradoxically, there is such an excess of heart that it becomes a kind of intellectual abstraction. We may respect the technical performance and the psychological subtlety, but, as in Poe's tales, we are uninvolved. Worse, it is difficult to take the book seriously. We watch the characters die, and we are not moved. We are not necessarily callous if we are not as angry as Melville was at the world and, perhaps most of all, at himself.

It is no wonder that the book made him "mad." Upstairs he wrote of parricide, incestuous bonds, sexual anxieties, and fear of insanity. Downstairs Maria Gansevoort Melville sat in the parlor, with his wife, the daughter of Allan Melvill's childhood friend. In his study Melville expressed his dreams of taking revenge upon his father, killing his mother, destroying a sister-wife and his betrothed. In the parlor two "toddlers" he fathered had to refrain from noisy outbursts which would disturb him, while he vented his destructive fantasies and verbalized his death fascination. After killing off Mrs. Glendinning, Melville had to dine with Maria Gansevoort Melville. Pierre kills the Apollo figure, Glendinning Stanly, whose name resembles Stanwix Melville, the recently arrived toddler. Glendinning Stanly also recalls the rival of his youth, Gansevoort Melville.

Another Apollo figure had recently "betrayed" Melville — Nathaniel Hawthorne.

"A Bond...
Passing the Love
of Woman"

For fifteen months Melville had basked in the aura cast by Nathaniel
Hawthorne and — even more important — in his own imaginative
heightening of that presence. As an idolator and a rival, in 1850 and
1851 he revised and rewrote a whaling story into a masterpiece, and
repaid a debt more personal than literary to the American Shakespeare. The review in *The Literary World* was the first of his love
offerings. *Moby-Dick* was the consummation of the relationship.
Then, seemingly abruptly, Melville learned of "finalities / Besides the
grave" — that the Hawthornes were leaving the Berkshires. His response was visceral, both in the Farewell Letter and in *Pierre*. Where
Ishmael-Melville maintains subtle and deliberately wrought balances
amid the complexities of *Moby-Dick*, Pierre-Melville erupts in a prose
that is often a parody of prose, a stylistic travesty that corresponds
to the hero's travesty. He tears all veils and like Ahab scorns all
restraints as he destroys everything he touches, including himself.

Pierre becomes an orgy of pain and despair. Self-love becomes self-hatred. The lacerating prose is self-laceration – or self-punishment – and it painfully records as it marks failure.

The first-person narrators of the early books protest the wrongs of "snivilization," but without losing faith either in the possibilities of social change or in themselves. They manage to indulge in playful self-mockery of their youthful indiscretions and their bumptious enthusiasm; they are not locked in despair. Pierre, on the other hand, is not playful. The tone is shrill in its anger, melodramatic in its self-pity; the tensions of his rage coil around him like a serpent. The narrator presents his "hero" as a fool almost from the outset, and Pierre later confirms the evolution – or fulfills the prophecy – when he proclaims himself "the fool of Truth, the fool of Virtue, the fool of Fate."

Pierre was written in anguish. The departure of Hawthorne wrote another chapter in the book of "betrayals" which began in his earliest years. Worse still, the separation, the loss of an idol, confirmed a frightening pattern of his life and at the same time exposed the futility, and perhaps stupidity, of his idealizations of men of flesh. In exposing his heart in his letters Melville offered to Hawthorne a gift which could only become a burden since it dictated the terms of the relationship and demanded reciprocation, which would have involved the kind of self-confession and candor that Hawthorne avoided in life and in art. The veils he inevitably and consistently drew in his fictions were the veils he drew in life. In *Mosses from an Old Manse*, that collection of tales which elicited a soul-wrenching reaction from Melville, Hawthorne comments somewhat roguishly, but accurately, upon his need to conceal: "So far as I am a man of really individual attributes, I veil my face; nor am I, nor have I ever been, one of those supremely hospitable people who serve up their hearts, delicately fried, with brain sauce, as a tidbit for their beloved public."

Beginning with the hyperbole in *The Literary World* and culminating in the equally extravagant language of the Farewell Letter in November 1851, Hawthorne received veneration such as one man rarely receives from another. In *Pierre*, as Henry A. Murray has noted, there are at a number of points echoes amounting sometimes to paraphrases of Melville's letters to Hawthorne. For fifteen months Hawthorne's magnetic influence emanated from a small red farmhouse at Stockbridge Bowl, six miles from the Melville home at Pittsfield. Isabel, who is Pierre's half-sister, "dwells in the little red farm-house, three miles from the village, on the slope toward the lake." Although Hawthorne himself was not overly impressed with the farmhouse, in *Pierre* it becomes a romantic dwelling: "But more

near, on the mild lake's hither shore, where it formed a long semi-
circular and scooped acclivity of corn-fields, there the small and low
red farm-house lay; its ancient roof a bed of brightest mosses; its
north front (from the north the moss-wind blows), also moss-
incrusted. . . ." Isabel's farmhouse has "three straight gigantic lin-
dens" as guardians; the only surviving photograph of the Hawthorne
house reveals three unidentifiable trees in the foreground as well as a
fir tree of which Sophia was fond. There was a two-story hen-coop
attached to the Hawthorne house; in *Pierre* there is a "lowly dairy-
shed" near one of the gables. Melville chose a red farmhouse as the
abode of a woman who was to transform Pierre's life before plunging
him into despair.

In the romance he echoes the agitated sentiments expressed in
his Farewell Letter. While their love remains untroubled, Pierre rhap-
sodizes to Lucy: "Thou art my heaven, Lucy; and here I lie thy
shepherd-king, watching for new eye-stars to rise in thee." Here he
recalled Hawthorne's "joy-giving and exultation-breeding letter"
after he had read and praised *Moby-Dick:* "In my proud, humble
way, — a shepherd-king, — I was lord of a little vale in the solitary
Crimea; but you have now given me the crown of India." When
Pierre is haunted by Isabel's face before she establishes her identity,
he resents this intrusion: "Mysterious girl! who art thou? by which
right snatchest thou thus my deepest thoughts? Take thy thin fingers
from me; — I am affianced, and not to thee. Leave me!" These lines
echo one of the most famous passages in the Farewell Letter:
"Whence come you, Hawthorne? By what right do you drink from
my flagon of life? And when I put it to my lips — lo, they are yours
and not mine."

Later Isabel, suspecting that his love has waned, fears to come
"too nigh," and Pierre asserts: "Too nigh to me, Isabel? Sun or dew,
thou fertilizest me! Can sunbeams or drops of dew come too nigh the
thing they warm and water? Then sit down by me, Isabel, and sit
close; wind in within my ribs, — if so thou canst, — that my one
frame may be the continent of two." Here Pierre mouths words from
the letter — "But I felt pantheistic then — your heart beat in my ribs
and mine in yours, and both in God's" — as well as from the article
in *The Literary World,* in which Melville confessed that "this Hawthorne has dropped germinous seeds into my soul."

After Glen Stanly stops writing affectionate letters to the
youthful Pierre, and tries to blunt the "preliminary love-friendship,"
the narrator comments: " . . . then the ardent words, 'My very' had
been prefixed to the reconsidered 'Dear Pierre;' a casual supposition,
which possibly, however unfounded, materially retarded any an-
swering warmth in Pierre, lest his generous flames should only em-

brace a flaunted feather." Pierre's anguish recalls Melville's pain when he wrote his Farewell: "Once you hugged the ugly Socrates because you saw the flame in the mouth and heard the rushing of the demon, — the familiar, — and recognized the sound; for you have heard it in your own solitudes."

Melville's love for Hawthorne, then, is echoed in the three loves in Pierre's life, Lucy, Isabel, and Glen Stanly.

He did not comment on *The Scarlet Letter* in *The Literary World,* in his letters, or apparently elsewhere in print. It may be only a coincidence, but an interesting one, that *Pierre* opens on a "morning in June," and that Hester Prynne emerges from "the prison door" "in this month of June" to accept her punishment as an adulterous woman. If *The Scarlet Letter* is not so much concerned with adulterous love as with Hester's betrayals — by parents who arrange an unnatural marriage, by a husband, Chillingworth, who abandons her to search for herbal remedies, and by her lover, Arthur Dimmesdale — so *Pierre*, in spite of the hero's "love" of two women, centers about the betrayals of males, first by his father, then by his friend Glen Stanly, next by his mother's suitor, Mr. Falsgrave, and finally by Plinlimmon.

One of the suitors of Mrs. Glendinning is the village parson, the Reverend Mr. Falsgrave. Delicate, effeminate in appearance, he wears on his bosom an "exquisitely cut cameo brooch, representing the allegorical union of the serpent and the dove." Although Falsgrave does not want to banish the fallen woman, Delly Ulver, as Mrs. Glendinning decrees with the certainty of a puritan magistrate, he, like Arthur Dimmesdale, lacks the courage of his ministerial convictions. In compromising his principles, he retains Mrs. Glendinning's ambiguous favor by surrendering the Christian spirit of forgiveness and betraying Pierre's youthful idealism. Surely Falsgrave's name was derived from Holgrave, the daguerreotypist in *The House of the Seven Gables* who abandons his voyeuristic profession and his socialist ideology to live in the Eden of Phoebe's sunshine. Interestingly, Holgrave, whose name in sound and syllables recalls Hawthorne's, degenerated into Falsgrave, one of the paternal figures who play Pierre false, as in Melville's eyes Hawthorne played him false.

A greater betrayer than Falsgrave, in Pierre's eyes, is a character that appears more than halfway through the novel. Plotinus Plinlimmon, like Pierre, is an author and "the Grand Master of a certain mystic Society among the Apostles," the literary group with which Pierre has a vague affiliation. On the seat of the carriage to New York Pierre discovers a pamphlet written by Plinlimmon and entitled "EI" ("If" in Greek). The narrator appears to minimize the pamphlet when he describes it as "a thin, tattered dried-fish thing; printed with blurred ink upon mean, sleazy paper." Despite its appearance Pierre becomes interested at once in what he knows, with the mysterious intuitions he is heir to, is "the profound intent of the writer of the sleazy rag pamphlet."

"EI" attempts to define two kinds of time, chronometrical and horological, the former referring to absolute or spiritual principles which exist outside of and transcend ordinary time, and the latter to earthly or clock time which is dominated by expediency and materialistic or nonspiritual considerations. The lecture establishes Plinlimmon as the theoretician who justifies Falsgrave's sophistical compromises: he offers consolation to those who believe in "the beauty of chronometrical excellence" as well as to those who practice what he calls "a virtuous expediency." Pierre's incomplete copy ends abruptly with two words: "Moreover: if —." The inconclusiveness is an appropriate conclusion for Plinlimmon's evasiveness and his unacknowledged atheism. Like Falsgrave, Plinlimmon indulges in what the narrator terms at another point "that great American bulwark and bore — elocution." At the same time the lecture is another one of Melville's virtuoso performances, like Father Mapple's sermon in *Moby-Dick*, in which he plays a verbal con game that invites the contradictory interpretations it has received.

Self-imprisoned in what the narrator calls "his own solitary closet," heated only by a pipe which, "passing straight through Isabel's chamber, entered the closet of Pierre at one corner" — a kind of "caloric" umbilical cord — the hero begins to write a novel. Soon Pierre finds himself watched by another occupant of the Apostles who turns out to be Plotinus Plinlimmon. "Through two panes of glass — his own and the stranger's," he becomes familiar with Plinlimmon's "blue-eyed, mystic-mild face" and finds himself magnetically drawn to "that remarkable face of repose, — repose neither divine nor human, nor any thing made up of either or both — but a repose separate and apart — a repose of a face by itself."

Plinlimmon's face and blue eyes hover over Pierre in response to a need which has nothing at all to do with the older man himself. At first Plinlimmon like a kind father seems to offer "repose" to Pierre's agitated spirits, but soon he begins "to domineer in a very remarkable manner." Then the face seems to become censorious: "Vain! vain! vain! . . . Fool! fool! fool! . . . Quit! quit! quit!" Now the face "says" with "a sort of malicious leer": "*Ass! ass! ass!*" Finally — "most terrible" — Pierre declares with a shudder, "the face knows that Isabel is not my wife! And that seems the reason it leers."

But the face "voices" only Pierre's projections of his panic. Plinlimmon himself never speaks except in the words of his pamphlet. In a need bordering on madness Pierre transforms Plinlimmon

into a father figure and cries out in the anguished tones of a child to
a parent. Plinlimmon's castigation is the self-castigation of a son who
in his own eyes has failed his father; the bitterness is a desperate
scream of rage against his "betrayer" and himself.

When Pierre meets Plinlimmon on the street, the older man lifts
his hat, bows gracefully, and passes on, without uttering a word.
"But Pierre was all confusion; he flushed, looked askance, stammered
with his hand at his hat to return the courtesy of the other; he
seemed thoroughly upset by the mere sight of the hat-lifting, gracefully bowing, gently-smiling, and most miraculously self-possessed,
non-benevolent man." Although Pierre rarely understates an opinion
or underplays an emotion, here and everywhere in his relationship
with Plinlimmon he appears to overreact. Like Billy Budd he becomes a stammering, blushing boy. Billy is at least falsely accused of
mutiny when he strikes out against Claggart in uncontrollable rage,
but Plinlimmon has nothing to do directly with Pierre and is not,
except by a wide stretch of plausibility, essential either to the action
or to the evolution of Pierre.

If, however, as many critics agree, Plinlimmon is a fictional
representation of Hawthorne, his artistic function is not necessarily
justified, but the impact of the blue-eyed, mystical face upon Pierre
at least becomes comprehensible, since we are then discussing the
impact of the Hawthorne-Melville relationship upon the novel.

Except for the addition of a moustache which Hawthorne did
not have in 1852, the description of the Grand Master — "a very
plain, composed, manly figure, with a countenance rather pale if any
thing, but quite clear and without wrinkle" — conjures up Nathaniel
Hawthorne. The description becomes a variation upon the Apollo
icon in Melville's writings.

> Though the brow and the beard, and the steadiness of the head and set-
> tledness of the step indicated mature age, yet the blue, bright, but still
> quiescent eye offered a very striking contrast. In that eye, the gay immor-
> tal youth Apollo, seemed enshrined; while on that ivory-throned brow, old
> Saturn cross-legged sat. The whole countenance of this man, the whole air
> and look of this man, expressed a cheerful content. Cheerful is the adjec-
> tive, for it was the contrary of gloom; content — perhaps acquiescence — is
> the substantive, for it was not Happiness or Delight. But while the personal
> look and air of this man were thus winning, there was still something
> latently visible in him which repelled. That something may best be
> characterized as non-Benevolence. Non-Benevolence seems the best
> word, for it was neither Malice nor Ill-will; but something passive. To
> crown all, a certain floating atmosphere seemed to invest and go along
> with this man. That atmosphere seems only renderable in words by
> the term Inscrutableness.

Unlike the extravagant earlier icons this one is tentative and qualified as the narrator seeks carefully for "the adjective" and "the substantive" which will adequately characterize Plinlimmon's physical stature and his personal and moral weaknesses. Almost every attribute is prefaced by *seem* in one form or another. The narrator struggles to be objective about the Apollo-Saturn figure, although his qualifications lead inevitably to the disparagement of Plinlimmon, his objectivity actually being ambivalence.

The ambivalence in *Pierre* was not evident in 1850 in Melville's articles in *The Literary World* or in the conversations reported by Sophia Hawthorne. "Mr. Hawthorne was the first person whose physical being appeared to him [Melville] wholly in harmony with the intellectual & spiritual. He said the sunny hair & the pensiveness, the symmetry of his face, the depth of eyes, 'the gleam – the shadow – & the peace supreme' all were in exact response to the high calm intellect, the glowing, deep heart – the purity of actual & spiritual life." Melville and others found "Nathaniel of Salem" "inscrutable" and believed that the somber attire "veiled" the man. But most observers were drawn to the blue eyes which, according to Bayard Taylor, breathed fire, or, in the words of a foreign novelist, Frederika Bremer: "Wonderful, wonderful eyes! They give, but receive not."

Pierre and *The Blithedale Romance* were written at the same time, at opposite ends of the state, in Pittsfield and West Newton. Although the authors may have discussed their romances before they separated, during the actual composition there was no contact, except for Melville's facetious comparison of *Pierre* to a "rural bowl of milk" in a letter to Sophia Hawthorne. Yet, as a number of commentators have pointed out, there are resemblances between the two works. Both writers draw upon autobiographical materials, Melville in the elaborate way dealt with in the preceding chapter, Hawthorne recalling his experiences at Brook Farm a decade earlier. Newton Arvin notes that Hollingsworth and Pierre are rabid idealists, fanatics or fools of virtue, and at the same time destroyers of women.

Both works have pairs of young women similar in appearance and personality. Priscilla in Hawthorne's romance and Lucy in *Pierre* are blonde, long-suffering, and self-sacrificing. Their respective counterparts, Zenobia and Isabel, are dark, erotic, egomaniacal women, both of whom are orphans, although Zenobia eventually recovers her father. Incest is not Hawthorne's subject, but Zenobia and Priscilla are sisters in love with the same man, Hollingsworth.

Pierre and Coverdale achieve some fame in their youth as authors of fashionable poems, but, aware of their limitations, both abandon poetry and take up the novel. Coverdale consistently minimizes himself by dwelling upon his timidity and his desire to be a spectator rather than an activist. The narrator of *Pierre* consigns his central character to fooldom almost from the first page. Coverdale manages to emerge from the ordeal relatively unscathed and to write an ironic record of the events twelve years later. Pierre dies, unsuccessful in love, life, and art — a pathetic fool.

Although Coverdale declares in the concluding chapter that he is in love with Priscilla, which may or may not be true, his involvement with Hollingsworth is more intense in the story, which as narrator he completely controls, than is his attachment to either of the sisters. Shortly after he arrives at the farm where the experiment in communal living takes place, Coverdale becomes ill and is nursed back to health by Hollingsworth, who, once a blacksmith, has "something of the woman moulded into the great, stalwart frame." Although Priscilla and Zenobia pursue Hollingsworth, women have little attraction for him. He disdains "petticoated monstrosities," women who refuse to be mothers and subordinates to men.   "I would call upon my own sex," he declaims, "to use its physical force, that unmistakeable evidence of sovereignty, to scourge them back within their proper bounds!" The love he withholds from women he offers to Coverdale first as a nurse and then as an associate in his crusade to reform criminals. This alliance, he insists to Coverdale, "offers you (what you have told me, over and over again, that you most need) a purpose in life. . . . Strike hands with me; and, from this moment, you shall never again feel the languor and vague wretchedness of an indolent or half-occupied man!" Hollingsworth disguises from himself that he seeks more than a disciple in an humanitarian cause. Suddenly his intellectualizations give way, and in a broken voice, with tears pouring down his face, he exposes his need for affection. "Coverdale," he murmurs, "there is not the man in this wide world, whom I can love as I could you. Do not forsake me!"

To escape Hollingsworth's "magnetism" Coverdale asks about the affections of the two sisters. "What have they to do with the proposal which I make you?" Hollingsworth demands, "after a moment of pregnant silence." "Will you devote yourself, and sacrifice all to this great end, and be my friend of friends, forever?" Within each sentence Hollingsworth wavers between authoritarian assertions and the pleas of a lover; between, in short, his two sexual roles. Now desperate and chagrined, Hollingsworth tries to subdue Coverdale with a command worthy of an Old Testament patriarch: "Be with me, or be against me! There is no third choice for you." Coverdale, "in the revulsion that followed a strenuous exercise of opposing will," dares to say, "No!"

In reliving the encounter as he writes *The Blithedale Romance*,

Coverdale explains his response:

> I never said the word . . . that cost me a thousandth part so hard an effort
> as did that one syllable. The heart-pang was not merely figurative, but an
> absolute torture of the breast. I was gazing steadfastly at Hollingsworth. It
> seemed to me that it struck him, too, like a bullet. A ghastly paleness —
> always so terrific on a swarthy face — overspread his features. There was a
> convulsive movement of his throat, as if he were forcing down some words
> that struggled and fought for utterance. Whether words of anger, or words
> of grief, I cannot tell; although, many and many a time, I have vainly
> tormented myself with conjecturing which of the two they were.

The chapter in which this exchange takes place is called "A
Crisis." It could have been called "The Crisis," for it is the pivotal
chapter in the book. Following the scene, Coverdale leaves for the
city, for "cozy" bachelor quarters which insulate him from Hollingsworth and others. As Coverdale runs away, so too does Hawthorne,
for in the rest of the romance the conflict between Hollingsworth
and Zenobia replaces the subject of male friendship.

If Melville comments upon his relationship with Hawthorne
through the characters of Plinlimmon and Pierre, it seems equally
plausible, as Dr. Murray suggests, that Hawthorne presents his version
through the characters of Hollingsworth and Coverdale.

Hollingsworth's physical appearance conjures up Melville as
Plinlimmon's does Hawthorne. Hollingsworth, we are informed, "was
then about thirty years old, but looked several years older, with his
great shaggy head, his heavy brow, his dark complexion, his abundant beard, and the rude strength with which his features seemed to
have been hammered out of iron, rather than chiselled or moulded
from any finer or softer material. His figure was not tall, but massive
and brawny." After Sophia Hawthorne met Melville she was charmed
by his forceful volatility and noted a contradiction between the absence of polish and a delicacy beneath the manly facade. Her portrait
closely resembles her husband's description of Hollingsworth: "As
for external polish, or mere courtesy of manner, he never possessed
more than a tolerably educated bear; although, in his gentler moods,
there was a tenderness in his voice, eyes, mouth, in his gesture, and in
every indescribable manifestion, which few men could resist, and no
women."

Although Coverdale is about the same age as Hollingsworth,
while Hawthorne was fifteen years older than Melville, this discrep-
ancy does not falsify the situation. For as the ardent pursuer, Melville placed Hawthorne in the feminine, passive role and conferred
upon him a youthfulness at odds with his chronological years.

It is interesting that in the fictional depictions of Hawthorne,

as Plinlimmon and Coverdale, both writers were in agreement. Plinlimmon and Coverdale are authors and voyeurs, given to observing
from windows or from protected retreats. Such spying is a recurrent theme in Hawthorne's tales. Reticent, Plinlimmon and Coverdale
cloak their personalities and keep their distance, which means that
they keep others at a distance. In their relationship Hawthorne maintained his "silence" before Melville's flood of words. Hawthorne
knew himself well. Before he married Sophia Peabody, he confessed
to an "external reserve" which shielded what he called his "delicacy." The barriers he placed between himself and others were deliberate. His coolness — what others saw as coldness — was his way of
protecting himself from the outside world which he, like many of the
characters in his tales, feared.

One of the major conflicts between Hollingsworth and Coverdale centers about their attitudes toward women. Similarly one of
the principal differences between Melville and Hawthorne appears in
the misogyny of the former and the latter's celebration of woman. In
The Blithedale Romance Hawthorne discusses a subject that pre-
occupies Melville, the bond between men. Coverdale asserts that
friendship can exist only between women: "There is nothing parallel
to this, I believe, — nothing so foolishly disinterested, and hardly
anything so beautiful — in the masculine nature, at whatever epoch
of life; or, if there be, a fine and rare development of character might
reasonably be looked for, from the youth who should prove himself
capable of such self-forgetful affection." In the scene in which
Hollingsworth makes his misogynistic pronouncements, he fails to
hear Coverdale's rejoinder or perhaps to take him seriously: "I have
never found it possible to suffer a bearded priest so near my heart
and conscience as to do me any spiritual good. . . . The task belongs
to woman. God meant it for her."

Years later, in *The Marble Faun*, Kenyon is the confidante of
the human statue Donatello, but he clearly defines the limits of the
involvement: "I do not pretend to be the guide and counsellor whom
Donatello needs; for, to mention no other obstacle, I am a man, and,
between man and man, there is always an insuperable gulf. They can
never quite grasp each other's hands; and therefore man never derives
any intimate help, any heart-sustenance, from his brother man, but
from woman — his mother, his sister, or his wife." Just as Kenyon
cannot "grasp" Donatello's hand, so Coverdale cannot "strike hands"
with Hollingsworth. Plinlimmon-Hawthorne bows to Pierre but does
not offer to shake hands.

If Coverdale is not successful in putting Hollingsworth out of
mind twelve years after their involvement at Blithedale, Hawthorne
did not banish Melville or the Berkshires when he moved to West

Newton. The artistic fissure in *The Blithedale Romance* — the unsatisfactory treatment of the male friendship theme when the emotional logic of the work demands deeper exploration — may be attributable to Hawthorne's troubled and mixed feelings toward Melville.

Since the events that transpired in 1851 left their marks on both men, we need to attempt a reconstruction of the emotional climate in which these two geniuses lived out their encounter.

Hawthorne came to Lenox spent and exhausted in 1850. *The Scarlet Letter* struggled into life, as one would expect, after months of pain. When Hawthorne read the final pages to Sophia and both wept, the tears were not shed solely for that martyr of puritanism, Hester Prynne. These were tears of relief and release, for after the loss of his position in the Salem Custom House and the death of his mother, Hawthorne restructured his badly shaken universe in an exquisitely structured romance and at the same time paid one of the loveliest tributes ever made to Mother. But in the enervation that followed the realization of his masterpiece he wanted to shake off the pain of creativity and the dust of Salem, Massachusetts. Restless, he sought a new beginning, away from his birthplace, from his years of seclusion in the "little room" which he rightly observed would be of importance to future biographers. He was impatient to settle into the red farmhouse in the Berkshires, but for weeks after he arrived he was overcome by lassitude. Sophia watched over him anxiously.

In the summer there was the exhilaration of the meeting with Melville, followed shortly by his deification in the pages of *The Literary World*. Then there were the early visits from Melville and the exchanges, one-sided as they often were, when Mr. Typee held forth in his manic manner. In the fall Hawthorne began *The House of the Seven Gables*. This most joyful book, an epithalamion to Sophia "Phoebe" Hawthorne, was wrung from pain. In November he complained to James T. Fields, his publisher, that "the book requires more care and thought than 'The Scarlet Letter.' " Sometimes the scenes and the mood would not come, or he could not find the words to realize his vision of a Dutch interior transferred to Salem. "Sometimes, when tired of it," he wrote, "it strikes me that the whole is an absurdity from beginning to end; but the fact is, in writing a romance, a man is always, or always ought to be, careering on the utmost verge of a precipitous absurdity, and the skill lies in coming as close as possible, without actually tumbling over."

The romance was completed in February 1851, and he was convinced, or so he said, that *The House of the Seven Gables* was a better and truer book than *The Scarlet Letter*. He allowed himself to be idle only for a short time. He saw the *House* through the press, assembled more tales and composed a preface to *The Snow-Image and Other Twice-Told Tales*, and wrote *A Wonder-Book for Girls and Boys*. Sometime in 1851 he had decided that his experiences at Brook Farm were to be the background of his next full-length romance. During these months he drove himself too hard, probably for many reasons, but partly perhaps because he now had to live up to Melville's proclamation that he was the American Shakespeare.

The demands of such unrelenting creativity and sheer hard work made him restless. As early as April 1851 he confessed to Duyckinck the need for "a relief from too profound repose" (which, coincidentally, happens to be the attribute of Plinlimmon that is especially irksome to Pierre). He did not look forward to another summer in the Berkshires. He wanted the city and "iced-creams and all kinds of iced liquors" which were "greatly preferable to the luke-warm basin of a brook, with its tadpoles and insects mingling in your draught." On May 18, he informed Henry Wadsworth Longfellow that "I need to smell the sea-breeze and dock mud, and to tread pavements." Although he was "as happy as mortal can be," he wrote, "sometimes my soul gets into a ferment, as it were, and becomes troublous and bubblous with too much peace and rest."

In his notebook in July Hawthorne complained of this "horrible, horrible, most hor-ri-ble climate." He was not ordinarily given in public or in private to such melodramatics. "I detest it! I detest it!! I de-test it!!!" he wailed. "I hate Berkshire with my whole soul, and would joyfully see the mountains laid flat . . . here, where I hoped for perfect health, I have for the first time been made sensible that I cannot with impunity encounter Nature in all her moods." Here Hawthorne lifted the veil and revealed openly the depression he was experiencing. Usually he denied himself such candor.

Later in the month he informed a friend, "I do not feel at home among these hills." Early in September he shared a secret with Fields: "I am sick to death of Berkshire." And then followed another admission: "for the first time since I was a boy, I have felt languid and dispirited during almost my whole residence here." What he told Fields was scarcely "a secret," unless, as seems likely, he had not made known to Sophia his decision to leave the Berkshires. Although she watched over him carefully, she had not noted in her letters to her family that Mr. Hawthorne was reflecting the mood of "THE POSTHUMOUS PAPERS OF A DECAPITATED SURVEYOR."

Unquestionably Hawthorne taxed his intellectual and physical energies in the fifteen months he spent at Lenox. Without the economic security of a government post he had real economic problems. He had no way of knowing that his romances would be popular successes or would provide an adequate income. Nor did the arrival of Rose ease his economic lot.

Two months after her birth he assured a friend that "she is to be the daughter of my age — the comfort (at least, so it is to be hoped) of my declining years." She was the last child he expected or intended to have. His words and his decision implied a feeling that for him life was closing in, that he was on the verge of old age. Perhaps he suffered only from exhaustion or from what is sometimes termed middle-aged depression, but whatever the cause or causes his spirits and resiliency were at low ebb. So, too, are Coverdale's in *The Blithedale Romance*.

Finally, there was Melville.

For months Hawthorne had received accolades such as few men receive, in print, in letters, and in conversation. On the one hand he was flattered; on the other hand the flattery was an assault. The praise in *The Literary World* was too extravagant, except in the eyes of Sophia Hawthorne. The florid and charged language of the letters could only have troubled a man who from his earliest years had trained himself to repress emotions, even in the intimacy of the family circle.

Sophia observed some of the personal exchanges between the "growing man" and the "Father Confessor," but the two men often sipped champagne and smoked cigars alone. What Melville said when they were the sole occupants of the Berkshire Ti and how Hawthorne responded to and handled Melville's volcanic outbursts, we can never know, since two extraordinarily articulate artists shrouded their conversations and their reactions in a silence that the passage of more than a century cannot disturb.

Since Hawthorne fulfilled Melville's icon of ideal male friendship, it is difficult to imagine that in conversation he could have concealed the affection he felt for a man who was a father and a brother come to life. Even though his passionate monologs may have been met by silence, Melville may not have construed the silence as rejection or disapproval. As Oliver Wendell Holmes observed after Hawthorne's death, "talking with him was almost like love-making, and his shy, beautiful soul had to be wooed from its bashful prudency like an unschooled maiden."

Melville, when his heart was engaged, was a fierce wooer. Similarly, the youthful protagonists in his writings — L. A. V., Tommo, Redburn, and the others — do not hesitate to assume the aggressive role of suitor. Hawthorne's heroes, on the other hand, shrink before commitment and retreat to their rooms and their veils.

Melville knew of Hawthorne's fears. In the copy of *Twice-Told Tales*, which his friend gave him on January 22, 1851, he marked the self-portrait in "Foot-prints on the Sea-shore," in which Hawthorne writes of himself: "From such a man, as if another self had scared me, I scramble hastily over the rocks, and take refuge in a nook which many a secret hour has given me a right to call my own." Melville may also have intuited that, despite the disclaimers in his fiction, Hawthorne shared his longings for a sensitive male friend. In a letter to a friend in 1850 Hawthorne articulated the longing clearly but carefully: "my theory is, that there [is] less indelicacy in speaking out your highest, deepest, tenderest emotions to the world at large than to almost any individual. You may be mistaken in the individual; but you cannot be mistaken in thinking that, somewhere among your fellow creatures, there is a heart that will receive yours into itself." Although he may have shared Melville's hunger for the ideal friend, he expected to establish no such relationship. He probably did everything possible not to become emotionally involved.

Even though Hawthorne kept Melville at a distance a great deal of the time, by delaying visits and other tactics, he was obviously attracted. If Hawthorne had found visits with Melville painful, he would not have spent two days in Pittsfield in March 1851. After spending a day with Melville and the Duyckinck brothers in August visiting a Shaker village, he was so exhilarated by the outing that he could not sleep that night and longed to be in Pittsfield.

Something occurred about this time in the relationship, possibly during Sophia's three-week absence from Lenox. Although Hawthorne had begun to complain about life in the Berkshires in April, in June Sophia informed her sister that "we wish to remain in Lenox two years more at least." Hawthorne's comments became more scathing and melodramatic during the summer, but he was negotiating for another place near the red farmhouse and Sophia had engaged a couple for the coming winter. On September 4 Sophia informed her sister Elizabeth that Hawthorne was delaying his trip to Boston: "he will not leave these beautiful days among the hills." He had hardly left Lenox when he wrote that he had engaged the home of Sophia's sister, Mrs. Horace Mann, in West Newton, which only a few months before they could not afford. On September 19 he referred elliptically to "our trouble" without explanation, since Sophia evidently understood what he meant. Writing from Salem on September 23, he said: "It does seem to me better to go; for we shall never be comfortable in Lenox again." On the same day Sophia wrote to Mrs. Mann: "Did Mr. Hawthorne tell you *all* the reasons why we are disenchanted of Lenox?" When on October 2 Sophia explained the sudden change in plans to her other sister, she admitted that "there are a great many reasons . . . & the most important one is the effect of the climate upon Mr. Hawthorne."

This was the first time she referred to Hawthorne's health, although he himself had spoken earlier of his languor. The explanation does not jibe with the admittedly vague references to "our trouble" and to disenchantment. Mrs. Hawthorne referred to an "overt act," without details, of their landlord's wife, Caroline Sturgis Tappan, who before her marriage in 1847 was an intimate of Margaret Fuller and Emerson, and apparently before and after marriage a most unconventional lady. She was friendly to Hawthorne while Sophia was in West Newton, but hostile to Sophia after her return.

Health, restlessness, economics, Mrs. Tappan — all may have contributed in some way to the hasty decision to leave. But, then there was Melville. Hawthorne could hardly have been expected to reveal to Sophia's innocent ears except in the most guarded way his fears concerning Melville's attachment, and certainly he made no allusion to "a proposal" or an "advance."

Over twenty years later, in *Clarel* (1876), Melville offered what may have been an account of what transpired in the summer of 1851. *Clarel* is a poetic version of Melville's journey to the Holy Land in 1856 and 1857. In Jerusalem, Clarel, a young theological student, meets and is magnetically drawn to a reserved man named Vine, who is a fictionalized treatment of Hawthorne. Clarel is puzzled by Vine's diffidence.

> *Like to the nunnery's denizen*
> *His virgin soul communed with men*
> *But through the wicket. Was it clear*
> *This coyness bordered not on fear —*
> *Fear or an apprehensive sense?*
> *Not wholly seemed it diffidence*
> *Recluse.*

The insight, while not unfair or unsympathetic, is probably indebted to Hawthorne's self-portrait in "Foot-prints on the Sea-shore" and perhaps to Holmes's allusion to "an unschooled maiden."

On the way to Sodom, in a secluded wood, Clarel muses as he watches Vine. He recalls "Prior advances unreturned," and longs "for communion true." He wants to say, but does not, "Give me thyself!" Afraid to make the verbal gesture which may be spurned, he continues to ruminate:

> *How pleasant in another*
> *Such sallies, or in thee, if said*
> *After confidings that should wed*
> *Our souls in one: — Ah, call me brother! —*
> *So feminine his passionate mood*

> *Which, long as hungering unfed,*
> *All else rejected or withstood.*

Then "Some inklings he let fall." The words he uses are not recorded, nor is Vine's reply, if indeed he makes one. All we know is
that "A shadow" comes over Vine's face.

Much later Clarel recalls "that repulsed advance" and freely
confesses that his heart is "hungering still, in deeper part / Unsatisfied." At last he defines the hunger, but in the form of a question:

> *Can be a bond*
> *(Thought he) as David sings in strain*
> *That dirges beauteous Jonathan,*
> *Passing the love of woman fond?*
> *And may experience but dull*
> *The longing for it?*

The hunger Clarel expresses is the same hunger that motivates
the quests of Tommo and Redburn, the passion of the article in *The
Literary World* in 1850, and the pages of *Pierre*. In *Clarel* Melville
still seeks "incorporation." The scenes in the poem also confirm
Hawthorne's veiled account of the relationship in *The Blithedale
Romance*. Hollingsworth's "proposal" is Clarel's "advance." Clarel's
celebration of male friendship Coverdale answers with perhaps too
much vehemence.

On the basis of the accounts in *The Blithedale Romance* and
Clarel we can arrive at a plausible reconstruction of what occurred in
1851. In their leisurely conversations which Melville always animated
with his nervous intensity as Hawthorne sat in "repose," the younger
man must have introduced the subject of male friendship, not once
but many times. The influence of Hawthorne's Apollonian beauty
and his fine sensibility must have elicited from Melville something
not unlike Hollingsworth's admission: "there is not the man in this
wide world whom I can love as I could you." Such a confession
Melville could not have made in a letter, where the act of recording
permits opportunity for second thoughts, hesitations, and finally evasiveness. In conversation or in an excited monolog, he may have
blurted out something like Hollingsworth's plea: "be my friend of
friends forever." Or perhaps he said, "Ah, call me brother."

No doubt a "shadow" crossed Hawthorne's face when he heard
the words, no matter how they were phrased. Such a plea he could
only have construed as an assault, an invasion of his privacy. He may
have checked Melville, but not with Coverdale's unequivocal "No!"
If he had spoken with such finality, no doubt *Moby-Dick* would have

been dedicated to someone else. As it was, Melville maniacally indulged himself in wild capers, like signing a letter "his X mark," visiting Hawthorne in a Spanish cavalier's costume, and cavorting in the company of the Duyckinck brothers during an August day that included a visit to a Shaker village.

The Duyckincks left for New York on August 14, and, after many changes of plan, Sophia Hawthorne returned on August 19 from West Newton. At the railroad station at Pittsfield she looked for "the face of Apollo," but Hawthorne had sent a neighbor to accompany her to the red farmhouse. It was probably about this time that "A Crisis" occurred when Melville made his "advance."

In September, as we have seen, suddenly the Hawthornes engaged Mrs. Mann's house in West Newton and made plans to move within two months. Hawthorne kept up appearances, as was to be expected of a man of iron. He accepted and read Melville's masterpiece, and then wrote a gracious letter in which he may have informed Melville for the first time of his departure.

Perhaps Hawthorne's praise of *Moby-Dick* revived Melville's expectation of a deep friendship. If such thoughts had not crossed his mind, surely he would have muted the eroticism in the Farewell Letter. The relationship of the two men did not end abruptly, like a novel, or with the suddenness of Coverdale's departure from Blithedale after his categorical rejection of Hollingsworth's offer. Letters continued for a year or more, and Melville visited Hawthorne in Concord in 1852. But a "shadow" had passed over the relationship.

When it came time to compose a dedication to *Pierre*, Melville chose "Greylock's Most Excellent Majesty": "for as such as I, dwelling with my loyal neighbors, the Maples and the Beeches, in the amphitheater over which his central majesty presides, have received his most bounteous and unstinted fertilizations." Such facetiousness strains to conceal the emptiness of a world in which his friends are trees, and "fertilizations" are rains and storms. The "impregnator," the "seedman" he had venerated in *The Literary World*, was gone.

As he wrote the dedication Melville must have recalled his proposal to climb the mountain with a companion who was to play Queequeg to his Ishmael. He could hardly have forgotten the graceful allusion in *A Wonder-Book for Girls and Boys* to "Herman Melville, shaping out the gigantic conception of his 'White Whale,' while the gigantic shape of Graylock looms upon him from his study-window."

Hawthorne wrote this description at the beginning of the summer of 1851, when Melville emotionally and artistically touched the heavens — before the world closed in upon him.

"Who Ain't a
Nobody?"

—The Short Stories

and

Israel Potter

The critical reception of *Mardi* in 1849 had stung Melville's pride, but the reception of *Pierre* was savage, with the critics venting their rage on the author, as in the romance Melville had vented his own rage.

A parody in *Godey's Lady Book* accurately singled out the mannered word-plays and the redundant adjectivitis from which the book suffers: "We have listened to its outbreathing of sweet-swarming sounds, and their melodious, mournful, wonderful, and unintelligible melodiousness has 'dropped like pendulous, glittering icicles,' with soft-ringing silveriness, upon our never-to-be-delighted-sufficiently organs of hearing; and, in the insignificant significancies of that deftly-stealing and wonderfully-serpentining melodiousness, we have found an infinite, unbounded, inexpressible mysteriousness of nothingness." In a Canadian review written in the form of a dialog, the critic was asked, "What is the nature of the story?" His reply was: "You might as well ask me to analyse the night-mare visions of an Alderman who after dining upon turtle and venison had wound up by supping upon lobsters and toasted cheese! The hero is a dreamy spoon, alike deficient in heart and brains." The book was attacked for its morbidity and its immorality. Even *The Literary World*, in a review presumably written by one of the Duyckincks, was offended because "The most immoral *moral* of the story, if it has any moral at all, seems to be the impracticability of virtue."

Another consistent theme in the reviews was concern for the author's sanity. The *Boston Post* termed *Pierre* "the craziest fiction extant. . . . it might be supposed to emanate from a lunatic hospital rather than from the quiet retreats of Berkshire." *The Southern Quarterly Review* made the same point with a directness that mocked the alleged decorum of the age: "That Herman Melville has gone 'clean daft,' is very much to be feared; certainly he has given us a very mad book, my masters." The reviewer could not contain himself or his offensiveness: "The sooner this author is put in ward the better. If trusted with himself, at all events give him no further trust in pen and ink, till the present fit has worn off."

The strained, mad prose was also censured. *The Athenæum* termed the style "a prolonged succession of spasms. . . . it is no refreshment after the daily toils and troubles of life, for a reader to be soused into a torrent rhapsody uttered in defiance of taste and sense." No contemporary reviewer recognized that the "spasms" married style to content in *Pierre*. The absurdity of the plot and the ambiguities of the subject matter demanded the stylistic excesses, though they defied common sense and the patience of readers. Even Fitz-James O'Brien, who wrote the most sensitive and penetrating appraisal of Melville in his own time, objected to the verbal excesses of *Pierre*: "Language is drunken and reeling. Style is antipodical, and marches on its head." For his "peculiar talents," O'Brien urged, "Let him diet himself for a year or two on Addison, and avoid Sir Thomas Browne, and there is little doubt but that he will make a notch on the American Pine." O'Brien preferred *White-Jacket* to *Moby-Dick*, *Omoo* to *Pierre*, largely because the earlier works evidenced a restraint that would have been incongruous in the later books.

There is no extant record of Melville's response to the critical blasts against *Pierre*, although they could only have hurt. He was accustomed to attacks upon the morality of his "wicked" books, and he was to continue to flout nineteenth-century decorum, but he was never again to write in the styles of *Moby-Dick* and *Pierre*. On the other hand he never again had subject matter that demanded the excesses of those two works. The simple style of his tales in the next three years was in part a return to the prose of *Typee* and *Omoo*, but it was also an adaptation to his audience of magazine readers as well as to the subject matter he dealt with. He still manipulated style to suit the demands of most dissimilar works like *Israel Potter* and *The Confidence-Man*. He was far more subtle than his critics.

That one reviewer after another spoke of his artistic decline seemed to confirm what he had written to Hawthorne in 1851, before he completed *Moby-Dick* — his fear that "I am now come to the inmost leaf of the bulb, and that shortly the flower must fall to the mould." The sales of the two books which he had wrung out of his guts confirmed his loss of favor. In the first eighteen months following publication of the American edition, *Moby-Dick* sold 2,300 copies. Eight months after the release of *Pierre*, Harper's reported that only 283 copies of an edition of 2,310 had been sold. (In Melville's lifetime *Pierre* produced royalties amounting to $157.)

Obviously authorship was providing an inadequate and uncertain livelihood for a man whose family increased every two years. How the Melvilles managed, even with Elizabeth's annual return from a trust fund, it is impossible to say, but Melville's tax statements reveal that he had $1,500 in the bank in 1852, $2,000 in 1853, and $2,500 in 1854. Included in these figures no doubt was the advance of $500 for *Pierre* and $300 in 1853 for a book about tortoises. The farm may have produced some income, and Maria Melville may have borne some of the household expenses, but the Melvilles must have lived frugally.

About three months after the publication of *Pierre* a family council at Arrowhead decided that Herman should seek a consular post in the new administration of Franklin Pierce. No doubt the decision was influenced by the fact that Nathaniel Hawthorne had written the campaign biography for his college chum and was to receive a diplomatic post as a reward. The Melvilles launched a campaign not unlike Gansevoort's in 1844 after the election of Polk. Peter Gansevoort asked his friends to write letters on Melville's behalf. Judge Shaw and his Boston associates joined in what became a deluge of recommendations. Hawthorne spoke to various officials in Washington. Although a large file of letters grew in support of his candidacy, Herman himself did little but observe the activities. His brother Allan took complete charge, even to discussing the matter on several occasions with Hawthorne and writing to Herman's father-in-law.

To guard its self-respect the family took the position publicly that it was not so much financial need as health that made a consular post necessary. His mother, with her customary exaggeration, was quite explicit: "The constant in-door confinement with little intermission to which Hermans occupation as author compels him, does not agree with him. This constant working of the brain, & excitement of the imagination, is wearing Herman out." When the Honolulu post was awarded to another applicant, the Melvilles (or at any rate Allan) were ready to settle for any post except those which provided no emoluments.

Melville evidently never voiced disappointment when his name was passed over. He was better qualified than many who received diplomatic sinecures, but he had no claims on politicians. As one of the people who wrote a recommendation observed, he "has not taken any part in politics since his residence in Pittsfield, and I believe has not attended the polls. I am not aware that he has made any public expression of his political opinions."

Although Melville was exhausted after he finished *Pierre*, there was no evidence in the letters of 1852 and 1853 of unusual depressed states or physical impairments. But after Hawthorne's departure from Lenox in November 1851 there was also no one to whom he exposed his heart. Since 1849 he had dedicated himself almost continuously to producing one book after another. After completing *Pierre* in late March or early April 1852, he did not plunge at once into another work. Not until the end of the year did he return to his study, and then perhaps for the first time he began a work which he could not finish. The abortive work was tied up with Hawthorne.

Hawthorne renewed the correspondence when he sent a presentation copy of *The Blithedale Romance* to Melville early in July 1852, and apparently included a note inviting him to Concord. Melville acknowledged the gift while declining the invitation in a letter written on July 17, after his return to Pittsfield following a two-week tour with Judge Shaw of Cape Cod, Martha's Vineyard, and Nantucket. He noted that everywhere he went people were reading new books by Hawthorne. He flattered his friend but said nothing of himself except that he had been "an utter idler and a savage" for the past three months. He was friendly and a trifle precious: "Do send me a specimen of your sand-hill, and a sunbeam from the countenance of Mrs: Hawthorne, and a vine from the curly arbor of Master Julian." But the passionate intensity of the letters of the previous years was missing, and the letter was signed "H Melville," not "Herman." On August 13 Melville sent Hawthorne a copy of *Pierre*. In the records which have survived there is no indication of the reactions of the two men to the romances which, as we have argued, commented upon their relationship in the Berkshires.

Along with the book Melville enclosed a lengthy account of a tale involving a woman named Agatha Hatch Robertson. Because of the resemblance of Agatha's story to "Wakefield," Hawthorne's strange account of a man who deserts his wife and lives, unknown to her, a block or so away for twenty years, Melville thought the material lay "very much in a vein, with which you are peculiarly familiar. To be plump, I think that in this matter you would make a better hand at it than I would." Melville could not refrain from offering a long explanation of how he would handle the tale, although he probably was aware that his advice could be construed as effrontery. "I do not therefore, My Dear Hawthorne, at all imagine that you will think that I am so silly as to flatter myself I am giving you anything of my own. I am but restoring to you your own property — which you would quickly enough have identified for yourself — had you but been on the spot as I happened to be."

On October 25 Melville offered another suggestion about the treatment of the Agatha story, and informed Hawthorne of the appearance of a guide book to the Berkshires entitled *Taghonic; or Letters and Legends about Our Summer Homes*, by J. E. A. Smith, in which "you are the most honored, being the most abused, and having the greatest space allotted you." Melville was praised by Smith, but a "Mr. Buckham of Lenox" censured Hawthorne's seclusion, his morbidity and coldness, and his unsympathetic treatment of puritans. Curiously, many of the contributors to the books were friends of Melville, including Smith, Mrs. Morewood, his neighbor, and John C. Hoadley, who was shortly to become his brother-in-law. Melville was not certain "when I shall see you. I shall lay eyes on you one of these days however." Then he added the kind of facetious remark that characterized his correspondence with Hawthorne: "Keep some Champagne or Gin for me," but the postscript was a grim witticism, essentially hostile: "If you find any *sand* in this letter, regard it as so many sands of my life, which run out as I was writing it."

A month later he spent a day with Hawthorne in Concord. At this meeting Hawthorne urged him to write the story of Agatha. A day or so later Melville wrote to say that he would undertake the task. "I invoke your blessing upon my endeavors; and breathe a fair wind upon me. I greatly enjoyed my visit to you, and hope that you reaped some corresponding pleasure."

On October 1, 1852, the editors of a new journal, *Putnam's Monthly Magazine*, sent Melville a circular letter asking him to become a contributor. For the first time in his career, unless "Fragments from a Writing Desk" is to be included, he undertook a medium which demanded compression and a control at variance with his tendency to permit his material to grow without check. He was also undertaking a form in which Hawthorne had demonstrated his mastery years earlier.

Melville began his version of the Agatha story in December, and it may have been the work his mother said was ready for the press in

April 1853. Since no manuscript survives, it would appear that he was unable to complete it. In 1853 he completed only two stories, "Bartleby the Scrivener," his masterpiece in the form, and "Cock-a-Doodle-Doo." On November 24th of that year he informed Harper & Brothers that he had been "prevented" from printing a work which he had completed in the preceding spring, presumably his account of Agatha, and now he had "pretty well on towards completion, another book — 300 pages, say — partly of nautical adventure, and partly — or, rather, chiefly, of Tortoise Hunting Adventure." Harper's gave him the requested advance of $300 in December, even though he was still in debt to the firm because earnings from his books had not paid off earlier advances. Toward the end of February, 1854, he informed the publisher that, "owing to a variety of causes," the manuscript was not ready. Yet "The Encantadas," which is a collection of sketches including the well-known one entitled "Two Sides to a Tortoise," began to appear in *Putnam's* in March and ran for three months.

Although Melville was unable to expand "The Encantadas" to book length, he did manage to finish in 1854 a long work called *Israel Potter*, which appeared in serial form in *Putnam's* and later as a book. In addition, he wrote five other tales in the same year. In 1855 he was seriously ill early in the year but composed five stories after his recovery. In 1856 he completed three tales and his last extended work in prose, *The Confidence-Man*.

Although the returns from the magazines do not seem large today, Melville was among the best paid writers of the era. He received $85 for "Bartleby," $37.50 for "The Bell-Tower," and $421.50 for *Israel Potter*. Payments, as was customary, were determined by the number of pages. If Melville occasionally padded, or at least did not compress rigorously, the reason is obvious.

Critical comments on the magazine works were usually kind, many reviewers maintaining that Melville had returned to his senses, which meant that he had returned to their standards. For Melville the form was new, the prose was for the most part simpler and leaner, partly because there were no Ahabs or Pierres exploding in rhetorical outbursts, but the subject matter was not substantially altered.

Melville's underworld was peopled with many demons, and the specter of failure would seem to have been one of the most frightening. In one way or another he presents in his short stories failures whose plights are sometimes rationalized, sometimes given an unconvincing aura of heroism which their enervation contradicts.

Jimmy Rose, a bachelor businessman as handsome as the youthful sailors, enjoys great success until two of his ships sink as they are coming into New York harbor. He is immediately ruined and, like

Timon of Athens, he is deserted by his friends. Eventually Jimmy "rose" from his poverty in that the bloom returns to his cheeks when the narrator sees him twenty-five years later. But the truth is that Jimmy is now a parasite upon the wealthy to whom he toadies for crusts of bread. As some critics have observed, "Jimmy Rose" may be a kind of tribute to Uncle Thomas Melvill, who managed to maintain some vestiges of self-respect and eccentric charm after his business reversals, although in middle life he had to accept the unpleasant recognition that he was unable to manage his farm in Pittsfield and that he was economically dependent upon his father. Herman knew his uncle's story well, but his father's better. The narrator of the tale is a youth and Rose about forty years of age when he fails. Allan Melvill was forty-eight when he became a bankrupt in 1830. It is hardly accidental that Allan's first failure occurred when a ship of which he was a part owner sank in 1811.

"The Fiddler" also appears to reverberate with allusions to Melville's own experiences. Hautboy until age twelve is a prodigy, fabulously successful as a violinist in America and in Europe. Then he vanishes only to reappear at age forty as a colorful raconteur and fiddler of folk music, blissfully satisfied, we are told, with his life as well as his obscurity. Once again, perhaps unconsciously, Melville refers to the fact that his world fell apart at age twelve. The narrator of the story is an unsuccessful writer who has had a poem rejected and is depressed that "immortal fame is not for me!" He comes to admire Hautboy's stamina in the face of adversity. But here and elsewhere, and especially in a trifle entitled "The Happy Failure," we are dealing with wish-fulfillment. Melville was whistling in the dark. No man in his early thirties, at the middle of the life journey, reconciles himself to seeing his career, and therefore his life, at an end. In 1851 Melville saw himself sharing Mount Olympus with Hawthorne, but in 1853 and 1854 he was adjusting himself, or so he intimated, to the happy life of a failure, although his failures are scarcely happy.

If in these tales the actors appear to be simpletons, it is because Melville is writing nonsense. If the stories are not convincing, it is because he was not honest with himself. It is no mistake that many of these stories about failures are artistic failures; Melville could not completely delude himself.

In "Cock-a-Doodle-Doo" he plays with obvious irony upon the Christian symbol of resurrection. Merrymusk, a happy but poor laborer, is the proud possessor of a rooster that crows with musical phrases worthy of a Beethoven. While Merrymusk and his family joyfully listen to the rooster, and refuse to sell it, they gladly starve to death. Once an alcoholic, Merrymusk is now addicted to the rooster. Bannadonna, the master builder in "The Bell-Tower," is killed by his own flawed creation, an ingenious clock which he constructs in the tower of a village church. The narrator of "I and My Chimney" attempts to preserve his chimney from his wife's designs to remodel the home and to destroy the only thing which appears to give the middle-aged man satisfaction. Benito Cereno loses control of his ship and his person to a group of slaves led by Babo. He sees his closest friend butchered by the blacks, and he is powerless to take revenge or even to take his own life. Bartleby, the clerk who "prefers not" to be a clerk or anything else, starves himself to death in what may be heroic defiance of the "establishment" (Wall Street) or psychosis.

In these tales the narrator identifies with the protagonists because he suffers from the same sense of failure. He too is a nonhero. The lawyer-narrator in "Bartleby," despite his professional success and the favor of John Jacob Astor, is almost as lonely and alienated as the scrivener. A bachelor, he has opted for Plinlimmon's compromise with the world's values, but he is willing to "adopt" Bartleby and take him into his home. The narrator of "Cock-a-Doodle-Doo" is as devoted to the rooster as Merrymusk; he is the only other person aware of the rooster's magical sounds. Like Ishmael, he is "too full of hypoes to sleep" and is subject to "doleful dumps."

Instead of embodying social norms, the narrators like their noncharacters are closer to the non-sense of a world without reason. They discard objectivity or detachment, conspire to befuddle issues and norms, and, like Ahab, make reality a mirror image of their anguish and flawed lives. The comic touches intended often to make the content palatable to a magazine audience turn into cruel mockery, and comedy no longer fulfills its traditional role as custodian of social values.

The scenes in the sketches which comprise "The Encantadas" are desolate in the extreme, the landscape littered with human and natural debris. In "Benito Cereno" gray and black are the primary colors: there are "Shadows present, foreshadowing deeper shadows to come." "The Bell-Tower" is set in the south of Europe, where we find "dank mould," "the black mossed stump of some immeasurable pine. . . . its dissolution leaves a mossy mound — last-flung shadow of the perished trunk." Everywhere — decay, disease, death. The desolation extends beyond the settings. The characters are for the most part amputations, caricatures of humanity.

The family is almost nonexistent, or, in "Cock-a-Doodle-Doo," huddled in a squalid little room gladly dying of starvation. Husband and wife are emotionally separated in "I and My Chimney." It is hinted that there may be something meaningful in the fact that Bartleby has worked in a Dead-Letter Office. The narrator of "Cock-a-Doodle-Doo," it is implied, has intimations of disaster after the loss of a "dear friend." Benito Cereno is incapacitated for living after the murder of his friend in the slave insurrection. In these tales friendship no longer substitutes for the family. It too is dead. Friendship is burlesqued in "Benito Cereno" and "Bartleby the Scrivener." Although Captain Delano is puzzled by the disorder and filth he finds aboard the slave ship, he is pleased to discover what appears to be a perfect master-servant relationship between Cereno and Babo. Babo never leaves Benito's side and cares for him like a child, but the truth kept from Delano is that Babo is in command of the ship but masquerades as an attentive servant. Sick at heart and harassed, Benito swoons into the waiting arms of Babo on at least seven occasions. This is the basic collapsing rhythm of the story. After Babo nicks Benito while shaving him, they shortly emerge, "Don Benito leaning on his servant as if nothing had happened," and Delano considers it "a sort of love-quarrel."

If Babo and Benito play out a charade that at any moment may end in the Spaniard's death, friendship is never realized in "Bartleby the Scrivener." After the lawyer hires Bartleby as a clerk in his legal firm, he attempts to befriend him in every possible way. He is annoyed but tolerant when his employee stops copying. He continues to provide him with a salary and shelter and at one point offers him a room in his own home. When Bartleby languishes in prison as a vagrant, the lawyer pays for special food and visits the most forlorn of men. Bartleby "prefers not to" have anything to do with the lawyer. If he scarcely touches life, he will permit no one to touch him. If he has been betrayed, except by the fact that he was born, we do not know about it since he discloses nothing about himself. If he refuses to receive aid, he gives nothing. His retreat into his own world provides the only shelter he apparently can tolerate. Lacking in self-trust, he places no trust in any man.

The most convivial group of people in these tales, excluding the dying Merrymusks, are the nine bachelors in "The Paradise of Bachelors" who gather at the London Inns of Court for feasts. In quarters once occupied by Knights-Templars, who at least had a mission, if a perverse one, they gorge themselves with the assistance of a servant named Socrates. Theirs is not a "symposium": they regale each other with banalities. Then they leave, arm-in-arm, each to go to his own quarters, some "to turn over the *Decameron* ere retiring." Child-men, they have regressed to oral delights and autoeroticism. Although Melville drew upon an experience he had in London in 1849, the sketch is a variation upon his account of the natives of Typee in the all-male Ti or upon the little group of kindred spirits who gather about Jack Chase in *White-Jacket*. As in the novels, the narrator becomes maudlin: "Ah! when I bethink me of the sweet hours there passed, enjoying such congenial hospitalities beneath these time-honored roofs, my heart only finds due utterance through poetry; and, with a sigh, I softly sing, 'Carry me back to old Virginny!' " Perhaps Melville wrote tongue in cheek, but male camaraderie elicited a sentimental response from him. Yet the bachelors in this sketch are isolates who periodically come out of their shells under the stimulation of food and drink.

"The Paradise of Bachelors" appeared with "The Tartarus of Maids" in *Harper's* in April 1855. In the second sketch the narrator identifies himself as a seedman and gives an account of a visit to a paper factory. The mills produce paper in nine minutes with apparatus that resembles the sexual reproductive organs. The tale is a grotesque mockery of the birth and sexual processes. The girls are not wives but passive virgins who lose their maidenheads to machinery and who give birth to foolscap.

The pair of tales dramatically illustrates the despair which possessed Melville and the emotional climate in which he wrote his short stories. During that period his family was increased by the birth of two daughters, Elizabeth on May 22, 1853, and Frances on March 2, 1855. "The Tartarus of Maids" may be a comment upon his wife's pregnancies as well as an unconscious admission of his own preference for male gatherings where sexuality, family, and responsibilities do not intrude.

Hunilla in "The Encantadas" is the only admirable woman in these tales and one of the few women to engage our hearts in Melville's writings. Deserted on an island, she endures the deaths of her husband and her brother and subsequently three years of ravishment by nature, with a silent stoicism that makes her a kind of feminine Bartleby. Most of the other women in the stories have the destructive characteristics of Mrs. Glendinning. In "I and My Chimney" the narrator defends himself and his twelve-foot chimney from the designs of a wife who is ready to use his illness and his passivity to get rid of the chimney so that she can remodel the house. As William Ellery Sedgwick pointed out long ago, the chimney, like White-Jacket's garment, is filled with nooks and crannies that in a sense make the husband independent of his spouse. Without the chimney he will be unmanned, his dependency upon his wife complete. The historical allusions make the wife a Judith and the husband a Holofernes, the chimney substituting for the latter's head. She is also likened to Sarah, who consigned Ishmael to the wilderness after the birth of Isaac. Since the legend is quite well established that Melville was writing about the chimney at Arrowhead and about his mother or Elizabeth Melville or both, the reference to Sarah justifies the earlier linkage of Mrs. Maria Gansevoort Melville to the biblical character. It is also not without significance that, as in the mistaken entry on the birth certificate of Stanwix or in the incestuous relationship of Pierre and Mrs. Glendinning, Melville castigated his mother but remained "married" to her.

Perhaps the bitterest and certainly the ugliest epithet and pun in the story occurs after the narrator discovers that his wife has been examining the ash-hole in the chimney as a possible hiding place of a missing treasure. "What devil, wife," the narrator asks, "prompted you to crawl into the ash-hole! Don't you know that St. Dunstan's devil emerged from the ash-hole?" This anal joke reveals better than anything else the narrator's (and Melville's) deep seated hostility and revulsion.

Primitive fears lie behind these stories. "I and My Chimney" is a not so funny phallic joke that the wife will remove what is most "personal" to the narrator, the chimney. Fearfully clinging to the chimney and his pipe, he does not leave home for seven years, as he succeeds in thwarting the castration threats of his phallic wife. "The Lightning-Rod Man" relates how a salesman attempts to sell the narrator a rod and even threatens the customer with the device when he encounters resistance to his sales pitch. As Richard Chase was the first to point out, the tale plays a variation upon the castration theme since the youth refuses "this monstrous idol of paternity" in order to escape "thralldom to his father." In "The Bell-Tower" Haman, the robot, kills his creator with a hammer. At Bannadonna's funeral a peasant tugs on the bell-rope, and as he does so "the groined belfry" crashes and the bell falls to the ground, as the "fathers" take their vengeance upon a man who plays at being God. The shaving scene in "Benito Cereno" less subtly points to castration, as does Benito's empty scabbard.

"The Tartarus of Maids" is an attack upon the evils of the nineteenth-century industrial system, but more frightening than the exploitation of the virgins, as Alvin Sandberg has pointed out, is the equation of the paper mill with coitus and birth. The machines are vaginas with teeth, the pistons are destructive phalluses, and the nine-minute process of paper manufacture is bloody and horrifying. The imagery originates in the child's confusion of the sexual act with a violent, destructive encounter in which love and emotion are lacking. In contrast with the narrator's more or less uncritical acceptance of the sterilities of those quaint oral simpletons in "The Paradise of Bachelors," is the compulsion to view sexuality in terms of infantile fears and to associate filth and ugliness with coitus and birth. The seedman wants to remain a bachelor, sexually pure and uncommitted.

Despite the comic surfaces of many of these short stories, perhaps intended as sop for the magazine audience, Melville depicts with almost frightening consistency a wasteland in which nothing grows and no one matures. The characters — or caricatures of humanity — are frozen, despite their chronological ages, in infantile responses or flee from life. Even the most complex of these "heroes," Benito Cereno, escapes from the tyranny of Babo, only to retreat to a monastery where the shadow of his former servant-master hovers over him until he dies a few months later, not yet thirty. In the masterpiece of these tales, "Bartleby the Scrivener," the comic beginning is but the foreground for Bartleby, who accomplishes the ultimate retreat or, more accurately, regression, to the tomb-womb.

One day out of nowhere, a "palidly neat, pitiably respectable, incurably forlorn" young clerk of unknown origins appears in a lawyer's office on Wall Street, and for a short time proves to be a diligent, even mechanical, clerk. Suddenly he "prefers not to" proofread briefs with the other copyists, and soon, for reasons which he never articulates, "prefers not to" do any work at all. The lawyer-narrator attempts to coax and wheedle his clerk, like an indulgent parent, and tolerates his behavior until the situation makes him the laughing stock among his colleagues. When Bartleby refuses to leave the premises, the lawyer moves his firm to another location. Soon Bartleby is dragged by force from the building to a prison where the lawyer visits him and attempts to ease his lot through the services of a grub-man. Bartleby refuses to eat: "I prefer not to dine to-day. . . . It would disagree with me; I am unused to dinners." Soon he lies dead from starvation.

> The round face of the grub-man peered upon me now. "His dinner is ready. Won't he dine to-day, either? Or does he live without dining?"
> "Lives without dining," said I, and closed the eyes.
> "Eh! — He's asleep, ain't he?"
> "With kings and counselors," murmured I.

As many commentators have noted, this is a tale of walls and Wall Street. The lawyer places Bartleby behind a screen in his office which limits his vision to white or black walls. After Bartleby refuses to copy, he has "dead-wall" reveries, and ends his life before the gloomy walls of the Tombs prison. Bartleby may be "walled in" by his society — or by life itself — but, as critics usually neglect to add, he is "walled in" by his own "preferences": he wills his death.

Even more pervasive than the wall imagery is the oral imagery: the tale is about eating and not eating, incorporating and not incorporating. Before Bartleby appears on the scene, we are amused by the eating habits of two clerks with the names of Turkey and Nippers. Their work habits change at noon, at dinner time: in the morning Turkey is an enthusiastic copyist and Nippers groans in his dyspepsia; after dinner Nippers works efficiently and Turkey bungles in an alcoholic haze. The two clerks are observed consistently in oral terms, as is a twelve-year-old lad named Ginger Nut, whose sole function in the office appears to be a "cake and apple purveyor." As the story unfolds it becomes clear that the narrator-lawyer acts as a nurturing parent to his clerks. He has adapted his office routine to the ingesting patterns of Turkey and Nippers, and soon he is worrying about the eating habits of Bartleby, whose diet consists of ginger-nuts.

When Bartleby refuses to copy or to accede to his employer's indulgences, he employs the tactics of a victim of anorexia nervosa. To punish the lawyer, the nurturing parent, he refuses to eat. There is no more effective and unsettling tactic than this for a child to get even, to cause parental anxiety and guilt. Denied the love and understanding which he craves and demands — the child denies himself nourishment. When Bartleby finds no gratifications in the world, when there is nothing left for him to incorporate, he curls up before the walls of the Tombs — "his knees drawn up, and lying on his side, his head touching the cold stones" — a fetal-like ball, as he returns to the womb of the eternal mother, death.

Beginning with the depiction of the Ti in *Typee* to the account of "The Paradise of Bachelors" at the Inns of Court, unencumbered or manic delight in Melville's writings is associated with feasting, usually in all-male society. The paradise Melville imagined with Hawthorne was to consist of an unending supply of champagne and ontological chatter. In his fiction the orgies are oral Edens, like the one briefly enjoyed by Pierre with his mother-sister. In "Bartleby the Scrivener" Melville unfolds with almost clinical rigidity the other side of paranoia, a depression so deep-rooted and encompassing that oral gratification is denied in order to effect what Hawthorne was later to characterize as a desire for self-annihilation.

Bartleby handles his overwhelming despair and rage by internalizing the hurt in his silence and his deliberate starvation. He punishes his body, his self-image — Narcissus peers at an emaciated body gradually becoming a corpse — but at the same time he leaves the lawyer-parent with feelings of guilt — "Ah, Bartleby! Ah, humanity!" Bartleby acts out in his rage the child's fantasy, which sometimes does not die in childhood, that when he dies the world, meaning his parents, will mourn him and at last give him the love and attention denied him in life.

The tale is profoundly autobiographical, not because of resemblances between the lawyer-narrator and members of Melville's family (lawyers like Allan and Gansevoort, Judge Shaw, and Peter Gansevoort) or because of what it reveals of Herman's emotional state following the creation of his masterpiece and the collapse of his friendship with Hawthorne. In this story Melville was commenting once again upon the death of Allan Melvill. Here Bartleby, the "son," leaves the "father" with the grief and guilt which Herman experienced in 1832. Bartleby and the lawyer are in the latter's words "sons of Adam" — which identifies the human and familial bond between them as well as the "predestinated" antagonism of father and son.

After the Melville revival began in the 1920s, two tales became favorites of commentators, "Bartleby the Scrivener" and "Benito Cereno," both of which have been endlessly analyzed. *Israel Potter*, however, has been for the most part ignored or quickly dismissed. Hawthorne made no such mistake when in *Our Old Home* he called *Israel Potter* an "excellent novel or biography." Hawthorne neglected to comment on the farcical nature of the work. The novel falters where, abandoning farce, Melville succumbed to his fondness for symbols and apocalyptic statements and to his addiction to wretched puns. The opening chapter is strewn with obvious symbols of death and disaster. Toward the conclusion when the author's interest may have waned as it sometimes did in many of his other works, he was not content to let his material speak for itself, and intruded platitudinous pessimistic utterances, drawn mostly from Ecclesiastes, which detracted from the story line and conflicted with the amoral and ahuman farcical tone. Despite these lapses *Israel Potter* is one of those neglected gems of the neglected American comic tradition.

In the fall of 1849 Melville acquired a little tract entitled *Life and Remarkable Adventures of Israel R. Potter*, published in 1824 by I. R. Potter. According to the title-page, Potter "was a soldier in the American Revolution, and took a distinguished part in the Battle of Bunker Hill . . . after which he was taken Prisoner by the British, conveyed to England, where for 30 years he obtained a livelihood for himself and family, by crying 'Old Chairs to Mend,' through the streets of London." Potter's pamphlet was designed to present his case for a government pension.

When five years later, in 1854, Melville was writing one story after another about failures, happy and otherwise, he apparently reread Potter's tract and decided to convert it into a farce about a pathetic fool who had a series of misadventures which took him from the Berkshires to England and France and finally back to the United States fifty years after the battle of Bunker Hill. Although Melville followed his source in the general outlines of his tale, he altered and expanded at will to suit his farcical purposes. There was no sentimentality in his treatment of poor Potter, who remains a bumpkin incapable of profiting in any way from his various escapades, and there was more than a little "wickedness" in the author's treatment of the historical figures he introduced into the plot.

Israel is a "plebeian . . . Œdipus," an eternal child-man who never succeeds in supplanting the father. The character's arrestment, emotional and genital, is brilliantly sustained (or arrested) in the farcical framework, which itself serves as an artistic arrestment.

When Israel's father opposes his marriage, the son does not defy the ban and run off with the lass; he goes off to make his fortune and to establish his manhood. When he returns home, three years older but no wiser and without a fortune, he is in no position to defy his father's continued opposition to marriage. Again he leaves, this time to try his hand at various jobs, including service as a harpooner aboard a whaling ship. When he arrives home about three years later, still the master of no trade, he discovers that the girl, not unwisely, has married. The pattern that emerges in these early scenes is destined to be Israel's life style: he is the passive victim of his own failures.

Israel goes off to war and fights manfully at Bunker Hill, but is taken prisoner and carried off to England. After he escapes, he meets up with English partisans of the Colonies who send him to France to deliver intelligence reports to Benjamin Franklin. Unlike the youth, Franklin is "Jack of all trades, master of each and mastered by none — the type and genius of his land." A "household Plato" and a descendant of Jacob and Hobbes, Franklin promptly proceeds to educate Israel according to the pragmatic adages of *Poor Richard's Almanac* and manages in the process to cheat the foolish youth of the toilet articles and wine placed in his room by the innkeeper and of a chambermaid who offers her services with a freedom which the young apostle of freedom does not (or psychologically cannot) understand. Israel laments but does nothing about his shoddy treatment.

John Paul Jones arrives upon the scene. Before he enters Franklin's room, Israel observes him pinching the not unwilling chambermaid. In order to avoid detection by the French, Jones hides for the night in Israel's room. As he paces back and forth like a rooster, Israel peeps and sees the naval commander expose his tattooed right arm in a mirror. In the morning Jones leaves, "with a light and dandified air, switching his gold-headed cane, and throwing a passing arm round all the pretty chambermaids . . . , kissing them resoundingly, as if saluting a frigate." Much later, when Israel is aboard his ship, now attired in a Scotch bonnet, Jones continues to play the rake.

Toward the conclusion of his wartime adventures Potter meets Ethan Allen, who has been brought to England as a prisoner. Although Allen physically resembles Israel — both, like Billy Budd, have flaxen hair — the general is a physical and verbal "lion." In a chapter entitled "Samson among the Philistines," Allen holds his captors at bay with his sarcastic taunts. Fashionable ladies call upon the American Samson, who "talks like a beau in a parlor" and cuts locks from his hair for the English Delilahs. Even in bonds Allen remains a potent sexual force.

The fathers — Mr. Potter, Franklin, Jones, and Allen — enjoy sexual conquests denied to Israel, who can only passively wait until marriage is forced upon him more by accident than by choice. Melville's farcical treatment of the historical figures may tarnish their greatness somewhat, but they enjoy the prerogatives of the maturity which they have earned, while Israel chronologically passes from boy's estate without becoming a man.

Although Israel is always in motion — usually in flight — his antics are kept in an infantile framework. He escapes twice from his English guards when he is a prisoner in England by pretending that he has to urinate. After he returns from his mission in France, Squire Woodcock hides him in the chimney and then dies of a stroke while Israel languishes for three days, passively awaiting his fate. When at long last he decides to do something about his incarceration, he dresses himself in the clothes of the dead man, not forgetting to examine himself in a mirror, then scares the servants out of their wits, and runs with little dignity and undue haste. Afraid that his clothes will give him away — besides, as a child-man he is not entitled to wear paternal garments — he exchanges clothes with a scarecrow and in the process assumes the attire of a fertility symbol. Almost at once his qualifications for this role are put to test when a suspicious farmer approaches. For a while Israel attempts to stare the farmer down, but when the prong of the pitchfork approaches his left eye, he takes to his legs — once more in flight.

Through some implausible shenanigans he seizes an enemy ship and turns it over to John Paul Jones, who calls him "my yellow lion" and invites Israel to share his cabin. They engage in an exchange of compliments and affection, but with the dubious or perverse erotic characteristics of the incestuous dialog in *Pierre* or of the "marriage" in *Moby-Dick.*

"I shall be a vice to your plans, Captain Paul. I will receive, but I won't let go, unless you alone loose the screw."

"Well said. To bed now; you ought to. I go on deck. Good night, ace of hearts."

"That is fitter for yourself, Captain Paul, lonely leader of the suit."

"Lonely? Aye, but number one cannot but be lonely, my trump."

"Again I give it back. Ace-of-trumps may it prove to you, Captain Paul; may it be impossible for you ever to be taken. But for me — poor deuce, a trey, that comes in your wake — any king or knave may take me, as before now the knaves have."

"Tut, tut, lad; never be more cheery for another than for yourself. But a fagged body fags the soul. To hammock, to hammock! while I go on deck to clap on more sail to your cradle."

And they separated for that night.

And so Israel finds in John Paul Jones the kind of friend or father the youths in Melville's novels seek. Jones combines the characteristics of Jack Chase and Queequeg. Like Chase he is a swashbuckling warrior addicted to literary pedantry. Like Queequeg he is a wellborn "barbarian" with "a sort of tattooing such as is seen only on thorough-going savage — deep blue, elaborate, labyrinthine, cabalistic." Attired in his Scotch bonnet, Jones plays father-mother to Israel: "To hammock, to hammock! while I go on deck to clap on more sail to your cradle."

When the war ends, America triumphs but Potter loses. Soon he is toiling in brickyards, "Half buried there in the pit, . . . poor Israel seemed some gravedigger, or churchyard man." After Israel escapes from this inferno, he of course does not find the Promised Land. At this point Melville calls him a "plebeian Lear or Œdipus" and in the same paragraph informs us that the roof of the hovel in which he lives collapses, "not leaving his faculties unaffected by the concussion of one of the rafters on his brain."

In the next paragraph it turns out that, when Israel has enough money for his passage to the United States, he is run over and taken into a bakery where the shop-girl treats him with such kindness "that in the end he thought his debt of gratitude could only be repaid by love. In a word, the money saved up for his ocean voyage was lavished upon a rash embarkation in wedlock." And so by accident dismasted, Israel finds himself trapped in matrimonial woe, a state for which he has no aptitude. In the next five pages Melville reports that "according to another well-known Malthusian enigma in human affairs, . . . eleven children were born to him in certain sixpenny garrets in Moorfields. One after the other, ten were buried." The wife is also buried, nameless in death as in life.

Years later "in his dismallest December, our veteran could still at intervals feel a momentary warmth in his topmost boughs." Israel decides to end his fifty years of exile. Accompanied by his only surviving son Benjamin, he returns to the United States, arriving at Bunker Hill on July 4, 1825. Israel is content to survey the battle-field from Copp's Hill, which is a cemetery. His son has difficulty in getting his father to leave the peaceful "mounds." Then Israel goes to his birthplace in western Massachusetts, where all he finds are the remains of a "tumbled chimney."

> "What are you looking at so, father?"
>
> " '*Father*!' Here," raking with his staff, "*my* father would sit, and here, my mother, and here I, little infant, would totter between, even as now, once again, on the very same spot, but in the unroofed air, I do. The ends meet. Plough away, friend."

Even as he "totters" toward Potter's Field, the poor old child, literally "unroofed," finds the epithet "father" unnatural and prefers to a status he has never achieved, the security of the infant. In the last paragraph we learn that the government — like Israel's father — rejects his appeal for a pension. The public permits "the record of his fortunes" to go out of print. "He died the same day that the oldest oak on his native hills was blown down."

As narrator Melville never takes Israel too seriously: he in effect kids the character and the subject matter, and thereby confines Israel to kid-dom. At three-score-and-ten Israel is still an infant. He has gone round and round — a nobody going nowhere. "Unroofed," he arrives at no wisdom, only at foolishness compounded. Behind such farce there is pain. It would seem to emerge from a sensibility deeply depressed, itself adrift like poor Israel Potter.

In "Hawthorne and His Mosses" Melville wrote an almost Whitmanesque sentence: "The world is as young to-day as when it was created; and this Vermont morning dew is as wet to my feet, as Eden's dew to Adam's." After the man he called his "angel" left the Berkshires, a deep depression dampened his spirits, or, in the words of one of his tales, "grief drizzles and drizzles down on my soul." His characters after 1851 are in fearful retreat, intent in one way or another upon self-annihilation. "Who ain't a nobody?" Israel Potter asks, and Hautboy, the fiddler who refuses "immortal fame," proclaims, "I am nobody forever and ever."

"The Whole World's
a Trick....
Ha! Ha!"

—*The Confidence Man*

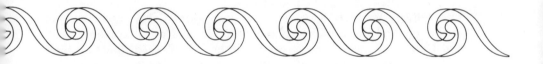

In a letter to Hawthorne in 1851 Melville almost abruptly voiced his feelings of despair: "Lord, when shall we be done changing?" he asked. "Ah! it's a long stage, and no inn in sight, and night coming, and the body cold." Darkness enfolded him in its cold embrace. There was no innkeeper in the inn. Perhaps there was no inn.

Neighbors and friends recognized the strain Melville placed upon his energies in his monomaniacal dedication while he wrote one book after another and in his gyrations in conversation from excited outbursts to moody silences. He complained of eyestrain while he was writing *Mardi*, and he was always delighted when he found a book in large type. After his long stints of writing, he read little in the evenings since the strain was too great, partly no doubt because of the uncertain light of lamps or candles and because of enervation. The discomforts and pain of eyestrain forced him to husband energies which he tended to squander recklessly, the body as it often does protecting the profligate from his own excesses. Given to such merciless self-examination, Melville sometimes found the insights too painful and the eyes rebelled. The body can frequently diagnose as effectively as the mind.

At the end of the day he sought to relieve the pinched body and nerves by doing various chores about the farm and by taking walks, and between bouts of creativity he worked hard in the fields in order to revitalize the muscles and to store up energies for his next artistic seizure. Gradually he held himself together by exertions of will worthy of an Ahab. As his works failed to win readers and as his family continued to grow, he found himself imprisoned like a Bartleby. The stories in *Putnam's* and *Harper's* provided a steady but modest income, but, as he recognized, he was compromising his artistic ideals in order to fill his purse. Worse, the failures of *Moby-Dick* and *Pierre* strained his self-confidence which, except in manic eruptions in letters to Hawthorne, was always faltering.

When in 1855 Melville's once magnificent physique began to fail him, bodily pain compounded his awareness of his artistic failure. In February 1855, according to his wife, "he had his first attack of severe rheumatism in his back — so that he was helpless." Perhaps she exaggerated slightly, or her memory deceived her, since Melville continued to submit manuscripts of short stories to *Putnam's Monthly*, although he may only have mailed works completed months earlier. In June he had an attack of sciatica, and his neighbor, Dr. Oliver Wendell Holmes, was summoned for consultation. Although Melville burlesqued the situation and the illness in "I and My Chimney," which he wrote while he convalesced, the *Berkshire County Eagle* on September 14 reported that he was "recovering from a severe illness." About the middle of September, accompanied by his mother, he left for a recuperative "jaunt" which included visits with her brothers. In times of trouble Mrs. Melville automatically sought out the Gansevoorts.

During his lengthy indisposition, the fourth and last child was born, on March 2, 1855. During the summer, according to the *Berkshire County Eagle*, the Insane Asylum Commission arrived in Pittsfield and examined various farm sites, including Melville's, as a possible location for a new asylum. At a community "fancy dress pic nic" in September, which the ill author attended, Elizabeth Melville, "as Cypherina Donothing, in a costume of cyphers, was no cypher, and although continually adding up cyphers to get at a sum of cyphers, found naught to amuse her; and was one of the most successful characters of the day, although she did nothing well." Elizabeth Melville rarely emerges in such a frivolous role. The wit behind the conception of the attire seems more characteristic of her husband's sense of futility, especially when one recalls that his next and last long prose work, *The Confidence-Man*, was to present his most awesome and blackest reductionism to a state of nothingness. If Melville convinced his wife to appear publicly in such a costume, he was truly a devious man. The attire was no less hilarious — and no less hostile — than the portrait of the dominating wife in "I and My Chimney," who, we recall, was probably patterned after his wife and his mother.

Late in October Melville went to Gansevoort, New York, to watch at the death-bed of his Aunt Catherine, whose husband had given him his name. During the winter he arranged for the publication of *The Piazza Tales*, which included "Bartleby," "Benito Cereno," "The Lightning-Rod Man," "The Encantadas," and "The Bell-Tower," all of which had appeared earlier in magazines. He prefaced the collection with an unpublished sketch entitled "The Piazza," which, like similar prefaces of Hawthorne, toys with the subject of illusion and reality. Here for the first time in print Melville refers to his illness of the preceding year, to the months spent in his chamber, and to his convalescence on the porch which he had added to Arrowhead shortly after he moved in.

Late in the winter or early in the spring of 1856 he began what was to be his last attempt to wrest a livelihood from authorship. On July 15 his sister Augusta was preparing a transcription for the printer. "I know nothing about it," his brother-in-law wrote, "but I have no great confidence in the success of his productions."

The despair and depression that suffuse *Pierre* and a tale like "Bartleby" reach their nadir in *The Confidence-Man*, a grim parable or dark joke which plays almost fiendish games around the words "trust" and "confidence." A cross-section of Americans in the 1850s from all classes and professions — beggars, students, clergymen, and intellectuals — are aboard a ship ironically named *Fidèle*, which sails from St. Louis down the Mississippi River. Although the narrator (himself a Confidence-Man, it will turn out) speaks of his "variety of characters," the passengers despite superficial differences in class status and education are undifferentiated, monochromatic, and for the most part not even accorded the dignity or individuation a name bestows. They are united in one great negation or monomania — self-interest. Their only truth, in spite of the platitudes they mouth, is deception, which in final analysis turns out to be self-deception. They participate in a joyless masquerade, thinking themselves free when they are actually slaves to the tyranny of their greed. The aphorisms of their unstated creed are: Suspect your neighbors as you suspect yourself; or Do others before they do you. Into this company of nonhumans will come a Confidence-Man who will assume many disguises, manipulating the passengers to his will as successfully as Ahab manipulates the crew of the *Pequod*. Where Ahab by virtue of his position and his rhetoric imposes a unity of purpose upon the sailors, the Confidence-Man points up and exploits the disunity or fragmentation in the lives of those aboard the *Fidèle*.

The locale in which the novel takes place recalled the lot of Herman Melville in 1840, when he went West, as far as the Mississippi River. At that time he was an ex-clerk, ex-teacher, a one-time sailor, and a former student of surveying. He had neither a livelihood nor the prospect of one. He was a nobody. On that trip, it will be recalled, he visited his father's brother, Thomas Melvill, that charming eccentric who could give the youth neither a job nor a model of confidence. Herman returned to New York, still a nobody. Dependent upon Gansevoort for support and afflicted with the "hypos," he signed aboard a whaling ship at the end of the year, an act of desperation which would one day result in a glorious novel.

The Confidence-Man opens "At sunrise on a first of April," or, in other words, at the birth of the day and of spring. But the birthday is April Fool's Day, that modern vulgarization and remnant of All Fool's Day and, still earlier, of the rites of spring extolling the return of the sun from darkness. In Melville's memory calendar April was not an auspicious time. In April 1837 Herman watched Gansevoort undergo the humiliation of bankruptcy, a failure in a business he inherited from an unsuccessful father. Seven years later, on April 3, 1846, Gansevoort, at the time fatally ill in London after seeing *Typee* through the press, wrote in what was to be his final oratorical display before he was silenced forever: "Selfishly speaking I never valued life much — it were impossible to value it less than I do now." We cannot be certain that Gansevoort's words reverberated in Herman's inner ear as he wrote, but the mood underlying *The Confidence-Man* closely approximates Gansevoort's despair. Ten years after his brother's premature death, Herman too was bankrupt, financially and emotionally, and in his own eyes seemed a failure.

The pilgrims in *The Canterbury Tales* assemble in the same season:

> *Whan that Aprille with his shoures soote,*
> *The droghte of March hath perced to the roote,*
> *And bathed every veyne in swich licour*
> *Of which vertu engendred is the flour. . . .*

Some of Chaucer's pilgrims are hypocrites or medieval confidence-men who crassly exploit for their ends those who naively or superstitiously trust in God and His institutions. But their machinations are balanced in lovely portraits of those who live lives of "vertu." In

Chaucer's world God still lives, and social and religious orders bind men together. In Melville's world God is dead, the unity of self-interest separates and estranges, and the "pilgrims" move not toward light or enlightenment but toward darkness or death.

The loose structure of *The Confidence-Man*, which allows for the interpolation of tales and episodes at will, may reflect the influence of Chaucer and of Sebastian Brandt's *Ship of Fools*, but, despite the fact that one tale could easily have been substituted for another or the order of events altered, the looseness is deceptive, a trick as it were. For, as in the seeming chaos of *Pierre*, the book is under the firm control of a master confidence-man, Herman Melville. On one level the book centers about monetary shenanigans of suspicious money-grubbers who live according to the golden rule of "No Trust," which is a recurrent slogan, and believe that "charity" begins and ends at home. They are true believers who are at heart Machiavellians. Here Melville satirizes, and the Confidence-Man exploits, a society which has transvalued values and hypocritically enshrined self-interest or greed. Beneath this traditional and even obvious attack on social man is a profound examination of confidence or trust on a personal, psychological level.

The Confidence-Man himself is truly one of Melville's most dazzling creations, blending God and Satan, Ishmael and Ahab, love and hate. Or perhaps we should say that he is a dazzling noncreation, since he has no identity, assuming eight or nine disguises in order to expose the hollowness of society and man. Because of his role he will have to resort to all the stereotyped trickery of con-men since the Garden of Eden. He will cheat those eager to get rich with seemingly honest get-rich-quick schemes. He will offer worthless medicine to the ill and the hypochondriacs, delighting in his sales pitch. He will explain diseases, diagnose symptoms, and eventually put out the lights. In the process he will sometimes demean himself like a Satan or a Mephistopheles. But at the same time he does not deceive himself as to the limitations and deceptiveness of self-interest or the confidence game. Because he retains *confidence in confidence* he is aware, as the fools are not, of the fractures in their lives. Yet he knows the absurdity of *confidence in confidence* in a world in which self-interest reigns and in which "The grand points of human nature are the same to-day as they were a thousand years ago. The only variability in them is in expression, not in feature."

Through his various disguises and his conversations the Confidence-Man will point up the heart of the human dilemma, although he will not be understood by characters imprisoned in their solipsistic worlds. He (and Melville too) will expose the futility of the youths in the earlier books who participate in what appears to be a rite of passage. In this work there is no rite of passage: there is nowhere to go.

At St. Louis at the beginning of the voyage the Confidence-Man as a youth or child-man boards the *Fidèle*. In appearance he is not unlike the handsome sailors or even Billy Budd: "His cheek was fair, his chin downy, his hair flaxen, his hat a white fur one, with a long fleecy nap." He is accompanied neither by porter nor by friend. "It was plain," we are informed, "that he was, in the extremest sense of the word, a stranger." The awesome language foretells that this is the most estranged of all the greenhorns — Tommo, Taji, Redburn, White-Jacket, Ishmael, and Pierre. They at least bear names, even if assumed ones in some instances. Worse, the youth as a mute must write slogans on boards, which turn out to be biblical texts. The passengers shrink from his petitions and his questions, and even suspect that he uses the Bible for his own purposes. They answer his pleas for guidance with hostility, by projecting their sickly suspicions and their perversions upon the cosmos. Since in relationship to the boy the passengers are parental surrogates, they are denying him the model every child needs; he is fated to be a "stranger" in "this strange world."

The mute, like an infant lacking the power of speech, cannot even voice his pain. When the Confidence-Man reappears as a cripple with a wooden leg, he gives visual form to his pain, and articulates the mute's despair in an angry outburst like that of an injured child: "You fools! . . . you flock of fools, under this captain of fools, is this ship of fools!" In his rage the cripple points up the fact that neither captain nor officers are in evidence, and that the *Fidèle*, as it were, is without authority or control. Surely it is significant and artistically appropriate that for the first time in Melville's novels there is no tyrant upholding a hierarchical or patriarchal system, which, even if perverted by an Ahab, provides a semblance of stability, a parody of familial structure and order. The greenhorns in the earlier works define themselves in their rebellions against authority, but in *The Confidence-Man* there is no way of achieving self-definition. A black cripple (the Confidence-Man in still another disguise) underscores the situation when he humbles himself according to a stereotyped formula, "Oh, sar, I am der dog widout massa." But he reveals a wisdom that eludes the white racists: they are not aware that they are "widout massa," without a unifying principle, external or internal, which will produce confidence in themselves and in the world.

This void in their lives makes it possible for the Confidence-Man both to exploit their emptiness and to play upon their self-righteousness. Now older and attired like the other passengers, the Confidence-Man engages in polemical discussions and tricks the fools into self-damaging admissions. In an exchange with a student who ostentatiously displays a copy of Tacitus, the Confidence-Man turns his attack upon the author into a commentary upon the modern age. "Without confidence himself, Tacitus destroys it in all his readers. Destroys confidence, paternal confidence, of which God knows that there is in this world none to spare. For, comparatively inexperienced as you are, my dear young friend, did you never observe how little, very little, confidence, there is? I mean between man and man – more particularly between stranger and stranger." The student is too pompous, and later too eager to get rich, to understand the Confidence-Man's point or his conclusion: "In a sad world it is the saddest fact."

In tricking a suspicious miser out of his money the Confidence-Man plays upon his greed so artfully that, "falling back now like an infant," the old man finally cries out like a child: "I confide, I confide; help, friend, my distrust!" The regression to an infantile state confirms, though the miser himself never achieves awareness, that the deprivation of his youth is now the deprivation of his age. As the Natural Bone-Setter the Confidence-Man speaks of "destitution, not of cash, but of confidence." Those fixated upon money have no understanding of emotional or spiritual destitution. In the role of the herb-doctor, the Confidence-Man offers his most acute diagnosis of the malaise afflicting the passengers aboard the *Fidèle*: "gladly seek the breast of that confidence begot in the tender time of your youth, blessed beyond telling if it returns to you in age." The passenger who wants a bottle of medicine to relieve his bodily pain, not a prescription for his psychic well being, makes the common-sense reply – "Go back to nurse again, eh? Second childhood, indeed. You are soft." He is unaware that so-called common sense is often nonsense, or at least beside the point.

What the Confidence-Man suggests, especially in his references to "the breast of confidence" and "paternal confidence," Erik Erikson has formulated in his sensitive analysis of childhood.

> Only a relatively "whole" society can vouchsafe to the infant, through the mother, an inner conviction that all the diffuse somatic experiences and all the confusing social cues of early life can be accommodated in a sense of continuity and sameness which gradually unites the inner and outer world. The ontological source of faith and hope which thus emerges I have called a *sense of basic trust*: it is the first and basic wholeness, for it seems to imply that the inside and the outside can be experienced as an interrelated goodness. *Basic mistrust*, then, is the sum of all those diffuse experiences which are not somehow successfully balanced by the experience of integration.

Through this trickster, then, Melville makes a perceptive comment upon mankind and also upon his own lot. For his self-confidence was dealt a shattering blow by his father's failure and sudden death. In *Young Man Luther* Erikson speaks of "the internalization of the father-son relationship; the concomitant crystallization of conscience; the safe establishment of an identity as a worker and a man; and the concomitant reaffirmation of basic trust."

Although his purposes are often devious, it is the Confidence-Man who attempts to establish ties of friendship among the strangers aboard the ship. In doing so he closely resembles the greenhorns of the earlier novels. At one point he says, "nothing like preserving in manhood the fraternal familiarities of youth. It proves the heart a rosy boy to the last," his words recalling the description of Pierre's "preliminary love-friendship." In two extended scenes the Confidence-Man, now with the impressive name of Charles Arnold Noble, attempts to establish comradely relationships first with a character ironically named Francis Goodman, whom some critics have identified with Hawthorne, and later with a young philosopher called Egbert, who is said to be a fictional travesty of Henry David Thoreau. In both episodes Noble alone reveals emotion: "with longing eyes," "eying him in tenderness," and "lovingly leaning towards him." Although he may be counterfeiting sentiment, his tender advances resemble those of Tommo to Marnoo, Redburn to Bolton and Carlo, Pierre to Glendinning Stanly. But since "the fraternal familiarities of youth" can only be simulated when boyhood is past, the scenes become charades of friendship. In each case the relationship collapses when Noble asks for a loan, or charity. Rosy boys have become suspicious men — or con-men. In one of the interpolated tales Orchis convinces a younger friend named China Aster to invest in spermaceti tallow for his candles and gives him money for this purpose with the promise that it can be repaid whenever it is convenient. But Orchis turns out to be a crafty money-lender and eventually forces China Aster into bankruptcy.

The depiction of friendship in *The Confidence-Man* takes on a deeper and sadder significance if we examine it in perspective. Beginning in 1839, there are pictures of successful friendships between "brothers" in *Typee*, *Redburn*, and *Moby-Dick*, or between "fathers and sons" in "Fragments from a Writing Desk," *Omoo*, *Mardi*, and *White-Jacket*. The theme achieves its fullest, happiest development in the "honeymoon" of Ishmael and Queequeg, during, that is, the happiest period of Melville's life. Then there was an abrupt change. In *Pierre* for the first time friendship turns to ashes in Glen Stanly's betrayal. Bartleby "prefers not to" accept the lawyer's advances, and the friendship of Benito Cereno and Babo is a brutal fraud. Israel

Potter is betrayed by almost everyone he comes in contact with. Finally in *The Confidence-Man* there are no connections, only charades. Reality and depression were dampening even Melville's fictional idealizations, which from the outset were, as he probably knew on some level of awareness, wish fulfillment.

After 1851 Melville's orphans are truly orphaned, which is but additional evidence that Hawthorne's departure from the Berkshires upset Melville's cosmos. It has been suggested, on admittedly slender evidence, that Orchis, who drives China Aster into bankruptcy through his betrayal, is a fictional counterfeit of Hawthorne. Since China Aster dies shortly after his business failure "with a wandering mind," not unlike Allan Melvill in 1832, the tale may also substantiate the thesis that Hawthorne's "betrayal" replicated Allan's. Whether Orchis or Goodman is Hawthorne will remain speculative, but it is hardly arguable that the name of the ship of fools recalls a Hawthorne tale which Melville found "deep as Dante," and from which, in that review he wrote after their meeting in 1850, he quoted a passage that in some respects reverberates throughout *The Confidence-Man*: " 'Faith!' shouted Goodman Brown, in a voice of agony and desperation; and the echoes of the forest mocked him, crying — 'Faith! Faith!' as if bewildered wretches were seeking her all through the wilderness."

As Melville's view of reality darkened in the 1850s, despair — or the "mildew" of Redburn's youth — took over. Ishmael demolishes philosophers and man-made syntheses with comic exuberance but without rancor. If *Israel Potter* debunks, Franklin is only wounded, not crippled. In *The Confidence-Man* the etching is more acid, the tone darker, and there is what amounts to character assassination. In Mark Winsome, "a kind of cross between a Yankee peddler and a Tartar priest" and "more a metaphysical merman than a feeling man," Melville demolishes with bitter glee Ralph Waldo Emerson, and his disciple Egbert, Henry David Thoreau. Winsome, "purely and coldly radiant as a prism," argues his optimistic creed speciously and denies charity to the first beggar that comes along. Egbert, beneath his idealistic patter and sophistry, is but another money-grubber. The unfeelingness of the characters is matched and magnified by the unfeeling satire. If Winsome and Egbert betray themselves, Melville betrays the greatness of Emerson and Thoreau. Yet the vilification is perhaps not without justification, or at least comprehensible, when we recall that this is a parable of a child rejected wherever he turns. Winsome and Egbert represent presumably the best of the larger world, but their philosophies are lies or empty words.

The last scene — and the last joke — occurs at night on April Fool's Day, in a cabin in which an old man sits at a white marble table, while in the bunks about the room other passengers, or phantoms, sleep. The man, a retired farmer, is spotlighted by "a solar lamp, . . . whose shade of ground glass was all round fancifully variegated, in transparency, with the image of a horned altar." The lighting creates "a halo" about the man as he sits reading the Bible. The Confidence-Man enters and soon is confounding (or conning) the old gentleman with quotations from Ecclesiastes which advise distrust of, rather than confidence in, mankind. After the farmer recovers from this unexpected attack upon the authority and consistency of the Bible, the two find themselves in agreement that, as the old man puts it, "to distrust the creature, is a kind of distrusting of the Creator" — which is, of course, a reinterpretation of the biblical passages but soon becomes hypocrisy.

At this moment a "juvenile peddler" enters carrying "a miniature mahogany door." (Melville ostentatiously clutters the scene with parodies of biblical passages.) "Go thy way with thy toys, child," the old man says to the youth, but soon he is conned into buying one gadget, or toy, after another, since his trust in mankind is verbal rather than genuine. First the peddler sells a lock to keep thieves out. Then a money belt, which in appearance resembles a truss. As a gift the youth hands the man a *Counterfeit Detector*," a book which will protect him against sharpsters. "Go, child — go, go!" the farmer observes. "Yes, child, — yes, yes," the boy replies in "roguish parody." The old man has the naiveté of youth, the lad the empirical wisdom of age. They are as one, however, in their lack of confidence, the lad being at least honest about the matter.

Next the Confidence-Man himself outdoes the youth. Before he retires for the evening the old man recalls that there is no life-preserver in his stateroom. The Confidence-Man gives him "a brown stool with a curved tin compartment underneath," which the old man does not recognize as a chamber pot. "This, I think, is a life-preserver, sir," the Confidence-Man says, "and a very good one, I should say, though I don't pretend to know much about such things, never using them myself." Carried away with his crude deception, the Confidence-Man declares, "you could have confidence in the stool for a special providence." "Then, good-night, good-night," the farmer replies, "and Providence have both of us in its good keeping." As the capitalization reveals, the old man converts the chamber pot into Providence, as cloaca becomes deity.

Suddenly a stench rises: "the waning light expired, and with it the waning flames of the horned altar, and the waning halo round the robed man's brow; while in the darkness which ensued, the [Confidence-Man] kindly led the old man away." And so the old man, his only security a chamber pot, disappears in the darkness as a stink pollutes the atmosphere. Martin Luther may have had a vision in an outhouse, but in *The Confidence-Man* there are only stink and extinction of light — and life. The narrator adds one line, signifying much or, more likely, since it is all a con-game, nothing: "Something further may follow of this Masquerade."

Some critics have devised elaborate allegorical explanations of this final scene, describing the old man as the Past, the Old God, or the Modern Christian, and the youth as Young America, Prometheus, or a latter-day Christian who accepts the death of God. Such constructions, however, con the text by transforming the calculated negations into a kind of affirmative resolution or "cheerful nihilism." The scene is a cruel *reductio ad absurdum*. All the noncharacters in the book cling to their fearful hollow shells, trusting no one, giving nothing to anyone without ulterior purpose. The old farmer embodies their nonlives as he clings possessively to the only thing that can protect him from disaster or death, a receptacle for his own feces.

If the trio in the final tableau are construed as representative of the three major divisions of the life span — youth, middle age, and old age — Melville's commentary is devastating. Age is hypocritical, fearful, and foolish. Middle-age indulges itself in dialectical and practical jokes or games, neither protecting age from youth's duplicities nor providing youth with a model or ego ideal. Youth, helpless when it is without guides, is out for a buck, leering knowingly at middle age and vengefully exploiting old age. It is a brutal scene, for three psychopaths are on the loose. If the past is a failure, and if the Confidence-Man and the peddler represent the present and the future, it is the same story continued, the same terrifying masquerade.

The suggestiveness of this last episode, which is apparently to become the first episode in another masquerade in an endless cycle of nothingness, is reinforced, as is generally the case in Melville's writing, by the style itself. Here in *The Confidence-Man* there are no rococo flourishes, stylistic involutions, and parodistic literary cadences such as one finds in *Pierre*. Absent too are the exclamation points which reflect the overstated, overanxious idealism and despair of L. A. V. or White-Jacket. The noncharacters are denied the grandeur accorded to Ahab even in his maddest flights of self-aggrandizement. Instead the sentences and paragraphs often resemble a lawyer's brief, studded with precedents from the past and twisting in short units to make logical what at bottom is illogical or playing upon words and meaning supposedly for the sake of clarification but actually for purposes of obfuscation. The following paragraph is not uncharacteristic:

Which animation, by the way, might seem more or less out of character in the man in gray, considering his unsprightly manner when first introduced, had he not already in certain after colloquies, given proof, in some degree, of the fact, that, with certain natures, a soberly continent air at times, so far from arguing emptiness of stuff, is good proof it is there, and plenty of it, because unwasted, and may be used the more effectively, too, when opportunity offers. What now follows on the part of the man in gray will still further exemplify, perhaps somewhat strikingly, the truth, or what appears to be such, of this remark.

As Alfred Kazin points out, the style is unwarmed by compassion, or, to state the situation in terms of Melville's deliberate tactic, it is as cold and detached as the strangers aboard the ship. Although Richard Chase argues that the style and the book are unified in "a dialectical movement of ideas," *The Confidence-Man* is not so much a novel of ideas — or even "a comedy of thought," as the narrator himself suggests at one point — as a deceptively cool masquerade for an overheated emotional response to the tricks life played upon one Herman Melville.

The impersonality of the style and the intrusions of the narrator at intervals to comment upon the nature of fiction and art create the illusion that the author is no more involved personally in his creation than are the characters with each other. But Melville as the artist is a confidence-man, if not the Confidence-Man. The parable he tells is not fiction so much as autobiography in fictional form. In a lengthy argument with the agent from the Philosophical Intelligence Office, the Confidence-Man describes the growth of youth in terms of his teeth, but in his levity and legalistic ingenuity he utters Melville's recurrent lament: "The second teeth follow, but do not come from the first; successors, not sons. The first teeth are not like the germ blossom of the apple, at once the father of, and incorporated into, the growth it foreruns; but they are thrust from their place by the independent undergrowth of the succeeding set — an illustration, by the way, which shows more for me than I meant, though not more than I wish." Which is but another way of describing how the abrupt death of Allan Melvill cheated Herman of the paternal blessing and conned him of confidence. And note, as in his description of Hawthorne, how poignantly and accurately the word *incorporated* points to the continuing frustration of his deepest longings.

That in *The Confidence-Man* Melville was reliving the pain of parental rejection is given additional substantiation in a passage that Melville saw fit to delete from the final text. The Mississippi River was likened to Abraham, "the father of a great multitude of men" — and of Ishmael. Melville left in the text a reference to Abraham's laughter when he was informed by an angel that the ninety-year-old Sarah would bear him a son, Isaac; a "miracle" that would lead eventually to Ishmael's banishment. The excised passage ended with a strange account of the relationship of the Missouri River to the Mississippi. "The Missouri sends rather a hostile element than a filial flow. Longer, stronger than the father of waters, like Jupiter he dethrones his sire and reigns in his stead." Here Melville voiced, without disguise, a parricidal wish. By means of these two mythic references in a two-page passage he had the father betray the son and the son overcome the father.

What was quite clear in the excised passage is somewhat veiled in the concluding scene, yet the brazen handling of the old man on the part of the Confidence-Man and the boy would appear to be an enactment of the oedipal drama, even to the suggested besmearing of the paternal figure. If, as we have conjectured, the Confidence-Man frequently speaks for Herman Melville, the old man's pious platitudes are reminiscent of Allan Melvill's, as is the gibberish of China Aster in the interval between bankruptcy and death. Over the years Melville frequently heard in his inner ear his father's mad outbursts before death. If he also recalled a helpless father in bed, his beautiful face wracked with pain, his eyes dim and staring, needing assistance to take care of his bodily functions, and the odor of a diseased, dying body, Herman's eyes and nostrils recorded an indelible event — the ugly death of a hero-father. At a time when he was having confirmation of his failure as an author — proof perhaps that he was the heir of a failure — and when he had small confidence in his "top-most greatness" which had begun to falter before he had finished *Moby-Dick*, or even in life itself, he may well have taken revenge upon a father who did not help him to man's estate. *The Confidence-Man* was, I suggest, the bitter retaliation of a son upon the paternal Confidence-Man. The final scene in the novel, not so coincidentally, occurs at the very hour at which Allan had died in 1832.

This final scene was also an attack upon an audience which had rejected him. Melville began his literary career in *Typee* with an opening chapter in which a native queen exposes her tattooed behind and puts the French navy to rout. Here it is an amusing anal assault upon prudes and readers who in the name of decorum deny that man sits on his buttocks. Redburn and later Israel Potter take childish revenge upon adults by exposing their behinds. Captain Riga after the *Highlander* docks in New York is confronted with the posteriors of a crew which topples him with a collective fart. With more subtlety, or greater disguise, Ishmael breaks winds in the first chapter of *Moby-Dick*, and later leads us through the Bower of the Arsacides. The childishly hostile retaliatory tactic becomes more pervasive in

The Confidence-Man, and appropriately so. These con-men, defiled by their preoccupation with money at the expense of everything else, receive the punishment they deserve: to wallow in their own feces.

At one point the merchant, flushed with wine, his lips trembling "with an imaginative and feminine sensibility," makes one of the bitterest pronouncements in a bitter book:

> "Ah," he cried, pushing his glass from him, "Ah, wine is good, and confidence is good; but can wine or confidence percolate down through all the stony strata of hard considerations, and drop warmly and ruddily into the cold cave of truth? Truth will *not* be comforted. Led by dear charity, lured by sweet hope, fond fancy essays this feat; but in vain; mere dreams and ideals, they explode in your hand, leaving naught but the scorching behind!"

The syntax of "scorching behind" is one of Melville's tricky passages, since "scorching" should refer back to the main clause, but the addition of "behind" deliberately places syntax and meaning in doubt. The bitterness is even greater when one notes that the phraseology recalls the passages in *The Literary World* about Hawthorne's impregnation of Melville's soul. In the outrageously unfair portrait of Emerson, Melville has Winsome introduce Egbert (Thoreau) as one who "can do more to enlighten one as to my theory, than I myself can by mere speech. Indeed," he says to Egbert, "it is by you that I myself best understand myself. For to every philosophy are certain rear parts, very important parts, and these, like the rear of one's head, are best seen by reflection."

At the conclusion of *The Confidence-Man* Melville comes full circle, from the queen's buttocks to the bedpan — associated with disease, dysfunctioning, and death. If readers were revolted — they were probably only indifferent since they weren't reading his books — that was a small matter. This final act of aggression in his prose exposed not so much Melville's enduring hates as his self-hatred. He did not spare Allan Melvill or anyone else, but least of all did he spare himself. The most memorable characters in his fiction are the haters — Jackson, Ahab, Bartleby, and Colonel Moredock, the Indian hater in *The Confidence-Man* — who are also self-haters.

If, as D. H. Lawrence asserts, Melville hated people, he also loved greatly: he loved Jack Chase, Nathaniel Hawthorne, and, above all, Allan Melvill. In his fear that he would be hurt, it sometimes seemed that he was only capable of hate, but he protected himself from the power of hurts in life and through his defensive prose and comic tactics in his art.

If the passengers aboard the *Fidèle* have no affect, never emerging into human status, and if the book lacks affect, as it does, Melville has succeeded in his artistic purpose, once more marrying prose and content. But the book also reveals that Melville himself in 1856 felt depleted and drained of emotion. He was close to self-annihilation.

"Doleful Doldrums"
—1856-1860

During the years at Arrowhead Melville took care of the farm. Like his Uncle Thomas, he was no farmer and evidently found the farm, despite its lovely setting in the shadow of Greylock, more a prison than a paradise. His mother was no doubt quite accurate when she observed, "the little petty cares, & annoyances, of the farm . . . are ever recurring & are so distasteful to him." On April 17, 1856, he advertised in the local newspaper that eighty acres were for sale, and in June he found a buyer who paid about $5,500. According to his sister "he was convinced that a residence in the country was not the thing for him, & could he have met with an opportunity of disposing of his place he would have done so."

During the summer, and probably earlier, Elizabeth Melville informed her family of her "great anxiety" about his "severe nervous affections." She accepted the medical verdict that Herman needed a sea voyage of four or five months. She and the two daughters were to stay with the Shaws in Boston, Malcolm with one of his aunts, and Stanwix with his grandmother at great-Uncle Herman's home in Gansevoort, New York. Melville's departure was delayed until the completion of a draft agreement with Dix & Edwards for the publication of *The Confidence-Man*. The contract was verbally approved on October 10, one day before Melville sailed.

While he waited in New York, his family scattered in three different homes, he evidently patched up his somewhat strained relations with Evert Duyckinck, whose coterie had been nastily satirized in *Pierre*. On October 1 Melville was at Duyckinck's — "fresh from his mountain charged to the muzzle with his sailor metaphysics and jargon of things unknowable." It was "a good stirring evening," during which — life imitating fiction — Melville related a story from the *Decameron*, and found release in what Duyckinck termed "an orgie of indecency and blasphemy." Eight days later there was another "Paradise of Bachelors" at the home of Daniel Shepherd, a lawyer like Allan and Herman's companion on a two-day "excursion of pleasure" near Lake George in August. According to Duyckinck, there was "good talk — Herman warming like an old sailor over the supper." On October 11 Duyckinck and Allan saw Herman off on the *Glasgow* — "Melville right hearty."

Between bachelor parties Melville managed to journey to Gansevoort to say good-bye to his mother. Apparently he did not make a special trip to Boston for a final farewell with Elizabeth or with Judge Shaw. Melville was always drawn to his mother, but the Judge's generosity made the trip possible: he advanced "fourteen or fifteen hundred dollars." The Judge advanced the funds, but Allan took charge of the arrangements for the voyage. More and more Herman's dependency upon Allan extended beyond contractual arrangements with publishers to personal matters. Allan, then, was replacing Allan Melvill and Gansevoort Melville as head of the family.

Melville offered no explanation as to why he chose the route he followed, but at thirty-seven he made some of the stops his father had made in his journey of 1818 at age thirty-six. Allan Melvill had landed at Liverpool and then had gone on to Scotland to visit the ancestral site of the Melvills. Herman disembarked at Glasgow, then went to Edinburgh, which was but forty miles from Fifeshire, the ancient family seat. Unlike his father he did not make the trip, nor did he seek out relatives. Where the father had found "just cause of pride, to revert back through ages to such ancestry," Herman, whatever he may have felt, said nothing about "a correspondent spirit of emulation in their descendants to the remotest posterity." Allan Melvill in 1818 had been exuberant, sentimental, proud; Herman Melville in 1856 was unsentimental, laconic, and depressed.

On November 8 he arrived in Liverpool. Although the most meaningful man in his life was now consul in that city, Melville did not immediately seek him out. He had an older debt to repay. For a day or so he wandered about the city, and "Looked at Nelson's statue, with peculiar emotion, mindful of 20 years ago." He was overtaken by memories and emotions. Liverpool was the place where he had learned the painful lesson that paternal guidebooks were obsolete, that the son had only his own two legs to travel on.

Such were the mysteries of chance, or fate, or coincidence, that in 1856 he visited the land of Melvill warriors, then looked with deep emotion at the statue of a wounded hero who had exerted an enormous attraction over his imagination for many years, and finally sought out the middle-aged Apollo who for fifteen months had provided him with the security and feeling of well-being he had not known since his father's death. Two days after his arrival he found Hawthorne at the consulate.

The meeting was awkward at first. Hawthorne attributed his own embarrassment to the fact that he had failed to obtain a consular post for Melville three years before. When he entered the office, Melville seemed to Hawthorne "a little paler, and perhaps a little sadder." He was attired "in a rough outside coat," which no doubt contrasted sharply with Hawthorne's fastidious and correct attire. Hawthorne observed that his friend had "his characteristic gravity and reserve of manners," which would appear to describe Hawthorne as much as Melville. After these two sensitive men, with their reticences and their memories of the strangely intense relationship five years earlier, got over their initial clumsiness, they found themselves "pretty much" — it was Hawthorne's qualification — on their "former terms of sociality and confidence."

Hawthorne invited Melville to stay at his home as long as he was in Liverpool. Melville arrived on November 11 with "the least little bit of a bundle, which . . . contained a night-shirt and a tooth-brush." Hawthorne noted his "very gentlemanly instincts in every respect, save that he is a little heterodox in the matter of clean linen." If Hawthorne felt obliged to record the fact, probably Sophia was even more troubled by Melville's appearance. She was not well at the time, as Melville noted in his journal, and her daughter Una implied that the visit was a strain upon her: "Mamma overtired herself during his visit, and was quite unwell for a day or two afterwards." That Sophia apparently did not comment on the visit, was in marked contrast with her excitement in the fall of 1850 when she saw the "growing man" for the first time.

Melville was laconic in his record of the visit: this time he was as terse and unemotional as Hawthorne had been in noting the trip to

Monument Mountain. On November 12, in Melville's words, the two friends "Took a long walk by the sea. Sands & grass. Wild & desolate. A strong wind. Good talk." Hawthorne noted the "long walk together," but in contrast with Melville's generalities, offered pictorial details. They "sat down in a hollow among the sand hills (sheltering ourselves from the high, cool wind) and smoked a cigar." It was not the Olympian setting which Melville dreamed of in one of his manic letters to Hawthorne, but it was a shelter which in appearance, as perhaps neither of them noted, resembled the mounds — or Saddleback — at the top of Mount Greylock. "Melville, as he always does," Hawthorne recorded, "began to reason of Providence and futurity, and of everything that lies beyond human ken." Not only was Melville repeating conversations of earlier years with Hawthorne, but he was reiterating themes he had discussed on board the ship crossing the Atlantic with an unnamed colonel — "fixed fate &c." — which in turn repeated similar conversations in 1849 when he traveled on the *Southampton* to England.

Melville's metaphysical ruminations eventually led him to say "he had 'pretty much made up his mind to be annihilated.' " Hawthorne was not alarmed by the threat of suicide: "but still he does not seem to rest in that anticipation; and, I think, will never rest until he gets hold of a definite belief." No comment ever made on Melville was to be more profound than what followed in Hawthorne's notebook:

> It is strange how he persists — and has persisted ever since I knew him, and probably long before — in wandering to and fro over these deserts, as dismal and monotonous as the sand hills amid which we were sitting. He can neither believe, nor be comfortable in his unbelief; and he is too honest and courageous not to try to do one or the other. If he were a religious man, he would be one of the most truly religious and reverential; he has a very high and noble nature, and better worth immortality than most of us.

Better almost than anything else this passage reveals the "magnetic" attraction the two men had for each other. Melville had intuitively chosen the man of all men who could empathize with his troubled spirit. For Melville resembled Ethan Brand, Chillingworth, Clifford, Hollingsworth, which is to say that he appealed meaningfully to one-half of Hawthorne's own nature. Melville also knew that his confessions had to be phrased in metaphysical or religious language in order to disguise and to distance the personal hurts hidden beneath the grandiose phrases. Neither man was able to unburden freely, that is, if Hawthorne were able to unburden at all. Although Hawthorne was perceptive, it is difficult to know how far he dared to pursue his perceptions.

Melville left the Hawthorne house two days later, on November 13, but continued to see his friend almost daily. They met at the consulate, lunched at Hawthorne's club, and toured Liverpool. They spent November 15 in Chester, where they took in the sights and sat "in a small snuggery" and "smoked a cigar and drank some stout, conversing the while with the landlord." Apparently there was no more talk of "annihilation," or perhaps Hawthorne made sure that there were no opportunities for confidences. The day before he sailed Melville admitted that "he did not anticipate much pleasure in his rambles, for that the spirit of adventure is gone out of him. He is certainly much overshadowed," Hawthorne added, "since I saw him last; but I hope he will brighten as he goes onward." On November 18 Melville sailed on the *Egyptian*. He left a trunk at the consulate, since he planned to return to Liverpool, and carried only "a carpet bag." Hawthorne considered this "the next best thing to going naked," although, he added, "we seldom see men of less criticizable manners than he."

And so once again Melville sailed from Liverpool. This time it was not the son in search of Allan Melvill. This time he searched for more ancient, mythic roots. It was Ishmael returning to the land of Abraham. In adolescence Melville journeyed to seek a Paradise in the South Seas, where Western sons could find no home in an alien culture and tradition. Now at thirty-seven, in the middle of the journey, he was traveling to the Holy Land, the birthplace of his hopes and doubts. Just as Israel Potter finds in the Promised Land after fifty years only desolation and ingratitude, so Melville was to discover Paradise Lost.

During his long sometimes tedious journey into the Mediterranean Sea, he kept a journal which was for the most part even more terse and unadorned than the journal of 1849. Unlike Thoreau, Emerson, or Hawthorne, he was satisfied with catalogs of sights and events, incomplete sentences, unpolished paragraphs. Apparently the notebook was intended only to jog his memory, and it did serve that purpose in many of the poems he was to write in later years. He obviously spent little time in making his recordings, sometimes writing two or three days after the events. Only rarely did he elaborate.

Although a pall hung over him, as Hawthorne observed, he tried to free himself by plunging vigorously into the role of a tourist. He rose early and walked until dusk. He missed few sights, and what really engaged him he visited several times. He visited cemeteries wherever he went, although gloomy sentiments peeped through only occasionally. He found the houses in Constantinople "So gloomy & grimy [it] seems as if a suicide hung from every rafter within" — a strange association which would occur only to someone suffering from depression. He was deeply moved when in Constantinople he saw "a woman over a new grave — no grass on it yet. Such abandonment of misery! Called to the dead, put her head down as close to it as possible; as if calling down a hatchway or cellar; besought — 'Why dont you speak to me? My God! — It is I! Ah, speak — but one word!' — All deaf. — So much for consolation. — This woman & her cries haunt me terribly." The next morning he "felt as if broken on the wheel."

In Egypt he took the customary trip to the pyramids. In his novels the pyramids were not architectural masterpieces but death motifs. As he approached the monuments he likened them to the vastness of the ocean, then to mountains: "Nothing in Nature gives such an idea of vastness." Then the lens, as it were, closed in: "View of persons ascending, Arab guides in flowing white mantles. Conducted as by angels up to heaven. Guides so tender." Abruptly he shifted focus to the tourists. "Resting. Pain in the chest. Exhaustion. Must hurry. None but the phlegmatic go deliberately. Old man with the spirits of youth — long looked for this chance — tried the ascent, half way — failed — brought down. Tried to go into the interior — fainted — brought out — leaned against the pyramid by the entrance — pale as death. Nothing so pathetic." As Melville recorded the scene, he gradually interpolated explanations which he had no way of knowing. The tourist, after all, was a silent stranger: "Too much for him; oppressed by the massiveness & mystery of the pyramids." And then the self-identification followed: "I myself too. A feeling of awe & terror came over me." Suddenly the guides were no longer "angels": "Dread of the Arabs. Offering to lead me into a side-hole. The Dust. Long arched way, — then down as in a coal shaft. Then as in mines, under the sea." Melville was overcome with terror. "I shudder at idea of ancient Egyptians. It was in these pyramids that was conceived the idea of Jehovah. Terrible mixture of the cunning and awful." Since Melville wrote this passage three days after the event, time provided no recollections in tranquility. Here were the manic rhythms of *Moby-Dick*. "Pyramids still loom before me — something vast, undefiled, incomprehensible, and awful." The desert was "more fearful to look at than ocean." These monuments of death were more terrifying than the white whale.

At last Ishmael reached the land of Abraham. There was no welcome for the prodigal orphan. Jerusalem was "A sickening cheat." The Holy Sepulchre was a "show-box" surrounded by "mildewed" walls. He visited the lepers — "Zion, this park, a dungheap." He wandered among tombs "till I began to think myself one of the possessed with devils." The Pool of Bethesda was "full of rubbish — sooty look & smell." He journeyed to the Dead Sea and to Bethlehem, but the rocky terrain of Judea depressed him: "Stony mountains & stony plains; stony torrents & stony roads; stony vales & stony fields, stony homes & stony tombs." He deleted the next phrase — "stony eyes & stony hearts." The Holy Land here and elsewhere in his journal was translated into the rhythms and disillusionment of *Pierre*, the repetitions pointing to his emotional enervation and the seeming overreactions to the scenes indicating something approaching panic. The man who hungered to believe found his hunger unassuaged. "No country will more quickly dissipate romantic expectations than Palestine — particularly Jerusalem. To some the disappointment is heart sickening."

At Joppa he wrote: "I am emphatically alone," and then added: "& begin to feel like Jonah." If he felt himself possessed by devils, he also fantasized himself in the dark loneliness of the whale's belly. He saw himself swallowed or "incorporated." After he was delayed in Joppa for six days, he commented: "The whole thing is half melancholy, half farcical — like all the rest of the world."

On the voyage to Greece he suffered "intolerable persecutions of bugs" and did not sleep for four nights. At Patmos he was, he confessed, "again afflicted with the great curse of modern travel — skepticism." At Patmos, where St. John had his apocalyptic visions, Melville did not achieve insight or illumination. He saw only the emptiness, within and without: "When my eye rested on arid heigth, spirit partook of the barrenness."

At Smyrna on the following day he had a "very bad neuralgia pain top of head." His spirits revived somewhat when the ship landed in Greece, but not until he was in Italy did he escape the ennui that afflicted him and find himself gradually caught up in the romance that is Italy. At first "Rome fell flat on me. Oppressively flat," but then during the month he stayed he was seized by the glories which he had known all his life from books and prints. At the Capitoline Museum, like Byron before him and Hawthorne and Henry James after him, he was moved by the statue of the Dying Gladiator. Then he saw for the first time the bust of Antinous, that "beautiful," somewhat hermaphroditic youthful favorite of the Emperor Hadrian. Two days later, on February 28, 1857, he saw the bas-relief of Antinous in the Villa Albani, and almost swooned before its loveliness, like Tommo at his meeting with Marnoo in *Typee*: "head like moss-rose with curls & buds — ... end of fillet on shoulder — ... hand full of flowers & eyeing them."

Early in March Melville suffered from eyestrain and for a few

days curbed his activities. Then on March 15 he was "attacked by
singular pain across chest & in back.... This day saw nothing,
learned nothing, enjoyed nothing, but suffered something." He
apparently recovered shortly and on March 20 left Rome. With improved spirits and guidebook in hand, he followed from city to city
the usual route, saw the usual sights, and voiced the usual super-
latives about the beauties of Italy. For the first time he was not
imprisoned in his depression. In Naples, in fact, he gave way to gaiety
when he met an "affable" young man named Antonio who became
his guide for several days. He recorded the bastardized English of the
youth as he listened to Antonio's observations about wealth, death,
and so forth. Melville concluded that the lad was a "good character
for Con Man," and quite obviously enjoyed "Floating about philoso-
phizing with Antonio the Merry."

When he saw da Vinci's famous fresco in Milan, he responded in
a most personal way: "Significance of the Last Supper. The joys of
the banquet soon depart. One shall betray me, one of you — men so
false — the glow of sociability is so evanescent, selfishness so lasting."
Which were not so much the thoughts of one great artist before one
of the masterpieces of an even greater artist, as of an all-too-human
disappointed idealist who could no more detach himself from the
content of da Vinci's painting than he could from the emotional
tensions of his own writings.

Melville went from Turin to Switzerland, then to Amsterdam by
way of Frankfort and Cologne. On April 26 he was in London, where
he revisited familiar sights and took in some new ones. Apparently
for the first time he saw the canvases of one of the greatest and most
innovative artists of the century, Joseph Turner, who had died in
1851. He deeply admired the luminous sunsets, "The Fighting of
Téméraire," "The Burial of Wilkie," and "The Shipwreck." As always, he was attracted to depictions of disaster and death, which also
haunted Turner. Then he went to Oxford, which he pronounced the
"Most interesting spot I have seen in England.... I know nothing
more fitted by mild & beautiful rebuke to chastise the presumptuous
ranting of Yankees."

On the following day, May 3, he made the obligatory visit to
Stratford-upon-Avon, where he completed the obligatory tour with
only a few comments: "Shakspeare's home — little old groggery
abandoned. — cheerless, melancholy Scrawl of names." On May 4 he
arrived in Liverpool, collected his trunk at the consulate, and on the
following morning "off for home."

Hawthorne and Melville met for the last time on May 4. Hawthorne made no entry in his notebooks; Melville confined himself to
two words, "Saw Hawthorne." Those two words were a kind of

epitaph of silence. Hawthorne may have been too busy with official business; Melville may have been in one of his depressed moods. Perhaps the silence resulted from one of those coincidences which haunted Melville's life and especially his relationship with Hawthorne. His memory calendar could not have forgotten that he had likened Nathaniel of Salem to William of Stratford in *The Literary World*. To have come from the birthplace of the greatest of artists into the presence of Hawthorne could only have evoked memories of those fateful fifteen months which saw the birth of *Moby-Dick*, the birth and death of a friendship, and the beginning of a decline in popularity and, worse, in his spirits and self-confidence. While Melville's reputation withered, Hawthorne had enjoyed one success after another, and now had the kind of sinecure denied his friend.

Melville could only have been envious if he learned from Hawthorne or the newspapers that just a few weeks earlier, on April 15, 1857, Hawthorne had been the principal speaker at the dedication of the William Brown Library in Liverpool. His introduction to the audience had been, ironically, as extravagant as Melville's review in *The Literary World*:

> His "Scarlet Letter" has struck to the heart of every man with whom it came in contact. He has built his house of "Seven Gables" in every town in England; and as for his "Twice-told Tales," we all wish they had been told ten times. (Applause.) Gentlemen, therefore, in giving you the health of that distinguished citizen of the United States, and that distinguished citizen of the literature of the world, I believe that you will join with me, and that you will feel you are in no degree derogating from the special purposes for which we have met together. (Applause.) . . . I give you "Nathaniel Hawthorne and the United States of America." (Loud and prolonged applause.)

Although it is always difficult to penetrate Hawthorne's veils, he may have enjoyed international renown, but he knew that, while he sat in his offices in Liverpool, he had completed no tales or romances. He may have even sensed that something went out of his life after he wrote *The Blithedale Romance* and after he had freed himself from the relationship with Melville. While Melville was on the continent, the agreement with the English publisher to bring out *The Confidence-Man* was signed, on March 20, 1857, by "Nathl Hawthorne, U. S. Consul, on behalf of Herman Melville." If Hawthorne wrote to Melville after reading *The Confidence-Man*, the letter was probably burned in one of those fires in which Melville tried to bury a past which of course he could not bury.

Melville landed in New York on May 20. He freely confessed what was no doubt self-evident: although his health was slightly improved, he had not shaken off the inner "mould." At home he discovered that his sister Augusta and Peter Gansevoort had undertaken another campaign to secure him a governmental post in the new administration after the elections of 1856. Augusta stated the family opinion on April 7: "We all feel that it is of the utmost importance that something should be done to prevent the necessity of Herman's writing as he has been obliged to for several years past. Were he to return to the sedentary life which that of an author writing for his support necessitates, he would risk the loss of all the benefit to his health which he has gained by his tour, & possibly become a confirmed invalid. Of this his physicians have warned him." Whether Augusta overstated the medical opinion we have no way of knowing, although the nonprofessional comments which have survived point to no such melodramatic conclusion that he was about to become a "confirmed invalid." If some doctor had sought to frighten the family and Melville himself by such a gloomy prediction, he had taken the wrong approach to a case which clearly involved depression. With the best of intentions, however, Augusta wanted Uncle Peter to obtain a position for Herman in the Custom-House in New York.

According to his brother-in-law, Lemuel Shaw, Jr., Melville agreed to the proposition and even promised not "to write any more at present." That Melville was no longer a resident of New York was an obstacle in obtaining a position, but probably his consistent abstention from politics was the determining factor. At any rate he was once again unsuccessful in his pursuit of a governmental post.

A month after his return to the United States, on June 24, he advertised that Arrowhead was for sale, and on July 3 signed a contract for the purchase of a property in Brooklyn. When in August it was clear that there were no purchasers for the farm, Allan arranged for the cancellation of the contract. He replied ambiguously, but consistently in terms of his promise to the family, to a letter from *The Atlantic Monthly* inviting him to contribute an article: "I shall be very happy to contribute, though I can not now name the day when I shall have any article ready." Now that he was freeing himself from the farm and from writing — or so he thought — he hit upon lecturing as a means of furnishing a livelihood. Allan immediately sought the guidance of G. W. Curtis, who had been editorial advisor to *Putnam's Monthly Magazine* and a successful lecturer. On September 15 Herman himself wrote to Curtis: "I have been trying to scratch my brains for a Lecture. What is a good, earnest subject? '*Daily progress of man towards a state of intellectual & moral perfec-*

tion, as evidenced in history of 5th Avenue & 5 Points.' " (The witticism referred to New York's most famous avenue and most infamous whorehouse district.)

Melville may have indulged in strained, self-conscious flippancy for a number of reasons. At a banquet after his return home his physician and neighbor, Oliver Wendell Holmes, had remarked that "a lecturer was a literary strumpet subject for a greater than whore's fee to prostitute himself." Melville's comment to Curtis also recalled a satirical passage in *Pierre* in which the "hero" is invited by the Urguhartian Club of Zadockprattsville to lecture on "Human Destiny." He may also have remembered Hawthorne's barbed reference in *The Blithedale Romance* to "that sober and pallid, or, rather, drab-colored, mode of winter-evening entertainment, the Lecture."

Despite his facetiousness Melville finally concocted a lecture based on his experiences in Italy which dealt with the "state of intellectual & moral perfection" of the Romans. He gave his lecture "Statues in Rome" sixteen times in such places as Boston, Cleveland, Detroit, Charlestown, and New Bedford. His fee was generally $50. After deducting expenses, he cleared $423.70, which amounted to about $26 for each lecture. In 1856 Emerson made about $1,700 on the lecture circuit, and Bayard Taylor, later the translator of Goethe and a popular raconteur, earned about $5,000 annually. In his careful examination of newspaper accounts, Merton M. Sealts, Jr., concludes that the response over-all was favorable. However, there were some harsh criticisms of his subject matter and his delivery. In Charleston a particularly nasty reviewer wrote: "His draughts upon the classical Dictionary were frequent and heavy, too heavy for the comfort and edification of his auditors. Some nervous people, therefore, left the hall; some read books and newspapers; some sought refuge in sleep, and some, to their praise be it spoken, seemed determined to use it as an appropriate occasion for self-discipline in the blessed virtue of patience." In Auburn, New York, the reporter attacked "his inexcusable blundering, sing-song, monotonous delivery. It was the most complete case of infanticide we ever heard of; he literally strangled his own child."

In the second season in 1858-59, he spoke on "The South Seas" to ten audiences. Despite the decline in the number of appearances he cleared $518. Again most of the reviews were favorable. The *Yonkers Examiner* found the lecture humorous and enjoyable, but criticized the delivery: "the closes of his sentences have a descending and rising cadence, which can be likened to nothing on earth but the graceful twist in a porcine afterpart." A letter to the same newspaper protested the absence of content and excitement in the lecture: "Job must have his disciples in Yonkers, and Bildad the Shuhuhite, from the placid Pacific has come to the rescue. Let us yawn!"

Despite the generally sympathetic press coverage, which may have been in part attributable to the general blandness of newspapers in reporting lectures, word must have gotten out that Melville was something less than dynamic on the platform. Only once was he invited for a return appearance, and in 1859-60 he could obtain only three engagements, for which he received $110. On the basis of the texts as reconstructed by Sealts from newspaper reviews, the public reaction was more than justified. The lecturer went steadily downhill from year to year. The first lecture, although the subject matter failed to interest many in the audience, was the best of the lot; his account of the South Seas was dull as well as bookish; and the third, "Traveling — Its Pleasures, Pains, and Profits," could only have produced yawns.

Although lecturing served the purpose of keeping Melville away from his desk for at least part of the year, and at the same time furnished an outlet for his restlessness, he was temperamentally and intellectually unsuited for the lyceum circuit. For one thing he had little genuine fondness for the citizens of Zadockprattsville. Like an incorrigible romantic, not without a dash of megalomania, he never recognized the immodesty of his desire to make audiences over in his own image. In addition, large gatherings of strangers, their eyes riveted on him, so intimidated him that he could not raise his eyes from the manuscript he was reading, and what natural grace and forcefulness he had disappeared in his sing-song delivery. Melville was unable on the lecture platform to resolve a conflict which had troubled him from the beginning, a desire for success and popularity and self-contempt because he had such a desire. Despite his fondness for "ontological heroics" on any occasion, he was not a profound or systematic thinker. He could not entertain his audience after the fashion of Bayard Taylor, nor could he rival Emerson in philosophical discussions either in the depth of his reading or in the exposition of his views. Misty as he may have sometimes been, Emerson at least thought in paragraphs; Melville felt in sentences.

The best of these lectures, "Statues in Rome," revealed Melville's weaknesses as a lecturer and a thinker. At the outset he asserted the democratic fallacy, which he certainly only half believed, that art was for the masses, or, in his words, that "Art strikes a chord in the lowest as well as in the highest; the rude and uncultivated feel its influence as well as the polite and polished." The reception of his own books, including his masterpiece, had demonstrated the obvious, that the citizens of Zadockprattsville did not scorn art; they were simply indifferent. As a child of romanticism he argued that art was superior to science, that progress was a delusion, and that modern civilization was inferior to that of the Romans: "Their virtues were great and noble, and these virtues made them great and noble." Again, "The deeds of the ancients were noble, and so are their arts." Since Melville was a religious man after his fashion, the speech was suffused with praise of a god of a religion long since dead. But Melville was as much in love with the famous sculpture of Apollo in the Vatican as he was with the Greek deity. Apollo, he proclaimed, is more beautiful than Venus, for "the Venus is of the earth, and the Apollo is divine." Modern man, he asserted, was not capable of producing such a sculptural monument as Apollo. Melville did not recognize that, like many of his generation, he was not clarifying matters by mixing esthetics and religion.

What his audiences could not have realized, as Melville himself may not have, was that he was using the lecture platform to defend, or to rationalize, his life-long attachment to the Apollonian ideal for personal more than esthetic reasons. In the earliest of his writings, "Fragments from a Writing Desk," it will be recalled, he clothed himself, or at any rate his central character, in Apollo's beauty in order to win M.'s affections. In extolling Apollo he was justifying his own search for an ideal relationship.

For a man who could not lift his eyes from the lectern the platform was a kind of scaffold. In the absence of eye contact Melville was as isolated from his audience as Father Mapple, who, upon climbing to the raised pulpit, pulls up his ladder after him. If Melville physically isolated himself, he compounded the separation by taking positions that could only offend conventionally religious sensibilities. He did just about everything necessary to insure his failure. He achieved his goal.

Although minor documents, the lectures are useful, particularly in the absence of other materials, in determining Melville's state of mind in the years before the Civil War. Two of the lectures dealt in somewhat fumbling, or indirect, ways with Edens or Paradises. Rome represented the Golden Age of civilization, Typee a primitive Paradise. It was clever to observe, as Melville did, that the Vatican was an index of the ancient world and the Washington Patent Office of the modern world, or that the Coliseum and the Crystal Palace in London revealed the "respective characters of ancients and moderns." These artfully chosen juxtapositions suggest that he was at this time radically alienated from his world, frightened by the power of the locomotive, or what would become Henry Adams's dynamo.

During the years he lectured, Melville's health apparently fluctuated, or at least the reports did. Just before he delivered his sixteenth lecture of the first season on February 23, 1858, Peter Gansevoort pronounced Herman "in excellent health & very fine spirits." But in the following month, according to his wife's memoir, "A severe attack of what he called a crick in his back laid him up at his Mothers in Gansevoort . . . and he never regained his former vigor & strength." He had complained of his back in 1856 in Liverpool and admitted to difficulty in walking. Later in 1858 George Duyckinck spoke of "an affection of the spine brought on by too many hours of brain work day after day." Yet Duyckinck found Melville "in good spirits," and in the same month Judge Shaw reported, "Herman is as well as I have seen him for years." A year later his sister Augusta claimed that he was "much stronger," which would indicate that he may have experienced a relapse in recent months. At the same time his neighbor Sarah Morewood admonished George Duyckinck: "Herman Melville is not well — do not call him moody, he is ill."

Two starry-eyed students at Williams College who came to Arrowhead in 1859 on their "first literary pilgrimage" were impressed by Melville's volubility on philosophical subjects, although he stubbornly refused to gratify their curiosity about the South Seas, which, unlike philosophy, did not appear in the academic curriculum. John Thomas Gulick, despite his years, noted that Melville "was evidently a disappointed man, soured by criticism and disgusted with the civilized world." The other visitor, Titus Munson Coan, pronounced the author "an Ishmael" who desired "to shut himself up in this cold North as a cloistered thinker."

Gulick made an interesting observation which no one else, so far as I can discover, was willing to record: "His countenance is slightly flushed with whiskey drinking, but not without expression." Others spoke of his amiability and loquacity over his cups and at the dinners the Duyckincks gave. Melville always called for champagne or gin in the happy days with Hawthorne, and his vision of a shared paradise included an abundance of alcoholic refreshment. Heavy drinking would not be surprising — a symptom, not a cause, of his depressed state.

Since lectures provided him with a small financial return, about the same in a given year as the return from his short stories, his economic situation was not changed. What made things easier was the income Elizabeth received. On November 8, 1858, at the beginning of the second lecture series, Shaw sent $100, "Believing that in providing your family supplies for the approaching winter, some pecuniary assistance may be wanted by you." A year later, in the fall of 1859, Melville gave Shaw a deed to Arrowhead, which had been purchased with the Judge's money and which, except for the acreage disposed of in 1856, he had not been able to sell. On May 15, 1860, Melville legally deeded the property to the Judge, who in turn conveyed it to his daughter. The result of the transaction was, in Shaw's phrasing, "to cancel and discharge all debt and pecuniary obligation of every description from you to myself." Now almost eighty with only a few years to live, Shaw was still providing for the Melvilles with genuine generosity which increased Herman's dependency upon his wife and her family, and which replicated Allan Melvill's dependency upon the Gansevoorts and Shaw.

Although Melville's life in these years was, on the basis of extant documents, as gray and drab as Bartleby's, marred by ill health and depression, the gloom lifted on the camping and hiking expeditions he undertook in the company of his brother Allan and other friends. In July 1859 Melville sent to one of Allan's law partners, Daniel Shepherd, who had written anonymously a novel entitled *Saratoga, A Story of 1787*, a letter which was actually a poem modeled after Marlowe's famous lyric: "Come, Shepherd, come and visit me." Although he was deliberately parodistic and a trifle heavy in his archness, he revealed once more, as he had in episode after episode in his novels and in his letters to Hawthorne, how important and meaningful male friendship was to him. In the poem he dreams of Jove's "laurel grove" and speaks in labored syntax of some kind of opposition to "friendship pure" — which may be his recognition that much as he desired "friendship pure" the world suspects its purity. Then he alludes playfully to Shepherd's (and his own) fondness for "Claret and Otard":

> Placed 'tween the two decanters, you,
> Like Alexander, your dear charmers view,
> And both so fair you find, you neither can eschew;
> — That's what they call an Alexandrine. . . .

Although it is not quite an Alexandrine, here, as in the male brothel scene in *Redburn*, Melville alludes obliquely to an ancient hero whose passions included wine and males. Of course the poem ends innocuously as a jest out of Marlowe and the pastoral tradition:

> Daniel Shepherd, come and rove —
>   Freely rove two faery dells,
> The one the Housatonic clove,
>   And that where genial Friendship dwells.

Once more, despite his bitter comments on friendship betrayed beginning in 1852, Melville melted into his affected diction before his thwarted desire.

As his poem to Shepherd indicates, he could not keep his promise to his family — not to write. A year earlier, in July 1858, George

Duyckinck reported that Melville was "busy on a new book," although at the time he did not know that it was to be a volume of verse. This was a secret between Herman and his wife. A decade earlier he had interspersed in *Mardi* undistinguished poems which revealed a defective ear, but he had not up to this time devoted serious attention to poetry. It remains questionable, as Robert Penn Warren had to admit in his reevaluation and praise of the poetry, that Melville really learned his craft, any more than he had really studied and mastered the narrative techniques of fiction. For the next few years Melville added to his library editions of many of the older English poets, some translations, but only rarely a volume by one of his contemporaries. Despite the "modernity" of his attitudes, at least in the eyes of some critics, he was conservative and traditional in his poetic taste. Two poems he submitted to an unidentified magazine on May 18, 1859, were rejected. Apparently not discouraged, he continued to compose poems, probably based on his journey to the Holy Land.

He had almost completed a volume of poetry when suddenly in May 1860 he decided to take a voyage with his brother Tom. Elizabeth Melville had not recopied the manuscript when Melville wrote hurriedly to Evert Duyckinck asking him "to lend something of an overseeing eye to the launching of this craft." At the same time he gave Allan Melville detailed instructions as to format, terms, and proofreading. "For God's sake," he commanded, "don't have *By the author of 'Typee' 'Piddledee' &c.* on the title-page." He concluded the letter with realistic forebodings which hid not at all what the book meant to him: "Of all human events, perhaps, the publication of a first volume of verses is the most insignificant, but though a matter of no moment to the world, it is still of some concern to the author." On June 19, while Melville was at sea, Charles Scribner returned the manuscript. Although the poems were "excellent," he wrote, "I doubt whether they would more than pay expenses."

Shaw in a sense made this voyage possible, as he had the preceding ones, after he arranged for the handsome property settlement upon Mrs. Melville. An eternal optimist, perhaps not unlike Captain Delano in "Benito Cereno," Shaw expected his son-in-law to benefit in health and spirits. Melville himself expected no miracles. "I anticipate," he wrote to Duyckinck, "as much pleasure as, at the age of fourty, one temperately can, in the voyage I am going" — the anticipation perhaps unwittingly reflected in the labored syntax.

The brothers were to sail to San Francisco, then to Manila, "& thence, I hardly know where." Herman sailed under Captain Thomas Melville, his favorite brother who bore the name of his favorite uncle, Thomas Melvill. Maria's last and favorite son, Tom had gone to sea at sixteen aboard the whaler *Theophilus Chase.* About the same weight and height, with the same brown hair, the brothers resembled each other closely. After fourteen years as a sailor Thomas had his own ship, having succeeded in a way of life which continued to attract Herman. That the ship was christened *Meteor* could only have heightened the romantic aura and excitement of the voyage which began in Boston on May 30, 1860.

Melville offered no explanation as to why he embarked on what could have been a lengthy voyage of a year or more in duration. There was, of course, the continuing problem of his health, physical and emotional, and people in the nineteenth century had a mystique about fresh air and travel. As Sealts suggests, there was his failure as a lecturer. He may have been exhausted after completing his volume of poems, since writing was a painful ordeal which he could not abandon, or he may have found life at Arrowhead more irksome than ever: Pittsfield suited his temperament and talents no more than it had Uncle Thomas's. Perhaps Melville — at least that part of his nature given to dreams — thought that the *Meteor* would take him to enchanted lands, but he also knew that the Encantadas were stony, bleak, murderous isles. Melville did not often deceive himself, but in his depressed state travel, if it offered nothing else, at least provided a change of scene.

A few months before he sailed he had underscored some lines in one of the ballads in Child's famous collection:

> *Away he goes with heavy heart;*
>   *His griefs he did conceale,*
> *And like a wise and prudent man,*
>   *To none did it reveale.*

He took along a small library of books. One of the books was *The Marble Faun*, a gift from his neighbor Sarah Morewood. Hawthorne had apparently forgotten to send a copy.

"All Fatherless
Seemed
the Human Soul"

—The Civil War
and
Battle-Pieces

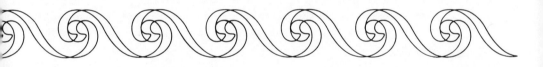

Melville became seasick the first night out and had a squeamish
stomach for almost three weeks. About the middle of June there
were no winds and the crew was afflicted with the "Doleful Doldrums." Until the winds returned the sailors were "given up to melancholy, and meditating darkly on the mysteries of Providence." The
voyager kept a journal but, as usual, confined himself to factual
matters for the most part, except when disaster struck, relating little
about his own feelings and almost nothing at all about life aboard the
Meteor. He played chess in the evenings with Tom, read when the sea
was calm, and evidently meditated darkly on fate.

The journey around Cape Horn recalled the voyages of the
1840s, particularly the trip aboard the *United States* which he had
recorded in *White-Jacket.* On August 9, one of the sailors named Ray
fell from the mast during a hail storm. His chum sat alone in a cabin
with the mangled body. " 'I have lost my best friend,' said he; and

then 'His mother will go crazy — she did not want to let him go, she feared something might happen.' " The following day after the simple burial at sea the sky was blue and the sea calm — "almost pleasant enough to atone for the gales, but not for Ray's fate, which belongs to that order of human events, which staggers those whom the Primal Philosophy hath not confirmed. — But little sorrow to the crew — all goes on as usual — I, too, read & think, & walk & eat & talk, as if nothing had happened — as if I did not know that death is indeed the King of Terrors." (In the background of the journal note one hears echoes of "The Death Craft," the sketch he published in 1839.)

If at age forty-one "the King of Terrors" stalked his meditations, Melville might at least have spared his eleven-year-old son Malcolm. When he wrote to his son he not only mentioned the incident but added grim details not recorded in his journal:

> Well, all at once, Uncle Tom saw something falling through the air, and then heard a thump, and then, — looking before him, saw a poor sailor lying dead on the deck. He had fallen from the yard, and was killed instantly. — His shipmates picked him up, and carried him under cover. By and by, when time could be spared, the sailmaker sewed up the body in a peice of sail-cloth, putting some iron balls — cannon balls — at the foot of it. And, when all was ready, the body was put on a plank, and carried to the ship's side in the prescence of all hands. Then Uncle Tom, as Captain, read a prayer out of the prayer-book, and at a given word, the sailors who held the plank tipped it up, and immediately the body slipped into the stormy ocean, and we saw it no more.

Profoundly moved, Melville evidently never thought for a moment of the effect such a tragedy would have upon a youth whose father was now far away from Pittsfield aboard a ship where death might overtake him at any time.

Toward the conclusion of the letter he spoke to Malcolm after the fashion of Allan, without the paternal clichés but with the kind of gratuitous advice that no son deserves: "I hope that you have called to mind what I said to you about your behaviour previous to my going away. I hope that you have been obedient to your mother, and helped her all you could, & saved her trouble. Now is the time to show what you are — whether you are a good, honorable boy, or a good-for-nothing one. Any boy, of your age, who disobeys his mother, or worries her, or is disrespectful to her — such a boy is a poor shabby fellow; and if you know any such boys, you ought to cut their acquaintance." A son as fragile as Malcolm appeared in a photograph taken in 1860 needed neither reminders of death nor injunctions to be manly. He needed the affectionate solicitude that his father himself never enjoyed. As things turned out, Malcolm was to have only seven more years of life.

On October 12 the *Meteor* arrived in San Francisco. Melville's health had not improved, and when Tom's orders were changed and there was doubt as to his destination, Herman set off alone for New York by way of Panama. He arrived in New York on November 12, at the very time — "whenever it is a damp, drizzly November in my soul" — that Ishmael takes to the sea to drive off "the spleen." At Christmas Herman wrote a ditty to "gallant Tom!" who at this time was on his way to England:

> *Thou that, duty-led, dost roam*
> *Far from thy shepherd-brother's home —*
> *Shearer of the ocean-foam!*
> *To whom one Christmas may not come, —*
>   *Of thee I think*
>   *Till on its brink*
> *The glass shows tears, beloved Tom!*

Although Herman no doubt merely wanted to say that Tom would celebrate Christmas at sea, his ambiguous phraseology — "To whom one Christmas may not come" — suggested that "the King of Terrors" managed to color his Christmas greeting to his favorite brother.

That winter Arrowhead and his family did not lighten his spirits, and in February Allan Melville undertook a concerted effort to obtain the consular post in Florence for Herman. Failing that, he proposed a position in the New York Custom-House. Once more Allan solicited the support of old family friends, including this time David Dudley Field, at whose home Hawthorne and Melville met for the first time in 1850. This time Herman actively involved himself in the campaign. He went to Washington shortly after Lincoln's inauguration, and met the president at a public reception. "Old Able is much better looking [than] I expected & younger looking. He shook hands like a good fellow — working hard at it like a man at sawing wood at so much per cord." When the post at Florence was awarded to an active Republican, Melville was willing to settle for Glasgow. But the administration passed him over and the spoils went as always to the faithful.

While Melville was in Washington, the venerable old Judge Shaw, now in his eightieth year, became critically ill. Shaw took a ride about Boston on March 30, returned for lunch and his customary nap, and later in the day died without a word in an easy chair. There was a "violent snow-storm" on the morning of the funeral, at which Allan Melvill's childhood friend was pronounced "A just man and one that feared God." Nine days later, on April 12, the shots fired at Fort Sumter plunged the nation into war.

On June 10 Melville was to take Stanwix to see the soldiers drill, but when passage to the barracks was blocked because of a fire, they took, in the words of his son, "a ride all through the Cemetery." Melville could not stay out of cemeteries. In August he went to see the uncle after whom he was named, Herman Gansevoort, who was seriously ill. He died on the following March 18, and four months later, on August 7, his brother Wessel Gansevoort passed away. On November 1, 1862, Priscilla Melvill, an unmarried aunt, died, leaving a legacy of $900 to Herman. Within a period of twenty months, then, a deeply depressed man recorded on his memory calendar four more fractures. He attempted to handle the losses by jest, or evasion, as in his remarks to Tom about "those sensible & sociable millions of good fellows all taking a good long friendly snooze together, under the sod — no quarrels, no imaginary grievances, no envies, heart-burnings, & thinking how much better that other chap is off — none of this: but all equally free-&-easy, they sleep away & reel off their nine knots an hour, in perfect amity."

Unable to face another winter in the bleak Berkshires, Melville took his family to New York in January 1862, and almost at once suffered an attack that made him "rheumatism-bound" for over two months. He summoned Evert Duyckinck to "settle the affairs of the universe" over "some whiskey punch." He continued to purchase volumes of poetry and through underscorings and marginal commentary to carry on his endless struggle with himself to resolve his religious doubts and confusion.

About April 15 he returned to Pittsfield and on the way stopped at Gansevoort to see the grave of Herman Gansevoort, whose burial he had been unable to attend. On May 21 he offered his home for sale. About this time he destroyed most of his poetry. "You will be pleased to learn," he wrote to Tom, "that I have disposed of a lot of it at a great bargain. In fact, a trunk-maker took the whole stock off my hands at ten cents the pound." His wit again originated in depression. As he compulsively pursued a fantasy which could only have been painful, since it confirmed the artistic sterility which had overtaken him in 1856, he recalled the fate of Plinlimmon's manuscript in *Pierre*: "So, When you buy a new trunk again, just peep at the lining & perhaps you may be rewarded by some glorious stanza stareing you in the face & claiming admiration."

Although there were no purchasers of Arrowhead, the Melvilles decided to move into Pittsfield for the winter. On November 7, as Melville was moving possessions to the new quarters, he was thrown from the carriage and broke his shoulder blade and injured some ribs. For the next four or five weeks he was laid up in great pain. In a bantering letter to his brother-in-law, Samuel Shaw, he averred that his recovery had convinced him that his life was of "some value." "I once, like other spoonies, cherished a loose sort of notion that I did not care to live very long. But I will frankly own that I have now no serious, no insuperable objections to a respectable longevity. I dont like the idea of being left out night after night in a cold church-yard." Perhaps at last the gloom was lifting, or so he hoped. (What he said here was almost an answer to Gansevoort's last letter in 1846: "Selfishly speaking I never valued life much — it were impossible to value it less than I do now.") But Melville's manic jesting cannot be completely trusted, certainly not the drawing toward the conclusion of the letter of a skull and crossbones — the skull, he claimed, wink-ing out of its left eye.

Eventually Allan decided to purchase Arrowhead as a summer home. Actually the farmhouse became part payment for a dwelling owned by Allan at 104 East 26th Street in New York. In October 1863 Herman returned to his "native place." To one correspondent he spoke of "a twelve years' visit in Berkshire." The stay in Pittsfield was hardly a "visit" and the period was thirteen years, not twelve, from 1850 to 1863.

The Melville boys did not go with their parents to New York. Malcolm, now fourteen, was sent to a boarding school in Newton Center, not too far from the Shaws in Boston. Stanwix, age twelve, attended school in Gansevoort, New York, under the supervision of his grandmother, who remained in Herman Gansevoort's house after his death. No one troubled to record why the youths were sent away to school; perhaps no one paid attention to the fact that once again the father voluntarily separated himself from his sons.

In his "native place" Melville presumably found some intellec-tual stimulation in the Duyckinck circle, but the Young Americans were now middle-aged. With the nation involved in a war that seemed endless neither art nor life could be carried on as usual. Melville wrote poetry occasionally, but with none of the urgency that con-sumed him when he was seeking a reputation as a writer of prose. On the one hand he was unable physically or mentally to endure the writing seizures of the past; on the other hand, since he was not an artist who slowly filed his works into perfection, he could not realize himself artistically without the total physical and intellectual com-mitment to his art. And so the days were long, and he was without a definite goal, artistic or personal. Like Melville, Hawthorne also drift-ed during the war years, unable to focus his talents or to rekindle his sagging energies.

After Melville's return to his birthplace, then, there was little evidence of increased vitality. A change of place is only a change of place; even one's birthplace can effect no transformation or elevate sunken spirits or renew depleted energies. He read a book at Duyckinck's request but declined to write a review: "tho I would like to please you, I have not spirit enough." These words were written on the "last day of 1863."

In April 1864 Allan and Herman decided to visit the battle-front. On one of those excursions characteristic of that strangely intimate war, they went to Vienna, Virginia, where their cousin, Colonel Henry Gansevoort, was stationed. Herman, as could have been anticipated, was exhilarated; he always was when he was sur-rounded by manly men engaged in manly pursuits. Or as he put it in one of his poems:

> *Nothing can lift the heart of man*
> *   Like manhood in a fellow-man.*
> *The thought of heaven's great King afar*
> *   But humbles us – too weak to scan,*
> *But manly greatness men can span,*
> *   And feel the bonds that draw.*

His letter of "thanks" to Henry Gansevoort also had that manic tone that male heroism always provoked: Henry was like the "sun," Mel-ville heard the neighing of Captain Brewster's "war-horses in my dreams," and he found pleasure in thinking of Edwin Lansing – all officers, it will be noted. He concluded with a peroration worthy of Jack Chase – or, more accurately, of Jack Chase's admirer:

> And now, Col. Gansevoort of the 13th N. Y. Cavalry, conceive me to be standing some paces from you, in an erect attitude and with manly bearing, giving you the military salute. Farewell. May two small but choice constellations of stars alight on your shoulders. . . . And after death . . . may that same name be transferred to heaven – bestowed upon some new planet or cluster of stars of the first magnitude. Farewell, my hero & God bless you

Upon his return to New York Melville suffered an acute attack of neuralgia in his eyes. After he heard that Gansevoort's superior, General Robert O. Tyler, had been wounded, he wrote what he must have considered a cheery letter: "I will not congratulate you, Gen-eral, upon your wound, but will reserve that for the scar, which will be equally glorious and not quite so irksome" – which was a peculiar and seemingly insensitive remark until one recalls Melville's fascination with scarred heroes like Lord Nelson and Captain Ahab. He hoped that the General was able to enjoy books and cigars and "(but this should have gone before) the sweet eyes of the sympathetic ladies, who, you know, have a natural weakness for heroes. How they must hover over you — the angels! — and how must your dreams be mingled of love and glory." Although Melville could not have known when he wrote that Tyler was to be lamed for life and his constitution shattered, anything would have been more appropriate than this bantering tone.

Shortly after his return from the front, on May 19, 1864, Nathaniel Hawthorne died suddenly in Plymouth, New Hampshire. There had been no communications between the two men after Melville sailed from Liverpool on May 5, 1857. No longer robust in health or in spirit, Hawthorne had been deeply troubled by the war. "The general heart-quake of the country," he wrote in *The Atlantic Monthly*, "long ago knocked at my cottage-door, and compelled me, reluctantly, to suspend the contemplation of certain fantasies, to which, according to my harmless custom, I was endeavoring to give a sufficiently life-like aspect to admit of their figuring in a romance." If Melville read the long article in *The Atlantic Monthly* in July 1862, no mention survives, although, as Robert Penn Warren points out, there are similarities in attitude and tone between Melville's poetry and Hawthorne's essay.

Elizabeth Melville informed her mother-in-law that Herman was "much shocked at hearing of Mr Hawthornes sudden death." Melville was to give beautiful expression to his feelings of loss and regret in a little poem simply called "Monody." Although he did not publish it until 1891, in the year of his own death, he may have written it in 1864 when he heard the news, or a year later, in May, when he was rereading *Mosses from an Old Manse*, that collection of tales which produced the impassioned confession in *The Literary World* in 1850. The twelve-line elegy was marred neither by archaic affectations nor by strangled syntax, which often crippled his verse. In death the affectionate bond was again clear and unequivocal, but the mystery of their parting still haunted him.

> To have known him, to have loved him
>   After loneless long;
> And then to be estranged in life,
>   And neither in the wrong;
> And now for death to set his seal —
>   Ease me, a little ease, my song!

By wintry hills his hermit-mound
The sheeted snow-drifts drape,
And houseless there the snow-bird flits
Beneath the fir-trees' crape:
Glazed now with ice the cloistral vine
That hid the shyest grape.

In April 1865, as the war was grinding to a close under the crushing leadership of Grant, Melville began to gather his poems about the war for a volume of verse. He read newspapers and magazine accounts of the battles and consulted the eight volumes of *The Rebellion Record*, which became an indispensable source. Only occasionally did he write out of his personal reactions to specific events. Lincoln's assassination led him to compose a ballad (an appropriate vehicle to express what he termed "the passion of the people" following the murder). The poem, although no doubt sincerely felt, is more preoccupied with vengeance upon the "parricides" than with Lincoln:

He lieth in his blood —
The father in his face;
They have killed him, the Forgiver —
The Avenger takes his place,
The Avenger wisely stern,
Who in righteousness shall do
What the heavens call him to,
And the parricides remand;
For they killed him in his kindness,
In their madness and their blindness,
And his blood is on their hand.

Battle-Pieces and Aspects of the War appeared in August 1866. During its composition Melville's health continued to be uncertain. After vacationing at his mother's home in the summer of 1865, he was reported to be "unusually well." Yet shortly before the book of poems appeared he was "looking thin & miserable." Perhaps the strain of writing a work "dedicated to the memory of the THREE HUNDRED THOUSAND who in the war for the maintenance of the union fell devotedly under the flag of their fathers," was too much for his depleted energies. If the war provided a "catharsis" for Melville, as some critics have suggested, the catharsis had short-lived and limited effects.

The book consists of over seventy poems more or less chronologically arranged, beginning with a tribute to John Brown ("The Portent") and concluding with "A Meditation." Most of the poems are short except for a lengthy account in about eight hundred lines of the escapades of Colonel Mosby entitled "The Scout toward Aldie." A prose Supplement at the conclusion is almost a prayer for renewal and rebirth, more eloquent than many of the poems: "Let us pray that the terrible historic tragedy of our time may not have been enacted without instructing our whole beloved country through terror and pity; and may fulfillment verify in the end those expectations which kindle the bards of Progress and Humanity."

In the seven reviews that appeared in succeeding months the critics sought to be fair, balancing praise and censure, although they were essentially in agreement as to Melville's limitations in poetry. One reviewer suggested that "he has written too rapidly to avoid great crudities. His poetry runs into the epileptic. His rhymes are fearful." The critic in *The Nation*, possibly Charles Eliot Norton, spoke of reading *Battle-Pieces* "with a certain melancholy. Nature did not make him a poet. His pages contain at best little more than the rough ore of poetry." The notice in *The Atlantic Monthly* asserted that events took on the reality of dreams, and that "tortured humanity" was "shedding, not words and blood, but words alone."

The opinions of these early reviewers stood unchallenged for the most part until recent decades when in the revival that restored Melville to the center of American literature his poems were reexamined. Although Robert Penn Warren was in large measure responsible for the reevaluation, he reiterated the technical reservations of Melville's contemporaries — "he is a poet of shreds and patches" who "did not master his craft." Despite reservation which would ordinarily be considered overwhelming, Warren in effect granted Melville exemption chiefly because he anticipated the tonalities and poetic practices of the age of T. S. Eliot. What contemporaries deemed failures of sympathy or feeling — Melville's impersonality, his distance, and his waveringly pessimistic stance — appealed to the modern sensibility.

It is pointless to dwell upon Melville's deficiencies in poetry: his ear failed him at some point in almost every poem he wrote. Although he lived through the war years, he wrote as a distant spectator, observing men and events through a telescope. The posture was honest, but the price was loss of immediacy and the feeling tone that one finds in Whitman's *Drum-Taps*. Sometimes Melville sought to place the Civil War in a timeless perspective, measuring modern warfare against the Miltonic or mythic past. He was capable of such anachronisms as placing the activities of the Confederate con artist, Colonel Mosby, in a setting straight out of Spenser:

> *By worn-out fields they cantered on —*
> > *Drear fields amid the woodlands wide;*
> *By cross-roads of some olden time,*
> *In which grew groves; by gate-stones down —*
> > *Grassed ruins of secluded pride:*
> > > *A strange lone land, long past the prime,*
> > > *Fit land for Mosby or for crime.*

Whatever artistic justification there may have been for intruding literature and myth in an account of the bloody war, a chill fell over the poetry. Either, like Ahab, Melville felt too deeply about the events to render them artistically, or he disguised his lack of empathy by recourse to bookish but stilted devices. For the first time he was describing situations and events in which he had no personal involvement.

"I muse upon my country's ills," he wrote, and he was successful in a few of his short poems. In "Shiloh" he does not attempt ironic juxtapositions and allows the movement of the swallows to dominate and to state the meaning of the poem.

> *Skimming lightly, wheeling still,*
> > *The swallows fly low*
> *Over the field in clouded days,*
> > *The forest-field of Shiloh —*
> *Over the field where April rain*
> *Solaced the parched ones stretched in pain*
> *Through the pause of night*
> *That followed the Sunday fight*
> > *Around the church of Shiloh —*
> *The church so lone, the log-built one,*
> *That echoed to many a parting groan*
> > *And natural prayer*
> > *Of dying foemen mingled there —*
> *Foemen at morn, but friends at eve —*
> > *Fame or country least their care:*
> *(What like a bullet can undeceive!)*
> > *But now they lie low,*
> *While over them the swallows skim,*
> > *And all is hushed at Shiloh.*

The effect at the conclusion of "Malvern Hill" is also moving:

> *We elms of Malvern Hill*
> > *Remember every thing;*

But sap the twig will fill:
Wag the world how it will,
Leaves must be green in Spring.

Here he is restating a memorable prose passage when the *Pequod* and Ahab vanish in the sea: "then all collapsed, and the great shroud of the sea rolled on as it rolled five thousand years ago."

The first poem in the collection is a superb picture of John Brown, even though it simplifies the complex actions of a complex fanatic:

Hanging from the beam,
   Slowly swaying (such the law),
Gaunt the shadow on your green,
   Shenandoah!
The cut is on the crown
(Lo, John Brown),
And the stabs shall heal no more.

Hidden in the cap
   Is the anguish none can draw;
So your future veils its face,
   Shenandoah!
But the streaming beard is shown
(Weird John Brown),
The meteor of the war.

If in his other poems he had achieved such compression and insight, limiting himself to monochromatic portraiture, Melville would indeed be the Civil War poet.

He recognized the changes that were mechanizing and depersonalizing warfare in "A Utilitarian View of the Monitor's Flight": "No passion; all went on by crank, / Pivot, and screw, / And calculations of caloric." Hawthorne had made the same point about the *Monitor* in 1862, characterizing it a "cheese-box." "All the pomp and splendor of naval warfare are gone by," he wrote. "Henceforth there must come up a race of enginemen and smoke-blackened cannoneers, who will hammer away at their enemies under the direction of a single pair of eyes; and even heroism — so deadly a gripe is Science laying on our noble possibilities — will become a quality of very minor importance."

Melville wrote: "All wars are boyish, and are fought by boys." Hawthorne lamented: "It is a pity that old men grow unfit for war, not only by their incapacity for new ideas, but by the peaceful and unadventurous tendencies that gradually possess themselves of the once turbulent disposition. . . . It is a pity; because it would be such an economy of human existence, if time-stricken people . . . could snatch from their juniors the exclusive privilege of carrying on the war." In "The March into Virginia," Melville, after his pessimistic observation about "boyish" wars, lapsed into strange naiveté: "So they gayly go to fight, / Chatting left and laughing right" — the sense perhaps conforming to the exigencies of meter and rhyme. Hawthorne, whose knowledge of combat was no greater than Melville's, was more realistic in his article in *The Atlantic Monthly*: "Set men face to face, with weapons in their hands, and they are as ready to slaughter one another now, . . . as in the rudest ages" — even to using skulls as drinking cups.

In Melville's "Ball's Bluff" the soldiers march "lustily" to battle, "Their hearts . . . fresh as clover in its prime," in the "breezy summer time." "Youth," he declares, "feels immortal," and then dies in battle. Such lines and descriptions are unreal and facilely ironic, even offensive. The soldiers were not Apollos, but freckled, homely, home-sick, fearful lads poorly trained and sometimes ineptly led and often ill-clad, going off to kill with a bravado that camouflaged anxieties and uncertainties. Hawthorne got at one of the frightening truths of war when he observed of a group of Confederate prisoners that they had not "the remotest comprehension of what they had been fighting for."

The failure, or inability, to particularize, *to see*, was Melville's most serious failure in these poems. He had to generalize, he could individualize neither an event nor a person. When he tried to draw a portrait, too often he ended up projecting his own despair and ideology upon the subject. "The College Colonel," one leg amputated and one arm crippled, returns home with his regiment after two years of battle. Sober in mien, he brings back the survivors, or "castaway sailors."

> There are welcoming shouts, and flags;
>   Old men off hat to the Boy,
> Wreaths from gay balconies fall at his feet,
>   But to him — there comes alloy.
>
> It is not that a leg is lost,
>   It is not that an arm is maimed,
> It is not that the fever has racked —
>   Self he has long disclaimed.
>
> But all through the Seven Days' Fight,
>   And deep in the Wilderness grim,

And in the field-hospital tent,
 And Petersburg crater, and dim
Lean brooding in Libby, there came —
 Ah heaven! — what truth *to him.*

Apparently the *"truth"* is stoical acceptance of what is, the capacity to endure and perhaps, if lucky, to survive. But in his emphasis upon *"truth,"* whatever it may mean, Melville missed the drama of this hero's lust for combat, the excitement of the life-death game that is warfare, the need to prove masculinity. He made no attempt imaginatively to depict the colonel's human contradictions.

The fractures in Melville's own life appeared in his poetry, particularly his wavering between belief and disbelief in a deity. At one moment God is old and cold, and doubt cries, "Ho ho, ho ho." Then God is as young as the ever-renewing earth, and finally He assumes a middle position:

YEA AND NAY —
EACH HATH HIS SAY;
BUT GOD HE KEEPS THE MIDDLE WAY.
NONE WAS BY
WHEN HE SPREAD THE SKY;
WISDOM IS VAIN, AND PROPHESY.

("The Conflict of Convictions")

At one moment Melville despairs of man's lot and then speaks of enlightenment "by the vollied glare." In another poem he worries that "the Founder's dream shall flee" after the war, but the next few lines make "the Founder's dream" and all dreams impossible, for "Age after age shall be / As age after age has been." But he cannot accept the finality of such a statement, and in the Supplement he presents a melioristic view: "Our institutions have a potent digestion, and may in time convert and assimilate to good all elements thrown in, however originally alien." Just as Ahab can blaspheme and adopt a most orthodox religious attitude, so Melville can espouse a statement that mocks his atheistic utterances:

Who weeps for the woeful City
 Let him weep for our guilty kind;
Who joys at her wild despairing —
 Christ, the Forgiver, convert his mind.

("The Swamp Angel")

Such are the fractures in Melville's thought. Whenever he killed off God, He rose again.

On the last day of his life Ahab makes one of his most personal confessions while speaking in the depersonalized third person: "Ahab never thinks; he only feels, feels, feels; *that's* tingling enough for mortal man!" Even in his most Shakespearean rhetoric Ahab's feelings emerge painfully but clearly. In *Battle-Pieces* Melville neither stamped the poems with his personality nor transcended the iciness of his telescopic distance. Where Ishmael surveys the cosmos from the masthead with rollicking wit and warmth, the poetry is frozen in despair: "And faces fixed, forefeeling death."

The disengagement from life evident in *The Confidence-Man* continued. The passage of ten years had not given Melville the "trust" he sought and needed. His eyes were turned, fearfully, inward, not outward. Uncertain of his craft and, worse, uncertain of life, he could scarcely be expected to find or to create in art what was missing in his soul, which he subsumed in one despairing line in his poems: "All fatherless seemed the human soul."

"The Perilous
Outpost
of the Sane"
—1866-1876

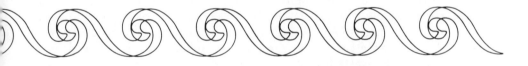

Two years after the publication of *Battle-Pieces* only 486 copies were sold, and in the next seven years there were only eleven purchasers. Melville's personal loss on the volume amounted to $400. For six years, following the last unsuccessful lecture season in 1859-60, he had earned nothing, except possibly small amounts of interest from investments. His dependency upon his wife and her family was as great and complete as poor Allan Melvill's upon the Gansevoorts.

Late in 1866, apparently without the usual assistance and organized efforts of family and friends, Melville did something to establish his independence. In Switzerland in 1857 he had met a New York merchant named Henry A. Smythe who later became a successful businessman and bank president. In 1866 President Johnson appointed him Collector of the Customs for the Port of New York. On November 28 Smythe recommended the appointment of Melville to the Custom-House, and on December 5 he took the loyalty oath.

The salary of four dollars a day at least reestablished his self-respect and sapped neither his brains nor his energies. Like Whitman, who at this time was in the Attorney General's office in Washington, Melville enjoyed the largesse of a government that created sinecures not for writers but as awards to political hacks in the notorious spoils system of the era. For the next nineteen years he remained incorruptible in an environment where graft was a way of life. One distinguished politician advised a friend, "If you have a son who won't lie or steal, don't for God's sake, put him in the New York Custom-House; he would soon lose those qualities there, and get other habits not half so virtuous." Apparently Melville was an "isolato" in governmental service as he had been on ships years earlier. There were periods of uncertainties about his position as administrations came and went, but he managed to keep his post.

Most of his duties in his new position were performed at the docks at the foot of Gansevoort Street, not too far from his birthplace and the scenes of his childhood. As an importer of yard goods his father had come to these docks in the days of his would-be prosperity and had sailed from them when he had retreated in humiliation to Albany after his bankruptcy in 1830. And so Melville had memories, some joyful, some sad, of other days, as he watched ships enter and leave the harbor. He had truly returned home.

At the Custom-House he held a post similar to Hawthorne's at Boston and later at Salem. If he was not to write with his friend's ironic detachment "POSTHUMOUS PAPERS OF A DECAPITATED SURVEYOR," in the preface to *The Scarlet Letter*, he became a living decapitated surveyor, an artist whom the public would in the next few decades almost completely forget.

For the first time in his married life Melville had a job that took him out of the house daily. In the eyes of the family he had at long last been normalized. They believed, as the naive often do, that regular employment would magically improve his health and lift his spirits. Within a few months after he started working, his mother pronounced Herman's health much improved "since he has been compelled to go out daily to attend to his business." Maria Gansevoort Melville did not to her dying day renounce her faith in the work ethic, ordained by God and the Gansevoorts.

Whatever physical and emotional well-being there may have been for Melville after he accepted the seeming security of the Custom-House, it was abruptly shattered by a gunshot nine months later, on September 11, 1867. On that day his first-born son Malcolm put a pistol to his head.

For eighteen months Malcolm had been employed in the insurance office run by Allan Melville's brother-in-law, a man whom

Grandmother Melville pronounced industrious, prompt, exact — in other words, of the "elect." With his salary of $200 annually Malcolm was now paying his own way, and he took to staying out late at nights. Herman reprimanded, took away his house key, ordered the door to the house locked at eleven o'clock.

Too young for service in the Civil War, the eighteen-year-old boy was apparently so enamored of what he had missed, or was so desirous of establishing his manhood, that he joined a volunteer regiment. Soon he was strutting about in a military uniform, and was so proud of his pistol that he kept it under his pillow at nights. Apparently he carried the gun about with him and was so anxious to show it off that the clerks in his office warned him to be more careful.

On September 10 Malcolm was out on the town with his friends. At eleven o'clock the door was locked, and Herman went to bed. The mother sat up. Malcolm did not come home until three o'clock. He had not been drinking, or so the family claimed. He did not get up the next morning although he answered when his sisters knocked. At the breakfast table the father ordered his wife to let the boy sleep. If he didn't want to stir himself, he could take "the consequences as a sort of punishment." Having delivered the age-old paternal verdict, Herman went off to the office at the foot of Gansevoort Street and left Elizabeth to handle the problem. During the day she knocked on Malcolm's door but there was no answer. She was not alarmed because he was a heavy sleeper. Later when she knocked again and tried the handle, she found the door locked. Nervously she waited for Herman's return. He was unusually late that day. When he finally arrived, he forced the door and found Malcolm on the bed in his night clothes, his pistol in his right hand and a hole in his right temple. He had been dead for several hours.

On the following day the jurors pronounced the act "Suicide . . . under temporary insanity of mind." According to the newspapers the parents "could not assign any cause for the suicidal act." A few days later, on September 16, perhaps after pressure for a retraction was brought by the Melvilles, the jurors publicly explained that it was not suicide but an accident.

Malcolm was buried in the Woodlawn Cemetery in the Bronx. His mother had him dressed in his military uniform in recognition of her son's momentary delight in the symbol of his maturity. According to one observer Elizabeth was "almost heart broken." According to Herman's sister, however, the father was "quite composed" and Elizabeth "had not shed a tear." But the first observer was more perceptive, particularly when she wrote: "I pity the poor parents — both Cousin Herman & Lizzie are of such nervous temperaments I should fear for *their peace of mind*." Herman kept up appearances, as one would expect. To his brother-in-law he wrote of his son's "gentle nature. Mackie never gave me a disrespectful word in his life, nor in any way ever failed in filialness." He agreed with his niece that Malcolm was "always obliging and affectionate, this was but of a piece with his whole nature and conduct."

If it was important for the public image to establish that Malcolm's act was an accident, Herman on some level of consciousness must have known that such acts are rarely accidents. He must also have recognized that Malcolm's act gave a horrible reality to a motif running through his fiction that revealed a personal preoccupation with suicide. Malcolm had, as it were, acted out his father's fantasy. At eighteen he was undoubtedly a dutiful son, as his grandmother, his cousin, and his father declared. Yet in taking his life he achieved what he had missed in life — attention and affection. He had punished himself but others too. What Melville perhaps did not realize was that the hostility which the suicide feels for a loved one he directs against himself.

The first-born son, Malcolm grew up in a household in which the father was monomaniacally dedicated to his writing. Sometimes it must have seemed to him that nothing else mattered to his father. Always moody and irascible, the father did not improve in disposition after the departure of Hawthorne from Lenox in 1851. Soon he was ill. Then he went abroad to regain his health. He returned, little improved in spirits, only to go off on the lecture circuit. Periodically members of the family gathered to discuss the father's health and economic prospects. When the family moved to New York in the 1860s, Malcolm was sent off to school near Boston. After he came to New York to stay with his family, the father was as restless, ill, and moody as ever. Malcolm went to work at seventeen. He joined a baseball team and was perhaps sowing some wild oats — only to be told abruptly and imperiously that he must be home by eleven o'clock.

Herman's favorite cousin termed him "a very strict parent," and her judgment was an outsider's. Only Malcolm and the other children knew the whole story. Even they did not realize how their father unwittingly imitated the stern sea captains who manhandled greenhorns into manhood aboard ships. If as a youth Herman fled authority, he later exercised it with a heavy hand. In *White-Jacket* he wrote fiercely against the tyrannical flogging aboard warships, but in a jocular letter to his brother Tom in 1862 he commended his treatment of "those young ones": "Strap them, I beseech you. You remember what the Bible says . . . about spareing the strap & spoiling the child."

Herman, like his father before him, managed to confuse his

children. On Christmas in 1865 he gave each child a bound volume of *Harper's Weekly*, which, with a similar gift to his wife, made up a five-year run of the journal — an unusual gift for children but of great practical use to him as he was composing *Battle-Pieces*. He showed similar insensitivity on the fifteenth birthday of Frances when he presented her with *The Buried Cities of Campania: or, Pompeii and Herculaneum*. Worse, indifferent to the tender feelings of children, he made them the butt of his wit. The youngest child Frances was humiliated when she asked her father what "property" meant and was promptly dubbed "Little Miss Property." When she cried her mother calmed her: "Papa doesn't mean anything. Run along to school." When in her twenties Frances entertained a suitor, the father came into the parlor, noisily slammed all the shutters, and asked the young man: "Do you prefer oatmeal or hominy for breakfast?" What a perfect illustration of the hostility behind much of Melville's wit!

Most important of all was the relationship at the center of family life, between father and mother. If we assume that incidents that occurred after Malcolm's death were characteristic of the relationship earlier, we can only conclude that the son as well as the other children witnessed the father, intentionally or not, demeaning the mother, who in turn was their defender against paternal tyranny. The father personally supervised the servants, particularly in the preparation of his oatmeal, and harried his wife constantly about the consistency of his coffee. According to Allan's daughter, "Herman was always challenging Elizabeth," deliberately exposing her lack of knowledge in intellectual matters as well as her inability to run a household.

One of Herman's relatives characterized Elizabeth as "thoroughly good but inefficient" — which may well have been at least partly accurate. But for the first six years of her married life she lived with her mother-in-law and four unmarried sisters-in-law. After the birth of Malcolm in 1849 there were for a time three generations under the same roof, a difficult situation at best. The Melvilles evidently complained that Elizabeth spent too much time in Boston with her father and her stepmother. She was there on many holidays and sometimes during confinement.

Perhaps because Judge Shaw's money was used to purchase their homes as well as to finance Herman's recuperative trips, Melville left financial matters in his wife's "inefficient" charge. As Elizabeth noted during the Custom-House years, "because Herman from his studious habits and tastes [is] unfitted for practical matters, all the *financial* management falls upon me." She also had to shield the children against the wit and moods of her husband. It was she who sat up and waited for Malcolm when he did not return until 3 A.M. It would be interesting to know whether Herman permitted her to voice her grief after Malcolm's death. Everything we know about him would indicate that he was the type of man who handled grief by silence.

Then there was the demonic fury and anxiety that possessed him when he was writing. He isolated himself according to a rigid schedule, appeared only for meals, commandeered whoever was available to copy his manuscripts. His sisters Helen and Augusta served this function for a period of time, as long as they remained under his roof. When he decided to go to sea in 1860, he left the manuscript of his poems with his wife, who was to supervise publication. As the years went by, his demands did not decrease. Elizabeth was almost frantic when he was getting *Clarel* ready for the press in 1876, and he did not hesitate to get Frances up at 2 A.M. to read proof. Herman's egomania was worthy of Ahab.

His extreme sensitivity forced Elizabeth to be careful about what she said, to be secretive, and sometimes to apologize for his unpredictable behavior. On one occasion when she was out of the city and Peter and Susan Gansevoort were in New York, she wrote to Susan: "If you see Herman, please do not tell him that I said he was *not well* — but if you think he looks well, I hope you will tell him so." Her instructions to Catherine Lansing revealed how delicately she had to handle her husband: "I want you *always* to mention Herman's name in your letters, especially if it is to say anything about coming down — *I* know your feeling is always right to him, and so does everyone else, but he is *morbidly* sensitive, poor fellow, and I always try (though I can't succeed to my sorrow) to smooth the fancied rough edges to him whenever I can — so I know you will understand why I mention it." At another time she included two letters in an envelope: "I have written you a note that Herman could see, as he wished, but want you to know how painful it is for me to write it, and also to have to give you the real cause." In the letter not seen by Herman she related the facts about his "frightfully nervous state." A few years later she was obliged to apologize to Mrs. Lansing: "It has laid heavily on my mind that the last part of your visit to New York was not as pleasant as it might have been and I have felt so sorry about it — but there is nothing to be said or done except to bow to inexorable fate."

Elizabeth's was a difficult lot, and in view of what she had to endure she complained little, at least in her letters, and did not wallow in self-pity. In order to live with Herman she had to accept his abuse, the anger which he projected on her, and to lie and to apologize in order to salve the feelings of relatives. If she was not "literary" or "intellectual," she had virtues more essential for the well-being and contentment both of her husband and her family. Economically and, more important, emotionally, she was the bulwark of the family.

About one other matter the family for the most part maintained a conspiracy of silence. It would appear that Herman at times leaned heavily on the bottle. At social gatherings his powers as a raconteur visibly improved over the wine and brandy, and, as some one has observed, orgies in Melville's writings are alcoholic rather than sexual. It was reported that his sisters felt "very badly" about his drinking, "but did not say much." According to one legend in the family, once in a drunken state Herman pushed Elizabeth down the stairs. He was not an alcoholic, but in the depressed states which became more marked after 1852 he apparently drank heavily at times.

The failures that overtook him in the 1850s — in his art, in friendship, and in the family — were reflected in the ailments which increased as the years passed and as the dark clouds of depression engulfed him. Elizabeth experienced similar psychosomatic disabilities. Just as Maria Gansevoort Melville became "nervous" and took to her bed in the 1820s when Allan Melvill failed to establish himself as a New York businessman, so Elizabeth also evidenced "nervousness." She had long been troubled by "rose fever," "a severe influenza lasting from six to eight weeks." About a year after Malcolm's death she complained of neuralgia and general weakness. In the 1870s she suffered from catarrh, and her step-brother in 1872 described her as "generally feeble" and "prematurely old." Elizabeth had never been robust, but her burdens were greater than her body could bear.

After the youth was buried, the Melvilles went to Arrowhead for ten days or so. Then they returned to their New York home, now a family of five. In December Herman complained of a kink in his back. During these days Elizabeth was particularly attentive to Stanwix, the child whose birth certificate established his grandmother as his mother. Stanwix went to pieces at Malcolm's funeral. In the following year he had trouble with deafness which Elizabeth, probably after medical consultation, attributed to "catarrhal weakness." It would be interesting to know whether the deafness began shortly after Malcolm's suicide. Stanwix was not in the house — he was at Arrowhead with his Uncle Allan — when Malcolm pulled the trigger.

In 1868 Stanwix was working in Uncle Allan's law office. "My deafness," he wrote, "had been a great trouble to me lately, but I am glad to say that it is getting better." The uncle he wrote to was Peter

Gansevoort, who had given Herman his first job as a clerk in Albany. Shortly Stanwix became restless and wanted to go before the mast. Evidently determined this time not to inflict the rigid discipline that characterized poor Malcolm's existence, his parents agreed, and on April 4, 1869, the lad sailed aboard a ship bound for Canton. From Shanghai Stanwix informed his family that his deafness had almost left him and that he liked life at sea. Early in January 1870 he jumped ship in London, and, except for a letter which his parents received in February, nothing was known about his whereabouts until he arrived in Boston on July 18, in good health and spirits, "a manly boy of nineteen."

Stanwix could not settle down. A year or so later he was off to Kansas, where he stayed with the Lansings, who were relatives of Catherine Gansevoort Lansing, Peter's daughter. Then he was back in New York and evidently worked as an apprentice in a dental office. In the spring of 1872 he returned to Kansas, stayed for a few weeks, and shortly began a year-long expedition during which he lived as a beachcomber, and narrowly escaped death, as he bummed about Cuba, Costa Rica, and Nicaragua. In March 1873 he was working for another dentist and looking forward to the independence a profession would bring. A month later he discovered that he was too nearsighted to operate "in the mouth." "Fate is against me in most of my undertakings," he declared. He sailed almost at once for California — "This time is going to decide my fortune." Eighteen months later he announced from a sheep farm in California that he had "been guilty of so many follies, and deaf to the counsel of older heads. . . . I hope to retrieve the past, & for better times in the future." In 1875 he returned to New York, to take up dentistry again, but he soon abandoned the profession as well as his home in order to return to California. Shortly he was planning to become a miner in the Black Hills, and wrote to the Shaws for a loan. Stanwix was now twenty-five.

He did not have his father's talents, only what his mother called "a demon of *restlessness*." It seemed as though he was following in Herman's footsteps, even to jumping ship and existing as a beachcomber, abandoning one job after another, traveling about the country and the world. When Stanwix needed financial assistance he turned to the son of Judge Shaw and to the son-in-law of Peter Gansevoort, to the successors of those who had rescued Herman at one time or another. Without genius Stanwix's escapades ended in pathetic, whining avowals in which, like the drunkard about to renounce the bottle, he promised to give up his follies. Unfortunately, fate was always against him.

The Melvilles lived quietly during the Custom-House years.

Since Herman did not seek out artists and writers, except for occasional evenings spent with Evert Duyckinck, he was a "retired" author whose existence the public would soon forget. He passed up most of the cultural events New York had to offer, but even in his younger days, unlike Whitman, he had not been an avid theater-goer. His limited social life pretty much centered about the family and its gatherings. Allan still practiced law in New York. Tom had married a lively, sociable woman and had abandoned the sea for a comfortable sinecure as head of the Sailors' Snug Harbor on Staten Island. The older Mrs. Melville maintained her brother's home in Gansevoort, but came to the city quite often. Catherine Lansing and her husband came down from Albany.

As Melville approached and then passed his fiftieth birthday, he experienced not only the disappointments of a father in his two sons but also the increasing awareness that he was shortly to be a lonely survivor. After the death of Malcolm, succeeding years seemed to become a calendar of deaths. His old friend, George Adler, the "crazy" professor whom he met on the voyage to London in 1849, died in a mental institution in 1868. His cousin Guert Gansevoort, the one who had achieved infamy after ordering the son of a cabinet officer hanged at sea, died in the same year. In 1871 Henry Sanford Gansevoort, the colonel whom Melville had visited at the front, passed on. Then death visited the immediate family. In 1872 Allan Melville died suddenly, apparently of tuberculosis. Two months later, on April 1, Maria Gansevoort Melville, at eighty-one still regal in her bearing and greatly beloved by her grandchildren except in Herman's family, died and was buried in Albany, next to Allan.

Elizabeth was in poor health at this time, depressed, and still grieving for Malcolm. As though 1872 had not tragedies enough, she suffered the loss through fire of a property in Boston which provided an annual return of $500 — a severe blow to their resources. Peter Gansevoort, however, made good the loss.

What Melville felt and thought as he experienced these contractions, these dissonances, he did not record for posterity, but at least he had the regularities and monotonies of his governmental post to provide a kind of buffer. Routine, the family was wont to maintain, was a safety valve. On April 4, 1873, Herman had a "sudden & severe illness" during one of Stanwix's temporary sojourns at home. Stanwix sailed for California on April 30, and within a few weeks Herman was completely recovered. Elizabeth almost made the association when she wrote: "Herman is quite well again now — you heard through Augusta, of his sudden & severe illness — and also of Stanny's going to California."

The family grew still smaller when Peter Gansevoort's second wife Susan died in 1874. In the following year Peter, the last of Maria's family, was seriously ill. During the summer he offered Melville $1,200 toward the publication of *Clarel.* In a real sense Peter made possible the publication of a work based on Herman's trip to the Holy Land which years before he had considered more appropriate material for his nephew's unsuccessful lecture career than an account of Roman antiquities. On January 4, 1876, on the day Melville signed a contract with the publisher, Peter died. In February Herman's unmarried sister Augusta, who had served as a copyist of the crudely spelled manuscripts in the early years of his literary career, became seriously ill. Herman "could hardly control his feelings while with her." Augusta died on April 4, four years after her mother, and was laid to rest in the family burial plot in Albany.

Despite this long foreground of deaths, familial disappointments, and depressions, *Clarel* was written and published on June 3, 1876, ten years after his first collection of poems. Because there was a conspiracy of silence, mandated by Herman, it is not known when he began to write what was to become one of the longest poems in the language. It could have been in the late 1860s or the early 1870s. Since he had only two-week vacations annually, he needed years in which to compose the eighteen thousand lines. Elizabeth did not confide what Herman was up to even to her stepmother until March 9, 1875: "Herman is pretty well and very busy — pray do not mention to any one that he is writing poetry — you know how such things spread and he would be very angry if he knew I had spoken of it." Peter Gansevoort did not learn of the manuscript apparently until the following summer, when he made one of his characteristically magnanimous gestures to his nephew.

After the contract was signed with G. P. Putnam & Sons, life in the Melville household became hectic. On February 2, 1876, Elizabeth advised Catherine Lansing that they could receive no visitors, not even Augusta and Fanny, the unmarried sisters. With this letter she enclosed a "painful" note, unknown to Herman, which gave "the real cause" for the denial of hospitality.

> The fact is, that Herman, poor fellow, is in such a frightfully nervous state, & particularly now with such an added strain on his mind, that I am actually *afraid* to have any one here for fear that he will be upset entirely, & not be able to go on with the printing — He was not willing to have even his own sisters here, and I had to write Augusta before she left Albany to that effect — that was the reason she changed her plan, and went to Tom's — If ever this dreadful *incubus* of a *book* (I call it so because it has undermined all our happiness) gets off Herman's shoulders I do hope he may be in better mental health — but at present I have reason to feel the

gravest concern & anxiety about it — to put it in mild phrase — please do not speak of it — you know how such things are exaggerated — & I will tell you more when I see you —

Perhaps Elizabeth was melodramatic or, understandably, alarmed since Herman was, as in the past, undergoing the throes of the damned as publication approached.

On April 22 the book was in galleys except for a few odds and ends. Melville agreed only after "the *very strong* representations" of the publishers to put his name on the title-page; once again he apparently wanted the protection of anonymity as well as the opportunity to be judged without reference to the books which he had almost come to hate — *Typee* and *Omoo*. After he consented to acknowledge authorship, he decided to dedicate the work to Peter Gansevoort. Elizabeth saw an end to the turbulence in the household: "I shall be so thankful when it is all finished and off of his mind, and cannot help hoping that his health will improve when he is released from this long continued mental strain." Bound copies were available on June 3. Melville inscribed one of the first copies to Elizabeth, "without whose assistance in manifold ways I hardly know how I could have got the book (under the circumstances) into shape, and finally through the press." Perhaps he remembered to thank his two daughters too. Frances, it will be recalled, was roused from bed at two in the morning to read proof. In the summer when Elizabeth and the two girls left the city early in order to obtain relief from hay fever, she shut up the house and sent Herman to her brother's apartment. "I think," she wrote, "the change will benefit him also — take him out of himself."

And so in circumstances that approximated the chaos described in *Pierre*, when the hero struggles to establish himself as a novelist after his youthful career as a poet, Melville launched his bid for poetic acclaim. His prefatory note offered an ambiguous defense of the book's lack of vitality and professed, in what can only be construed as an authorial fib, indifference to its success.

> If during the period in which this work has remained unpublished, though not undivulged, any of its properties have by a natural process exhaled; it yet retains, I trust, enough of original life to redeem it at least from vapidity. Be that as it may, I here dismiss the book — content beforehand with whatever future awaits it.

"Life
an Unfulfilled
Romance"
—*Clarel*

Clarel is Melville's poetic restatement of the subject matter of his
prose. Twenty years after the publication of his last sustained
narrative, *The Confidence-Man*, he related once again the fable of an
unformed youth in search of security in a world which has no security to offer. Clarel, a theological student, is the brother of Tommo,
Taji, Redburn, White-Jacket, Ishmael, and Pierre. He is an orphan —
"bereft while still young," and, like most of his "brothers," has a
kind of hermaphroditic beauty — "in feature fine, / Yet pale, and all
but feminine / But for the eye and serious brow." The likeness, as
always, is to the delicate beauty of Gansevoort Melville or Apollo.
Like his predecessors Clarel is a well-born Ishmael, adrift and alone, a
passive observer for the most part as the other characters discuss the
nineteenth-century crisis of faith. Although he has apparently completed his theological training, Clarel, his doubt unresolved, is seeking
a mentor.

The search is for more than intellectual or religious guidance; it is, as we learn at the beginning of the poem, "Longing for solacement of mate." The phrasing is awkward and almost evasive because Melville did not dare to state unequivocally, either to his readers or to himself, that the manifest or philosophical theme of his poem — the quest for faith — is actually subordinated to the latent theme — the quest for a "mate." Transplanted to the stoney, and Holy Land, Clarel's is the search of Tommo and the others, except that he has a brief, abortive romance with a young lady named Ruth. He is saved from a marriage which he unconsciously does not want, as Walter E., Bezanson points out, by her death.

In a sense the poem is a kind of dance of Eros and Thanatos, but a dance that leads to no resolution. The characters are to meet and to go on a pilgrimage, to reveal their needs in friendships which are to be ephemeral, and then to separate, their longings unsatisfied, the quest another failure. There are to be drinking bouts and hilarity in which bonds are seemingly established, only to be severed when the evening ends, as transient as the bubbles of the wine. Clarel's fate is the Melvillean fate and arrestment: at the end of the journey he is "another orphan."

At the beginning of the poem, Clarel wanders about Jerusalem until he comes to an inn run by a Black Jew named Abdon — "The lone man marked his lonelier guest." Abdon, as it turns out, is descended from one of the ten lost tribes — "Lost children in the wood of time." The innkeeper has been a wanderer, adrift in his faith, truly another lost child. He is the first of the father figures that have nothing to offer to Clarel. In ruminating on nineteenth-century doubt and his uncertainty, Clarel puts the situation in the form of a strange but revealing question, which Melville italicizes, "*And can the Father be?*" Almost the first historical spot that Clarel visits is the synagogue where "Joseph, Mary, and the BOY, / Whose hand the mother's held," when Jesus, at twelve, had not only his faith but also his family. If in the background reverberates Melville's lot at that same age, in the foreground the modern situation is depicted in a familial image: "O, bickering family bereft, / Was feud the heritage He left?" The age is "bereft" of family as Clarel is "bereft" of mother and sisters.

As the youth wanders beyond Jerusalem's walls to the site where two disciples who accompanied Jesus on the road to Emmaus had their doubts resolved by the Savior Himself, he, silently, voices his despair:

I too, I too; could I but meet
Some stranger of a lore replete,

Who, marking how my looks betray
The dumb thoughts clogging here my feet,
Would question me, expound and prove,
And make my heart to burn with love —
Emmaus were no dream to-day!

Nehemiah, a wanderer who hails from Narragansett, answers the unspoken plea when he offers Clarel a guide — the Bible. The old man is
a millenarian who believes the world is about to be "re-imparadised."
Nehemiah can cipher out the time of Jesus' second coming but does
not know the time of day, and he nods as he reads the Bible.
Through his visions Nehemiah transcends his anguish and offers to be
Clarel's companion: "With me divide the scrip of love." "Grateful for
the human claim," Clarel cannot find an answer to his own need, or
place much trust, in a harmless old man who, with ironic appropriateness, will walk to his own death in his sleep one night. Nehemiah's
book is as useless as the guidebook Redburn inherits from his father.
    Clarel is more powerfully drawn to a handsome youth named
Celio, who is endowed with "Absalom's locks but Æsop's hump."
Although the young men never speak to each other except through
their troubled eyes, and Celio suddenly dies, Clarel finds in him

A second self . . . ,
But stronger — with the heart to brave
All questions on that primal ground
Laid bare by faith's receding waves.

Presumably Celio is "stronger" because he dares, as Clarel does not,
to break with religion and with an aristocratic family intent upon
placing him in a conventional mold. Invariably the Melvillean "hero"
is drawn to males of surpassing beauty or with physical deformities
or both.
    Near the *"Sepulchre of Kings"* Clarel encounters a middle-aged
man, and suddenly the sometimes pedestrian verse comes alive and
turns amorous. Clarel beholds a frieze and Melville unfolds an icon:

But who is he uncovered seen,
Profound in shadow of the tomb
Reclined, with meditative mien
Intent upon the tracery?
A low wind waves his Lydian hair:
A funeral man, yet richly fair —
Fair as the sabled violets be.
    The frieze and this secluded one,

Retaining each a separate tone,
Beauty yet harmonized in grace
And contrast to the barren place.
    But noting that he was discerned,
Salute the stranger made, then turned
And shy passed forth in obvious state
Of one who would keep separate.

The two men do not speak. As with Celio the bond is the eyes. The silence is a brilliant touch. For Clarel is seeing the physical incarnation of his fantasy, and Melville is once more hymning the magnetic attraction of "the shyest grape," Nathaniel Hawthorne.

For a while the man who attracts Clarel like a magnet is without a name. Suddenly he is baptized — "Name him — Vine" — in phraseology that recalls the opening sentence of *Moby-Dick* and, in turn, its source in one of Hawthorne's earliest tales, "The Gentle Boy": " 'Friend,' replied the little boy, in a sweet though faltering voice, 'they call me Ilbrahim, and my home is here.' "

Shortly Vine's rival appears, a man more imposing physically, bronzed, outgoing, acquainted "With dædal life in boats and tents, / A messmate of the elements." When the pilgrimage is organized later, Rolfe becomes the natural leader. While Vine pursues his own way, usually in the rear and separated from the other travelers, Rolfe rides majestically on his horse: "Sat Indian-like, in pliant way, / As if he were an Osage scout, / Or Gaucho of the Paraguay." Because Rolfe subsequently relates events similar to those which Melville records in *Typee*, he is often identified with the author. Although he may be an idealized version of the young Melville, he has characteristics — the affability, the learning, the charisma of a leader — that belong to another of Melville's idols, Jack Chase. As Rolfe is more virile than the elf-like Vine, so the balding Apollo of the seas, "noble" Jack Chase, was more muscularly impressive than the shy Apollo of Salem, Nathaniel Hawthorne. It was one of the many coincidences in Melville's life-journey that after he wrote his apotheosis of Chase in *White-Jacket*, he met Hawthorne, whom he promptly and passionately apotheosized in the pages of *The Literary World*. The poem in effect repeats the life situation as Clarel looks from Rolfe to Vine.

Peers, peers — yes, needs that these must pair.
Clarel was young. In promise fine,
To him here first were brought together
Exceptional natures. . . .

Unlike Chaucer's pilgrimage, Melville's excludes women, and Clarel's journey resembles the flights of his sailor predecessors to the all-male environment aboard ships. In addition to Vine and Rolfe the pilgrims include such opposites as Derwent, an Anglican who retains his faith by glossing over doubts, and Mortmain, a disenchanted revolutionary who, like Ahab, is intent upon self-annihilation. Although Clarel recognizes Mortmain's destructive tendencies, the attraction is great, perhaps because of similar tendencies in himself, and he rejects Derwent's faith as "an over-easy glove." Mortmain, like Ahab and Bartleby, is enwombed in his solipsistic universe and can offer nothing to anyone except paralyzing despair. Derwent, like Nehemiah, offers Clarel "the scrip of love." "Paternally my sympathies run — / Toward you I yearn," he declares, but the youth, like Melville, will have none of the "Yea Gentry."

Since Clarel cannot penetrate Vine's reserve, and feels rebuffed by his silence, he turns to Rolfe, finding him

> Sterling — yes,
> Despite illogical wild range
> Of brain and heart's impulsive counterchange.

Although Rolfe is often the spokesman for Melville's doubts about religion, society, and art, Clarel has, as the passage confirms, reservations that keep him from surrendering to the sway of Rolfe, whose verbalizations turn out to be not as magnetic as Vine's silence. The drabness of the stoney countryside through which the pilgrims pass, and of the unending conversations which end too often in a despair that itself is "an over-easy glove," is relieved with the appearance of a Cypriote, a young hedonist who is given a lyric which was one of Melville's favorites:

> "Noble gods at the board
> Where lord unto lord
> Light pushes the care-killing wine:
> Urbane in their pleasure,
> Superb in their leisure —
> Lax ease —
> Lax ease after labor divine!
>
> "Golden ages eternal,
> Autumnal, supernal,
> Deep mellow their temper serene:
> The rose by their gate
> Shall it yield unto fate?
> They are gods —

They are gods and their garlands keep green.
  "Ever blandly adore them;
  But spare to implore them;
They rest, they discharge them from time;
  Yet believe, light believe
  They would succor, reprieve —
    Nay, retrieve —
Might but revelers pause in the prime!"

The Cypriote, like Celio, Clarel himself, and the handsome sailors in the earlier writings, embodies ideal beauty, or homoerotic fantasy: "Young he was, and graced / With fortunate aspect, such as draws / Hearts to good will by natural laws." In a brief phrase the youth's physicality is captured: "in the saddle free / A thigh he lolled."

The appearance of the Cypriote is the prelude to the first of several bachelors' paradises. The first of these revels is led by two men from Lesbos. One offers Derwent wine as he sings, "Quaff it, sweetheart, I and you." The other, a mountaineer "Barbaric in his hardy grace" and "a rare symposiarch," offers Rolfe his hand in "vinous fellowship." Alone as usual, Vine cuts through the literary homosexual haze to observe, "'tis Ahab's court." Almost in confirmation of Vine's forebodings, one of the Lesbians sings of Cybele, the orgiastic goddess, Rolfe waltzes with one of the pagans, and Derwent pushes his knees under the table closer to his companion's. Toward the conclusion of the orgy, Vine against his wishes is compelled to sing; he sings not of Eros but of amaranths and death. That night, unable to sleep, Rolfe and Clarel walk about in the silent town, and the youth finds the older man's candid but relentless attacks upon men and their faiths too harsh: "Revulsion came." He even suspects that Rolfe's "Manysidedness" is hollow. Clarel does not admit the obvious: he is repelled by, or perhaps fearful of, Rolfe's sensual freedom.

To counterbalance the Lesbians, and to correct their hedonistic perspective, there appears a Wandering Jew, "More lonely than an only god" and fearful of his sanity; or an Agath, "ocean's wrinkled son" and a tattooed "sea-Solomon"; or an Ungar, a bitter and scarred veteran of the Civil War, "A wandering Ishmael from the West." Clarel, always respectful and always passive, listens to their bitter tales and observes their turbulent faces, but their despair offers no clarification, the self-hate which they project upon the world being a perverse kind of self-indulgence. He is beginning to learn that whatever answers there may be to life's muddle he will have to discover for himself.

What may man know?
(Here pondered Clarel) let him rule —
Pull down, build up, creed, system, school,
And reason's endless battle wage,
Make and remake his verbiage —
But solve the world! Scarce that he'll do:
Too wild it is, too wonderful.
Since this world, then, can baffle so —
Our natural harbor — it were strange
If that alleged, which is afar,
Should not confound us when we range
In revery where its problems are. —

When the pilgrims arrive at Bethlehem, at the birthplace of "the BOY," once again a maniacal mood begins to pervade, innocently set off at the appearance of a young Franciscan monk. Salvaterra is an "Isaac," with "damsel-eyes," "like a maid in lily of youth" — another hermaphrodite, this time in clerical garb. Although Rolfe voices reservations about Salvaterra's manliness, both Derwent and Clarel are strongly attracted. Clarel says: "I would / I were his mate, . . . / Such faith to have." But he cannot be the Franciscan's "mate" any more than he can be Vine's. In Bethlehem Rolfe and Derwent, both of whom Clarel has rejected on one score or another, establish a "brotherly" relationship. "A bond we have," Derwent exclaims, slipping his arm into Rolfe's. Although the end of the journey is near, Clarel has yet to establish a "bond."

Abruptly the narrator himself intrudes to announce, "the satyr's chord is strung," which heralds the appearance of a prodigal named Lyonese. A French Jew who denies his origins and a salesman of luxuries, Lyonese has a "mobile face, voluptuous air." A satyr in contrast with the saintly Salvaterra, married to the senses rather than to God, he informs Clarel of his friendship with the Muscovite — "Locked friends we were." He sings lusty, seductive songs and expounds on the sexual-mystical meanings of the Song of Solomon. Once more Clarel stands in awe of an overpowering male beauty:

Then first he marked the clustering hair
Which on the bright and shapely brow
At middle part grew slantly low:
Rich, tumbled, chestnut hood of curls,
Like to a Polynesian girl's. . . .

That night Clarel has a dream in which he is embraced by Salvaterra and Lyonese, the religious and pagan hermaphrodites.

On the following day the Muscovite, "Mateless now," appears and speaks of "a juicy little fellow — / A Seckel pear, so small and mellow." The atmosphere becomes increasingly sensualized. When Clarel admits that he shared a cell with Lyonese the night before, the Muscovite cannot resist an innuendo, more bald than the baldest puns in *Moby-Dick*: "And, doubtless, into chat ye slid." When Clarel acknowledges that at first Lyonese refused to talk "but afterwards gave way," the Muscovite observes, " 'Indeed?' — with meaning smile." After the hedonists depart — and Melville moves away from a relationship which is transparently homosexual — a pall descends upon the pilgrims. Clarel experiences "the reign / Of reveries vague," and wonders whether he has been "infected" by Lyonese and his friend.

It is now Easter week. Clarel says farewell to the pilgrims, saving for last the one first in his heart, Vine. If Clarel has not exactly been reborn like "the BOY," he has reached the stage of development or maturity, if such it is, at which the Melvillean fable invariably concludes. After his unsuccessful search for "a mate," he is supposedly more or less ready to go it alone, although he is still a "lacquey," dependent rather than active. His seeming self-reliance is little more than resignation before life's inevitabilities. If the "hero" jumps ambiguously into maturity, Melville's concluding lines are equally ambiguous, since the melioristic position he states does not emerge from the prevailingly pessimistic attitude evident in the poem or from the unsuccessful relationships of the characters.

> *If Luther's day expand to Darwin's year,*
> *Shall that exclude the hope — foreclose the fear?*
> . . . .
>   *Yea, ape and angel, strife and old debate —*
> *The harps of heaven and dreary gongs of hell;*
> *Science the feud can only aggravate —*
> *No umpire she betwixt the chimes and knell:*
> *The running battle of the star and clod*
> *Shall run forever — if there be no God.*
> . . . .
>   *Then keep thy heart, though yet but ill-resigned —*
> *Clarel, thy heart, the issues there but mind;*
> *That like the crocus budding through the snow —*
> *That like a swimmer rising from the deep —*
> *That like a burning secret which doth go*
> *Even from the bosom that would hoard and keep;*
> *Emerge thou mayst from the last whelming sea,*
> *And prove that death but routs life into victory.*

The lines wobble uncertainly in what appears to be a somewhat qualified Emersonian affirmation or even at times an almost orthodox religious statement. But they do not come to grips with Clarel's orphan-like state and evade the emotional core of the poem, the longing for a "mate," for friendship in a friendless universe. Melville fell back on his intellectual defenses.

In recalling the journey to the Holy Land, Melville could not escape the memory of Hawthorne, who, anxiously concerned about his friend's health and desire for annihilation, saw him leave from Liverpool for the Mediterranean, and in the following year watched him board a steamer bound for America. Hawthorne's farewells provided a frame for Melville's lonely expedition. When the men parted in May 1857, Melville knew that his journey to Jerusalem had failed to meet what were unrealizable expectations, and, no doubt more important, that his relationship with Hawthorne could not be revived.

But the memory of Hawthorne was not silent. Perhaps when he wrote "Monody," that delicately wrought elegy to the "shyest grape," Melville thought that he was putting a period to a relationship that physically had ended in May 1857, but he was mistaken. Between 1868 and 1872 he acquired through gift or purchase at least six works of Hawthorne's: *Our Old Home*, *Passages from the American Note-books*, a second copy of *The Scarlet Letter*, *The Snow-Image and Other Twice-Told Tales*, *Passages from the French and Italian Note-books*, and *Septimius Felton*. *Passages from the English Note-books of Nathaniel Hawthorne*, which was published in 1870, was also in his library. Although the date of acquisition is unknown, the probabilities are that he read it while he was writing *Clarel*. If so, he learned for the first time how Hawthorne had reacted to their discussions before he had set out for the Holy Land. In Mrs. Hawthorne's severely abridged version, she recorded that "Melville, as he always does, began to reason of Providence and futurity, and of everything that lies beyond human ken." Sophia's sense of decorum and tact led her to excise her husband's report that Melville expressed a desire "to be annihilated" as well as Hawthorne's opinion that Melville could not be "comfortable in his unbelief." The account as she adapted it abruptly jumped to the flattering conclusion: Melville "has a very high and noble nature, and better worth immortality than most of us." Unless Sophia's elisions made him suspect bowdlerization, Melville could not fault Hawthorne's unrestrained praise.

When he began to recreate in his poem what had been a lonely tour of the Holy Land, he superimposed upon reality a fantasy of a tour in the company of Nathaniel Hawthorne. Ostensibly and intellectually he was attempting to come to terms with "the BOY," but emotionally he was again a youth in what he wanted to be an idyllic relationship with "Nathaniel of Salem." Behind the fantasy in the Holy Land were the experiences which had taken place in the Berkshires in 1850 and 1851. The relationship which began on Monument Mountain and continued in the shadows of Mount Greylock was to be replayed in the stoney, arid wastes of Palestine — an appropriate physical setting for a friendship which even in fantasy could not be fulfilled.

While the various characters in *Clarel* attempt "to reason of Providence and futurity, and of everything that lies beyond human ken," Clarel is a listener rather than a participant. He is more interested in a "mate" than in intellectual matters. When Melville in 1856 talked of such matters to Hawthorne, he no doubt secretly longed to reestablish the old bond of something more than polite friendship. In the fantasy he created he had Hawthorne all to himself in a relationship which in his customary fashion excluded women and, in particular perhaps, Sophia Hawthorne. This transposition conformed to his wish but was false to a man whose dependency upon and dedication to women were among his most marked characteristics. Melville without women is a conceivable portrait; Hawthorne without women is unimaginable. The fantasy in *Clarel* repeats the vision embodied in that letter in which Melville and Hawthorne drank ambrosial wine together on Mount Olympus. But this time the dream, tempered by what had transpired in the intervening years, begins, not on Monument Mountain or Mount Olympus, but at the Tomb of Kings, the most famous sepulchre in Jerusalem. (Interestingly, in the early pages of the poem Jerusalem is shortened to Salem.) The second meeting of Clarel and Vine takes place at "The Site of the Passion," or Gethsemane. Not inappropriately, given the setting as well as the course of the Melville-Hawthorne relationship, Nehemiah reads aloud the biblical account of Judas' betrayal. Vine and Clarel are not to succeed where Hawthorne and Melville failed.

At these early meetings, when the contact is limited to the eyes, Clarel worships before the beauty of the older man, whose "Lydian hair" is gently tossed by a "low wind" and who, wearing Hawthorne's black attire, is "Fair as the sabled violets be." The imagery recaptures insistently the tone of the impassioned review of *Mosses from an Old Manse* in *The Literary World*. When Vine departs from the Tomb of Kings, Clarel ascends a hill that is likened to "Franconian land, / The marvel of the Pass," which, as Bezanson notes, is a thinly disguised reference to Franconia Notch and to the site of Hawthorne's tale of "The Great Stone Face." The touch is at the same time delicate and poignant.

In the extended icon that follows Vine's baptism the narrator dwells upon the powerful physical attraction of Vine — "the ripe flush, Venetian mould" and the "opulent softness." Not unexpectedly, Apollo is invoked, although Vine's is not a pagan but a "virgin soul" and underneath "reigned austere / Control of self." In the narrator's eyes the lush beauty of Vine becomes "coyness," a strong seductive force which, he asserts, is not checked "by moral sway" but "by doubt, if happiness through clay / Be reachable." Vine is inhibited because of "Fear or an apprehensive sense."

Ordinarily Vine is "rapt . . . in remoteness," but sometimes he emerges from his shell to indulge in "freakish mockery" of monks or tourists. This "Ambiguous elfishness," not unlike Ariel's or Pearl's in *The Scarlet Letter*, reveals a detachment bordering on hostility of a man who, like many of the characters in Hawthorne's tales, prefers the role of spectator or voyeur. At one point Clarel recognizes and (silently) chastises the cowardly aggressiveness of Vine, which recalls the furtive behavior of Coverdale in *The Blithedale Romance*: "Paul Pry? and in Gethsemane?" As the other pilgrims endlessly luxuriate in their spiritual and personal conflicts, Vine abstains from the discussions or has recourse to what the narrator terms a laconic "irony": "Hard for a fountain to refrain." (The fountain image would appear to refer to a recurrent one in Hawthorne's writings.) Except for a relatively brief attraction to Rolfe, Clarel turns from the others to Vine's "few words . . . suggestive more / Of choicer treasures."

Whether Vine is an accurate portrait of Hawthorne is essentially beside the point: it is an accurate portrait of Melville's Hawthorne. If he misses Hawthorne's self-irony and genuine playfulness as well as other aspects of a complex personality, the characterization of Vine remains a fascinating summation of Melville's views. Twenty-five years later Melville found pleasure, and no doubt some pleasurable pain, in reliving those fifteen months during which he pursued a tremulous, aloof man who simultaneously aroused and checked his passionate nature. Twelve years after his death Hawthorne's beauty and memory were undimmed. Hawthorne had died without commenting directly, at least in print, upon a relationship and a pursuit which could have been to him only an embarrassment. Melville, if he did not penetrate deeply into the mysteries of his dead friend's personality, finally in *Clarel* made clear why he had termed Hawthorne an "impregnator" twenty-five years earlier. That ardent review necessarily dwelt on the esthetic and intellectual attractions; in *Clarel* Melville recorded the physical attractions.

During the pilgrimage Vine remains in a self-imposed isolation. While others talk he remains silent, or occasionally intrudes a comment "with timorous air / Of virgin tact." When the other pilgrims

are depressed by the stoney landscape and the aridity of the country,
Vine is not "infected," and when the travelers sing joyously, Vine
blushes as he joins the group. "Was joy a novelty?" the narrator
inquires. Then one day in a sylvan setting reminiscent of the forest
scene in *The Scarlet Letter*, the most erotic moment in nineteenth-
century American literature, or of that meeting in 1851 in Love
Grove near Lenox, Clarel comes upon Vine.

> *As were Venetian slats between,*
> *He espied him through a leafy screen,*
> *Luxurious there in umbrage thrown,*
> *Light sprays above his temples blown —*
> *The river through the green retreat*
> *Hurrying, reveling by his feet.*
> > *Vine looked an overture, but said*
> *Nothing, till Clarel leaned — half laid —*
> *Beside him. . . .*

Suddenly the older man begins to talk, of "Short life and merry!" and
of an Arab chieftain as a member of the "Clan of outcast Hagar."
Not inadvertently, Melville had Vine invoke the biblical myth with
which he had identified his own outcast nature, particularly in the
book dedicated to Hawthorne, *Moby-Dick*. Ravished by Vine's voice
and the natural setting, Clarel is magnetically drawn: "So pure, so
virginal in shrine / Of true unworldliness looked Vine." Although
"prior advances" have been "unreturned," Clarel

> > *yearned —*
> *O, now but for communion true*
> *And close; let go each alien theme;*
> *Give me thyself!*

Vine, not "suspecting Clarel's thrill / Of personal longing," rambles
on. Clarel listens but thinks of

> > *confidings that should wed*
> *Our souls in one: — Ah, call me* brother!

As Clarel silently longs for the fusion articulated in the Farewell
Letter twenty-five years earlier — "your heart beat in my ribs and
mine in yours" — the narrator defines the state as "feminine his
passionate mood" and as "hungering unfed." Then —

> *Some inklings he let fall. But no:*
> *Here over Vine there slid a change —*
> *A shadow, such as thin may show*
> *Gliding along the mountain-range*
> *And deepening in the gorge below.*

Clarel, or the narrator, offers a series of speculations to account for Vine's rejection.

> *Does Vine's rebukeful dusking say —*
> *Why, on this vernal bank to-day,*
> *Why bring oblations of thy pain*
> *To one who hath his share? here fain*
> *Would lap him in a chance reprieve?*
> *Lives none can help ye; that believe.*
> *Art thou the first soul tried by doubt?*
> *Shalt prove the last? Go, live it out.*

At last he comes to the heart of the matter and of the situation:

> *But for thy fonder dream of love*
> *In man toward man — the soul's caress —*
> *The negatives of flesh should prove*
> *Analogies of non-cordialness*
> *In spirit.*

When, rebuffed and ashamed, Clarel glances up, he detects, or thinks he detects,

> *serious softness in those eyes*
> *Bent on him. Shyly they withdraw.*
> *Enslaver, wouldst thou but fool me*
> *With bitter-sweet, sly sorcery,*
> *Pride's pastime? or wouldst thou indeed,*
> *Since things unspoken may impede,*
> *Let flow thy nature but for bar? —*

Clarel chooses to believe that Vine fears to return his affection. So too it would appear that Melville believed Hawthorne had encouraged through silence and his shy presence an intimacy or a bond which, when articulated, had caused "shadows" to cross his face. Whether Melville related fact or wish we of course will never know. Lovers are rarely reliable observers, but Hawthorne's reticences were perhaps suspect too. Vine's reaction causes Clarel to say to himself:

Nay, dizzard, sick these feelings are;
How findest place within thy heart
For such solicitudes apart
From Ruth?

After the wordless rebuff relations between Vine and Clarel are somewhat cooler. One character terms Vine "a poor nun's pining hen," a comment which recalls Melville's in a letter in 1851: "He does'nt patronise the butcher — he needs roast-beef, done rare." No longer are Vine's words "suggestive more / Of choicer treasures," but he is "one / Whose race of thoughts long since was run." Vine's neutrality becomes irksome: "Nor sided he with anything." Then one day Clarel discovers Vine "quivering" in fear.

> *He wore that nameless look*
> *About the mouth — so hard to brook —*
> *Which in the Cenci portrait shows,*
> *Lost in each copy, oil or print;*
> *Lost, or else slurred, as 'twere a hint*
> *Which if received, few might sustain:*
> *A trembling over of small throes*
> *In weak swoll'n lips, which to restrain*
> *Desire is none, nor any rein.*

Both Melville and Hawthorne were fascinated by Guido's famous portrait and the incestuous subject matter. It is referred to in a climactic scene toward the end of *Pierre* and plays an important part in *The Marble Faun*. If Melville read the copy of *Passages from the French and Italian Note-books of Nathaniel Hawthorne* which he had acquired in 1872, he knew that Hawthorne had gone to see the portrait at least four times. Melville was hinting at some dark recess of Hawthorne's nature, perhaps that Hawthorne shared Ethan Brand's secret and unpardonable sin. After this moment of recognition, obscure as it is, Clarel noiselessly slips aside: "No more need dream of winning Vine / Or coming at his mystery." But the words are belied by Clarel's subsequent actions as well as by the narrator's continued explorations of Hawthorne's psyche.

At the first of the two banquets Vine blushes when he is called on for a tale or a song, in language reminiscent of "Monody" and of earlier scenes in the poem:

> *"Ambushed in leaves we spy your grape,"*
> *Cried Derwent; "black but juicy one —*
> *A song!"*

The imagery here is consistent with the oral framework in which Melville from *The Literary World* to *Clarel* placed Hawthorne. Although Vine is repeatedly chided for "shy prying into men," Clarel is a Coverdale too, both in the scene in which the allusion to the Cenci portrait is introduced and later in an elaborate episode where various characters comment upon a date tree. In both scenes Clarel recalls Vine's rejection but his own continuing preoccupation with Vine, to whom he is attracted as he is not to any of the other pilgrims.

> and his glance
> Rested on Vine, his reveries flow
> Recalling that repulsed advance
> He knew by Jordan in the wood,
> And the enigma unsubdued —
> Possessing Ruth, nor less his heart
> Aye hungering still, in deeper part
> Unsatisfied. Can be a bond
> (Thought he) as David sings in strain
> That dirges beauteous Jonathan,
> Passing the love of woman fond?
> And may experience but dull
> The longing for it? Can time teach?

Clarel does not answer his own questions, nor did Melville, although his preoccupation with male friendship throughout his life in effect answered the last question, "Can time teach?"

Clarel is disappointed when Rolfe voices reservations about Salvaterra's manhood, but after Vine abandons his neutrality and elfishness to offer a sensitive appraisal of the monk, Clarel is once again ravished by the comments "Breathed now by that exceptional one / In unconstraint." It is, as it were, with Vine's blessing that Clarel in his dreams that night embraces Salvaterra and Lyonese. Vine resembles Salvaterra, the priest, in attire and in self-restraint, and Lyonese in his "opulent" physicality and in his worldly attitude toward religion.

At the end of the journey in the Holy Land Clarel's final farewell is reserved for Vine, and the narrator characterizes the fictional or poetic relationship in words — "Friendly they tarried — blameless went" — that recall the opening lines of "Monody" in which Melville summarizes the real-life relationship with Hawthorne —

> To have known him, to have loved him
> After loneness long;

And then to be estranged in life,
    And neither in the wrong. . . .

The lines that follow in *Clarel* are, then, a twofold benediction:

Life, avaricious, still demands
Her own, and more; the world is rent
With partings.

"Keep True
to the Dreams of
thy Youth"

If Melville did not expect acclaim following the publication of *Clarel*, he was not disappointed. (In 1884 he pronounced it "eminently adapted for unpopularity.") Yet after the hours, the energy, the personal investment he had put into the longest poem in American literature, he could hardly have accepted without pain the critical rebuffs and the silence. He had consistently maintained after the failure of *Mardi* that fame held no interest for him, but the posture seems suspect. There was the alternative of silence, the Bartleby stance, but in the remaining years of his life he continued to write, perhaps somewhat compulsively.

Mostly as a social isolate, Melville lived out his life in the modest house on 26th Street in New York City, which was no Arrowhead or Gansevoort mansion. In the front hall there was a colored engraving of the Bay of Naples, and Naples was recalled in poems like "After the Pleasure Party." In the parlor was a marble bust of Antinous, the beautiful page and favorite of the Emperor Hadrian, who at twenty-one drowned himself in the Nile. In Rome, years before, Melville had been magnetically attracted to the bust of a youth who corresponded to the icon of the handsome sailor. In the back parlor hung the J. O. Eaton portrait of Melville which, probably because of the half light, frightened his granddaughter, who always avoided the room. The portrait, painted in 1870, was much too benign to have produced such a response, unless the granddaughter was bringing other associations to her confrontation with the oil painting.

There was an iron-trimmed porch on the second floor, where Melville sat with his pipe and a cane, which, according to the grandchild, was "his most constant companion." (Here is additional confirmation of the identity of the narrator of "I and My Chimney.") Near where he sat was a match holder in the form of a red and blue china butterfly. Melville amused the grandchildren by looking to see whether the butterfly had flown away. It became an oft-repeated joke.

Also on the second floor was his study-bedroom which faced north, like the study at Arrowhead. The granddaughter spoke of "his own dark privacy" in characterizing the room. It was a carpetless room, gloomy and monastic in appearance. There was a small black iron bed covered with dark cretonne, which could have come from Pierre's study. A great mahogany desk had four shelves of books, on top of which were "strange plaster heads that peered along the ceiling level." The writing surface was "a pebbled green-paper," an interesting juxtaposition in view of the recurrent polarity in his writings of the sea and the green land. Underneath the open desk on a side wall, almost out of sight, was pasted a motto, "Keep true to the dreams of thy youth." The grandchildren were seldom invited in, although there was always a small bag of figs on the desk.

Nearby was Elizabeth Melville's bedroom, sunny and comfortable. The bed was white, "like other people's," in the words of her granddaughter. There was a sewing machine as well as a big armchair in which Melville sat when he left his own room. Here he was affability itself, at least on some occasions, allowing the children to pull on his thick beard. Although Elizabeth suffered from depressions and various physical ailments in the 1870s and 1880s, as did her husband, at least she did not encase herself in a funereal or ascetic environment.

Although some critics have convinced themselves that in *Clarel* Melville moved toward reconciliation and even a modest or limited affirmation, achieving a catharsis both literary and personal, the heart of the poem relates the fruitless search of Clarel for personal connections or bonds; and Melville's quest did not end in 1876 in quiescent resignation. What he called "these inexplicable fleshly bonds" were too much with him. In writing to his favorite brother-in-law, John C. Hoadley, in 1877, he attempted to banter, but twice referred to his age. "You are young," he wrote, "but I am verging upon three-score, and at times a certain lassitude steals over me – in fact, a disinclination for doing anything except the indispensable. At such moments," he continued, "the problem of the universe seems a humbug, . . . and the – well, nepenthe seems all-in-all." Later in the day he added a postscript to the letter: "It is a queer sort of an absurd scribble, but if it evidences good-fellowship and good feeling, it serves the purpose. You are young (as I said before) but I aint; and at my years, and with my disposition, or rather, constitution, one gets to care less and less for everything except downright good feeling. Life is so short, and so ridiculous and irrational (from a certain point of view) that one knows not what to make of it, unless – well, finish the sentence for yourself." Before he sent this letter there was still another addition: "N.B. *I aint crazy*." The one he reassured was himself.

A few months later, in June 1877, Mrs. Melville informed Peter Gansevoort's daughter of Herman's gratitude for the legacy of $500 from his uncle's estate, and then wrote: "poor fellow he has so much mental suffering to undergo (and oh how *all* unnecessary) I am re-joiced when anything comes into his life to give him even a moment's relief." Mrs. Melville was afraid to leave Herman alone that summer "in his state of mental health," but she managed to arrange a pleas-ant two-week vacation for him while she and her two daughters went to the mountains to obtain relief from hay fever.

While Elizabeth worried, Herman wrote bantering letters which appeared to contradict her evaluation. Yet in the midst of his seeming playfulness his disillusion sometimes emerged. In discussing his theory of leisure, for example, he exclaimed: "They talk of the *dignity of work*. Bosh. True Work is the *necessity* of poor humanity's earthly condition. The dignity is in leisure." Then he added with the hyperbole of inverted Calvinism: "Besides, 99 hundredths of all the *work* done in this world is either foolish and unnecessary, or harmful and wicked." The next sentence, in Melville's characteristic rhythm, attempted to mitigate the despair: "But bless my heart! I am scrib-bling here at a pretty rate."

It was a household in which depression and physical disability afflicted most of the members with the exception of Frances, who in 1878 announced her engagement to Henry B. Thomas. In May of that year Herman had his first attack of erysipelas, and for a while was unable to write. Later in the year Stanwix was confined to a hospital in Sacramento, California. The luckless son was still drifting from job to job, and from hope to hope, and occasionally borrowing money from Lemuel Shaw, Jr. Although Herman never referred to Stanwix in his extant letters, Elizabeth tried to reassure herself: "he has seen some very hard times, and deserves much credit for his pluck and patience under difficulties and disappointments."

Early in 1879 Elizabeth was having "one of her 'run down' turns," as she described her situation, and was hardly able to guide her pencil. Unlike her sister Frances, Bessie was almost an invalid. Not only did she suffer from the hay fever which incapacitated her mother in the summer, but her arthritis was crippling, the doctor at one time suggesting that her fingers be straightened "*by force.*" The family always discussed Bessie's ailments in physical terms, although they would appear to be in part psychosomatic. In 1884, Herman had "a kind of Rheumatic gout," and at the end of the year Bessie had a "severe attack of 'muscular rheumatism.' "

Mrs. Melville suffered with her own ailments and her children's, but she had always had Boston to escape to several times during the year. After her stepmother, Hope Savage Shaw, died in August 1879, even that retreat was denied to her. Later in the same year she was not "robust" enough, in Herman's words, to undertake a trip to Albany. Frances's engagement, however, dissipated some of the gloom in the household. As Elizabeth noted almost quaintly, "Fanny has finally struck flag and surrendered the citadel, and of course is as happy as happy can be." Before the wedding took place on April 5, 1880, the Melvilles entertained the prospective son-in-law at dinners amounting to New York-style orgies over which Herman presided with almost manic glee.

A memorable crab dinner became part of the family lore. Herman was at the head of the table, a board and hammer in front of him. Crabs were brought from the kitchen, and then the hammer went to work. In a strange accompaniment to the explosions of the hammer Herman spouted whatever came to mind. Everyone was stuffed long before Herman's hunger and oratory were appeased. Whenever the incident was mentioned later Elizabeth rolled her eyes and sighed. At another premarital feast the staple was baked potatoes which Herman consumed with the gusto of a Roman banqueteer. How many potatoes he ate no one could remember!

Shortly after Melville entered the seventh decade of his life, he termed himself "an — old fogy," who had to endure not only a gradual decline in physical vigor but also the loss of one intimate after another. A year earlier, in 1878, with the death of Evert Duyckinck, Melville lost his oldest literary friend, the man who had supervised the publication of his first book and had introduced him to Hawthorne. When his favorite brother Tom suffered a sudden and fatal heart attack on March 5, 1884, Herman became the only surviving male in the family. A year later his sister Frances died, and on October 21, 1886, John C. Hoadley. In 1888 Helen Griggs, the oldest sister who had arranged the marriage of Elizabeth and Herman, died within seven months of her husband. Herman was left with only one sister, Catherine, Hoadley's widow, who was to be the last of Allan Melvill's family.

Stanwix, the "omoo" of the family, died in San Francisco on February 23, 1886, at age thirty-five. He had continued to drift from position to position, always convincing himself that at last fate would smile upon him, until, weakened by tuberculosis, he had to be hospitalized. Elizabeth, her sister-in-law noted, was "unable to find solace for her grief — it was *so* hard, — the sickness and death so far away!" She was denied the solace of burying the last of her two sons. What Herman's reaction was there is no way of knowing; probably he veiled his grief in silence. Perhaps, as Robert Penn Warren has suggested, Stanwix's death led to the transformation of *Billy Budd, Sailor* into the story of a father-son relationship in which Captain Vere becomes a surrogate for Allan Melvill and Herman Melville.

Judge Shaw, though dead for many years, was to make his presence felt even in the closing years of Herman's life. When Lemuel Shaw, Jr., died in 1884 his estate was placed at $323,450. The three Melville children received $2,000 each, and eventually Elizabeth was bequeathed $33,516. Elizabeth inherited almost $2,500 from her mother's sister, Martha B. Maret, and at the death of Mrs. Maret's daughter, Mrs. Ellen Gifford, there were bequests of $15,000 to Elizabeth, $8,000 to Herman, and $3,000 to the two daughters. In addition, there were monies from the estate of Herman's sister Frances as well as from the sale of Uncle Herman's home in Gansevoort, New York. But, as Mrs. Metcalf perceptively notes, the economic well-being had a price. If Elizabeth was able to give Herman $25 each month for the purchase of prints and books, and if because of the various legacies it was possible eventually for Herman to retire from the Custom-House, it was for the most part Shaw money that made these things possible; if there was gratitude, there was also the continuing dependency upon his wife's family.

Life at the Custom-House went its monotonous course. In 1877 he almost lost his position after a change in the national administration; he survived, but the working hours were increased. In the following year he was transferred to a post at 76th Street and the East River, where he remained for the next seven years. Apparently in 1885 there was a rumor that he would be relieved of his position. Elizabeth urged the Lansings to use their influence with the new administration in Washington. "The *occupation*," she reasoned, "is a great thing for him — and he could not take any other post that required head work, & sitting at a desk." Then she warned, in her usual fashion: "but *do not let* Herman know that the subject has been mentioned between us." Six months later, to the same correspondents she reported that Herman had resigned from the Custom-House on December 31, because "for a year or so past he has found the duties too onerous for a man of his years." She noted his "exhaustion, both mental and physical" which she had not mentioned earlier.

Meanwhile Frances Thomas was asserting the life principle with the birth of three daughters before her father's death. Eleanor, the first child, who was christened "Tittery-Eye" by her grandfather, later dedicated a great deal of her life to the establishment of her grandfather's fame; as Eleanor Melville Metcalf, she made family records available to scholars and biographers. In *Herman Melville, Cycle and Epicycle* (1953) she not only printed extant materials but also recorded family anecdotes. According to Mrs. Metcalf, one spring day in 1887 Herman took his four-year-old granddaughter to Madison Square for a walk and then absent-mindedly went off without the child. When he realized his mistake, he retraced his steps, only to find the girl making her way home contentedly. Mrs. Metcalf also recalled sitting in an armchair on Herman's knees as he related ghost stories and she squeezed his wiry beard. He intimidated her into eating her oatmeal with the admonition, "Jack Smoke will come down the chimney and take what you leave!" The grandchildren also knew the gloomy moods that led him to predict that they, like his own children, would turn against him when they grew up.

All his life Melville had been filled with restless energy, and, predictably, there was little change in his autumn years. He liked to ride the ferries in the Hudson River and in the New York harbor. His son-in-law sometimes accompanied him while he moved impatiently from one seat to another, and rode back and forth on the ferry as though he were in search of something. When Julian Hawthorne visited him in 1883, he noted that Melville, pale and nervous, got out of his chair frequently and with a stick that had a hook at the end opened and closed the window. Alone, he wandered in and out of second-hand bookstores, seeking unusual books at bargain prices, never talking much to the clerks. In the winter of 1888, once again alone, he went to Bermuda on what was to be his last voyage. During a blizzard off the coast of Florida he had to crawl "around on hands & knees," which surely demonstrated that at sixty-eight he was still hardy. On the passenger list of the *S. S. Trinidad* appeared the entry: "H Melville 37 Merchant." The entry would appear to have been another of his pranks, since he could scarcely pass for thirty-seven, which was the age of his merchant father at his birth.

In 1888 he was writing and revising *Billy Budd, Sailor* into what in its final form would be a study of a father-son relationship, and at the same time he was writing poems looking nostalgically to his past. Except for the publication of a condensed version of "The Haglets" in the *New-York Daily Tribune* of May 17, 1885, he did nothing in these years to keep his name before the public.

Yet he was not completely forgotten. In 1877 William J. Linton included in *Poetry of America* two poems from *Battle-Pieces*, "Sheridan at Cedar Creek" and "Shiloh, A Requiem." In 1882 Melville rejected an invitation to join the Authors' Club, apparently, according to Charles DeKay, on the grounds that "his nerves could no longer stand large gatherings." Brander Matthews, later professor of literature at Columbia University, recalled seeing Melville at the Club on several occasions — "an unobtrusive personality, with a vague air of being somehow out of place in our changing and chattering groups." W. Clark Russell, an expatriate living in England, the author of nautical tales, and a one-time sailor, pronounced Melville the "first" of "the poets of the deep" in the September 1884 issue of *The Contemporary Review*. Two years later he began a correspondence with Melville that was to continue until 1891.

He claimed that Melville's "reputation here [in England] is very great. It is hard to meet a man whose opinion as a reader is worth having who does not speak of your works in such terms as he might hesitate to employ with all his patriotism, towards many renowned English writers." Russell allowed his own enthusiasm to lead him to overstatement; sales of Melville's books picked up slightly in England in the 1880s, but there was no rush to the bookshops. In 1885 Robert Buchanan, who achieved notoriety as the author of "The Fleshly School of Poetry," published a poem in *The Academy* called "Socrates in Camden, With A Look Round," which in its jingling fashion told of his visit with Walt Whitman in Camden and of his futile search for Melville in New York.

> Meantime my sun-like music-maker [Whitman],
>   Shines solitary and apart;
>
> . . . .
> While Melville, sea-compelling man,
> Before whose wand Leviathan
> Rose hoary white upon the Deep,
> With awful sounds that stirred its sleep,
> Melville, whose magic drew Typee,
> Radiant as Venus, from the sea,

Sits all forgotten or ignored,
While haberdashers are adored!
He, ignorant of the drapers' trade,
 Indifferent to the art of dress,
Pictured the glorious South-sea maid
 Almost in mother nakedness —
Without a hat, or boot, or stocking,
A want of dress to most so shocking,
With just one chemisette to dress her
She lives, — and still shall live, God bless her!
 While heaven repeats the thunder of it,
 Long as the White Whale ploughs it through,
The shape my sea-magician drew
 Shall still endure, or I'm no prophet!

The poem pleased Melville: "It is the insight of genius and the fresh mind."

Buchanan's poem almost for the first time — the exceptions being Whitman's brief but favorable reviews of *Typee* and *Omoo* — linked the names of the two great New York artists who were born in the same year. In his only recorded comment Melville limited himself to acknowledging Buchanan's truthfulness: "The tribute to Walt Whitman has the ring of strong sincerity." Apparently he read his contemporary's poetry about this time, since in 1888 he spoke "so much of Whitman" to Edmund Clarence Stedman, a well-established critic of the era, that Stedman sent him his chapter on Whitman in *A Library of American Literature*. What Melville thought of the poetry of the most radical voice in American literature there is no way of knowing, and Whitman in his mature years had nothing to say of Melville. A meeting between "Socrates" and "Triton," to borrow Buchanan's terminology, ignites the imagination, and would have provided a fascinating counterpoint to the meeting of Mr. Noble Melancholy and New Neptune, but it was not destined to occur.

If toward the end of his career Whitman was given to "backward glances," so, too, was Melville. In 1888, at his own expense in an edition limited to twenty-five copies, Melville published *John Marr and Other Sailors*, exactly twelve years after the appearance of *Clarel*. Here for the first time he printed poetry that drew upon his experiences at sea. John Marr, a former sailor and another of Melville's orphans, has retired from the sea and lives in a small prairie town. After the death of his wife and child, he finds himself in an environment where no one in the Gilded Age is interested in his yarns of the sea. Now middle-aged, he yearns for the "chummies" of his youth:

> *Ye float around me, form and feature:* —
> *Tattooings, ear-rings, love-locks curled;*
> *Barbarians of man's simpler nature,*
> *Unworldly servers of the world.*

(The description foreshadows the appearance of Billy Budd.) Tenderly Marr recalls a funeral at sea —

> *A beat, a heart-beat musters all,*
> *One heart-beat at heart-core* —

and longs

> *to clasp, retain;*
> *To see you at the halyard's main* —
> *To hear your chorus once again!*

The longest poem in the collection, "Bridegroom Dick," is filled with similar nostalgia, as Dick tells the "old woman" (his wife) for the nth time of his days at sea, "boozing now on by-gone years." After the passing of years he clings to the baptismal name he has received at sea — "Bridegroom Dick lieutenants dubbed me." Although toward the end of the poem he asks his wife to "buss me in good fashion; / A died-down candle will flicker in the snuff," his body may belong to his wife, but his heart belongs to his sailor pals.

> *My pipe is smoked out, and the grog runs slack;*
> *But booze away, wife, at your blessed Bohea;*
> *This empty can here must needs solace me* —
> *Nay, sweetheart, nay; I take that back;*
> *Dick drinks from your eyes and he finds no lack!*

Comically, like so many of the others in the novels, Dick creates an oral paradise.

In "Jack Roy" Melville recalls Jack Chase, to whom he was to dedicate *Billy Budd, Sailor*, and again, as in *White-Jacket*, confers upon Chase a heroism which his high jinks scarcely merit:

> *Larking with thy life, if a joy but a toy,*
> *Heroic in thy levity wert thou, Jack Roy.*

"To Ned" memorializes Richard Greene, or Toby of *Typee*, and that island in the South Seas is once more an Eden far removed from modern American "Pelf and Trade." In this recreation there are no cannibals, no tattoo doctors, no Mow-Mows, the fog of nostalgia obliterating anxieties and fears. Though most of the poems are sentimental, even a trifle saccharine, a few like "The Maldive Shark" and "The Berg" present the by now familiar dark side of Melville's view, but flounder in a too-easy pessimism. The terror of the shark with "serrated teeth" — "Pale ravener of horrible meat" — withers beneath the contrived irony. Even the abyss in "The Berg" is but a picture, only superficially felt.

> *Hard Berg (methought), so cold, so vast,*
> *With mortal damps self-overcast;*
> *Exhaling still thy dankish breath —*
> *Adrift dissolving, bound for death;*
> *Though lumpish thou, a lumbering one —*
> *A lumbering lubbard loitering slow,*
> *Impingers rue thee and go down,*
> *Sounding thy precipice below,*
> *Nor stir the slimy slug that sprawls*
> *Along thy dead indifference of walls.*

The poems in *John Marr* are for the most part flaccid and in final analysis tedious, lacking the dynamics and emotional gyrations of his prose. Melville dedicated the volume to Russell, and in 1890 Russell inscribed *An Ocean Tragedy* to "the Author of 'Typee,' 'Omoo,' 'Moby-Dick,' 'Redburn,' and other productions which top the list of sea literature in the English tongue."

One of the manuscripts which Melville revised after his retirement in 1885 consisted of prose essays (printed posthumously as "Burgundy Club Sketches") and poems with the title of "Marquis de Grandvin." Apparently he began to compose the book in 1876 and projected a work in which prose would alternate with verse and in which there would be two main characters or narrators, the Marquis de Grandvin and John Gentian. Like the poems in *John Marr*, this collection emphasizes a longing for a Golden Age. Discontent with the present age is explicit:

> *Never comes the mart's intrusive roar,*
> *Nor heard the shriek that starts the train,*
> *Nor teasing telegraph clicks again,*
> *No news is cried, and hurry is no more —*

With obviously contrived gaiety the Marquis de Grandvin laments:

> *Utility reigns — Ah, well-a-way!*
> *And bustles along in Bentham's shoes.*

Later another character speaks of "This cabbage *Utility, parbleu!*"
Only toward the conclusion does "Rose, the flower of flowers,"
appear to correct the perspective —

Ah, let time's present time suffice,
No Past pertains to Paradise.

Like the melioristic conclusion of *Clarel* or the espousal of "THE
MIDDLE WAY" in "The Conflict of Convictions" in *Battle-Pieces*, the
correction carries little conviction after the unrelieved indictment of
the present and uncritical (and even unhistorical) glorification of the
past. In 1885 Melville informed James Billson, a young English admirer, that he was "neither pessimist nor optomist," but that he
admired poems such as James Thomson's "The City of the Dreadful
Night" "if for nothing else than as a counterpoise to the exorbitant
hopefulness, juvenile and shallow, that makes such a bluster in these
days — at least, in some quarters."

Marquis de Grandvin, a bachelor and "a patrician of hereditary
rank," presides over the Burgundy Club, and is a habitué of "most of
the Fifth Avenue clubs," the clubs which Melville himself would have
nothing to do with. The Burgundy Club is a Ti transferred from
Typee to New York and similarly a gathering place for the well-born.
As Grandvin's name suggests, he is a kind of modern Bacchus, who,
unlike his mythic counterpart, has nothing much to do with the
opposite sex. The Burgundy Club is the last refuge for the embattled
male. Women are excluded, Grandvin explains, because they have "a
constitutional incapacity for good-fellowship, that is, in the masculine acceptation of the term." Although the ladies are said to admire
the Marquis, their admiration "hardly extends to such of his qualities
as partake of the Grand Style, as one may say, the highly elevated
style; a style apparently demanding for its due appreciation a robust
habit, in short, the masculine habit." Men like Grandvin, we learn,
are "wedded to enjoyment, and hence productive, . . . They have a
suggestion of the potentialities in the unvitiated Adam, a creature,
according to hallowed authority, originally created but a little lower
than the angels." Which is an extraordinary statement if it is to be
taken seriously — "the unvitiated Adam" presumably being the
asexual creature before the appearance of woman with her sexual
demands and the attendant sapping of the male. Billy Budd, as we
shall see, was to be an "unvitiated Adam."

Like King Mehevi's associates in Typee, all of whom are Apollonian in appearance, Grandvin's fellowship is a similar figment of
fantasy: "Almost invariably these men have physical beauty; and the
moral charm is in keeping with that, apparently a spontaneous ema-

nation from it. It is as golden wine down in a golden chalice, where, seen through the lustre suffusing the shadow, the delicious fluid looks to be the exuded gathered sap of the precious metal." As such a passage reveals, in his art Melville continued to escape to and romanticize male society. Similarly there was no diminution through the years of the misogynistic note sounded in a tale like "I and My Chimney," where the narrator protects his sacred chimney and precious pipe against the schemes of his wife, the eternal predatory Eve.

The chief disciple of Grandvin is John Gentian, another bachelor, who is known as "Major Gentian, or the Dean, or the Major, or Jack." Gentian, then, is still another version of "noble" Jack Chase. At the same time, as Merton M. Sealts, Jr. observes, he embodies many characteristics of Melville himself, the same descent on both sides of the family from heroes in the Revolutionary War as well as similar personal and literary friends, including a fondness for the writings of Nathaniel Hawthorne. Gentian is the author of a "famous" work entitled "Afternoon in Naples." When it is praised he invariably answers, as did Melville when *Typee* was mentioned, "Pshaw!" for he has an "indifference to any reputation except that old-fashioned one of being a man of honour."

Like Rolfe in *Clarel*, Gentian fuses Chase and Melville, the romantic dream and reality, the icon of fantasy and the person. In a description which he apparently intended to delete Melville wrote: "To the last thou wilt be Jack Gentian; not too dignified to be humane; a democrat, though less of the stump than the heart. And should mortal decline come — which Heaven long defer — and the Black Brunswicker lay seige to thee in thy bachelor tower, thy compatriots, those who best know the true temper of thy genial spirit, would still call thee *Jack* as in the days of their youth, and though debility should then tongue-tie thee, thou wouldst still respond to them out of thy waning eyes." When we recall that Melville had neither seen nor heard from Chase since 1844, the impact of Jack was truly extraordinary. Since Chase and Melville become one in the recreations here and in *Clarel*, the declaration — "Dean of the Burgundians, but I love thee!" — is, amusingly, not only love but also self-love.

In its unfinished form this collection of essays and verse goes nowhere in particular, except to illustrate, wickedly, a facetious remark of one of the bachelors in the Burgundy Club: "But you know second childhood has a natural affinity for the first." Once more, for the last time but one, Melville was dealing in the characterizations of Grandvin and Gentian with an implied father-son relationship. Jack Gentian, we are told, "belongs to a transplanted shoot of Southern stock," presumably from Virginia. The author of "Hawthorne and His Mosses," we recall, masquerades as a Virginian. If there is, then, something of Melville in the character of Gentian, and if Grandvin is kin to Vine and therefore to Hawthorne, "the shyest grape," the parallels, despite some fuzziness of language, are clarified in a passage in which Hawthorne is introduced by means of a pun on the title of *Our Old Home*, his account of his years in England. The words "filial appreciation" in the passage make the identification clear.

> Highly, Major, didst thou relish that title whereby, as regards so many of us Americans, a rare son of New England with happiest simplicity desig-nated that Elder England, from which his progenitor came — *Our Old Name*. But if thy filial appreciation of the historic Past has something of Nathaniel Hawthorne in it, the medium, Dean, through which thou re-callest it, viewing it as through an irradiated vapour, this is not without a touch of *our incomparable friend*, the Marquis.

In the summer of 1883 Melville was visited by Hawthorne's only son, Julian, who was seeking material about the "red-letter days" in the Berkshires for his two-volume biography, *Nathaniel Hawthorne and His Wife*. As a child Julian had been fond of Melville, who had even written a playful note to the lad after the Hawthornes had left Lenox. If Julian can be trusted — he commented on the interview on four separate occasions between 1901 and 1922, but not until a decade after Melville's death — it was an awkward meeting.

Melville's reply to Julian's letter requesting the visit was cordial but the salutation read, "Dear Mr. Hawthorne." "He greeted me kindly, with a low voice and restrained manner," Julian wrote. In *Hawthorne and His Circle* Melville was described as "pale, sombre, nervous, but little touched by age," yet in another account he was "a melancholy and pale wraith of what he had been in his prime." While Melville kept opening and closing the window, Julian asked about his father's letters: "He said, with a melancholy gesture, that they had all been destroyed long since, as if implying that the less said or preserved, the better!"

Although Melville reiterated "the highest admiration for my father's genius, and a deep affection for him personally," Julian spoke of "incoherent talk" and "reason to suspect . . . a vein of insanity." In another article he observed that Melville seemed "partly to reach out for companionship in the dark region into which his mind was sinking." These apparent overstatements, unless Julian's presence triggered a rush of painful memories and emotions, may have been provoked by Melville's reference to "some secret in my father's life which had never been revealed, and which accounted for the gloomy passages in his books." Julian's rejoinder was sharp — "It was characteristic in him to imagine so; there were many secrets in his own career" — although in his final sentence Julian tempered his indignation: "But there were few honester or more lovable men than Herman Melville." Elizabeth purchased a copy of *Nathaniel Hawthorne and His Wife* in 1885, but Melville made no recorded comments. A cousin, however, wondered, "I should think some of the allusions would be very trying to a person of his sensitive nature."

After Melville began in 1886 his first sustained work in prose since 1856, he complained of eyestrain as he had during the writing of *Moby-Dick* and *Pierre*. He drew up a will on June 11, 1888. In the following year he acknowledged that his "vigor sensibly declines. What little of it is left I husband for certain matters as yet incomplete, and which indeed may never be completed." A month later, in January 1890, he excused himself for his delay in not replying to a letter because of "Illness." In April of the same year he had a second attack of erysipelas "which weakened him considerably," Elizabeth noted. In January 1891 he "walked 3/4 of a mile in a bitter cold air," and then took to his bed. By the end of the month, if not earlier, he was about, going to the library and purchasing some of Schopenhauer's books.

About the end of May he delivered the manuscript of *Timoleon* to the Caxton Press, which was to print at the author's expense an edition of twenty-five copies. The volume included poems written probably in the late 1850s after his trip to Palestine and as recently as the past year. It included "Monody," his elegy to Hawthorne, as well as "After the Pleasure Party." The latter is a puzzling poem, somewhat muddy in conception, probably deliberately so, since Melville was apparently seeking to transcend the sexes and sexual drives for a purer, asexual state.

While critics have sought to unravel the ambiguities of "After the Pleasure Party," with results that can only be termed inconclusive, they have neglected the poem which provided the book with its title. "Timoleon," which is based in part on one of Plutarch's *Lives*, tells of the rivalry of two brothers for the love of the mother, who prefers Timophanes, the first born. As rendered by Melville, the mother becomes a later embodiment of Mrs. Glendinning, who, we remember, was a fictional portrait of his mother. Timophanes develops into a tyrant, and when he continues in his despotic course despite Timoleon's entreaties, the younger brother slays him to save the state from his tyranny.

For years self-outcast, he but meets
In shades his playfellow's reproachful face.
        Estranged through one transcendent deed
From common membership in mart,
In severance he is like a head
Pale after battle trunkless found apart.

Timoleon begins to quarrel "with gods" who do not reward "just" men like himself, but his quarrel immediately turns into a plea —

        O, tell at last,
    Are earnest natures staggering here
    But fatherless shadows from no substance cast? —

which is the plea that reverberates throughout Melville's writings. Then Timoleon asks for "some little sign":

    Me reassure, nor let me be
    Like a lone dog that for a master cries.

At last Corinth recalls Timoleon:

    Not slayer of thy brother, no,
    But savior of the state, Jove's soldier, man divine.

The state lifts the ban, but Timoleon lives on his "adopted shore"; the stain of fratricide remains.

If in the last year of his life he wrote of his now ancient rivalry with Gansevoort, he was also to give fictional form once more to his ties to Allan Melvill.

"Child-Man"
—*Billy Budd, Sailor*

Like Jacob with the angel, Melville wrestled with the manuscript of *Billy Budd, Sailor.* For five years beginning in 1886 he sought to complete his last extended work in prose, but when he wrote "End of Book" on April 19, 1891, the manuscript was in such a disorderly state that readers had to wait until 1962 for an accurate transcription of what he was unable to shape into final form.

In his first incarnation Budd was an older sailor, probably not unlike Bridegroom Dick, seeking boozily to recapture the aura of the past. As Melville contemplated his creation he was dissatisfied, his heart not fully engaged, until a vision of an incomparably beautiful youth possessed, or repossessed him, and the figment was baptized Billy Budd.

Billy was another, and final, embodiment of L. A. V., Tommo, Redburn, and the others. Then, in the next stage of the manuscript's evolution, from the shadows of Jackson, Blount, and Ahab, emerged

John Claggart, master-at-arms, and Claggart's innate depravity was counterpointed with innate goodness, worldly experience with primeval innocence. In the final stages Melville created, or recreated, in the tradition of M. and the good fathers of his earlier writings, his most complex character, Edward Fairfax Vere, who was to be perplexed not only by his role as a captain of a battleship allegedly threatened by mutiny during wartime, but also by his obligations in another role he assumes.

Although *Billy Budd, Sailor* is placed in historical time, in the year 1798 when the English and the French were engaged in naval warfare, and Lord Nelson was master of the seas, it transcends history for the timelessness of fable, specifically the fable that haunted Melville's writings. The warfare is not between nations for supremacy on the seas but between father and son in the eternal warfare to determine succession.

In the course of the evolution of the tale into its seemingly final form it became a love story, the familiar love story in Melville's books. Now enfeebled in health and by age, and without male heirs after the death of Stanwix in 1886, Melville fell in love with his artifact, or, perhaps more accurately, renewed and restated his love for the icon of the handsome youth, the wish fulfillment of his narcissistic needs and imagination. If in the tale Vere and Claggart are in love with Billy, the one as "father" and the other as rival, their love is exceeded by that of the author. Billy is truly Melville's love child, the recipient of pent-up affections and feelings which in life he could, sadly, give to no one, except perhaps to Nathaniel Hawthorne.

Another orphan and a bastard, but of good birth, Billy is twenty-one, illiterate, inarticulate, but a singer. He is a blue-eyed, blonde-haired, rosy-cheeked cherub whose very presence causes reason to abdicate and purity to reign, at least temporarily. Caressing the youth like an overfond father, Melville elevated him to transcendant heights. To glorify this superyouth Melville plundered classical, biblical, and other sources for epithets. Upon Billy is bestowed the muscularity and beauty of such Greek figures as Alexander, Apollo, Hercules, and Achilles. He is the "young Adam before the Fall," David, Joseph, and Isaac. Since this orphan "was found in a pretty silk-lined basket hanging one morning from the knocker of a good man's door in Bristol," he is probably to be equated with Moses too. Like Queequeg, he is an "upright barbarian." More familiarly he is compared to a St. Bernard dog and to a blood horse. Burly crews and authoritarian officers call him "rose" or "jewel" or "beauty."

Like Marnoo and the others Billy incorporates both sexes — the most magnificent hermaphrodite of all Melville's hermaphrodites. The face is "feminine in purity of natural complexion." It has "that humane look of reposeful good nature" of the statues of Hercules, although the muscular body "was subtly modified by another and pervasive quality. The ear, small and shapely, the arch of the foot, the curve in mouth and nostril, even the indurated hand dyed to the orange-tawny of the toucan's bill, a hand telling alike of the halyards and tar bucket, but, above all, something in the mobile expression, and every chance attitude and movement, something suggestive of a mother eminently favored by Love and the Graces." Billy has only one flaw, a tendency to stutter in moments of crisis, and in this respect, we are informed, he resembles the beautiful but flawed Georgiana in Hawthorne's tale "The Birthmark." Although Billy strikes a man dead with his fists, he is immediately likened to "a condemned vestal priestess."

A wrinkled old sailor named the Dansker "in freak of patriarchal irony," we are told, "substituted *Baby* for Billy." The baptism is most appropriate, since, despite the lad's heroic affinities, age, and experiences as a sailor, he is and remains, as the text states, "a child-man." His innocence is untested and unsullied like a baby's. It is as though Melville kept him arrested except for the flowering of his late adolescent physical beauty. Billy's intellectual capacity is qualified by a devastating clause "such as it was." Later Melville explains that part of Billy's charm is the absence of "mental superiority tending to excite an invidious feeling." At another point he speaks of the youth's "simple-mindedness," which may at the same time point to his innocence and his foolishness. Since on the one hand Melville compares Billy to classical and biblical heroes and gods who combined beauty and intelligence, these deliberate qualifications of his intelligence point to an awareness that Billy is without flesh and bones. But it is folly to ask for consistency in the depiction of an icon which springs not from the intellect but from feelings.

During his service aboard the *Rights-of-Man* Billy becomes in the eyes of the crew and its officers a "jewel" because he brings peace to a faction-ridden ship. Overcome by his radiant beauty, the crew becomes a "happy family": "Not that he preached to them or said or did anything in particular; but a virtue went out of him, sugaring the sour ones." Melville would have us believe that Billy equals virtue equals nurturing mother ("sugaring"). Billy's mettle and chastity are tested when an envious sailor named Red Whiskers "under pretense of showing Billy just whence a sirloin steak was cut ... insultingly gave him a dig under the ribs." To this provocation — and exploration of his genitality — Billy responds by giving the sailor a "drubbing," or, perhaps more accurately, a spanking. After he is punished Red Whiskers loves Billy like the others. The crew protects the lad as though he is a sacred child or, to shift the image, a queen bee. "Some of 'em," we read, "do his washing, darn his old trousers for him; the carpenter is at odd times making a pretty little chest of drawers for him." If Billy is constantly shifting sexual roles, sometimes the leader and sometimes the infant, the crew also plays both sexual roles.

After Billy is transferred from the *Rights-of-Man* to the *Bellipotent*, a warship ready for battle, he enters a larger world which will put his beauty and innocence to a severe test. Following the baptism of Baby Budd, the Dansker assumes the role of a good father – in Melville's mythic analogy he plays Chiron to Achilles – but he does not explain the machinations of Claggart to a youth incapable of understanding evil. This failure makes the Dansker into an ineffectual father, or perhaps Billy like Redburn must learn to rely upon his own resources. Life aboard the *Bellipotent* bewilders Billy because, although every one appears to love him – and like a child's Billy's existence is dependent upon being loved – there are rumors that Claggart is "down" on him.

"His portrait I essay, but shall never hit it," the narrator observes of Claggart, who is to be the dark-haired antagonist of the blonde sailor. Claggart is thirty-five, with small hands unaccustomed to physical labor and with features like those "on a Greek medallion." "His brow was of the sort phrenologically associated with more than average intellect; silken jet curls partly clustering over it, making a foil to the pallor below." Yet the chin resembles those of certain famous historical traitors, and his eyes glitter and glow hypnotically. From Gothic melodrama, Iago, Milton's Satan, Hawthorne's Chillingworth or Westervelt, but primarily from allegory and the primitive landscape of the unconscious, Claggart emerges to play the role of the villain, endowed not only with good looks but also with intelligence and insight.

Like Red Whiskers, Claggart is envious of Billy's charm and good nature, and, even more than the other sailors, he is fiercely aware of the youth's "significant personal beauty." One day when the ship lurches Billy spills his bowl of soup and the "greasy liquid" streams across Claggart's path. "Pausing, he was about to ejaculate something hasty at the sailor, but checked himself, and pointing down to the streaming soup, playfully tapped him from behind with his rattan, saying in a low musical voice peculiar to him at times, 'Handsomely done, my lad! And handsome is as handsome did it, too!' " As a number of critics have indicated, this sexually suggestive episode hints at Claggart's homosexual tendencies. Billy, of course, construes the words and the tap of the rattan as proof of Claggart's affection, without understanding the sexual innuendo in the "equivocal words."

By denying Billy the powers of logos and dwelling upon his

physical attractions, Melville confers upon him the powers of Eros. Billy is not so much a charismatic presence as an erotic magnet. The epithets — "rose" and so forth — emphasize his bisexual nature, and the seemingly learned and heroic allusions to Alexander, Apollo, Hercules, and Achilles are to bisexuals, most of whom were more attracted to males than to women. Even Claggart is Saul to Billy's David. This aspect of the drama largely remains unwritten, for obvious reasons. Instead of dealing with the Saul-David attraction, Melville deflects attention by introducing an analogy to Milton's Satan when he writes "of soft yearning, as if Claggart could even have loved Billy but for fate and ban."

When Claggart reports to Captain Vere that a certain sailor is plotting mutiny, the name of the culprit is, significantly, not Baby or Billy Budd but William Budd. Here for the first time Budd is both a morally and sexually mature male. When Vere expresses astonishment, Claggart replies: "You have but noted his fair cheeks. A man-trap may be under the ruddy-tipped daisies." At this moment Vere recalls Billy's first appearance on the *Bellipotent* as "a fine specimen of the *genus homo*, who in the nude might have posed for a statue of young Adam before the Fall" — which in itself is an unusually erotic response of a stranger (and a captain) to a handsome sailor. In the confrontation scene, when Billy and Claggart are brought face to face and the master-at-arms makes his accusation, the specific charges and evidence are not stated. Instead, Claggart is described in the act of committing a kind of rape of the youth.

If Billy has charmed and soothed sailors, and especially Claggart, because of his beauty, Claggart retaliates by attempting to overpower that beauty by means of his eyes, in an extraordinary scene of displacement. "Claggart deliberately advanced within short range of Billy and, mesmerically looking him in the eye, briefly recapitulated the accusation." Billy stands "impaled and gagged," as Claggart's eyes lose their "wonted rich violet color blurring into a muddy purple." The "serpent fascination" of the eyes changes into "the paralyzing lurch of the torpedo fish." Billy is "transfixed," "gesturing and gurgling," "a condemned vestal priestess in the moment of being buried alive, and in the first struggle against suffocation."

At this point Captain Vere emerges from the background to assume the pivotal role in the drama. A bachelor, like Billy of uncertain but aristocratic origins, Vere is over forty, old enough, we are later instructed, to be Billy's father. Unlike the usual despotic captains in Melville's books, Vangs, Riga, and Claret, for example, he is characterized by "dreaminess of mood," and is nicknamed "Starry Vere." Moreover, "He loved books, never going to sea without a newly replenished library, compact but of the best." Like Melville he is particularly fond of Montaigne. "A dry and bookish gentleman" in the eyes of his detractors, Vere has the learning characteristic in Melville's fantasy of the good father, whether it is M., Jack Chase, or Glendinning. Vere's library would appear to be Allan Melvill's.

After Claggart's verbal and ocular assault upon Billy, Vere commands, "Speak, man! . . . Speak! Defend yourself!" The youth, "transfixed," can only gurgle and stutter. At this moment Vere, who knows nothing of Billy's "vocal impediment," recalls "a bright young schoolmate of his whom he had once seen struck by much the same startling impotence in the act of eagerly rising in the class to be foremost in response to a testing question put to it by the master." With this realization there is a sudden transformation in Vere's roles.

> Going close up to the young sailor, and laying a soothing hand on his shoulder, he said, "There is no hurry, my boy. Take your time, take your time." Contrary to the effect intended, these words so fatherly in tone, doubtless touching Billy's heart to the quick, prompted yet more violent efforts at utterance — efforts soon ending for the time in confirming the paralysis, and bringing to his face an expression which was as a crucifixion to behold. The next instant, quick as the flame from a discharged cannon at night, his right arm shot out, and Claggart dropped to the deck. Whether intentionally or but owing to the young athlete's superior height, the blow had taken effect full upon the forehead, so shapely and intellectual-looking a feature in the master-at-arms; so that the body fell over lengthwise, like a heavy plank tilted from erectness. A gasp or two, and he lay motionless.

Captain Vere is now by his own action Father Vere. When Vere becomes the father, Claggart and Billy are no longer sailors but sons in rivalry for his favor and blessing. Claggart manifestly is charging mutiny but latently is accusing the younger son or brother of plotting the father's overthrow. When Vere touches Billy paternally, it is a caress desired but at the same time intolerable, for Billy cannot endure tactile contact, as evidenced in the earlier scene with Red Whiskers. When Billy strikes Claggart with a furious blow to the forehead, he puts out the "evil eye" of his enemy-rival, but at the same time the blow is displaced, since Billy is prohibited from striking the father. After Claggart is struck and lies on the deck "a dead snake," Vere covers his face with his hand in silent recognition of the displaced blow.

Allusions to Satan or ominous utterances like Vere's "Fated boy" obscure the underlying drama which is suggested rather than delineated. The situation in "Timoleon" is repeated, the younger son slaying an older brother. If the poem recalls the rivalry of Gansevoort and Herman, so does the novel, since Claggart has the verbal facility of Gansevoort and Billy resembles Herman in his embarrassed, stumbling speech. If Vere is Allan Melvill, he is also, as Richard Chase proposes, Herman Melville, not only as the father of two sons whose lives ended tragically but also as "the devourer of his own childhood" in that he endlessly and compulsively reenacted in his writings the hurts of his youth. In the character of Billy, Melville was, in Chase's words, "overwhelmingly moved with pity for . . . an image of himself."

When Vere slowly uncovers his face, like a moon emerging from an eclipse (the analogy is Melville's), "The father in him, manifested towards Billy thus far in the scene, was replaced by the military disciplinarian." Although Vere seeks to revert to his former role as captain, he is intellectually and viscerally shaken. He seizes the surgeon's arm "convulsively." His manner is "excited" and he is given to "passionate interjections" and "excited exclamations" in his "unwonted agitation." At times he lapses, like Billy himself, into "mere incoherencies." The surgeon, perplexed by Vere's sudden erratic behavior, wonders, "Was he unhinged?" Captain Vere's "mental disturbances" would appear to be out of proportion, an extraordinary overreaction to an accidental murder, but as Father Vere, now a participant and indeed the pivot of the action, the response is not extreme but awesomely realistic. Up to this point in his life Vere has been insulated and defended by his official position and by his intellectual and bookish nature. Like Ahab when he allows feelings about his abandoned wife and son to intrude upon his monomaniacal quest, Vere almost goes mad in the sudden collapse of his controls. His emotions are not unlike what Melville must have felt as he helplessly watched one son become a suicide and the other wreck his life.

With the dead unburied Claggart in one compartment and Billy confined in another, Vere hastily assembles a court in the room in which the murder has occurred. In such cases as Billy's the usual procedure under the rules of the English navy was to refer the matter to a superior, but Vere insists on trial and conviction at once, although he does not credit Claggart's allegations. As captain of the *Bellipotent* he has nothing to fear, but as a father in an oedipal conflict he, like every father and every son, is bewildered by conflicting emotions: as a father to protect himself from his successor and as a former son to relive his guilt.

After Vere presents the case to the court, Billy says: "Captain Vere tells the truth. It is just as Captain Vere says, but it is not as the master-at-arms said. I have eaten the King's bread and I am true to the King." And Vere replies: "I believe you, my man," "his voice indicating a suppressed emotion not otherwise betrayed." During the proceedings Billy's face has "a look in its dumb expressiveness not unlike that which a dog of generous breed might turn upon his master." In contrast with Billy's passivity, Vere evidences "a mental disturbance." After a strange pun — he refers to Claggart as cut off by a "lasting tongue-tie" — Vere instructs the court as to its duty, but in contrasting a court martial and the Last Assizes, he illustrates by using the language of the oedipal struggle. "We proceed under the laws of the Mutiny Act," he advises the judges. "In feature no child can resemble his father more than that Act resembles in spirit the thing from which it derives — War. . . . And the Mutiny Act, War's child, takes after the father. Budd's intent or non-intent is nothing to the purpose." Nor, as he does not add, is intention a mitigating factor in the ancient father-son relationship. Under the unyielding eyes of Vere the judges condemn Billy and order him hanged on the following morning.

After the trial Vere visits Billy Budd in his compartment, but "what took place at this interview was never known." Although in this tale Melville is the omniscient narrator, he deliberately does not dramatize potentially the greatest and most human scene in his fiction. Throughout his writings he had been preoccupied with this moment, this meeting of father and son, and nowhere else had he led his readers so inevitably toward the confrontation. But evasion — or silence like Bartleby's — was "predestinated." Technically Melville had an uncertain command of dialog, as one would expect in view of his difficulties in human relationships, except in parodistic situations where hostile wit had free sway. Nowhere in his books does a character grow in awareness through interaction with another, wiser character. Ishmael triumphs as a solitary survivor without confrontation (or even a word) with Ahab. Perhaps unconsciously, Melville protected himself from depicting the meeting between father and son by creating in Bartleby a character who retreats into silence and in Billy one who is inarticulate, though godlike in appearance. But there is still a more personal explanation. Since his own father had been snatched from him and even deprived at the end of his mental faculties, Melville was not able here or in *Pierre* or elsewhere to depict what he had not experienced — reconciliation with the father.

We are informed that "Vere in end may have developed the passions sometimes latent under an exterior stoical or indifferent." The narrator suggests that Vere is old enough to have been Billy's father, and some critics have toyed with the possibility of literal paternity, although the fable does not depend upon such coincidence or literalness, surrogates accomplishing the same purpose. Besides, Melville at this point introduces the Abraham myth: "The austere devotee of military duty, letting himself melt back into what remains primeval in our formalized humanity, may in end have caught Billy to his heart, even as Abraham may have caught young Isaac on the brink of resolutely offering him up in obedience to the exacting behest." Here, as Richard Chase was the first to point out, Melville's orphan is Isaac rather than Ishmael, and the foundling would seem to achieve a reconciliation with the father.

This final use of his recurrent biblical myth is more symbolic or artistic than convincing psychologically. It tampers with the myth, for, unlike Isaac, Billy is not destined to succeed Abraham as the patriarch. He is to die "another orphan." Even the invocation of Jesus later, when Billy is enshrined in the memories of sailors, is artful evasion: Billy becomes a lovely artifact, without human relevancy.

That evening Billy sleeps soundly, free after his "healing" interview with Vere of the "agony, mainly proceeding from a generous young heart's virgin experience of the diabolical incarnate." This awkward phrasing of allegory gives way to a realistic description "of a slumbering child in the cradle when the warm hearth-glow of the still chamber at night plays on the dimples that at whiles mysteriously form in the cheek, silently coming and going there." This is truly Baby Budd. Like an infant he has no fear of death, if he can conceive of death at all. The chaplain enters "to bring home to him the thought of salvation and a Savior." Although the youth eats the King's bread, he does not accept Christianity's wafer. Yielding his dogmatic faith to the power of the youth's transcendent beauty, the chaplain kisses Baby Budd, logos yielding once again to eros.

On the next morning, the hemp about his neck, "At the penultimate moment, his words, his only ones, words wholly unobstructed in the utterance, were these: 'God bless Captain Vere!' " Like "the clear melody of a singing bird on the point of launching from a twig," the syllables "had a phenomenal effect, not unenhanced by the rare personal beauty of the young sailor, spiritualized now through late experience so poignantly profound." Nature itself pays homage to Budd's magnanimity of spirit: "At the same moment it chanced that the vapory fleece hanging low in the East was shot through with a soft glory as of the fleece of the Lamb of God seen in mystical vision, and simultaneously therewith, watched by the wedged mass of upturned faces, Billy ascended; and, ascending, took the full rose of the dawn."

Nowhere else in his writings did Melville paint in such poetic and apocalyptic tonalities, although there was some straining for painterly effects. But with the alternating movement characteristic of *Moby-Dick* and his life, the eternal wavering between certainty and distrust, the apotheosis of Baby Budd is abruptly corrected in the next paragraph, the poetry almost collapsing into seemingly unnecessary factuality. "In the pinioned figure arrived at the yard-end, to the wonder of all no motion was apparent." To make the point inescapably clear, in Chapter 26 the purser and the surgeon discuss realistically and scientifically this "phenomenal" case of a hanged man's dying without the usual involuntary orgasm. Longing in one part of his being for transcendental leaps into mystical or pantheistic states but locked in his skepticism and his hurts, Melville knew that his fable was but a fable, and that Billy's triumph is the triumph of his lovely, lonely artifact. Melville settled, as he must, for artistic sublimation.

Billy achieves presumably complete happiness when he utters his final words of forgiveness, "God bless Captain Vere!" and in so doing imitates "the BOY" that Clarel seeks. But such self-transcendence evades the oedipal conflict. Billy, unlike his predecessors in Melville's writings, wins the father's love. He becomes Isaac, at a price that he willingly, even joyously, pays: he remains forever arrested as a "child-man." He welcomes the arrestment, accepts castration.

The power of the drama — its enormous pull on readers, particularly on "sons" — is not the fiction of apotheosis but the affective reverberations caused by a father's betrayal which no son perhaps can ever forgive. Bartleby rages against himself and the lawyer, Billy blesses Captain Vere, yet both youths in their different ways welcome the release of death — there is no more growing up to do — and both leave the paternal figures to suffer guilt.

Billy's fate confirms that the hermaphroditic icon is life-denying, or, more kindly, life-evading. Billy and all the handsome sailors want out from adult heterosexuality: they want to be neither husbands nor fathers. The underscored references to Billy's impotency — his neuter state, as it were — reveal all too clearly that behind the icon or fantasy lay the author's fear of genitality and his disgust with the insatiable demands of sexual urges. From the beginning to his last work, Melville wanted to transcend a sexuality which he found anxiety-producing, as his sometimes scatological wit undoubtedly evidences. Billy in death leaps the vexed human state, just as L. A. V. in Melville's first work flees the Lansingburgh belles for the safety and security of M.'s library.

In its final elaboration, or embellishment, the icon establishes the narcissism, which, as Melville hints in the opening chapter of *Moby-Dick*, may be "the key to it all." Narcissus, we recall, perished of self-love.

Some time after Billy's hanging Captain Vere is fatally wounded and on his deathbed, "under the influence of that magical drug," which frees him from pain and reality, utters, "Billy Budd, Billy Budd." In a similar scene in *Pierre*, Mr. Glendinning, in his seemingly mad ravings, calls for an unknown daughter and spurns his second-born child. Perhaps on his deathbed in his rambling Allan Melvill uttered Gansevoort's name.

If Allan Melvill and Gansevoort hovered over *Billy Budd, Sailor*, so did the other two men who played important roles as surrogates. The book was to be "Dedicated to Jack Chase / Englishman / Wherever that great heart may now be / Here on Earth or harbored in Paradise." Curiously, John Claggart has the same initials, which may point to some ambivalence, or at least recognition that Melville had consistently idealized a man who lacked stability and was, ironically, disrated in the year in which *White-Jacket* appeared.

Nathaniel Hawthorne makes his presence felt even more insistently than Chase. There is, as noted earlier, the specific reference to "The Birthmark," one of the tales in *Mosses from an Old Manse*, which Melville read shortly before the two men met in 1850. In Hawthorne's story Aylmer, an alchemist who cannot be "weaned" from science "by any second passion," suddenly marries Georgiana and shortly afterwards becomes so troubled by a birthmark on her face that he attempts to remove it by means of a potion which takes her life — a fate which in his sexual anxiety he unconsciously desires. In Melville's tale Billy is given Georgiana's overwhelming beauty, and Claggart and Vere assume Aylmer's destructive role. It may have been in 1850 or in the late 1880s that Melville underscored this passage in "The Birthmark":

> ... [Aylmer's] most splendid successes were almost invariably failures, if compared with the ideal at which he aimed. ... [Aylmer's journal] was the sad confession, and continual exemplification, of the short-comings of the composite man — the spirit burthened with clay and working in matter; and of *the despair that assails the higher nature*, at finding itself so miserably thwarted by the earthly part. Perhaps every man of genius, in whatever sphere, might recognize the image of his own experience in Aylmer's journal.

Melville recognized Hawthorne's identification with both Georgiana and Aylmer; similarly in his last tale he identified with both Billy and Vere.

When at their meeting Vere and Billy become Abraham and Isaac, the text reads:

> But there is no telling the sacrament, seldom if in any case revealed to the gadding world, wherever under circumstances at all akin to those here

attempted to be set forth two of great Nature's nobler order embrace. There is privacy at the time, inviolable to the survivor; and holy oblivion, the sequel to each diviner magnanimity, providentially covers all at last.

As Hayford and Sealts point out in their edition of the novel, the phraseology and the rapture recall Melville's elation in the Farewell Letter written in November 1851 after Hawthorne had read *Moby-Dick*.

> In me divine magnanimities are spontaneous and instantaneous — catch them while you can. The world goes round and round, and the other side comes up. So now I can't write what I felt. But I felt pantheistic then — your heart beat in my ribs and mine in yours, and both in God's. A sense of unspeakable security is in me this moment, on account of your having understood the book. I have written a wicked book, and feel as spotless as the lamb.

After Billy's death sailors cherish relics from the *Bellipotent*, which in their eyes becomes a sacred vessel as Billy becomes a sacred memory. His glory is celebrated in a popular ballad entitled "Billy in the Darbies":

> *Fathoms down, fathoms deep, how I'll dream fast asleep.*
> *I feel it stealing now. Sentry, are you there?*
> *Just ease these darbies at the wrist,*
> *And roll me over fair!*
> *I am sleepy, and the cozy weeds about me twist.*

The words resonate, as Billy, like Bartleby, snuggles into the womb. To the end Melville remained true to the unfulfilled dreams of his youth.

Epilogue

In June 1891 Elizabeth Melville was preparing to go to Fire Island for relief from her "rose cold," though she was worried that Herman would "get very impatient" in her absence. When her husband's health began to decline, she changed her plans. In July Dr. Everett S. Warren took charge, and at 12:30 A.M. on September 28, 1891, Herman Melville died of "Cardiac dilatation, Mitral regurgitation . . . Contributory Asthenia," as the death certificate stated.

The obituaries in the newspapers were brief, noting with unfailing regularity that Melville's popularity had ended about 1852, that his most popular work was *Typee*, and that, as *The Press* noted, "even his own generation has long thought him dead, so quiet have been the later years of his life."

A short service was held on September 30 at 104 East 26th Street. The Reverend Mr. Theodore C. Williams of All Souls' Church officiated.

Melville was buried in Woodlawn Cemetery, in the northern part of the Bronx, near Yonkers. A rolling, sylvan site, it was and remains a fashionable burial ground. In the midst of monuments and mausoleums there is a small marble stone:

HERMAN MELVILLE.
Born August 1, 1819.
Died September 28, 1891.

The decoration is simple — a scroll, a quill pen, and a vine.

Bibliography

The Writings of Herman Melville. The Northwestern-Newberry Edition, eds. Harrison Hayford, Hershel Parker, and G. Thomas Tanselle. Evanston, 1968-   . [Published to date: *Typee*, 1968; *Omoo*, 1968; *Redburn*, 1969; *Mardi*, 1970; *White-Jacket*, 1970; *Pierre*, 1971.]

The Works of Herman Melville. Standard Edition. 16 vols. London, 1922-24.

The Battle-Pieces of Herman Melville. Ed. Hennig Cohen. New York, 1963.

Billy Budd, Sailor. Eds. Harrison Hayford and Merton M. Sealts, Jr. Chicago, 1962.

Clarel: A Poem and Pilgrimage in the Holy Land. Ed. Walter E. Bezanson. New York, 1960.

Collected Poems of Herman Melville. Ed. Howard P. Vincent. Chicago, 1947.

The Confidence-Man: His Masquerade. Ed. Elizabeth S. Foster. New York, 1954.

"Hawthorne and His Mosses." *The Literary World*, 7 (August 17, 1850), 125-27; (August 24), 145-47.

His Fifty Years of Exile (Israel Potter). Ed. Lewis Leary. New York, 1957.

Journal of a Visit to London and the Continent. Ed. Eleanor Melville Metcalf. Cambridge, Mass., 1948.

Journal of a Visit to Europe and the Levant. Ed. Howard C. Horsford. Princeton, 1955.

The Letters of Herman Melville. Eds. Merrell R. Davis and William H. Gilman. New Haven, 1960.

Moby-Dick. Eds. Harrison Hayford and Hershel Parker. New York, 1967.

Moby-Dick. Eds. Luther S. Mansfield and Howard P. Vincent. New York, 1962.

Piazza Tales. Ed. Egbert S. Oliver. New York, 1962.

Pierre: or, The Ambiguities. Ed. Henry A. Murray. New York, 1962.

Selected Poems of Herman Melville. Ed. Robert Penn Warren. New York, 1970.

[Melville, Gansevoort]. "An Albany Journal by Gansevoort Melville." Ed. Jay Leyda. *Boston Public Library Quarterly*, 2 (1950), 327-47.

—————. *Gansevoort Melville's 1846 London Journal*." Ed. Hershel Parker. The New York Public Library, 1966.

Allen, Gay Wilson. *Melville and His World*. New York, 1971.

Anderson, Charles Roberts. *Melville in the South Seas*. New York, 1939; reprinted 1966.

Arvin, Newton. *Herman Melville*. New York, 1950.

Barber, Patricia. "Herman Melville's House in Brooklyn." *American Literature*, 45 (1973), 433-34.

Berthoff, Warner. *The Example of Melville*. Princeton, 1962.

Birdsall, Richard D. "Berkshire's Golden Age." *The American Quarterly*, 8 (1956), 328-55.

Bowen, Merlin. *The Long Encounter – Self and Experience in the Writings of Herman Melville*. Chicago, 1960.

Brodtkorb, Jr., Paul. *Ishmael's White World – A Phenomenological Reading of "Moby-Dick."* New Haven, 1965.

Charvat, William. "Melville's Income." *American Literature*, 15 (1944), 251-61.

Chase, Richard. *Herman Melville: A Critical Study*. New York, 1949.

—————, ed. *Melville: A Collection of Critical Essays*. Englewood Cliffs, 1962.

Davis, Merrell R. *Melville's Mardi – A Chartless Voyage*. New Haven, 1952.

Erikson, Erik H. *Identity: Youth and Crisis*. New York, 1968.

—————. *Young Man Luther: A Study in Psychoanalysis and History*. New York, 1958.

Fiedler, Leslie A. *Love and Death in the American Novel*. New York, 1960.

Fields, James T. *Yesterdays with Authors* (1870). New York, 1970.

Fredericks, John T. "Symbol and Theme in Melville's *Israel Potter*." *Modern Fiction Studies*, 8 (1962), 265-75.

Gilman, William H. *Melville's Early Life and "Redburn."* New York, 1951.

Gross, Theodore L., and Stanley Wertheim, eds. *Hawthorne, Melville, Stephen*

Crane — A Critical Bibliography. New York, 1971.

Hawthorne, Julian. *Hawthorne and His Circle*. New York, 1903.

————. *Nathaniel Hawthorne and His Wife*. 2 vols. Boston, 1885.

Hawthorne, Nathaniel. *The Complete Works*. 13 vols. Boston, 1898.

————. *The Centenary Edition*. Ohio State University Press, 1962-Volumes 1-8.

————. "Hawthorne's Speech to the Friends of the William Brown Library, 15 April 1857." *The Nathaniel Hawthorne Journal 1972*, ed. C. E. Frazer Clark, Jr. Washington, 1973.

————. *Love Letters of Nathaniel Hawthorne* (1907). Washington, 1972.

Hayford, Harrison. "The Significance of Melville's 'Agatha' Letters." *English Literary History*, 13 (1946), 299-310.

Hayford, Harrison, and Merrell R. Davis. "Herman Melville as Office-Seeker." *Modern Language Quarterly*, 10 (1949), 168-83, 377-88.

Howard, Leon. *Herman Melville: A Biography*. Berkeley, 1951.

Jerman, Bernard R. " 'With Real Admiration': More Correspondence between Melville and Bentley." *American Literature*, 25 (1954), 307-13.

Kazin, Alfred. "On Melville as Scripture." *Partisan Review*, 17 (1950), 67-75.

Kenny, Alice P. *The Gansevoorts of Albany: Dutch Patricians in the Upper Hudson Valley*. Syracuse, 1969.

————. " 'Evidences of Regard': Three Generations of American Love Letters." *Bulletin of the New York Public Library*, 76 (1972), 92-119.

Larrabee, Harold A. "Herman Melville's Early Years in Albany." *New York History*, 15 (1934), 144-59.

Lathrop, Rose Hawthorne. *Memories of Hawthorne*. Boston, 1897.

Lawrence, D. H. *Studies in Classic American Literature*. New York, 1923.

Lebowitz, Alan. *Progress into Silence: A Study of Melville's Heroes*. Bloomington, 1970.

Lévi-Strauss, Claude. *The Savage Mind*. Chicago, 1966.

Levin, Harry. *The Power of Blackness: Hawthorne, Poe, Melville*. New York, 1958.

Leyda, Jay. *The Melville Log: A Documentary Life of Herman Melville, 1819-1891*. 2 vols. New York, 1951.

Logan, John. "Psychological Motifs in Melville's *Pierre*." *The Minnesota Review*, 7 (1967), 325-30.

Lueders, Edward G. "The Melville-Hawthorne Relationship in *Pierre* and *The Blithedale Romance*." *The Western Humanities Review*, 4 (1950), 323-34.

Mansfield, Luther Stearns. "Glimpses of Herman Melville's Life in Pittsfield, 1850-1851 — Some Unpublished Letters of Evert A. Duyckinck." *American Literature*, 9 (1937), 26-48.

Marx, Leo. *The Machine in the Garden — Technology and the Pastoral Ideal in America*. New York, 1964.

Mathews, Cornelius. "Several Days in Berkshire." *The Literary World*, 7 (August 24, 1850), 145-47; (August 31), 166; (September 7), 185-86.

Matthiessen, F. O. *American Renaissance: Art and Expression in the Age of Emerson and Whitman.* New York, 1941.

Mayoux, Jean-Jacques. *Melville.* Trans. John Ashbery. New York, 1960.

Metcalf, Eleanor Melville. *Herman Melville, Cycle and Epicycle.* Cambridge, 1953.

Miller, Perry. *The Raven and the Whale: The War of Words and Wits in the Era of Poe and Melville.* New York, 1956.

Olson, Charles. *Call Me Ishmael.* New York, 1947.

Paltsits, Victor Hugo, ed. "Family Correspondence of Herman Melville, 1830-1904." *Bulletin of the New York Public Library*, 33 (1929), 507-25, 575-625.

Parker, Hershel, and Harrison Hayford, eds. *Moby-Dick as Doubloon: Essays and Extracts (1851-1970).* New York, 1970.

————. "Gansevoort Melville's Role in the Campaign of 1844." *New York Historical Society Quarterly*, 49 (1965), 143-73.

————, ed. *The Recognition of Herman Melville: Selected Criticism Since 1846.* Ann Arbor, 1967.

Petrullo, Helen B. "The Neurotic Hero of *Typee*." *The American Imago*, 12 (1955), 317-23.

Polk, James K. *The Diary of James K. Polk.* Ed. Milo Milton Quaife. 2 vols. Chicago, 1910.

Rosenberry, Edward H. *Melville and the Comic Spirit.* Cambridge, Mass., 1955.

Rosenheim, F. "Flight from Home: Some Episodes in the Life of Herman Melville." *The American Imago*, 1 (1940), 1-30.

Sandberg, Alvin. *The Quest for Love and the Quest for Revenge in Herman Melville.* Unpublished dissertation, New York University, 1970.

Schroeter, James. "*Redburn* and the Failure of Mythic Criticism." *American Literature*, 39 (1967), 279-97.

Sealts, Merton M., Jr. "The Ghost of Major Melvill." *The New England Quarterly*, 30 (1957), 291-306.

————. *Melville as Lecturer.* Cambridge, Mass., 1957.

————. "Melville's Burgundy Club Sketches." *Harvard Library Bulletin*, 12 (1958), 253-67.

————. *Melville's Reading – A Check-list of Books Owned and Borrowed.* Madison, 1966.

Sedgwick, William Ellery. *Herman Melville: The Tragedy of Mind.* Cambridge, Mass., 1944.

Seelye, John. *Melville: The Ironic Diagram.* Evanston, 1970.

Shneidman, Edwin S. "The Deaths of Herman Melville," in *Melville & Hawthorne in the Berkshires*, ed. Howard P. Vincent. Kent State, 1968.

Star, Morris. "A Checklist of Portraits of Herman Melville." *Bulletin of the New York Public Library*, 71 (1967), 468-73.

Stern, Milton R. *The Fine Hammered Steel of Herman Melville.* Urbana, 1957.

Tanselle, G. Thomas. "The Sales of Melville's Books." *Harvard Library Bulletin*, 17 (1969), 195-215.

Tharp, Louise Hall. *The Peabody Sisters of Salem*. Boston, 1950.

Thompson, Lawrance. *Melville's Quarrel with God*. Princeton, 1952.

Travis, Mildred K. "*Mardi*: Melville's Allegory of Love." *Emerson Society Quarterly*, 45 (II Quarter 1966), 88-94.

Vincent, Howard P. *The Tailoring of Melville's "White-Jacket."* Evanston, 1970.

————. *The Trying-Out of "Moby-Dick."* Carbondale, 1949.

Warren, Robert Penn. "Melville the Poet," in *Selected Essays of Robert Penn Warren*. New York, 1958.

Weaver, Raymond M. *Herman Melville, Mariner and Mystic*. New York, 1921.

Index